Wheel Series 1

*THE PERFECTION OF WISDOM
IN EIGHT THOUSAND LINES
& ITS VERSE SUMMARY*

translated by Edward Conze

Four Seasons Foundation
Bolinas, California

Book design by Zoe Brown

Tripitaka   Selections, Eng.
Sutrapitaka   "   '
Prajnaparamita   "   '
Sancayagatha   "   '

Second printing, with corrections, 1975

ISBN 0-87704-048-6 (cloth)

ISBN 0-87704-049-4 (paper)

Library of Congress Catalog Card No.: 72-76540

The Wheel Series is edited by Donald Allen, published by the
Four Seasons Foundation, and distributed by Book People,
2940 Seventh Street, Berkeley, California 94710

CONTENTS

PREFACE

The Two Versions

In this book the reader finds the same text presented in two versions, once in verse and once in prose. For early Mahayana[1] Sutras that was quite a normal procedure. Generally speaking the versified versions are earlier, and in all cases they have been revised less than those in prose. The reason lies in that the verses are in dialect, the prose in generally correct Sanskrit. The dialect is nowadays known as "Buddhist Hybrid Sanskrit," a term adopted by Professor F. Edgerton who first compiled its grammar and dictionary.[2] The verses are often difficult to construe, and require close comparison with the Tibetan translations which reflect the knowhow of the Indian pandits of the ninth century. Nevertheless most of my translation should be regarded as fairly reliable, and there are serious doubts only about the rendering of I 7, II 13 and XX 13, which so far no amount of discussions with fellow scholars has dispersed.

The Ratnaguna

The verse form of this Sutra is handed down to us under the name of *Prajñāpāramitā-Ratnaguṇasaṃcayagāthā*[3] (abbreviated as *Rgs*), which consists of 302 "Verses on the Perfection of Wisdom Which Is the Storehouse of Precious Virtues," the virtuous qualities being, as the Chinese translation adds, those of the "Mother of the Buddhas." The text has acquired this title only fairly late in its history, for references to it occur only at XXIX 3 (*idaṃ guṇasaṃcayānām*) and XXVII 6 (*ayu vihāra guṇe ratānām*), i.e. in the latest portions of the text. But Haribhadra, its editor, has not made it up from these hints because two verses from it are quoted by Candrakirti (ca 600) under the title of *Ārya-Saṃcayagāthā*.[4]

Unfortunately our present text is not the original one. It has been tampered with in the eighth century when, under the Buddhist Pala dynasty, which then ruled Bihar, the great expert on Prajnaparamita, Haribhadra, either rearranged[5] the verses or, perhaps, only divided them into chapters. Regrettably the Chinese translators also missed the original text and produced only a tardy and none too reliable translation of Haribhadra's revision in A.D. 1001. But the verses themselves, as distinct from their arrangement, cannot have been altered very much because their archaic language and metre would resist fundamental changes. Although some of the poem's charm evaporates in translation, it nevertheless comes through as a human and vital statement of early Mahayana Buddhism, simple and straightforward, pithy and direct. Not unnaturally the *Ratnaguna* is still very popular in Tibet where it is usually found in conjunction with two other works of an edifying character, the "Vows of Samantabha-dra" and "The Recitation of Manjusri's Attributes."

In my view the 41 verses of the first two chapters constitute the original *Prajñāpāramitā* which may well go back to 100 B.C. and of which all the others are elaborations. Elsewhere I have given an analytical survey of their contents.[6] These chapters form one single text held together by the constant recurrence of the refrain "and that is the practice of wisdom, the highest perfection" (*eshā sa prajñā-vara-pāramitāya caryā*) and termi-nated by a fitting conclusion in II 13.[7] In fact the title of the original document was probably "the practice (*caryā*) of Perfect Wisdom," just as in China the first P.P. text had been the *Tao-hsing*, "the practice of the Way," in one fascicle[8] and as in the three earliest Chinese translations the first chapter was called "practice (of the Way)," and not, as now, "the practice of the knowledge of all modes."[9]

At the other end there are 52 verses which have no counterpart in the *Ashta* at all. In the main they are a separate treatise which deals, in reverse order, with the five perfections which lead up to the perfection of wis-dom,[10] and which was appended to the existing *Rgs* so as to bring the number of chapters from 28 to a total of 32. For the rest, 33 more *Rgs* verses are absent from the *Ashta*.[11] They concern mostly similes.

Of special interest are the similes in chapter XX which deal with the following particularly abstruse subject: It is one of the most distinguishing features of a "Bodhisattva" that he can postpone his entrance into Nirvana so as to help living beings. Technically this is expressed by saying that "he does not realize the Reality-limit (*bhūta-koṭi*)." "Reality-limit" had for a while been one of the more obscure synonyms of "Nirvana," but now by a shift in meaning it becomes identified with the inferior hinayanistic Nir-vana of the Arhat as distinct from the full and final Nirvana of a Bud-dha.[12] Tradition also knew three "doors to deliverance"—emptiness, the signless and the wishless—which are three kinds of meditation which lead straight to Nirvana. Chapter XX now tries to explain (bracketed pages 370-81) how these can be practised without the undesirable side-effect of the person quitting the world by disappearing into the basically selfish hinayanistic Nirvana. Most readers will find the similes of *Rgs* more con-vincing than the apparent rationality of the *Ashta.*

On the other hand, large chunks of the *Ashta* are unrepresented in the *Ratnaguna*. They are roughly 240 pages out of 529.[13] It is not always quite clear why they should be missing. Some obviously are absent be-cause they were added to the Sutra after the completion of *Rgs*. They are, as I have suggested elsewhere,[14] chapters XXIX to XXXII, as well as large portions of chapters XIII, XIX to XXVIII, and so on. Others could prob-

ably by no stretch of the imagination be subjected to poetical treatment,
such as the attempts to probe the mind of the All-knowing in chapter XII,
the rather monotonous rhapsodies on Suchness in chapter XVI, or the
sometimes prosy enumerations of Mara's misdeeds in chapters XI, XVII
328-32, and XXIV 416-21. It is also quite possible that some parts of *Rgs*
are later than the prose text of the *Ashta* and that their authors did not
aim at reproducing all the points of the argument, step by step, but were
content to pick out a sentence here or there.

The Ashta

Now as to the Sutra itself. First its title. *Aṣṭasāhasrikā Prajñāpāramitā*[15]
(abbreviated as *Ashta* or *A*) means "The Perfection of Wisdom in Eight
Thousand Lines," or *ślokas.* A *śloka* is used to indicate a unit of 32
syllables. The Cambridge manuscript Add 866 of A.D. 1008 gives the
actual number of *ślokas* after each chapter, and added together they are
exactly 8,411. Religious people are inclined to attribute their holy scrip-
tures to divine inspiration, and they do not like to think of them as a
historical sequence of utterances made by fallible men. The faithful in
India and the Buddhist world in general assumed that all the P.P. Sutras
are equally the word of the Buddha, more or less abbreviated according to
the faculty of understanding of the people and their zeal and spiritual
maturity.[16] The first was that in 8,000 lines, or rather its precursor. This
was then expanded into 10,000, 18,000, 25,000 and 100,000 *ślokas;* and
after that it was contracted to 2,500, 700, 500, 300 (*The Diamond Sutra*),
150, 25 (*The Heart Sutra*), and finally into one syllable ("A"). They are all
anonymous and date between A.D. 50 and 700.

In its language our Sutra is almost pure Sanskrit. The date of its
composition can be inferred to some extent from the Chinese translations.
The first was Lokakshema's "P.P. Sutra of the Practice of the Way" in
A.D. 179. At that time "the *sūtra* had already assumed the basic format
preserved in the Sanskrit, and no chapters are left out completely."[17] But
even that must have grown over one or two centuries because it contains
many sections omitted in the *Ratnaguna* (see above at note 14) which
reflects an earlier state of the text from which even Lokakshema's version
was derived. After Lokakshema we can follow the further growth and
modifications of the text in China over eight centuries.[18] The current
Sanskrit text which we have translated here is that of the Pala manuscripts
which are dated between A.D. 1000 and 1150. They are confirmed by the
Tibetan translation (ca A.D. 850) and closely agree with Danapala's Chi-
nese translation of A.D. 985 and to some extent already with one of

Hsüan-tsang's translations (Taisho 220[4], ca A.D. 650). In fact so much effort has been devoted to this greatly revered scripture that its text is unusually well established. From India we have more old manuscripts of it than of any other Mahayana scripture. In China "it was the first philosophical text to be translated from the Mahayana literature into Chinese"[19] and it was translated no fewer than seven times. The colophon of the Tibetan translation in the Kanjur shows the exceptional care taken of it over the centuries by some of the greatest names of Tibetan scholarship: —it was first translated ca 850; then again in 1020; then compared with many Indian Mss and commentaries and revised in 1030, in 1075 and again in 1500.

The Speakers

The Sutras of the Mahayana are dialogues. One must know the conventions behind their presentation, because what matters is not only what is said but who says it. First there are three of the best known of the "disciples" of the historical Buddha, technically known as "auditors" (*śrāvaka*, from *śru*, to hear), because they have heard the doctrine directly from the Buddha's lips. They are Subhuti, Sariputra and Ananda.

Where *Subhūti* talks it is the Buddha himself who speaks through him. Subhuti was one of the "eighty great disciples" of the tradition of the Elders who was outstanding for his practice of friendliness, or lovingkindness. In the older Buddhism, charity (*maitrī*) had been a minor and subordinate virtue. It is characteristic of the Mahayana that its representative should now be placed above all the other disciples. In addition, Subhuti was celebrated for his being "the foremost of those who dwell in Peace,"[20] (a formula which implies that he avoided all strife by not contending at all,) and also for practising the contemplation of dharmas as empty.[21] He is the principal channel through whom the Buddha's inspiration travels downwards. The theory is stated quite clearly at *Rgs* I 2-4 (=*A* I 4), and also at *A* I 25, II 44. It is the Buddha's might (*anubhāva*), his "sustaining power" (*adhiṣṭhāna*), or as we might say, his "grace" which leads to his revelation of the true doctrine, either through his own words or through inspired men as his mouthpiece. These men in their turn gain access to the revelation by their holy lives and their spiritual and meditational practices. And in this Sutra Subhuti is the most important of them.

On the other hand, *Śāriputra*[22] had been for the Elders the first of those who excelled in wisdom. "Wisdom" is here a term for the "Abhidharma" which had grown up in the community about three centuries after the death of the Buddha. The Abhi-dharma, or "higher doctrine," was a system of meditation which analysed and classified all those processes and events in the conditioned world which could be held to affect salvation. Obsessed with this task Sariputra is now depicted as being blind to the One Ultimate Truth, of being incapable of getting away from his preoccupation with multiplicity and dualities, and of facing the undifferentiated oneness of emptiness. It is his very insight into the absence of self in all conditioned things which now prevents him from comprehending the relation of the self to the Absolute (as e.g. at *A* VIII 187-88). It is as an advocate of a lesser vision that he asks his often puzzled questions, and he is no longer "the second Buddha" of the older tradition which also knew him as the "field marshall of the doctrine," and of whom it had been said that "just as the eldest son of a king turns his wheel (i.e. rules) as his father did, so you, Sariputra, turn the wheel of the supreme Dharma (i.e. teach) as perfectly as I have done."[23]

Ānanda speaks eight times.[24] He had been the Buddha's personal attendant for thirty years, and his devotion to the Buddha's person was proverbial. He had heard all the Buddha's discourses. In consequence he was known as "the treasurer of the Dharma," and there was something quite miraculous about his retentive memory and it was "said of him that he could take in without missing a single syllable 60,000 lines uttered by the Buddha and that he could speak eight words when an ordinary person speaks one."[25] In the list of the "great disciples"[26] he is the one who is foremost for his great learning (literally: having heard much, *bahu-śruta*). He is also reputed to have recited in front of 499 Arhats at the first "council" of Rajagriha, which took place one year after the Buddha's demise, all the Sutras, or texts dealing with Dharma ('doctrine' or 'truth'), whereas Upali recited the texts on Vinaya, i.e. monastic discipline. In the *Ashta* on two occasions Ananda authenticates the Sutra on P.P. which is specially entrusted to him by the Buddha.[27]

In addition to these three disciples there is Pūrṇa at *A* I 20, 24, II 40 and XVI 319. The other *dramatis personae* are Maitreya, the coming Buddha, and Sakra, the chief of gods.

Maitreya speaks twice — at VI 135-54 and XIX 359-60. The first time he explains an exceedingly obscure metaphysical problem concerning the transfer of merit, and the second time his testimony is solicited because he has had firsthand experience of the matter in hand.

The Buddhist treatment of the brahminical gods (*deva*) is governed by two considerations: —the one is to stress in every way their inferiority to the Lord Buddha, and the other is the conviction that intellectually they are not particularly bright, as a result of their being altogether too happy and long-lived. They are the Indian counterpart of the Greek "immortals," and there are 27 classes of them, distributed among the "triple world": —six on the plane of sense-desire, seventeen on the plane of form and four on the formless plane. The gods who figure in the Sutras are those on the plane of sense-desire, whose sensuous and even libidinous interests make them feel a certain kinship with mankind. The lowest are the four "Great Kings" or "World-Guardians," and the second from below are the "gods of the Thirty-three," whose chief is Indra, the old warrior god of the Aryan invaders, who in Buddhist texts is usually called *Śakra*,[28] chief of the gods (*devānām indra*), and is often addressed as *Kauśika* because he is the tutelary divinity of the brahminic clan of the Kuśika. He and his retinue live on the summit of Mount Sumeru, in a palace called Vaijayanta (XI 236-37) from which they can repel the incursions of their hereditary enemies, the Asuras (III 72), and which has a huge meeting hall, called Sudharmā (*A* IV 94-95) and is surrounded by parks with miraculous trees and wonderful elephants. In this heavenly realm the Buddha's mother had been reborn for a while, and the Buddha went up there to preach her the Abhidharma. Sakra is a very frequent interlocutor in Buddhist Sutras of all kinds, but he is acutely aware of his intellectual shortcomings. At *A* XXIII 415 he admits that "I myself am quite incapable of uttering anything relevant on the subject of Bodhisattvas." When he talks sense he does so because and when inspired by the Buddha (*A* XXIII 414, XXVI 438), but very often he reflects the bewilderment of those who are not yet very far advanced.

Relation to Preceding Literature

In its very first sentence the text proclaims itself as a Sutra of the traditional type. "Thus have I heard at one time"—the "I" here is Ananda, who is supposed to have recited also this Sutra soon after the Buddha's Nirvana. That is, of course, a pious fiction which did not prevent others from taunting the authors of these Sutras with being mere "poets."[29] This is an allusion to a well-known saying in the scriptures of the older schools[30] which had contrasted the new-fangled fabrications of "poets," or "novelists" as we might say, with "the Sutras taught by the Tathagata himself, which are deep, deep in meaning, supramundane, with emptiness for their message." The scene of the sermons is said to be near Rajagriha, on the Gṛdhrakūṭa-parvata, Mount Vulture Peak, a particularly desolate district, all stones and empty air. This location likewise is clearly unhistorical. Modern scholars still disagree on the place of origin of the *Prajñāparamitā*. Some seek it in the Dravidian South, some in the Northwest and some in the Deccan. But none would look for it on the Vulture Peak in

Magadha, the heartland of the old dispensation.

Direct *quotations* from previous Sutras are very rare. Of great importance is the one at *A* I 8-9 (= *Rgs* I 7) about the wanderer Śreṇika. It provides us with the link which connects the new revelation with the old,[31] and shows that the P.P. continues a tradition within the community which meant to leave room for an Absolute in man, and saw the religious quest as a hunt for his true self and as an attempt to realize, or to reveal, the Tathagata in his own heart. Two further quotations are untraced, but most go back to the scriptures of the Elders. They occur at *A* XI 246 and XII 256.[32] A third, at IV 94, concerning the Dharma-body, is obviously a late addition to the text [33] and must refer to some Mahayana scripture. In other cases [34] we are not sure whether we have to deal with quotations from the actual literature of the Elders, or just with Buddhist commonplaces cherished in Mahayana circles.

Traditional phrases play a large part in all oral literature. In Homer's poems, for instance, stereotyped phrases account for about one third of the total. E. Lamotte has collected a number of such phrases,[35] and I use this opportunity to draw attention to some more. They are mostly synonyms which are often difficult to reproduce in English, but which at that time were highly valued for providing a traditional flavour to those familiar with the *Nikāyas* and *Āgamas* and which are elaborate ways of expressing such ideas as "encourage," "fearlessness," "worship," or "learning,"[36] or cumbersome formulas for gifts [37] or earthquakes,[38] etc.

Likewise, the *mythological characters* are those of the old Sutras of the Elders: —e.g., the four World-Guardians (II 33, XXIII 414), Sakra and his entourage (see above), and the Tushita gods (XIV 285, XXVIII 459); Maitreya (also at VIII 199, IX 200, XIV 285, XXXII 529) and Dipankara (II 48, XIX 368-69); Mara [39] and his hosts (III 49), the yakshas (II 38) and a variety of deities from the Hindu pantheon.[40] And the Vajrapani of XVII 333 is the great yaksha "with the thunderbolt in his hand" who is a kind of guardian angel of the Buddha and is familiar to us from sculptures and frescoes as one who follows the Buddha so as to discomfort his detractors with his *vajra*; but he is not the Mahayana Bodhisattva of the same name who belongs to the family of Akshobhya. The few references to Mahayana deities belonging to the cycle of the Buddha Akshobhya are later intrustions,[41] and so are those belonging to the story of Sadāprarudita (e.g. XXX 481). Also the few *historical* and *geographical* allusions are all to items familiar from the scriptures of the Elders: —the kings Bimbisara and Prasenajit and the tribes of the Licchavi and the Sakya (III 78); the great disciples at II 40; the town of Dipavati (II 48) as well as the Jambudvipa continent and (Su)meru, the mountain.[42]

The Topics and Their Treatment

A survey of the main topics is given in the Appendix. One should, of course, bear in mind that the contents of the Sutra are of unequal age. Quite late, for instances, are chapters XXX to XXXI, which are really an edifying tale (*avadāna*) tucked on at the end. Hsüan-tsang (A.D. 650) omitted it from the *Ashta* altogether and appended it to the version in 100,000 lines.[43] This story has over the course of time been altered more extensively than any other part of the Sutra.[44] In fact, the rearrangements and sermonic paddings which have taken place have obscured the original intention of the story of Ever-weeping, severely damaged its clarity and sequence, and destroyed much of its literary merit and dramatic quality. In its earlier versions[45] it is the simple story of the symbolic journey of the Bodhisattva to find the P.P., and Ever-Weeping is a typical saintly hero figure of a kind which Joseph Campbell has so ably described in his *Hero with a Thousand Faces* (1949), —a 'Call' is followed by a journey, a fight with a very powerful foe, help from supernatural agents and feminine figures and, finally, the heroic quest accomplished, he penetrates, accompanied by a retinue of people, to the source of wisdom and returns with his trophy.

But even in the more strictly doctrinal portions there has been much development. It may be useful to briefly indicate some of the criteria by which the later accretions in P.P. Sutras can be detected.[46] What we find in later layers is 1. increasing sectarianism, with all the rancour, invective and polemics that that implies; 2. increasing scholasticism and the insertion of longer and longer Abhidharma lists;[47] 3. growing stress on skill in means, and on its subsidiaries such as the Bodhisattva's Vow and the four means of conversion, and its logical consequences, such as the distinction between provisional and ultimate truth; 4. a growing concern with the Buddhism of faith, with its celestial Buddhas and Bodhisattvas and their Buddha-fields; 5. a tendency towards verbosity, repetitiveness and overelaboration; 6. lamentations over the decline of the Dharma; 7. expositions of the hidden meaning which become the more frequent the more the original meaning becomes obscured;[48] 8. any reference to the Dharmabody of the Buddha as anything different from a term for the collection of his teachings; 9. a more and more detailed doctrine of the graded stages (*bhūmi*) of a Bodhisattva's career.

The English Translation

The translation of *The Perfection of Wisdom in Eight Thousand Lines* was completed in 1951, and first published in 1958 by the Asiatic Society of Calcutta as no. 284, or 1578, of their Bibliotheca Indica. (It is said to have been reprinted in 1970, but no copy of the reprint has reached me.) In the present edition numerous corrections have been introduced. My intentions can be seen from the original Preface, which I reproduce here as it stands.

"A literal, word by word translation of the Prajnaparamita is tiresome to read, and practically unintelligible to any one who does not have the Sanskrit original before him. If ever there was a case where the letter kills the spirit, it is here. The Sutra itself was meant to be memorized, the translation is meant to be read. Lengthy repetitions, stereotyped phrases, and the piling up of synonyms were of great assistance to memory, but they irritate and distract the modern reader, and obscure from him the meaning of the text. This translation aims at bringing out the meaning of the Sutra, often with the aid of Haribhadra's commentary, and it keeps as close to the text as is compatible with intelligibility. The reproduction of the literary conventions and of the stylistic peculiarities of Buddhist Sanskrit diction was not one of my aims. It would be of little, or no, value to scholars, and it bewilders the general reader."

In one passage, i.e. at XII 256-72, the disquisition on how the Buddha knows the minds of beings is quite incomprehensible in the Sutra text. I have therefore freely interpolated the comments of Haribhadra's *Abhisamayālaṅkārāloka.*

As to the abbreviations, an "etc." indicates either a list of dharmas or other items, or a string of synonyms. "Form, etc." means, "form, feelings, perceptions, impulses and consciousness," and it might have been better to translate as "the five skandhas" throughout. At XX 376, 378 "faith, etc." refers to the five cardinal virtues, i.e. faith, vigour, mindfulness, concentration and wisdom; and likewise at XX 378 "friendliness, etc." indicates the four boundless states, i.e. friendliness, compassion, sympathetic joy and impartiality. At III 62 "flowers, etc." refers to a list of gifts found on III 57; and "take up, etc." at III 56 is spelled out in full at XXII 398 and elsewhere. "Name, etc." at XXVII 449, 452 stands for "name, clan, power, appearance and form," as at XXVII 449. At 11 35 the three "etc., until we come to" are parts of the original text, whereas the later "etc., to" is my own. I clearly assumed that readers would look at the Sanskrit text.

My translation of the *Verses on the Perfection of Wisdom* is based on E. Obermiller's text of the *Ratnaguna* (Bibliotheca Buddhica XXIX, 1937), as corrected by me in *Indo-Iranian Reprints* (V, 1960) and in the *Indo-Iranian Journal* IV, 1960, pp. 37-58, by Prof. E. Edgerton in *Indo-Iranian Journal* V, 1961, pp. 1-18 and by Dr. R. O. Meisezahl in *Oriens* 17,

1964, 289-301. I have added section headings, but the reader should bear in mind that they form no part of the text. The translation of the first two chapters appeared originally in *The Middle Way* XXXII 4, 1958, pp. 136-41, and for it I adopted a kind of rhythm. The remainder is rendered quite literally, and generally speaking the division of the lines corresponds to that of the original. The whole translation was first published in 1962 by the International Academy of Indian Culture, of New Delhi, in *Indo-Asian Studies*, part 1, edited by Prof. Raghu Vira, pp. 126-78, and for a time bound offprints were available from Luzac & Co. of London.

Aids to the Study of the Sutra

These profound texts are hard to understand without a commentary, and no Indian would ever have tried to do so. The best is Haribhadra's *Abhisamayālaṅkārāloka*, ed. by U. Wogihara in 1932-35. It has remained so far untranslated, but has guided my interpretation on many occasions. Three Indian commentaries to the *Rgs* are preserved in Tibetan translations, but I have not consulted them. For the technical terms the most useful book is Har Dayal, *The Bodhisattva Doctrine in Buddhist Sanskrit Literature*, 1932, reprinted in India in 1970 by Banarsidass. For the philosophical background my *Buddhist Thought in India*, 1962, is the most up-to-date survey. Very much the most valuable source book for P.P. texts in general is Nagarjuna's "Explanation of the Large Perfection of Wisdom," preserved only in Chinese and partly translated (i.e. chapters 1-42) into French by Etienne Lamotte, as *Le Traité de la grande vertu de sagesse*, 3 vols., 1944, 1949 and 1970.

Niruktipratisamvid, or knowledge of languages, is traditionally given as one of the attributes of an effective Bodhisattva. Those English-speaking people who want to probe into the intellectual profundities of Mahayana Buddhism must at present try to master two languages: Sanskrit and French. As for the first, it is of course not altogether indispensable, but it certainly helps to acquire at least some idea of how Sanskrit words are constructed. I will give just one single rather obvious example which will illustrate that *Prajñāpāramitā* Buddhism is not a religion suitable for the brainless.

The disquisitions in chapter XVI on Suchness and the Tathagata cannot convincingly be transposed into English and are better appreciated by those who have some awareness of the Sanskrit background. For Suchness is *tatha-tā*, i.e. *tathā* = such, plus *-tā*, to designate an abstract noun. A variant is *tathā-tva*, "Thusness." To take something in its Suchness is to take it such as it is, i.e. without adding anything to it or subtracting anything from it. Furthermore, *tathā-gata* is an epithet of the Buddha. This may be construed as *tathā-gata,* thus gone," or *tathā-āgata,* "thus come," i.e. come or gone such as the other Buddhas have come or gone. But, and here is the rub, like many other Buddhist technical terms, *Tathā-gata* may well be the Sanskritisation of a Prakrit [49] word. Just as *tathatā* designates true reality in general, so the word which developed into "Tathagata"[50] designated the true self, the true reality within man, the kind of person whom the Buddhist doctrine tries to produce, a Buddha, a Tathā-gata, who "has come to the real Truth," or "who has gone there," i.e. to liberation, his true goal.

Conclusion

In this Preface I have contented myself with describing the scriptures which we lay before the public as *literary* documents, relating them to other literary documents which may contribute to their understanding. If there had been room for it, one might also have written about their general background from the standpoint of the *history of ideas,* and shown what factors combined to change the face of Buddhism about the beginning of the Christian era.

Finally one could also treat them as *spiritual* documents which are still capable of releasing spiritual insights among people separated from their original authors by two thousand years and vast disparities in intellectual and material culture. There is, however, a certain absurdity about interpreting spiritual matters in the abstract and in general terms, since everything depends on concrete conditions and the actual persons and their circumstances. Some will regard this literature as rather strange and alien, and may long for something more homespun. They will, I hope, allow me to retort with a remark that so endeared me to my students at Berkeley. Asked what Buddhism should do to become more acceptable to Americans, I used to enumerate with a smile a few concessions one might perhaps make respectively to the feminist, democratic, hedonistic, primitivistic and anti-intellectual tendencies of American society. Though in the end I invariably recovered my nerve and reminded my listeners that it is not so much a matter of the Dharma adjusting itself to become adaptable to Americans, but of Americans changing and transforming themselves sufficiently to become acceptable to the Lord Buddha.

E.C.

[1] *Mahā-yāna,* 'great vehicle.' Opposite *hīna-yāna,* 'inferior vehicle.' Both arose about the beginning of the Christian era. What preceded them for 500 years was neither 'Hinayana' nor 'Mahayana,' and should be called the doctrine of the Elders. *—Sūtra* = a sermon attributed to the Buddha.

[2] Published in 1953. Reprinted 1970 in India.

[3] Bibliographical notes on all the P.P. (abbreviation of *Prajñāpāramitā*) texts up to 1960 in E. Conze, *The Prajñāpāramitā Literature,* 1960; up to 1971 in P. Beautrix, *Bibliographie de la littérature Prajñāpāramitā,* 1971.

[4] Verses xx 5 and ii 3d in *Prasannapadā,* ed. de la Vallée-Poussin, 1903-14, vii, 166-67.

[5] *Suvihita.* So in the second of two final verses omitted in the translation as being clearly the work of Haribhadra himself.

[6] In 1960. Reprinted in *Thirty Years of Buddhist Studies,* 1968, 124-30.

[7] Looking again at this verse I find that my translation is rather free and perhaps unduly interpretative. The Sanskrit just says: "Thus speaks the Jina, an uncontradicted speaker: 'When I was (not deprived [so *A*]) of this supreme perfection, Then, etc." My translation is, however, partly suggested by the Tibetan.

[8] Kajiyoshi and Hikata (xxxvi-xxxvii), it is true, have doubted Seng-yu's statement on this, but without giving convincing reasons.

[9] *Sarva-ākāra-jñatā-caryā.* "Knowledge of all modes" is a late scholastic term for the omniscience of the Buddha as distinct from that of other saints. The *Ashta* always uses the simpler term "all-knowledge," except at xxx 507.

[10] About these see my *Selected Sayings from the Perfection of Wisdom,* 1955, 62-70.

[11] They are iii 8; v 5-8; vii 7; ix 1; xii 6-9; xix 3-5; xx 5-7, 11, 13, 15, 17-20; xxi 8; xxii 6; xxiii 1, 3; xxiv 2, 6; xxvi 2, 3; xxvii 8. Five further verses are in doubt, i.e. v 2, xiv 1, xx 12, 14, 16.

[12] The *locus classicus* for this distinction is the 5th chapter of the *Saddharmapuṇḍarīka,* translated in *Thirty Years,* etc. 104-22.

[13] For the list see my *Prajñāpāramitā Literature* 17.

[14] See my article on "The Composition of the *Aṣṭasāhasrikā Prajñāpāramitā*" (1952), reprinted in *Thirty Years,* etc., 168-84, especially 179-82, and also my *Prajñāpāramitā Literature,* 15-16.

[15] It was edited by R. Mitra in 1888, and we give the pages of his edition in brackets. At page 464 he omitted one palmleaf, and page 464a indicates that missing page which I have restored from the original now in Oxford and of which the Sanskrit can be found in my *Thirty Years,* 183-84.

[16] The usual attitude of the Mahayanistic faithful can be gathered from Buston's admirable *History of Buddhism,* translated by E. Obermiller, II, 1932, 48-51. Likewise in China, when Chih Tun (ca 350) noticed discrepancies between the version in 25,000 and that in 8,000 lines he concluded that "the Greater and Lesser Prajnapara-

mita issue from a prime source, whose text, numbering six hundred thousand words, now moves about India but has never come to China." Trans. H. Hurvitz *JAOS* 88, 1968, 255.

[17] Lewis Lancaster's dissertation, *An Analysis of the Aṣṭasāhasrikā-prajñāpāramitā-sūtra from the Chinese Translations.* University of Wisconsin, 1968, 317.

[18] For a detailed concordance see Lancaster's dissertation, 326-73.

[19] So Lancaster, 32, who refers to 10 Catalogues.

[20] E.g. i 6, 20; *Diamond Sutra* 9e. For the meaning of this somewhat cryptic term see my *Vajracchedikā Prajñāpāramitā*, 1957, 97-98, and *Buddhist Wisdom Books*, 1958, 45.

[21] Nagarjuna, *Ta chih tu lun*, 356a, quot. Migot, 489. See also *Ashta* xxvii 454.

[22] Most of the information available about Sariputra has been collected by A. Migot in "Un grand disciple du Bouddha: Śāriputra," *BEFEO* 1955, 405-554. See also my *Buddhist Wisdom Books*, 1958, 81-82, and my *Prajñāpāramitā Literature* 13-14. —He speaks at i; ii 37-38, 43-44; iii 77; vii 170-73, 176-77, 181-83; viii 187-88, 190; x 212-13; xvi 309-20; xix 356-61; xxvii 444.

[23] *Samyutta Nikāya* viii 7.

[24] At ii 40, iii 80-81, iv 98, xix 365-69, xxiii 414, xxiv 416-23, xxviii 458-64a, xxxii 528.

[25] *Encyclopedia of Buddhism*, ed. G. P. Malalasekera, i 4, 1965, 531.

[26] *Anguttara Nikāya* i 23-26; *Ekottarāgama* T 125.

[27] I.e. xxviii 460, 14-464a, xxxii 527, 15. There is none of this in *Rgs*.

[28] Sanskrit for 'powerful,' 'mighty.' —See Ch. Godage, "The Place of Indra in Early Buddhism," *University of Ceylon Review*, April 1945, 41-72. The occasions on which he speaks are listed in my *Materials for a Dictionary of the Prajñāpāramitā Literature*, 1967, 378.

[29] *Ashta* xvii 328.

[30] For the sources see E. Lamotte, *Histoire du Bouddhisme Indien*, 1958, 180.

[31] For the details see my *The Large Sutra on Perfect Wisdom*, I, 1961, xxvi-xxvii.

[32] For the first see *Anguttara Nikāya* i 34-35, and *Milindapañha* 142.6. For the second *Samyutta Nikāya* iv 52 and *Abhidharmakośavyākhyā* 23.

[33] It is omitted in *Rgs*. All the "Dharma-body" passages (see List of Topics) are missing in the early Chinese translations "except for the rather literal idea of 'collection of the *sūtras* of the Buddha.'" Lancaster, 92-100, 130, 154.

[34] I.e. xviii 346, 347; xix 356, 357, 358; xxii 405.

[35] "Relevé des formules et des clichés" in *L'enseignement de Vimalakīrti*, 1962, 481-83.

[36] *Samdarśayati samādāpayati samuttejayati sampraharṣayati,* e.g. viii 190, xxx 489, 510. Cf. *sandassati samādapeti samuttejeti sampahamseti* at *Samyutta Nikāya* i, 209, etc. *—nottrasyati na samtrasyati na samtrāsam āpadyate,* e.g. xxii 406, or: *na samsīdati na-avalīyate na samlīyate na viprsthībhavati nottrasyati,* etc. i 5, 7-8, 10; xxvi 441; xxviii 446. *—satkaroti gurukaroti mānayati pūjayati arcayati apacāyati* xxii 402. *—śrotavyā udgrahītavyā dhārayitavyā vācayitavyā paryavāptavyā pravartayitavyā* i 6.

[37] At iii 57; xxii 403; xxx 501, 505, 507; xxxii 528-29.

[38] xvi 309, xxxi 516.

[39] Most places for Mara in *Ashta* can be found on page 320 of my *Materials.* We may add *A* xx 373 and for *Rgs:* i 18; iii 1; xi 2, 3, 6, 8, 10; xvii 4; xx 4; xxi 2, 3-5, 7; xxiv 1, 3, 4; xxvii 2, 3.

[40] At ii 48, viii 198, xvii 313, xxvii 446-47.

[41] See my *Thirty Years* 172-75.

[42] Jambudvipa: ix 203, xvii 336, xxii 401, xxiii 410, xxv 431. —Sumeru: xxvi 435, xxix 477-78, xxx 492, xxxi 525-26.

[43] T 220(1), vol. 6, 1059: 16 — 1073:1.

[44] See L. Lancaster's dissertation, pages 199-309.

[45] In Lokakshema A.D. 179 and Chih-Ch'ien A.D. 225; the translations of A.D. 408, 660 and 985 agree more with the Sanskrit.

[46] For much material on this topic see R. Hikata, *Suvikrāntavikrāmi-pariprcchā Prajñāpāramitā,* 1958, xxxi-xxxvi and L. Lancaster's dissertation, pages 32-198.

[47] In *Rgs* the five skandhas are throughout held to be sufficient for analysis. And so it was in the early Chinese translations, Lancaster 138.

[48] See my *Thirty Years* 142.

[49] *Saṃ-s-kṛta:* artificially made, in accordance with the rules of the grammarians. *Pra-kṛta:* natural, language of the people.

[50] For the discussion on this see: E. Lamotte, *Le traité de la grande vertu de sagesse,* I, 1944, 126; Har Dayal 321-22; D. S. Ruegg in *Journal Asiatique* 1955, 163-70.

VERSES ON THE PERFECTION OF WISDOM

CONTENTS

TABLE OF CONTENTS

Homage to all the Buddhas and Bodhisattvas!

Thereupon the Lord, in order to gladden the four assemblies, and to further lighten up this perfection of wisdom, preached at that time the following verses:

Chapter 1

Preliminary Admonition

1. "Call forth as much as you can of love, of respect and of faith!
   Remove the obstructing defilements, and clear away all your taints!
   Listen to the Perfect Wisdom of the gentle Buddhas,
   Taught for the weal of the world, for heroic spirits intended!

The Source of Subhuti's Authority [4]¹

2. The rivers all in this Roseapple Island,
   Which cause the flowers to grow, the fruits, the herbs and trees,
   They all derive from the might of the king of the Nagas,
   From the Dragon residing in Lake Anopatapta,² his magical power.
3. Just so, whatever Dharmas the Jina's disciples³ establish,
   Whatever they teach, whatever adroitly explain—
   Concerning the work of the holy which leads to the fullness of bliss,
   And also the fruit of this work—it is the Tathagata's doing.
4. For whatever the Jina has taught, the Guide to the Dharma,
   His pupils, if genuine, have well been trained in it.
   From direct experience, derived from their training, they teach it,
   Their teaching stems but from the might of the Buddhas, and not
       their own power.

The Basic Teachings [5-18]

5. No wisdom can we get hold of, no highest perfection,
   No Bodhisattva, no thought of enlightenment either.
   When told of this, if not bewildered and in no way anxious,
   A Bodhisattva courses in the Well-Gone's wisdom.
6. In form, in feeling, will, perception and awareness⁴
   Nowhere in them they find a place to rest on.

Without a home they wander, dharmas never hold them,
Nor do they grasp at them—the Jina's Bodhi they are bound to gain.

7. The wanderer Srenika[5] in his gnosis of the truth
Could find no basis, though the skandhas had not been undone.
Just so the Bodhisattva, when he comprehends the dharmas as he
    should
Does not retire into Blessed Rest.[6] In wisdom then he dwells.

8. What is this wisdom, whose and whence, he queries,
And then he finds that all these dharmas are entirely empty.
Uncowed and fearless in the face of that discovery
Not far from Bodhi is that Bodhi-being then.

9. To course[7] in the skandhas, in form, in feeling, in perception,
Will and so on, and fail to consider them wisely;
Or to imagine these skandhas as being empty;
Means to course in the sign,[8] the track of non-production ignored.

10. But when he does not course in form, in feeling, or perception,
In will or consciousness, but wanders without home,
Remaining unaware of coursing firm in wisdom,
His thoughts on non-production—then the best of all the calming
    trances cleaves to him.

11. Through that the Bodhisattva now dwells tranquil in himself,
His future Buddhahood assured by antecedent Buddhas.
Whether absorbed in trance, or whether outside it, he minds not.
For of things as they are he knows the essential original nature.

12. Coursing thus he courses in the wisdom of the Sugatas,[9]
And yet he does not apprehend the dharmas in which he courses.
This coursing he wisely knows as a no-coursing,
That is his practice of wisdom, the highest perfection.

13. What exists not, that non-existent the foolish imagine;
Non-existence as well as existence they fashion.
As dharmic facts existence and non-existence are both not real.
A Bodhisattva goes forth [10] when wisely he knows this.

14. If he knows the five skandhas as like an illusion,
But makes not illusion one thing, and the skandhas another;
If, freed from the notion of multiple things, he courses in peace —
Then that is his practice of wisdom, the highest perfection.

15. Those with good teachers as well as deep insight,
Cannot be frightened on hearing the Mother's deep tenets.
But those with bad teachers, who can be misled by others,
Are ruined thereby, as an unbaked pot when in contact with moisture.

Three Key Terms Defined [18-24]

16. What is the reason why we speak of 'Bodhisattvas'?
    Desirous to extinguish all attachment, and to cut it off,
    True non-attachment, or the Bodhi of the Jinas is their future lot.
    'Beings who strive for Bodhi' are they therefore called.
17. What is the reason why 'Great Beings' are so called?
    They rise to the highest place above a great number of people;
    And of a great number of people they cut off mistaken views.
    That is why we come to speak of them as 'Great Beings.'
18. Great as a giver, as a thinker, as a power,
    He mounts upon the vessel[11] of the Supreme Jinas.
    Armed with the great armour he'll subdue Mara the artful.
    These are the reasons why 'Great Beings' are so called.
19. This gnosis shows him all beings as like an illusion,
    Resembling a great crowd of people, conjured up at the crossroads,
    By a magician, who then cuts off many thousands of heads;
    He knows this whole living world as a mock show, and yet remains
       without fear.
20. Form, perception, feeling, will and awareness
    Are ununited, never bound, cannot be freed.
    Uncowed in his thought he marches on to his Bodhi,
    That for the highest of men is the best of all armours.
21. What then again is 'the vessel that leads to the Bodhi'?
    Mounted upon it one guides to Nirvana all beings.
    Great is that vessel, immense, vast like the vastness of space.
    Those who travel upon it are carried to safety, delight and ease.

The Transcendental Nature of Bodhisattvas [24-31]

22. Thus transcending the world, he eludes our apprehensions.[12]
    'He goes to Nirvana,' but no one can say where he went to.
    A fire's extinguished, but where, do we ask, has it gone to?[13]
    Likewise, how can we find him who has found the Rest of the
       Blessed?
23. The Bodhisattva's past, his future and his present must elude us,
    Time's three dimensions nowhere touch him.
    Quite pure he is, free from conditions, unimpeded.
    That is his practice of wisdom, the highest perfection.
24. Wise Bodhisattvas, coursing thus, reflect on non-production,
    And yet, while doing so, engender in themselves the great compassion,

Which is, however, free from any notion of a being.
Thereby they practise wisdom, the highest perfection.

25. But when the notion of suffering and beings leads him to think:
'Suffering I shall remove, the weal of the world I shall work!'
Beings are then imagined, a self is imagined, —
The practice of wisdom, the highest perfection, is lacking.

26. He wisely knows that all that lives is unproduced as he himself is;
He knows that all that is no more exists than he or any beings.
The unproduced and the produced are not distinguished,
That is the practice of wisdom, the highest perfection.

27. All words for things in use in this world must be left behind,
All things produced and made must be transcended —
The deathless, the supreme, incomparable gnosis is then won.
That is the sense in which we speak of perfect wisdom.

28. When free from doubts the Bodhisattva carries on his practice,
As skilled in wisdom he is known to dwell.
All dharmas are not really there, their essential original nature is
    empty.
To comprehend that is the practice of wisdom, perfection supreme.

Chapter II

Where Bodhisattvas Stand [35-37]

1. He does not stand in form, perception or in feeling,
   In will or consciousness, in any skandha whatsoever.
   In Dharma's true nature alone he is standing.
   Then that is his practice of wisdom, the highest perfection.
2. Change and no change, suffering and ease, the self and not-self,
   The lovely and repulsive[14] — just one Suchness in this Emptiness they
   are.
   And so he takes not his stand on the fruit which he won, which is
   threefold —
   That of an Arhat, a Single Buddha, a Buddha fully enlightened.
3. The Leader himself was not stationed in the realm which is free
   from conditions,
   Nor in the things which are under conditions, but freely he wandered
   without a home:
   Just so, without a support or a basis a Bodhisattva is standing.
   A position devoid of a basis has that position been called by the Jina.

Wherein Bodhisattvas Train [38-43]

4. Those who wish to become the Sugata's Disciples,
   Or Pratyekabuddhas, or likewise, Kings of the Dharma —
   Without resort to this Patience[15] they cannot reach their respective
   goals.
   They move across, but their eyes are not on the other shore.
5. Those who teach dharma, and those who listen when it is being
   taught;
   Those who have won the fruit of an Arhat, a Single Buddha, or a
   world-saviour;
   And the Nirvana obtained by the wise and the learned —
   Mere illusions, mere dreams — so has the Tathagata taught us.
6. Four kinds of persons are not alarmed by this teaching:
   Sons of the Jina skilled in the truths; saints unable to turn back,[16]
   Arhats free from defilements and taints, and rid of their doubts;
   Those whom good teachers mature are reckoned the fourth kind.
7. Coursing thus, the wise and learned Bodhisattva,
   Trains not for Arhatship, nor on the level of Pratyekabuddhas.
   In the Budha-dharma alone he trains for the sake of all-knowledge.

No training is his training, and no one is trained in this training.
8. Increase or decrease of forms is not the aim of this training,
   Nor does he set out to acquire various dharmas.
   All-knowledge alone he can hope to acquire by this training.
   To that he goes forth when he trains in this training, and delights in its
      virtues.

The Facts of Existence [44-47]

9. Forms are not wisdom, nor is wisdom found in form,
   In consciousness, perceptions, feeling, or in will.
   They are not wisdom, and no wisdom is in them.
   Like space it is, without a break or crack.
10. Of all objective supports the essential original nature is boundless;
    Of beings likewise the essential original nature is boundless.
    As the essential original nature of space has no limits,
    Just so the wisdom of the World-knowers is boundless.
11. 'Perceptions'—mere words, so the Leaders have told us;
    Perceptions forsaken and gone, and the door is open to the Beyond.
    Those who succeed in ridding themselves of perceptions,
    They, having reached the Beyond, fulfil the Teacher's
       commandments.
12. If for aeons countless as the sands of the Ganges
    The Leader would himself continue to pronounce the word 'being':
    Still, pure from the very start,[17] no being could ever result from his
       speaking.
    That is the practice of wisdom, the highest perfection."

Conclusion

13. And so the Jina concludes his preaching, and finally tells us:
    "When all I said and did at last agreed with perfect wisdom,
    Then this prediction I received from Him who went before me:[18]
    'Fully enlightened, at a future time thou shalt a Buddha be!' "

Chapter III

The Merit Derived from Perfect Wisdom [49-70]

1.　"One who will take up this Perfection of Wisdom,
　　Wherein the Saviours course, and constantly study it;
　　Fire, poison, sword and water cannot harm him,
　　And also Mara finds no entrance, nor his host.
2.　Someone may for the Sugata who went to rest build Stupas,
　　Made of the seven precious things, and worship them;
　　Until thousands of *kotis* of fields are filled with these Stupas
　　Of the Sugata, countless as the sands of the Ganges;
3.　And like him as many beings again as there are in endless kotis of
　　　　fields,
　　They all would do worship, without doing anything else, —
　　With heavenly flowers and the best perfumes and unguents, —
　　Let us reckon for aeons in the three periods, and still more than that:
4.　But if someone else had copied this book, the Mother of the Sugatas,
　　From which come forth the Guides with the ten powers,
　　Would bear it in mind, revere it with flowers and unguents, —
　　An infinitesimal portion of his merit would have those who had given
　　　　worship to the Stupas.

Perfect Wisdom a Great Lore [73-74]

5.　This Perfection of Wisdom of the Jinas is a great lore,
　　Appeasing dharmas making for sorrow and ill in many a world of
　　　　beings.
　　The Saviours of the World in the past, and in the future, and those
　　　　[now] in the ten directions,
　　They have, by training in this lore, become the supreme physicians.
6.　And [also] those who course in the practice of pity and concern for
　　　　the welfare of others,
　　They, the wise, by having trained in this lore, will experience
　　　　enlightenment.
　　Those who have conditioned happiness, and those who have
　　　　unconditioned happiness,
　　All their happiness should be known as having issued from this.

Perfect Wisdom and the Other Five Perfections [81-82]

7.　Gems exist potentially scattered in the earth,

And, when conditions are favourable, they grow in great variety:
All the qualities of enlightenment [that are in] the five perfections,
They all grow from the perfection of wisdom.

8. Wherever, we know, the Universal Monarch may travel,
   There is all the army of all the seven precious things:
   Wherever there is this perfection of wisdom of the Jinas,
   There also all dharmas of good quality are brought along."

Chapter IV

Relative Value of Relics and Perfect Wisdom [94-99]

1. Asked a question by the Jina, Sakra answered:
   "If I could have Buddhafields like the sands of the river Ganges,
   All of them filled to the top with the relics of the Jinas:
   Nevertheless I would still take this wisdom, the foremost of the
       perfections.
2. For what reason? It is not that I lack in respect for the relics,
   But they are worshipped because they are fostered by wisdom.
   Just as every man who is supported by the king gets worship,
   Just so the Buddha-relics, because they are supported by the
       perfection of wisdom.

Simile of the Wishing Jewel [96-99]

3. A precious gem, in possession of all qualities, priceless,
   The basket in which it may be, should be paid homage to;
   Even when it has been taken out, the basket continues to emit its
       radiance:
   Such are the qualities of that gem.
4. Just so it is with the qualities of wisdom, the foremost perfection,
   Which gain worship for the relics of the Jina even after he has gone to
       rest.
   Therefore let him who wants to win the Jina-qualities
   Take up the perfection of wisdom. She is the liberation."

Perfect Wisdom and the Other Five Perfections [100-101]

5. [The Lord then said:] "Wisdom controls him who gives gifts,
   And also morality, patience, vigour and concentration.
   She takes hold of the wholesome dharmas so that they may not be
       lost.
   She alone is also the one who reveals all dharmas.

Simile of the Shadows [101]

6. There are in Jambudvipa many thousands of kotis of trees,
   Of different species, manifold and different in form;
   And yet there would not also be a difference between their shadows,

But when one speaks they are all equally reckoned as shadows:
7.   Just so do these five perfections of the Jinas
     Have their name from the perfection of wisdom:
     When they are being turned over into all-knowledge,
     The name of enlightenment provides one single principle for all the six
          of them.

Chapter V

The Counterfeit and the True Perfection of Wisdom [112-13]

1. When a Bodhisattva [falsely] reveals form, perception, feeling, will,
    Or thought as impermanent [claiming that they are destroyed], —
    In the counterfeit [perfection of wisdom] he courses, considering not
        wisely;
    Because the learned never effect the destruction of a dharma.
2. Wherein of form, of feeling, or perception,
    Or consciousness, or will there is no apprehension:
    By the method of emptiness and non-production [he] cognizes all
        dharmas.
    This is the practice of wisdom, the foremost perfection.

Perfect Wisdom Greater Than Any Other Spiritual Gift [122-23]

3. If someone would discipline in Arhatship as many beings
    As there are in fields equal to the sands of the river Ganges:
    And if someone else, having copied this perfection of wisdom,
    Would give the book to another being, —his would be the more
        distinguished merit.
4. For what reason? The supreme Teachers, trained in this,
    Make all dharmas intelligible in this emptiness.
    When they have learned that[19] the Disciples speedily experience their
        own kind of emancipation,
    Others experience Pratyekabuddha-enlightenment, others again the
        Buddha-enlightenment.

Importance of the Thought of Enlightenment

5. Where there is no sprout, there can in the world be no tree.
    How can therein be the production of branches, leaves, fruits or
        flowers?
    Without the aspiration for enlightenment there is no possibility of a
        Jina in the world.
    How then could Sakra, Brahma, fruit and disciples manifest
        themselves?
6. When the orb of the sun sends forth a multitude of light,
    Then beings exert themselves in doing their work:

So, when the thought of enlightenment has come into being for the
    sake of knowing the world,[20]
Through its cognition all the dharmas of quality are assembled.

7.   If there were no Chief of the Serpents in his Anavatapta [Lake],
    How could there be here in Jambudvipa a flowing along of the rivers?
    And if there were no rivers, fruits and flowers could not possibly be,
    And there would also be no manifold jewels in the oceans.

8.   So, if there were no thought of enlightenment, how could there be
    The flowing along of the cognition of the Tathagata in all these
        worlds?
    And if there is no cognition, there can be no growth of the virtues,
    No enlightenment, nor the oceanlike dharmas of the Buddha.

The Sun and the Firefly

9.   If all the light-emitting animals everywhere in this world
    Would, for the purpose of illumination, shed light:
    One single ray, issued from the orb of the sun, outshines them all,
    And infinitesimal would be all the luster of the hosts of light-emitting
        animals.

Chapter VI

Supreme Merit of Dedication and Jubilation [135]

1. However much merit the hosts of Disciples may beget,
    Associated with giving, morality, and [meditational] development:
    But if a Bodhisattva rejoices with one single thought,
    There would [by comparison] be no mass of merit in all the hosts of
        the Disciples.

The Range of Jubilation [135-38]

2. If we take the niyutas of kotis of Buddhas, who have gone by in the
        past period of time,
    And those who just now abide in endlessly many thousands of kotis
        of Buddha-fields;
    And also those Saviours of the world who, having gone to Parinirvana,
    Will demonstrate the jewel of Dharma for the sake of the complete
        extinction of suffering;
3. If we consider the merit of those Jinas during the period
    Beginning with the first production of the thought of the foremost
        enlightenment,
    Until the time of the extinction of the good Dharma of the Guides, —
    And the dharmas connected with the perfections, and also the
        Buddha-dharmas;
4. And also the merit of the offspring of the Buddhas, and of the
        Disciples,
    Be they in training or adepts, with outflows or without, —
    Having heaped it all up, the Bodhisattva rejoices at it,
    And turns it all over to the enlightenment which is linked with the
        weal of the world.

True and False Turning over [142-58]

5. When in one who turns over there proceeds the perception of a thought,
    Or if the turning over of the perception of enlightenment involves the
        perception of a being:
    Established in perception, false views, and thought, it is tied by the
        triple attachment.
    It does not become turned over to those who apprehend it.
6. But when he thus cognizes: These dharmas are extinct and stopped,

And wherein they are turned over, that is also extinct;
Nor is ever anywhere a dharma turned over into a dharma:
Then it does become turned over in one who thus considers wisely.

7.   When he makes a sign, he does not turn over [to enlightenment],
But if [he turns to it as] the signless, [that] becomes turned over into
  enlightenment.
Just as though food mixed with poison were good to eat,
So has the taking of pure dharmas as a basis been spoken of by the
  Jina.

8.   Therefore thus should one train in turning over:
As the Jinas wisely know that wholesome [root], —
Its class as it is, its origins as they are, its characteristics as they are, —
Thus do I rejoice [in that wholesome root], thus do I turn [it] over.

9.   And thus turning merit over into enlightenment,
He does not upset the Buddha, one who preaches what the Jina has
  taught.
As many as there are in the world Bodhisattvas who lean on a basis
All of them surpasses the hero who turns over in this way.

Chapter VII

Perfect Wisdom Guides the Other Perfections [172]

1. How can those niyutas of kotis of born-blind, who are without a
       guide,
   Who are not conversant with the way, find an entrance to the city?
   Without wisdom these five perfections are eyeless:
   Those who are without the guide are unable to experience
       enlightenment.
2. When they are taken hold of by wisdom,
   Then, having gained the eye, do they get that designation [i.e.
       'perfection'].
   It is like a [religious] painting [of a deity or a saint] which is
       complete except for the eyes.
   Only after the eyes are painted in does one get one's fee.

The Attitude to Dharmas and to the Self [172-75]

3. When one who develops wisdom to the end does not seize on the least
       dharma,
   Conditioned or unconditioned, dark or bright;
   Then one comes to speak in the world of the perfection of wisdom,
   [Which is like] space, wherein nothing real whatsoever is established.
4. When he thinks, 'I course in the wisdom of the Jinas,
   I will set free niyutas of beings touched by many ills':
   This Bodhisattva is one who imagines the notion of beings,
   And this is not the practice of wisdom, the foremost perfection.

Faith in the Perfection of Wisdom [176-79]

5. The Bodhisattva who has observed this foremost perfection,
   When in the past he served [the Buddhas], is learned and does not
       doubt:
   As soon as he has heard it he will again recognise the Teacher,
   And he will swiftly understand the Peaceful Calm of enlightenment.
6. Though in the past he has honoured millions of Buddhas, and served
       them,
   If without faith in the Jina's perfection of wisdom,
   Hearing of it, he will cast it away, one of small intelligence;
   After he cast it away, he will go to the Avici Hell, and no one can save
       him.

7.   Therefore, have faith in this Mother of all the Jinas,
     If you wish to experience the utmost Buddha-cognition:
     Let him be like a merchant, who has travelled to the treasure island,
     And who, having lost his goods[21] would [nevertheless] again return
        [to it].

Chapter VIII

The Meaning of Purity [186-95]

1. The purity of form should be known from the purity of the fruit.
   From the purity of form and fruit is the purity of all-knowledge.
   The purity of all-knowledge and of the fruit, and the purity of form:
   As with the sameness of the space-element, they are not broken nor
      cut apart.
2. Having transcended what belongs to the triple world, the
      Bodhisattvas,
   [Although their] defilements [are] removed, exhibit [their] rebirth;
   [Although] freed from decay, illness and death, they exhibit
      decease, —
   This is the perfection of wisdom in which course the constantly wise.
3. This world is attached to the mud of name-and-form.
   The wheel of birth-and-death revolves, similar to a wind-wheel.
   Having cognized the revolving world as like a snare for wild beasts
   The wise roam about similar to the birds in space.
4. He who, coursing perfectly pure, does not course in form,
   Nor in consciousness, perception, feeling or will;
   Thus coursing he shuns all attachments.
   Freed from attachments he courses in the wisdom of the Sugatas.

Chapter IX

All-round Purity [200-201]

1. Thus coursing, the wise and learned Bodhisattva,
   Having cut off his attachments, marches on unattached to the world.
   As the sun, released from the planet Rahu, blazes forth,
   Or, as fire, let loose, burns up grass, log and forest.
2. The Bodhisattva sees that all dharmas and the Perfection of Wisdom
   Are pure, perfectly pure, in their essential original nature.
   But he does not seize on one who sees, nor on all dharmas.
   This is the practice of wisdom, the foremost perfection."

Chapter X

Qualifications for Perfect Wisdom [211-13]

1. Sakra, King of Gods, asks the Jina:
    "Coursing in wisdom, how is the Bodhisattva 'engaged in' it?"
    "Who is 'joined' to not the least thing whatsoever, be it skandha, or
        element,
    He who is 'engaged' thus, that Bodhisattva is 'joined' [to wisdom].
2. As one set out for long in the vehicle should that being be known,
    As one who has done his duty under many niyutas of kotis of Buddhas,
    Who, when he has heard that these dharmas are fictitious and like an
        illusion,
    Does not hesitate, but makes efforts to train himself.

The Simile of a Village [215-16]

3. If a man [coming out of] a wilderness extending over many miles
    Would see cowherds, or boundary lines, or woods:
    He [then] regains his breath, and has no [more] fear of thieves:
    [For he knows that] these are signs that a village or city is quite near:
4. Just so the one who searches for enlightenment, when he learns of this
        wisdom,
    The foremost perfection of the Jinas, and gets hold of it:
    He regains his breath, and he has no [more] fear,
    Not even that of [falling on] the level of an Arhat or the level of a
        Pratyekabuddha.

The Simile of the Ocean [216-17]

5. As long as a man who travels to the watery ocean in order to see it,
    Still sees the trees and forests of the Himalayas, [he is far from it].
    But when he no longer sees these signs, he becomes free from doubt,
        [and knows that]
    'Quite near is the great ocean, it is not too far away':
6. Just so should be known one who has set out for the foremost
        enlightenment,
    And who is learning about this perfection of wisdom of the Jinas.
    Although he is not one who has face to face been predicted by the
        Leader,
    He knows that 'before long I will experience the Buddha-

enlightenment.'

The Simile of Spring [217]

7.   In beautiful springtime, when the stalks and leaves have come out,
     From the branches will, before long, come forth [more] leaves, and
         fruits and flowers:
     One who has been taken in hand by this perfection of wisdom,
     Before long he will attain the foremost enlightenment of the Leaders.

The Simile of the Pregnant Woman [218]

8.   When a pregnant woman is all astir with pains,
     One should know that the time has come for her to give birth:
     Just so will the Bodhisattva, if on hearing of the wisdom of the Jinas
     He beholds her with delight and zest, speedily experience
         enlightenment."

How to Dwell in Perfect Wisdom [219-20]

9.   "When the Yogin is coursing in wisdom, the supreme perfection,
     He does not see the growth of form, nor its diminution.
     If someone does not see dharma, nor no-dharma, nor the
         Dharma-element[22]
     And if he does not experience the Blessed Rest, then he dwells in
         wisdom.
10. When he courses therein, he does not imagine the Buddhadharmas,
     Nor the powers, nor the roads to psychic power, nor does he imagine
         the peaceful calm of enlightenment.
     Not discriminating, free from constructions, coursing on resolutely,
     This is the practice of wisdom, the foremost perfection."

Chapter XI

The Theme [232]

1. Subhuti asks the Buddha, the moon of the Doctrine:
   "Will there be any obstacles to the precious qualities?"
   "Many obstacles there will be," preaches the Teacher.
   "Of them I will proclaim only a few:

Various Obstacles [232-33]

2. Diverse and manifold flashes of ideas will arise in him
   When he copies out this wisdom, the perfection of the Jinas.
   Then again they will speedily vanish, like lightning,
   Without benefit to the weal of the world. This is one deed of Mara.
3. And he may have some doubts when it is being taught:
   'My name is not proclaimed by the Leader therein;
   Nor are the circumstances of my birth; nor my birthplace or clan.'
   Because of that they will not listen, and reject it. That also is Mara's
         deed.

The Bodhisattva-path and the Disciple-path [234-39]

4. Just as, in his ignorance, someone would give up the root,
   And prefer, the deluded, the branches and foliage;
   [Or] as one who, when he had got an elephant, would want an
         elephant's foot instead; —
   Thus would be one who, having heard the Prajnaparamita, would wish
         for the Sutras [of the Disciples instead].
5. Just as one who had got superior food of a hundred [different] tastes,
   Would, although he has got the best food of all, nevertheless seek for
         inferior food.
   So would be a Bodhisattva who, having got this perfection,
   Would seek for enlightenment on the level of an Arhat.

More Obstacles [242-43]

6. They will want honour, they will want gain,
   In their hearts longing for them, intent on familiarity with the families
         [of the faithful].
   Having spurned what is right [Dharma], they will do what is wrong;

Having left the right path, they have gone on to a wrong road. This
    also is Mara's deed.
7. Even though at first they have produced faith,
    Keen to hear this most excellent dharma;
    When they find that the dharma-preacher is disinclined to do his
        work,
    They will go away, devoid of joy and very sad.

Mara's Deeds and the Buddha's Help [248-52]

8. When these deeds of Mara will take place,
    Together with many other diverse and manifold obstacles,
    Then many monks will be troubled thereby,
    And will not bear in mind this Prajnaparamita.
9. Where there are jewels which are priceless
    And hard to get, their owners invariably have many foes.
    Just so this wisdom, the foremost perfection of the Jinas,
    Is the Dharma-jewel hard to get, and [connected with] many troubles.
10. When a being has newly set out in the vehicle, and is limited in his
        intelligence,
    He does not [at once] obtain this Dharma-jewel, hard to get.
    Mara will then be zealous to cause obstacles.
    But the Buddhas in the ten directions will be intent on helping.

Chapter XII

Perfect Wisdom the Mother of the Buddhas [253-57]

1. If a mother with many sons had fallen ill,
   They all, sad in mind, would busy themselves about her:
   Just so also the Buddhas in the world-systems in the ten directions
   Bring to mind this perfection of wisdom as their mother.
2. The Saviours of the world who were in the past, and also those that
   are [just now] in the ten directions,
   Have issued from her, and so will the future ones be.
   She is the one who shows the world [for what it is], she is the
   genetrix, the mother of the Jinas,
   And she reveals the thoughts and actions of other beings.

How the Tathagata Knows the World [270-74]

3. The Suchness of the world, the Suchness of the Arhats,
   The Suchness of Pratyekabuddhas, and the Suchness of the Jinas, —
   As just one single Suchness free from existence, unaltering,
   Has the perfection of wisdom been understood by the Tathagata.
4. Whether the wise abide in the world, or whether they have gone to
   final Nirvana,
   Firmly established remains this fixed sequence of Dharmahood:
   'Dharmas are empty.'
   It is that Suchness (*tathatā*) which the Bodhisattvas understand.
   Therefore then have the Buddhas been given the name of
   'Tathagatas.'
5. This is the sphere of the Guides, with their own powers,
   Who reside in the delightful forests of the perfection of wisdom.
   Although they fetch suffering beings out of the three places of woe,
   Yet they never have anywhere the notion of a being.

Similes about the Buddha

6. When a lion, residing in his mountain cave,
   Roars fearlessly, the lesser beasts are made to tremble:
   Likewise, when the Lion of Men, depending on the perfection of
   wisdom,
   Roars fearlessly, the many heretics are made to tremble.
7. Just as the rays of the sun, supported by the ether,
   Dry up this earth, and do reveal its form:

Just so the king of the Dharma, supported by the perfection of
    wisdom,
Dries up the river of craving and reveals the dharma.

The Tathagata's Vision of Dharma

8. Wherein there is no vision of form, no vision of feelings,
    No vision of perception, no vision of will,
    No vision of consciousness, thought or mind,
    This has been expounded as the vision of Dharma by the Tathagata.
9. A vision in space is a being, so they declare.
    A vision like that of space, so should you consider that object!
    Thus has the vision of Dharma been expounded by the Tathagata.
    But it is not possible to report on that vision by definite statements
        [that differ from it].

Chapter XIII

Simile of the King and His Ministers [281]

1. Who sees thus, he sees all dharmas.
   When the minister does everything, the king is evenminded.
   Whatever Buddha-actions there are, whatever dharmas of the
      Disciples,
   It is the perfection of wisdom which effects them all.
2. A king does not travel to villages or into the countryside;
   But in his own home is the meeting-place where he assembles all:
   Just so the Bodhisattva does not move away from the dharmic nature
      of dharmas,
   But he assembles all the qualities in the Buddha-dharmas.[23]

Chapter XIV

The Bodhisattva and Enlightenment [284-86]

1. The Bodhisattva who has firm faith in the Sugata,
    Who is resolutely intent on the supreme perfection of wisdom;
    Gone beyond the two levels of the Disciples and Pratyekabuddhas,
    He will swiftly attain, unhindered, the enlightenment of the Jinas.

The Simile of the Ship [286-87]

2. When a ship breaks up in the ocean,
    Those who do not get hold of a corpse, a stick or a log,
    Go to their destruction in the midst of the water, without having
        gained the shore;
    But those who hold on to something, travel to the other shore and
        reach it:
3. Just so those who, although endowed with some faith and in
        possession of some serenity,
    Reject the perfection of wisdom, the mother:
    In the ocean of birth-and-death they must wander about for ever and
        ever,
    In birth, decay, death, sorrow, turmoil, and the breaking up [of
        limbs].
4. But those who have been taken hold of by the supreme wisdom,
    Skilled in seeing the own-being of existence, seers of ultimate reality:
    They are persons worthy of the vehicle who have collected the wealth
        of merit and cognition.
    They will speedily experience the exceedingly wonderful Sugata-
        enlightenment.

The Simile of the Jar [287-88]

5. It is as if someone would transport water in an unbaked jar;
    One should know that it will break quickly, because it does not hold
        the water well.
    But when water is transported in a fully baked jar, that on the way
    It might break there is no fear, and it gets safely to the house:
6. Although the Bodhisattva be full of faith,
    If deficient in wisdom he swiftly reaches destruction.
    But when taken hold of by both faith and by wisdom,
    Gone beyond the two levels he will attain the supreme enlightenment.

The Simile of the Two Ships [288-90]

7. A ship, which is not well got ready, in the ocean
    Goes to destruction, together with its goods and merchants.
    But when a ship is well got ready, and well joined together,
    Then it does not break up, and all the goods get to the [other] shore.
8. Just so a Bodhisattva, exalted in faith,
    But deficient in wisdom, swiftly comes to a failure in enlightenment.
    But when he is well joined to wisdom, the foremost perfection,
    He experiences, unharmed and uninjured, the enlightenment of the
        Jinas.

The Simile of the Aged Man [290-91]

9. An aged man, ailing, one hundred and twenty years old,
    Although he may have got up, is not capable of walking on his own;
    But when two men, both to his right and left, have taken hold of him
    He does not feel any fear of falling, and he moves along at ease:
10. Just so a Bodhisattva, who is weak in wisdom,
    Although he sets out, he breaks down midway;
    But when he is taken hold of by skilful means and by the best
        wisdom,
    Then he does not break down: he experiences the enlightenment of
        the mightiest of men.

Chapter XV

The Beginner and the Good Friends [292-93]

1. The Bodhisattvas who stand on the stage of beginners,
   Who with resolute intention have set out for the supreme
         enlightenment of a Buddha,
   They, the discerning, should, as good pupils intent on respect for their
         Gurus, —
   Always tend their spiritual teachers [who are their 'good friends'].
2. For what reason? From that [tending] come the qualities of the
         learned.
   They [the good friends] [are those who] instruct in the perfection of
         wisdom.
   Thus preaches the Jina, the holder of all the best qualities:
   'Dependent on the good friend are the Buddha-dharmas.'

How a Bodhisattva Helps Beings [293-301]

3. Giving, morality, also patience and vigour,
   The concentrations and wisdom should be turned over into
         enlightenment.
   But one should not grab at enlightenment, having considered [it as
         belonging to] the skandhas.
   It is thus that it should be demonstrated to beginners.
4. Coursing thus, the Oceans of Qualities, the Moons of the doctrine
   Become the shelter of the world, its refuge, and its place of rest;
   The means of salvation [route], the intelligence, the islands, leaders
         who desire its welfare;
   The light, the torch, teachers of the foremost Dharma, imperturbable.
5. An armour difficult to wear the greatly determined put on;
   But they are not armed with the skandhas, elements or sense-fields;
   They are free from the notion of the three vehicles, and have not
         taken hold of it;
   They are irreversible, immovable, and steadfast in their character.
6. Being thus endowed with dharma, unimpeded,
   Freed from hesitations, perplexity and consternation, intent on what
         is beneficial,
   Having heard the perfection of wisdom, they do not despair.
   They should be known as incapable of being led astray by others, as
         irreversible.

Perfect Wisdom and Its Conflict with the World [304-5]

7. Deep is this dharma of the Leaders, hard to see,
    Nor is it obtained by anyone, nor do they reach it.
    For that reason, when he has obtained enlightenment, the Benevolent
        and Compassionate
    Becomes unconcerned, — 'what body of beings will cognize this?'
8. For beings delight in a place to settle in, they are eager for
        sense-objects,
    Bent on grasping, unintelligent, and quite blinded.
    The Dharma should be attained as nothing to settle in and as nothing
        to grasp.
    Its conflict with the world is manifest.

Chapter XVI

On Suchness [306-8]

1. The space-element in the eastern direction, and in the southern,
   And so in the western and northern directions is boundless;
   Above and below, in the ten directions, as far as it goes
   There is no multiplicity, and no difference is attained.
2. Past Suchness, future Suchness,
   Present Suchness, the Suchness of the Arhats,
   The Suchness of all dharmas, the Suchness of the Jinas, —
   All that is the Dharma-Suchness, and no difference is attained.

Wisdom and Skill in Means [309-11]

3. If a Bodhisattva wishes to reach this
   Enlightenment of the Sugatas, free from differentiated dharmas,
   He should practise the perfection of wisdom, joined to skill in means.
   Without wisdom there is not the attainment of the Leaders of men.
4. A bird with a frame one hundred and fifty miles large
   Would have little strength if its wings were lost or feeble:
   If it should jump down to Jambudvipa from the abodes of the Gods
       of the Thirty-three,
   It would travel to its destruction.
5. Even if he would procure these five perfections of the Jinas
   For many niyutas of kotis of aeons,
   And would all the time tend the world with an infinite abundance of
       vows; —
   If he is without skill in means, deficient in wisdom, he falls into
       Discipleship.

The Desirable Attitude to Other Beings [321-22]

6. If he wishes to go forth into this Buddha-cognition,
   He [should have] an even mind towards the whole world, the notion
       of father and mother [towards all beings];
   He should exert himself with a thought of benevolence, and a friendly
       mind;
   Amenable and straight, he should be soft in his speech."

Chapter XVII

The Theme [323]

1. The Elder Subhuti questions the Saviour of the World:
   "Teach the characteristics of those who are secluded in Peace, of the
       Oceans of Qualities,
   How they become irreversible, and of great might.
   Declare, O Jina, their qualities, merely by way of outline!"

Qualities of Irreversible Bodhisattvas [323-38]

2. "They are free from the perception of multiplicity; they speak suitably;
   They do not take refuge with outside Sramanas or Brahmanas.
   The wise have avoided for all time the three places of woe,
   And they are practised in the ten wholesome paths of action.
3. Free from self-interest they instruct the world in Dharma.
   They take delight in the Dharma. They always speak gently.
   Standing, walking, lying down, sitting, they are fully conscious [of
       what they are doing].
   They walk along looking ahead only one yoke, their thoughts not
       wandering about.
4. They wear garments clean and unsoiled. They become pure through
       the threefold detachment.[24]
   Majestic men they want no gain, but always Dharma.
   They have passed beyond Mara's realms. Others cannot lead them
       astray.
   They meditate in the four trances, but they do not use those trances
       as a support [for a better rebirth].
5. They do not want fame, their hearts are not overcome by anger.
   As householders they remain constantly unattached to their entire
       property.
   They do not seek to earn their livelihood in the wrong way,
   Through bewitchment-spells, or the spells which are the work of
       women.
6. Nor do they [earn a living by] tell[ing] plausible lies to men and
       women.
   Practised in the quite detached wisdom, the best of perfections,
   Free from quarrels and disputes, their thoughts firmly friendly,
   They want [to see] the all-knowing, their thoughts always inclined
       towards the religion.

7.   They have avoided the barbarous populations of outlying districts, of
          the border regions.
       They are free from doubts about their own stage, always fashioned
          like Meru.
       For the sake of Dharma they renounce their very life, intent on their
          practice.
       These should be wisely known as the characteristics of the irreversible.

Chapter XVIII

Deep Stations [342-43]

1. Deep are form, feeling and will,
   Consciousness and perception; signless in their essential original
       nature, and calm.
   Like one who tries to reach the bottom of the ocean with a stalk,
   So, when the skandhas have been considered with wisdom, one does
       not get to the bottom of them.
2. When a Bodhisattva thus understands that these dharmas
   In the deep vehicle are in the ultimate sense stainless;
   Wherein there is neither skandha, nor sense-field, nor element,
   How can there be to him the attainment of his own merit anywhere?

The Simile of the Woman [343-44]

3. As a man, preoccupied with matters of greed, had made a date
   With a woman, and would, not having met her, indulge in many
       thoughts;
   As many preoccupations as he would have [in his mind] during a day,
   For so many aeons does a Bodhisattva strive to reach his goal.

Considerations of Merit [344-46]

4. If a Bodhisattva would for many thousands of kotis of aeons
   Give spotless gifts, and would equally guard his morality.
   And if another one were to preach the dharma associated with
       wisdom, the foremost perfection, —
   The merit from giving and morality would [by comparison] be
       infinitesimal.
5. When a Bodhisattva, having meditated on the foremost wisdom,
   Emerged therefrom [i.e. that meditation] preaches the stainless
       Dharma,
   And turns over also [the merit from] that to the enlightenment linked
       to the weal of the world:
   There is nothing that is lovely in the triple world that could become
       equal to him.
6. And just that merit is declared to be just worthless,
   And likewise empty, insignificant, void and unsubstantial.
   Thus coursing he courses in the wisdom of the Sugatas.

Coursing [thus] he acquires immeasurable merit.

No Growth or Diminution [347-51]

7. As mere talk he cognizes all these dharmas
    Which the Buddha has demonstrated, practised and revealed.
    Though he may teach for many niyutas of kotis of aeons,
    Yet the Dharma-element does not get exhausted nor does it increase.
8. And as to these five perfections of the Jinas.
    These dharmas also have been proclaimed as mere words.
    The Bodhisattva who turns over, without putting his mind to it,
    Does not fail;[25] but he experiences the supreme Buddha-
        enlightenment.

Chapter XIX

Conditioned Coproduction and the Simile of the Lamp [352-53]

1.   The wick of a burning oil lamp, —it is not by the first incidence [of
          the flame]
      That the wick is burned [away]; nor is it burned [away] when [that
          incidence] is not, without it.
      Nor is the wick burned [away] by the last incidence of the flame,
      And also when that last flame is not does the lamp wick not burn
          away.
2.   By the first thought [of enlightenment] one does not experience the
          foremost enlightenment,
      And again, when that is not there, one is not able to experience it;
      Nor does the last thought arrive at the Bliss,
      Nor again, when it is not there, is one able to reach it.

The Simile of the Seed and the Fruit

3.   From a seed trees, fruits, and flowers come forth;
      When it is obstructed, or absent, then there is no tree from it.
      Just so the first thought is, of course, the foundation of
          enlightenment;
      But when it is obstructed or absent, there is no enlightenment from it.
4.   Conditioned by seeds grow barley, rice and so on;
      Their fruits are in these [seeds], and yet they are not in them.
      When this enlightenment of the Jinas arises,
      What takes place is an illusion, which in its own-being is without
          existence.

The Simile of the Water Drops

5.   Water drops fill a water jar drop by drop,
      Gradually, from the first incidence to the last one.
      Just so the first thought is the [initial] cause of supreme
          enlightenment;
      Gradually are the bright qualities fulfilled in the Buddhas.

The Meaning of Emptiness [356-61]

6.   He courses in dharmas as empty, signless and wishless;
      But he does not experience the Blessed Rest, nor does he course in a

sign:
As a skilful ferryman goes from this [shore] to the other shore,
But does not stand at either end, nor does he stand in the great flood.
7.   Thus coursing, the Bodhisattva also does not think:
'Predestined by those who have the ten powers, may I experience
        enlightenment!'
Nor is he trembling [because he sees that] enlightenment is here not
        anything.
Thus coursing he becomes one who courses in the wisdom of the
        Sugatas.

The Attitude to Places Which Might Inspire Fear [361-64]

8.   When they have seen a world which is a wilderness, full of famine and
        disease,
They have no fear, and go on putting on the armour.
For the wise are always joined to the limit which is further on.
They do not produce the least fatigue in their minds.

Chapter XX

The Three Doors to Deliverance, and the Buddha-dharmas [370-71]

1. Furthermore, the Bodhisattva who courses in the wisdom of the Jinas
    Cognizes these skandhas as unproduced, as empty from the beginning.
    Even during the time that unconcentrated he views in compassion the
        world of beings,
    He does not become destitute of the Buddha-dharmas.

The Simile of the Hero [371-74]

2. A skilful man, endowed with all qualities,
    Powerful, unassailable, well-qualified, instructed in many arts,
    Perfect in archery, devoted to many crafts,
    Perfect in knowing the various forms of magical illusion, keen on the
        welfare of the world
3. He takes his mother and father, together with his sons and daughters
    And enters a wilderness, full of many hostile forces.
    He conjures up many men, heroic champions,
    Gets away safely, and again goes back to his home;
4. Just so at that time when a wise Bodhisattva
    Extends the great friendliness to all in the world of beings,
    Having passed beyond the four Maras, and the two levels,
    He permanently abides in the best of concentrations, but he does not
        experience enlightenment.

The Simile of the Cosmos

5. Supported by space is air, and [by that] the mass of water;
    By that again is supported this great earth and the [living] world.
    If the foundation of the enjoyment of the deeds of beings
    Is thus established in space, how can one think of that object?[26]
6. Just so the Bodhisattva, who is established in emptiness
    Manifests manifold and various works to beings in the world,
    And his vows and cognitions are a force which sustains beings.
    But he does not experience the Blessed Rest; for emptiness is not a
        place to stand on.
7. At the time when the wise and learned Bodhisattva
    Courses in this most excellent quietude of the concentration on
        emptiness,
    During that time no sign should be exalted,

Nor should he stand in the signless; for he is one who courses calm
and quiet.

The Simile of the Flying Bird [374]

8. A flying bird has no footing in the intermediate space.
    It does not stand on it, nor does it fall to the ground.
    So the Bodhisattva who courses in the doors to freedom
    Neither experiences the Blessed Rest, nor does he course in the sign.

The Simile of the Archer [374-75]

9. As a man trained in archery shoots an arrow upwards,
    And then again other arrows in [quick] succession,
    Without giving [a chance] to the first one to fall to the ground
    Until he wishes the arrow to fall to the ground.
10. Just so someone who courses in wisdom, the best of perfections,
    And who accomplishes wisdom, skill in means, the powers and the
        ability to work wonders:
    As long as these wholesome roots remain unfulfilled
    So long he does not obtain that most excellent emptiness.

The Simile of the Twin Miracle

11. A monk endowed with the most excellent ability to work wonders
    Standing in the sky performs the twin miracle:
    He exhibits the coming and going, the lying down and the sitting;
    But he cannot be made to desist, nor does he feel exhausted however
        long he may be in it.
12. Just so the wise Bodhisattva, standing in emptiness,
    Perfect in cognition and the ability to work wonders, wandering
        without a home,
    Manifests an endless variety of works to the world,
    But he cannot be worn down, nor does he feel exhausted for kotis of
        aeons.

The Simile of the Parachutes

13. It is as with some men who have stood on a high cliff;
    If they held a parachute in each hand and would jump off into space,
    Their bodies, once they had left the high cliffs,

Would go on falling until they had reached the ground.[27]
14. Just so the wise Bodhisattva, having stood in compassion,
    Having taken hold of the two parachutes of skill in means and of
        wisdom,
    Considers dharmas as empty, signless and wishless;
    Though he does not experience the Blessed Rest, he nevertheless sees
        the dharmas.

The Simile of the Merchant and the Jewel Island

15. Someone, desirous of jewels, has travelled to the treasure island,
    And, having obtained the jewels, he would again return home.
    Although in those circumstances the merchant lives quite happily,
    Yet he bears in mind the hosts of his suffering kinsmen:
16. Just so the Bodhisattva who has travelled to the treasure isle of
        Emptiness,
    And has obtained the trances, faculties and powers;
    Although he could experience the Blessed Rest, wholly delighting in
        it,
    He would bear in mind all suffering beings.

The Simile of the Merchant and His Journey

17. As a merchant, interested in business, goes into the cities,
    Market towns and villages, which he comes across on his way, so as to
        get acquainted with them;
    But he neither abides therein, nor in the treasure island;
    But he, the discerning, becomes skilful in the path [which leads] to
        his home.[28]
18. Just so the wise Bodhisattvas who become skilful everywhere
    In the cognition and emancipation of the Disciples and
        Pratyekabuddhas,
    They abide not therein, nor in the Buddha-cognition,
    Nor in what is conditioned. Wise as to the path becomes the one who
        knows the method.

The Bodhisattva Undefinable

19. At the time when he has communed with the world in friendliness,
    And courses in the concentrations on emptiness, the signless and the
        wishless:

It is impossible that he either would [have an inclination to] reach the
    Blessed Rest,
Or that he could be defined by the conditioned.

20. As a magically created man, or one who has made his body invisible,
    Cannot be defined by words:
    Just so the Bodhisattva who courses in the doors to freedom
    Can also not be defined by words.

The Doors to Deliverance and the Irreversible Stage [379]

21. If on being questioned about the practice and the faculties
    A Bodhisattva does not effect the revelation of deep dharmas
    Which are empty and signless, if he fails to indicate the dharmas
        peculiar to
    The irreversible stage, he should not be known as one who has been
        predicted.

Tokens of Irreversibility [380-84]

22. Not the level of an Arhat nor the Pratyekabuddha-level,
    Nor what belongs to the triple world does he long for in his dreams;
    But he sees the Buddhas, and himself as one who preaches Dharma to
        the world:
    Predicted as 'irreversible' should he then be known.

23. Having seen in his dreams the beings who are in the three places of
        woe,
    He makes the vow, 'May I that very instant abolish the places of
        woe!'
    If, through the power of his declaration of the Truth, he appeases
        even a mass of fire:
    Predicted as 'irreversible' should he then be known.

24. Those possessed by ghosts, with various diseases, in the world of
        mortals,
    Through the power of his declaration of the Truth he appeases them,
        he who is benevolent and compassionate.
    Nor does there arise to him any self-consciousness or pride:
    Predicted as 'irreversible' should he then be known.

Chapter XXI

Pride and Other Deeds of Mara [385-91]

1. But when there arises in him the conceit, 'I have been predestined
   [Because] by [my] declaration of the Truth manifold things get
   accomplished,'
   When a Bodhisattva sets himself above other [Bodhisattvas] as one
   who has been predestined,
   One should know that he stands in conceit, and has little intelligence.
2. Again, as to the power of the name, Mara, having approached,
   Will say [to him]: 'This is your name.'
   The lineage of [your] father and mother for seven generations
   backwards he runs through;
   'When you are a Buddha, this will then be your name!'
3. If he is one who has behaved in accordance with the ascetic practices,
   a devoted Yogin,
   [Mara will tell him:] 'Formerly [in your past lives] you have also had
   these very same qualities.'
   The Bodhisattva who, on hearing this, becomes conceited,
   One should know him to be possessed by Mara, of little intelligence.

Faults in Connection with Detachment [391-95]

4. Though he might practise quite detached from villages or cities in a
   mountain cave,
   In a remote forest, or in isolated woods, —
   The Bodhisattva who exalts himself, who deprecates others,
   One should know him to be possessed by Mara, of little intelligence.
5. Although they may constantly dwell in a village, a royal city [or] a
   market town;
   If therein they do not generate longing for the vehicle of the Arhats
   and Pratyekabuddhas,
   But are devoted to enlightenment for the sake of maturing beings:
   Then this has been preached as the detachment of the Sugata's sons.
6. Though he may reside in mountain caves, five hundred miles wide,
   Infested with wild beasts, for many kotis of years:
   That Bodhisattva does not know this [true] detachment
   If he dwells contaminated by conceit.
7. When he feels superior to Bodhisattvas who practise for the weal of
   the world,

And who have attained the concentrations, emancipations, faculties,
   trances and powers,
On the ground that they do not course in the detachment of the
   remote forest, —
Of him the Jina has said that 'he is established in Mara's sphere.'
8.   Whether he dwells in the neighbourhood of a village, or in the remote
        forest:
     If he is free from the thought of the twofold vehicle and fixed on the
        supreme enlightenment,
     Then this is the detachment of those who have set out for the weal of
        the world.
     As one whose self is extinct should that Bodhisattva be considered.

Chapter XXII

The Good Friends and the Perfections [396-99]

1. Therefore then the learned who has slain pride,
   Who seeks with weighty resolution for the best enlightenment,
   Should, as one attends upon a physician to be cured of a multitude of
      ailments,
   Attend upon the good friend, undaunted.
2. The Buddhas, the Bodhisattvas who have set out for the best
      enlightenment,
   And [those who have] these perfections have been enumerated as
      'the good friends.'
   It is they who instruct them [i.e. the Bodhisattvas] in these
      progressive stages,
   For a double reason they [quickly] understand the Buddha-
      enlightenment.
3. The past and future Jinas, and those who stand [just now] in all the
      ten directions,
   They all [have] this perfection for their path, and no other.
   As a splendid illumination, as a torch, as a light, as the Teacher
   Have these perfections been described to those who have set out for
      the best enlightenment.
4. As he cognizes the perfection of wisdom through the mark of
      emptiness,
   So by the same mark he cognizes all these dharmas;
   When he wisely knows dharmas as empty, as without marks,
   In coursing thus he courses in the wisdom of the Sugatas.

Defilement and Purification [400]

5. In want of food, indulging in imagination, beings
   Always wander about in birth-and-death, their minds attached.
   Both I and Mine as dharmas are unreal and empty.
   By his own self has the fool become entangled in space.
6. As someone who suspects that he has been poisoned
   May well be struck down, although no poison has got into his
      stomach;
   Just so the fool who has admitted into himself [the notions of] I and
      Mine
   Is forced by that quite unreal notion of an I to undergo birth and
      death again and again.

7. Where one takes notice, there is defilement, so it has been revealed;
    The non-apprehension of I and Mine has been called purification.
    But there is herein no one who is defiled or who is cleansed.
    Then the Bodhisattva has understood the perfection of wisdom.

The Supreme Merit of Perfect Wisdom [401-2]

8. If as many beings as there are here in the entire Jambudvipa
    Would all, having aspired for the foremost enlightenment,
    And having given gifts for many thousands of kotis of years
    Dedicate it all to the enlightenment linked to the weal of the world;
9. But if someone else, practised in wisdom, the foremost perfection,
    Would for even one single day comply with it:
    An infinitesimal merit would here that heap of giving bring.
    Therefore the undaunted should always plunge into wisdom.

Compassion and Perfect Wisdom [402-4]

10. When the Yogin courses in wisdom, the best of perfections,
    He engenders the great compassion, but no notion of a being.
    Then the wise becomes worthy of the offerings of the whole world,
    He never fruitlessly consumes the alms of the realm.
11. The Bodhisattva who wishes to set free the gods and men,
    Bound for so long, and the beings in the three places of woe,
    And to manifest to the world of beings the broad path to the other
            shore,
    Should be devoted to the perfection of wisdom by day and by night.

The Simile of the Pearl of Great Price [404-5]

12. A man who had gained at some time a very fine jewel
    Which he had not got before, would be contented.
    If, as soon as he had gained it, he would lose it again through
            carelessness,
    He would be sorry and constantly hankering after
            the jewel.
13. Just so the Yogin who has set out for the best enlightenment
    Should not get parted from the perfection of wisdom, which is
            comparable to a jewel,
    Seizing the jewel which he has gained, with growing energy
    He moves forward, and swiftly he comes to the [state of] Bliss.

Chapter XXIII

The Superior Position of Bodhisattvas [413]

1. When the sun rises, free from clouds and one blaze of rays,
   Having dispelled the entire blinding and confusing darkness,
   It outshines all animals such as glowworms,
   And also all the hosts of the stars, and the lustre of the moon.
2. Just so the wise Bodhisattva, who courses in wisdom, the foremost
       perfection:
   Having destroyed the jungle of views,
   The Bodhisattva who courses in emptiness and the signless
   Very much surpasses the whole world, as well as the Arhats and
       Pratyekabuddhas.

The Simile of the King and the Crown Prince

3. Just as the son of a king, a giver of wealth, desiring the welfare [of
       others],
   Becomes a person of authority among all, much sought after.
   For even now he makes [many] beings happy,
   How much more so when he will be established as the resourceful
       [ruler] of the kingdom!
4. Just so the wise Bodhisattva, who courses in wisdom,
   A donor of the deathless, dear to gods and men.
   Already now he is interested in the happiness of [many] beings,
   How much more so when he will be established as king of the
       Dharma!

Chapter XXIV

How Mara is Discomforted and Defeated [416-17]

1. But Mara at that time becomes like one who feels a thorn in his flesh,
   Afflicted with sorrow, miserable, displeased, of little stamina.
   [He manifests]²⁹ a conflagration on the horizon, he hurls a meteor,
       in order to cause fear,
   'How can this Bodhisattva be made to become despondent in his
       mind!'
2. When the wise become resolutely intent,
   Day and night beholding the meaning of wisdom, the foremost
       perfection,
   Then their bodies, thoughts and speech become [free] like a bird in
       the sky.
   How can the Kinsman of Darkness gain entrance to them?

What Makes Mara Contented [420]

3. When a Bodhisattva has taken to quarrels and disputes,
   And when the thoughts [of two Bodhisattvas] become mutually
       conflicting and angry,
   Then Mara becomes contented, and supremely elated, [thinking:]
   'Both these remain far distant from the cognition of the Jinas.
4. Both these remain far distant [from it], comparable to malignant
       demons;
   Both these will effect for themselves a waning of their pledge.
   Those who are full of hate, deficient in patience, how can they have
       enlightenment?' —
   Then Mara becomes contented, together with his host.

The Bodhisattva's Pride and Repentance [420]

5. If a Bodhisattva who has not had his prediction
   Should have angry thoughts for one who has had it, and should bring
       about a dispute:
   For as many moments as he persists in his obstinate faulty thoughts,
   For so many aeons he must again put on the armour.
6. Then he sets up mindfulness, and [he reflects], 'These are
       unwholesome thoughts;
   By means of the perfection of patience do the Buddhas experience
       enlightenment.'

He confesses his fault, and afterwards he restrains himself,
Or he desists, and trains himself in this Buddha-dharma.

Chapter XXV

How a Bodhisattva Is Trained [424-30]

1. When he trains himself, he does not anywhere approach a training,
   Nor does he get at one who trains, or at the dharmas which
      [constitute] training.
   Who trains himself, without discriminating between both, —training
      and no-training, —
   He trains himself in this Buddha-dharma.
2. The Bodhisattva who thus cognizes this training,
   He does not ever become deficient in training, or immoral.
   Having found pleasure in them, he trains himself in these
      Buddha-dharmas.
   He trains himself, skilful in [the superior] training, but without
      apprehending anything,
3. When they train thus in wisdom, to the wise shedders of light
   Not even one single thought arises that is unwholesome:
   As when the sun goes through the sky, before the impact of its rays
   No darkness can maintain itself in the intermediate space.

Perfect Wisdom Comprehends All the Perfections [430-31]

4. For those who have effected a training in the perfection of wisdom
   All the [other] perfections are comprehended in it.
   As in the false view of individuality all the sixty-two false views
   Are included, so are these perfections [included in the perfection of
      wisdom].
5. As when the life faculty has been stopped
   Also all the other faculties that may exist are stopped:
   Just so, when the best of the wise course in wisdom,
   All these perfections have been said to be therein comprehended.

Bodhisattvas and Disciples [432-33]

6. In all the qualities of the Disciples and likewise of the
      Pratyekabuddhas,
   The wise Bodhisattva becomes trained:
   But he does not stand in them, nor does he long for them.
   'In that [also] should I be trained,' [he thinks]. In that sense he
      trains himself [in them].

Chapter XXVI

Rejoicing and Perfect Wisdom [435-36]

1. If someone resolutely rejoices in the productions of thought
   [Of a Bodhisattva who] has set out for the best enlightenment and is
       irreversible [from it];
   One might [measure] the Merus in up to a trichiliocosm by comparing
       them [with a tip of straw],[30]
   But not that merit derived from rejoicing.
2. They rejoice at the heap of merit of all beings that there are,
   Who desire what is wholesome, [and] who want emancipation.
   When for the weal of beings they have reached the infinite qualities of
       a Jina,
   They will give the Dharma to the world for the complete extinction of
       suffering.
3. The Bodhisattva who, not discriminating, comprehends
   All dharmas as empty, signless and unimpeded,
   Without any dualism he seeks in wisdom for enlightenment.
   Devoted to the foremost perfection of wisdom is that Yogin.

The Simile of Space and the Firmament [441]

4. An obstruction of the space-element by the firmament
   Cannot be found anywhere by anyone.
   Just so the wise Bodhisattva, coursing in wisdom,
   Is just like open space, and he courses calmly quiet.

The Simile of the People Created by Magic [441-42]

5. As it does not occur to a man whom a magician has conjured up
       [when he looks at the audience]:
   'I will please those people,' and nevertheless he performs his work;
   They see him exhibiting manifold illusory works,
   Although he has no body, thought, or name.
6. Just so it never occurs to one who courses in wisdom:
   'Having known enlightenment I will set free the world!'
   In his various rebirths he is associated with manifold works,
   Which he manifests like magical illusions, but he does not course in
       false discrimination.

The Simile of the Buddha's Magical Creations [442-43]

7.   As a Buddha's magical creation performs a Buddha's work,
     But, when he does so, no thought of self-conceit arises in him:
     Just so the wise Bodhisattva, who courses in wisdom,
     Manifests all works, comparable to a fictitious magical illusion.

The Simile of the Machine [443]

8.   An expert and experienced mason has made a wooden apparatus;
     Comparable to a man or a woman it performs here all its works.
     Just so the wise Bodhisattva, coursing in wisdom,
     Performs all his work by his cognition, but without discrimination.   '

Chapter XXVII

The Bodhisattva Worthy of Homage [446-47]

1. To the wise, who courses thus, many congregations of gods,
   Having bent forth their outstretched hands, in respectful salutation, will pay homage.
   The Buddhas also, as many as there are in the world-systems in the ten directions,
   Effect the proclamation of the garland of the praises of his qualities.

Mara Is Powerless against Certain Bodhisattvas [447-49]

2. If as many beings as there are in the fields countless like the sands of the Ganges
   Would all, let us assume, become Maras;
   And if every single hair on their bodies would again magically create a snare,
   They all could not hinder the wise.
3. For four reasons does the powerful and wise Bodhisattva
   Become unassailable by the four Maras, [and] unshakable:
   He becomes one who dwells in the empty; and yet he is not one who abandons beings;
   He acts as he speaks; he is sustained by the Sugatas.

The True Attitude to Suchness [452-54]

4. The Bodhisattva who resolutely believes when this perfection of wisdom,
   The mother of the Tathagatas, is being taught,
   And who practises the progressive path with resolution,
   He should be known as having well set out towards all-knowledge.
5. But he does not come to a standing place in the Suchness of the Dharma-element.
   He becomes as one who, like a cloud, stands in the sky without anywhere to stand on,
   As a sorcerer who, like a bird, rides on the wind which offers him no support,
   Or as one who, by the force of his spells, miraculously produces on a tree full-blown flowers out of season.

The Bodhisattva Dwells Supreme [454-56]

6. The wise and learned Bodhisattva who courses thus
    Does not get at one who wakes up to enlightenment, nor also at the
      Buddha-dharmas,
    Nor at one who demonstrates, nor also at one who loves and sees the
      Dharma.
    This is the dwelling of those who desire calm, of those who delight in
      the precious qualities.
7. As many as there are the dwellings of Disciples and Pratyekabuddhas,
    Associated with the peace and happiness of calm concentration:
    With the exception of the Arhat-liberation of the Tathagatas
    This dwelling is among all the foremost and the unsurpassed.

How and Why One Should Dwell in Emptiness [456]

8. A bird dwells in space, but does not fall down.
    A fish dwells amidst water, but does not die.[31]
    Just so the Bodhisattva who through the trances and powers has gone
      beyond,
    Dwells in the empty, but does not reach the Blessed Rest.
9. One who wants to go to the summit of the qualities of all beings,
    To experience the best, the exceedingly wonderful, Buddha-cognition,
    To give the best gift of the highest and supreme Dharma,
    He should resort to this best dwelling of those who bring benefit.

Chapter XXVIII

Who Trains in Perfect Wisdom Trains in Buddhahood [466]

1. Of all the trainings which have been revealed by the Leader,
   This teaching is the best and unsurpassed.
   One who, wise in all trainings, wishes to go Beyond,
   He should train in this perfection of wisdom, in the Buddha-training.

Inexhaustibility of Perfect Wisdom [464-71]

2. This is the best receptacle, the storehouse of the supreme Dharma,
   The treasury of happiness and ease of those people who belong to the
      clan of the Buddhas.
   The past and future world saviours, [and those who are at present] in
      the ten directions,
   They have come forth from this, and yet the Dharma-element does
      not get exhausted.
3. As many trees, fruits, flowers and forest trees as there are,
   They all have come out of the earth and originate in it.
   And yet the earth does not undergo exhaustion, or growth,
   It does not get tired, does not dwindle away, making no
      discrimination.[32]
4. The Buddha's offspring, the Disciples and Pratyekabuddhas,
   The gods, and the dharmas which lead to the ease and happiness of all
      the world, —as many as there are,
   They all have issued from wisdom, the foremost perfection,
   And yet wisdom does not ever get exhausted, nor does it increase.
5. As many beings as there are in the low, middle and high [regions of
      the] world,
   They have all, so has the Sugata said, been brought about by
      ignorance.
   The machinery of ill is kept going by the full complement of the
      conditions,
   And yet the machinery of ignorance does not get exhausted, nor does
      it grow.
6. As many roots of skilful devices as there are, or doors and methods of
      cognition,
   They all have issued from wisdom, the foremost perfection.
   The machinery of cognition is kept going by the full complement of
      conditions,

And yet the perfection of wisdom does not increase or become
   diminished.

Conditioned Coproduction [468-70]

7.   But the Bodhisattva who understands conditioned coproduction as
         non-production
   And this wisdom as non-extinction:
   As the rays of the sun freed from the covering of the clouds,
   So he has dispelled the covering of ignorance, and become one
         Self-Existent.

Chapter XXIX

The Perfection of Concentration

1. Those of great might who dwell in the four Trances
   Do not make them into a place to settle down in, nor into a home.
   But these four Trances, with their limbs, will in their turn become
   The basis for the attainment of the supreme and unsurpassed
        enlightenment.
2. One who is established in the Trances becomes one who obtains the
        foremost wisdom;
   And also when he experiences the four most excellent Formless
        Trances,
   He makes these Trances subservient to the best and foremost
        enlightenment.
   But it is not for the extinction of the outflows that the Bodhisattva
        trains himself in these.
3. Astonishing and wonderful is this accumulation of precious qualities.
   When they have dwelled in Trance and Concentration, there is then no
        sign.
   When the personality of those who have stood therein breaks up,
   They are reborn again in the world of sense-desire, as [and where]
        they had intended.
4. As some man from Jambudvipa who had in the past been a god,
   Would, after reaching again the highest abodes of the gods,
   See the apartments contained in them
   And would then again come back, and not make his home therein;
5. Just so those Bodhisattvas, bearers of the best qualities,
   Having dwelt in Trance and Concentration, Yogins who have exerted
        themselves,
   Become again established in the sense-world, unstained
   As the lotus in water, independent of the dharmas of the fools.
6. Except in order to mature beings, to purify the [Buddha-] field,
   To fulfil these perfections, the Great-souled ones
   Do not strive after rebirth in the formless world,
   Lest there be a loss of the perfections and of the qualities of
        enlightenment therein.
7. It is as if some man, having found a deposit of jewels,
   Would not generate longing in his intelligence with regard to it.
   At some other time he may acquire a few of them;

Having taken hold of them, having entered his home, he would not be
covetous [for any more?].

8. Just so the wise Bodhisattvas who have gained
The calm concentration of the four Trances, which gives joy and ease,
Having let go the acquisition of the joy and ease of Trance and
concentration,
They enter again into the sensuous world, compassionate for all that
lives.

9. When a Bodhisattva dwells in the concentration of the Trances,
He generates no longing in his intelligence for the vehicle of the
Arhats and Pratyekabuddhas:
[For then] he becomes unconcentrated, in his thought distracted and
puffed up,
He has lost the qualities of a Buddha, a sailor who suffers shipwreck.

10. Although he applies himself to the five sense-qualities, —
To form and sound, and likewise smell, and taste, and touch, —
When free from the vehicle of the Arhats and Pratyekabuddhas, the
joyous Bodhisattva
Should, a hero, be wisely known as being constantly concentrated.

The Perfection of Vigour

11. They have pure and courageous minds and are linked to other beings
and persons,
[When] they are practising the excellent perfection of Vigour.
As a maid servant is submissive to her master who is not subject to
anyone else,
So do the firmly wise submit to subjection by all beings.

12. The servant does not answer back to her master,
Even when abused, struck, or beaten.
Exceedingly trembling in mind, and overcome by fear,
She thinks, 'He surely will kill me for that!'

13. Just so the Bodhisattva who has set out for the foremost
enlightenment,
Should behave towards the entire world like a true servant.
Thereupon he obtains enlightenment, and the fulfilment of the
qualities takes place.
Fire, which has arisen from grass and sticks, [then] burns them up.

14. Having renounced a happy destiny for himself,
Practising his duty towards other beings, day and night, in his thought
free from hesitation:

Like a mother, ministering to [her] only child,
He abides in his resolute intention unexhausted.

Chapter XXX

1. The Bodhisattva who intends to wander about in birth-and-death for
   [a] long [time],
   A Yogin devoted to the purification of the [Buddha-] field for the
   welfare of beings,
   And who does not produce the least thought of fatigue,
   He is endowed with the perfection of vigour, and undaunted.
2. If the unwise Bodhisattva counts the kotis of aeons,
   And has the notion that it is long until the full attainment of
   enlightenment, he is bound to suffer,
   And for a long time he will be suffering while moving unto Dharma.
   Therefore he is inferior in the perfection of vigour, and essentially
   indolent.
3. Beginning with the production of the first thought of the foremost
   enlightenment,
   Until in the end he reaches the unsurpassed Bliss,
   If night and day he would persevere single-mindedly,
   The wise and learned should be known as one who has put forth
   vigour.
4. If someone would say, 'On condition that you have shattered Mount
   Sumeru,
   You will be one who will attain to the foremost enlightenment,'
   And if he [then] effects a thought of fatigue or limitation [to his
   efforts],
   Then that Bodhisattva is affected by indolence.
5. But when there arises to him the mindful thought, 'That is nothing
   difficult.
   In a mere moment Sumeru [will] break up into dust,'
   Then the wise Bodhisattva becomes one who puts forth vigour.
   Before long he will attain the foremost enlightenment of the Leaders.
6. If he would exert himself with body, thought and speech, [thinking]
   'Having matured [it] I will work the weal of the world,'
   Then, established in the notion of a self, he is affected by indolence.
   He is as far distant from the meditational development of not-self as
   the sky is from the ground.
7. When one has no notion of either body, or thought, or a being,
   Standing rid of perception, coursing in the non-dual Dharma, —
   That has been called by Him who bestows benefits the perfection of
   vigour

Of those who desire the blissful, imperishable, foremost enlightment.

The Perfection of Patience

8. When he hears someone else speaking to him harshly and offensively
The wise Bodhisattva remains quite at ease and contented.
[He thinks:] 'Who speaks? Who hears? How, to whom, by whom?'
The discerning is [then] devoted to the foremost perfection of
patience.

9. If a Bodhisattva, devoted to the precious Dharma, remains patient, —
And if someone else would give the trichiliocosm filled with precious
things
To the Buddhas, Knowers of the world, and to the Arhats and
Pratyekabuddhas, —
Infinitesimal only will be [by comparison] the merit from that heap
of gifts.

10. The personality of one who is established in patience is completely
purified,
Exalted by the thirty-two marks, [it becomes] boundless.
He preaches the best empty Dharma to beings.
Dear to the entire world do the patient and discerning become.

11. If someone had taken a basket containing sandalwood power,
And, with respect and affection, strewed it over the Bodhisattva;
And if a second one were to throw live coals over his head, —
He should produce a mind equal to both of them.

12. Having thus been patient, the wise and learned Bodhisattva
Dedicates that production of thought to the foremost enlightenment.
The hero who remains patient in all the worlds, surpasses
Whatever Arhats and Pratyekabuddhas there may be in the world of
beings.

13. Again, one who is patient should produce a thought [thus]:
'In the hells, in the world of animals and in the Yama world there are
many ills.
With the sense-pleasures as cause one must experience much that
causes displeasure.
Better, for the sake of enlightenment, to be patient today!'

14. 'Whip, stick, sword, murder, imprisonment, and blows,
Decapitation, and amputation of ears, hands and feet, and of nose,
As many ills as there are in the world, [all] that I [will] endure,'
[When he thinks thus, then] the Bodhisattva stands in the perfection
of patience.

Chapter XXXI

The Perfection of Morality

1. By morality those who hanker after calm are lifted up,
   Established in the sphere of those with the ten powers, unbroken in
     their morality.
   How ever many actions of restraint they comply with,
   They dedicate them to enlightenment for the benefit of all beings.

2. If he generates a longing for the enlightenment of Arhats and
     Pratyekabuddhas,
   He becomes immoral, unwise, and likewise faulty in his coursing.
   But when one turns over [all one's merit] into the utmost Bliss of
     enlightenment,
   Then one is established in the perfection of morality, [although]
     joined to the sense-qualities.

3. The Dharma from which come the qualities of the enlightenment of
     the Gentle,
   That is the object of the morality of those who are endowed with the
     qualities of Dharma.
   The Dharma which [involves] the loss of the qualities of the
     enlightenment of those who act for the weal of the world,
   As immorality has that been proclaimed by the Leader.

4. When a Bodhisattva tastes of the five sense-qualities,
   But has gone for refuge to the Buddha, the Dharma, and the holy
     Samgha
   And has turned his attention towards all-knowledge, [thinking] 'I will
     become a Buddha,' —
   As established in the perfection of morality should that discerning one
     be known.

5. If, when coursing for kotis of aeons in the ten paths of wholesome
     action,
   He engenders a longing for Arhatship or Pratyekabuddhahood,
   Then he becomes one whose morality is broken, and faulty in his
     morality.
   Weightier than an offence deserving expulsion is such a production of
     thought.

6. When he guards morality, he turns [the resulting merit] over to the
     foremost enlightenment,
   But he does not feel conceited about that, nor does he exalt himself.
   When he has got rid of the notion of I and the notion of other beings,

Established in the perfection of morality is that Bodhisattva called.
7. If a Bodhisattva, coursing in the path of the Jinas,
   Makes [a difference between] these beings as observers of morality
       and those as of bad morality,
   Intent on the perception of multiplicity he is perfectly immoral.
   He is faulty in his morality, not perfectly pure in it.
8. He who has no notion of I and no notion of a being,
   He has performed the withdrawal from perception, [and] he has no
       [need for] restraint.
   One who minds neither about restraint nor about non-restraint,
   He has been proclaimed by the Leader as restrained by morality.

The Perfection of Giving

9. But one who, endowed with morality, a pure being,
   Becomes unconcerned about anything that may be dear or undear, —
   If, when he renounces head, hands and feet his thought remains
       undejected,
   He becomes one who gives up all he has, always uncowed.
10. And having known the essential original nature of dharmas as void and
       without self,
    He would renounce his own flesh, undejected in thought,
    To say nothing of his renouncing of property and gold.
    It is impossible that he should act from meanness.
11. Through the notion of I comes about a sense of ownership about
       property, as well as greed;
    How can the deluded have the resolve to renunciation?
    The mean are reborn in the world of the Pretas,
    Or if as humans, then they are poor.
12. Then the Bodhisattva, having understood why these beings are
       poverty-stricken,
    Becomes resolved on giving, always a generous giver.
    When he has given away the four Continents, well adorned, as if
       they were just spittle,
    He becomes elated, for he has not kept the Continents.
13. Having given gifts, the wise and learned Bodhisattva,
    Having brought to mind all the beings that there are in the triple
       world,
    Becomes to all of them a donor, and he turns over
    That gift into the most excellent enlightenment, for the weal of the
       world.

14. When he has given a gift, he does not make it into a basis or support.
And he does never expect any reward from it.
Having thus renounced, he becomes a wise renouncer of all.
The little he has renounced becomes much and immeasurable.

15. If all the beings in the entire triple world, as many as there are
Would, let us assume, give gifts for endless aeons,
To the Buddhas, Knowers of the world, to Arhats and
    Pratyekabuddhas,
But would wish for the virtues of the Disciples; —

16. And if a Bodhisattva, wise and skilled in means,
Would rejoice at the foundation of their meritorious deed,
And would, for the weal of beings, turn it over into the best and most
    excellent enlightenment, —
By having turned over he surpasses the [merit of the] entire world.

17. If there were a large heap of spurious glass jewels,
One single gem of lapis lazuli surpasses it all:
Just so the Bodhisattva, who rejoices, surpasses
The [merit from the] whole vast heap of gifts of the entire world.

18. If the Bodhisattva, when giving gifts to the world
Remains unaffected by a sense of ownership or by affection for his
    property,
From that his wholesome root grows into something of great might:
As the moon, in the absence of cloud, is a circle of radiant light in the
    bright half of the lunar month.

Chapter XXXII

Rewards of the Six Perfections

1. Through Giving a Bodhisattva cuts off rebirth as a Preta.
   He also cuts off poverty, and likewise all the defilements.
   When he courses in it [i.e. giving] he gains infinite and abundant
      wealth.
   Through [his] giving he matures beings in trouble.
2. Through Morality he avoids rebirth as one of the many animals,
   And also the eight untoward moments; he constantly gains rebirth at
      an auspicious moment.
   Through Patience he gains a perfect and exalted body,
   With golden skin, dear to the world to look at.
3. Through Vigour he does not incur the loss of the bright qualities.
   He gains the storehouse of the infinite cognition of the Jinas.
   Through Trance he casts off the sense-qualities in disgust,
   He acquires the "lore," the superknowledges and concentrations.
4. Having, through Wisdom, comprehended the essential original nature
      of dharmas,
   He completely transcends the triple world and the states of woe.
   Having turned the precious wheel of the Mightiest of Men,
   He demonstrates Dharma to the world for the complete extinction of
      ill.
5. When the Bodhisattva has fulfilled these dharmas,
   He then still receives the purity of the field and the purity of [the]
      beings [in it].
   He also receives the lineage of the Buddha, the lineage of the Dharma,
   And likewise the lineage of the Samgha. He receives all dharmas."

Conclusion

6. The supreme physician who accords medical treatment to the sickness
      of the world,
   Has taught this exposition of wisdom which is the path to
      enlightenment.
   It is called "The Path to enlightenment which is the 'Accumulation of
      Precious Qualities,' "
   And it has been taught so that all beings might reach that Path.

[1] Numbers in brackets refer to corresponding pages of R. Mitra's edition of the *Ashta.*

[2] According to Indian mythology, rain is the work of Nagas, i.e. Serpents or Dragons, who live in lakes, etc. *Anopatapta* is the Prakrit form, used in this text, of the Sanskrit word *Anavatapta*, which means 'cool," and refers to the famous Lake Manasarowara in the Himalayas.

[3] "Jina," the "Victorious One," a name of the Buddha. In the second line of this verse the Buddha is also called "The Great Bull," an epithet I have omitted in the translation.

[4] "Awareness," the fifth skandha, more usually "consciousness."

[5] Srenika Vatsagotra was a "Wanderer," i.e. a non-Buddhist ascetic, whose conversations with the Buddha form one section of the *Samyuktāgama* of the Sarvastivadins. On one occasion (*Samy.* no. 105, pp. 31c-32) Srenika raised the question of the "true self," which he identified with the Tathagata. The Buddha told him that the Tathagata could not be found in the skandhas, outside the skandhas, or in the absence of the skandhas. In a supreme act of faith Srenika was willing to accept the Tathagata in spite of the fact that he could not be related to any of the skandhas.

[6] The "Blessed Rest" means the Nirvana which excludes the world of suffering, and the Bodhisattva should not "retire into" it, should not "cleave to" it.

[7] "To course" means "to be attentive to," "to treat as real."

[8] "Sign" is a technical term for the object of false perception. This difficult word has been explained in *Buddhist Wisdom Books* p. 27, and in my Rome edition of the *Vajracchedikā*, 1957, 106-7.

[9] Su-gata, "Well-Gone," a name for the Buddha.

[10] "Goes forth," i.e. to enlightenment.

[11] "Vessel," more usually "vehicle."

[12] "Apprehensions" here means "attempts to apprehend him, to get hold of him."

[13] In other words, the process which follows its extinction is beyond the range of observation. The simile of the fire refers to *Sutta Nipāta* (1074, 1076): "As flame flung on by force of wind / Comes to its end, reaches what none / Can sum; the silent sage, released, / From name-and-form, goes to the goal, / Reaches the state that none can sum. / When all conditions are removed, / All ways of telling also are removed."

[14] This list refers to the four "perverted views."

[15] Here understood as an intellectual virtue, which enables us to accept without undue perturbation the fact that nothing at all exists in any true sense of the word.

[16] At one stage of their career the saints can no longer turn back on enlightenment, but are bound to proceed until they become Arhats, Pratyekabuddhas or Buddhas.

[17] "Pure" here means "empty."

[18] I.e. the Buddha Dipankara, Sakyamuni's 24th predecessor, who prophesied his future Buddhahood. For the full story see *Buddhist Scriptures*, 1959, pp. 20-24.

[19] I.e. the emptiness, or the Dharma.

[20] The translation of this line is uncertain. The Tibetan may perhaps mean: "For the cognition of the wise has the thought of enlightenment come into being in the world."

[21] Used up his merchandise?

[22] So the Tibetan. Perhaps, "but only the Dharma-element"?

[23] The Tibetan has, "on the Buddha-stage."

[24] I.e. purity of body, speech and mind.

[25] *na ca hīyate*. In *Ashta* it is Suchness of which it is said that *na parihīyate*.

[26] The Tibetan seems to construe: "If the foundation . . . is like this, / How can it have its standing place in space? / Reflect on that object!"

[27] This is a tentative translation, and the text seems to require emendation.

[28] The Tibetan understands: the discerning also does not abide in his home, but becomes skilful in the path.

[29] Added from *Ashta: upadarśayati*.

[30] Added from *Ashta*. Tibetan: "It would be easier to weigh Mount Meru in a balance, than to find the measure of the merit from that act of rejoicing."

[31] Tibetan: "is not drowned."

[32] I.e. all this makes no difference to it.

*THE PERFECTION OF WISDOM
IN EIGHT THOUSAND LINES*

CONTENTS

Chapter I

THE PRACTICE OF THE KNOWLEDGE OF ALL MODES

1. INTRODUCTION

Thus have I heard at one time. The Lord dwelt at Rajagriha, on the Vulture Peak, together with a great gathering of monks, with 1,250 monks, all of them Arhats,—their outflows dried up, undefiled, fully controlled, quite freed in their hearts, well freed and wise, thoroughbreds, great Serpents, their work done, their task accomplished, their burden laid down, their own weal accomplished, with the fetters that bound them to becoming extinguished, their hearts well freed by right understanding, in perfect control of their whole minds—with the exception of one single person, i.e., the Venerable Ananda.

The Lord said to the Venerable Subhuti, the Elder: Make it clear now, Subhuti, to the Bodhisattvas, the great beings, starting from perfect wisdom, how the Bodhisattvas, the great beings go forth into perfect wisdom!

Thereupon the Venerable *Sariputra* thought to himself: [4] Will that Venerable Subhuti, the Elder, expound perfect wisdom of himself, through the operation and force of his own power of revealing wisdom, or through the Buddha's might?

The Venerable *Subhuti*, who knew, through the Buddha's might, that the Venerable Sariputra was in such wise discoursing in his heart, said to the Venerable Sariputra: Whatever, Venerable Sariputra, the Lord's Disciples teach, all that is to be known as the Tathagata's work. For in the dharma demonstrated by the Tathagata they train themselves, they realise its true nature, they hold it in mind. Thereafter nothing that they teach contradicts the true nature of dharma. It is just an outpouring of the Tathagata's demonstration of dharma. Whatever those sons of good family may expound as the nature of dharma, that they do not bring into contradiction with the actual nature of dharma.

2. THE EXTINCTION OF SELF

Thereupon the Venerable *Subhuti*, by the Buddha's might, said to the Lord: The Lord has said, 'Make it clear now, Subhuti, to the Bodhisattvas, the great beings, starting from perfect wisdom, how the Bodhisattvas, the great beings go forth into perfect wisdom!' When one speaks of a 'Bodhisattva,' what dharma does that word 'Bodhisattva' denote? I do not, O

Lord, see that dharma 'Bodhisattva' [5], nor a dharma called 'perfect wisdom.' Since I neither find, nor apprehend, nor see a dharma 'Bodhisattva,' nor a 'perfect wisdom,' what Bodhisattva shall I instruct and admonish in what perfect wisdom? And yet, O Lord, if, when this is pointed out, a Bodhisattva's heart does not become cowed, nor stolid, does not despair nor despond, if he does not turn away or become dejected, does not tremble, is not frightened or terrified, it is just this Bodhisattva, this great being who should be instructed in perfect wisdom. It is precisely this that should be recognised as the perfect wisdom of that Bodhisattva, as his instruction in perfect wisdom. When he thus stands firm, that is his instruction and admonition. Morever, when a Bodhisattva courses in perfect wisdom and develops it, he should so train himself that he does not pride himself on that thought of enlightenment [with which he has begun his career]. That thought is no thought, since in its essential original nature thought is transparently luminous.

Sariputra: That thought which is no thought, is that something which is?

Subhuti: Does there exist, or can one apprehend in this state of absence of thought either a 'there is' or a 'there is not'?

Sariputra: No, not that. [6]

Subhuti: Was it then a suitable question when the Venerable Sariputra asked whether that thought which is no thought is something which is?

Sariputra: What then is this state of absence of thought?

Subhuti: It is without modification or discrimination.

Sariputra: Well do you expound this, Subhuti, you whom the Lord has declared to be the foremost of those who dwell in Peace. And for that reason [i.e. because he does not pride himself on that thought of enlightenment] should a Bodhisattva be considered as incapable of turning away from full enlightenment, and as one who will never cease from taking perfect wisdom to heart. Whether one wants to train on the level of Disciple, or Pratyekabuddha, or Bodhisattva,—one should listen to this perfection of wisdom, take it up, bear it in mind, recite it, study it, spread it among others, and in this very perfection of wisdom should one be trained and exert oneself. In this very perfection of wisdom should one endowed with skill in means exert himself, with the aim of procuring all the dharmas which constitute a Bodhisattva. [7] In just this perfection of wisdom all the dharmas which constitute a Bodhisattva, and in which he should be trained and exert himself, are indicated in full detail. He who wants to train for full enlightenment should also listen, etc., to this perfection of wisdom. One who is endowed with skill in means should exert himself in just this perfection of wisdom, with the aim of procuring all the dharmas which constitute a Buddha.

Subhuti: I who do not find anything to correspond to the word 'Bodhisattva,' or to the words 'perfect wisdom,'—which Bodhisattva should I then instruct and admonish in which perfect wisdom? It would surely be regrettable if I, unable to find the thing itself, should merely in words cause a Bodhisattva to arise and to pass away. Moreover, what is thus designated is not continuous nor not-continuous, not discontinuous or not-discontinuous. And why? Because it does not exist. That is why it is not continuous nor not-continuous, not discontinuous or not-discontinuous. A Bodhisattva who does not become afraid when this deep and perfect wisdom is being taught [8] should be recognized as not lacking in perfect wisdom, as standing at the irreversible stage of a Bodhisattva, standing firmly, in consequence of not taking his stand anywhere. Moreover, a Bodhisattva who courses in perfect wisdom and develops it, should not stand in form, etc. Because, when he stands in form, etc., he courses in its formative influence, and not in perfect wisdom. For, while he courses in formative influences, he cannot gain perfect wisdom, nor exert himself upon it, nor fulfil it. When he does not fulfil perfect wisdom, he cannot go forth to all-knowledge, so long as he remains one who tries to appropriate the essentially elusive. For in perfect wisdom form is not appropriated. But the non-appropriation of form, etc., is not form, etc. And perfect wisdom also cannot be appropriated. It is thus that a Bodhisattva should course in this perfect wisdom. This concentrated insight of a Bodhisattva is called 'the non-appropriation of all dharmas.' It is vast, noble, unlimited and steady, not shared by any of the Disciples or Pratyekabuddhas. The state of all-knowledge itself cannot be taken hold of, because it cannot be seized through a sign. If it could be seized through a sign, then Srenika, the Wanderer, would not have gained faith in this our religion. Srenika, the Wanderer, believed resolutely in this cognition of the all-knowing, and as a 'faith-follower' he [9] entered on a cognition with a limited scope. He did not take hold of form, etc. Nor did he review that cognition with joyful zest and pleasure. He viewed it neither as inside form, etc., nor as outside, nor as both inside and outside, nor as other than form, etc. In this scripture passage, Srenika, the Wanderer, as one who always resolutely believes in this cognition of the all-knowing, is called a faith-follower. He took the true nature of dharmas as his standard, and resolutely believed in the signless, so that he did not take hold of any dharma, nor apprehend any dharma, which he could have appropriated or released. He did not even care about Nirvana. This also should be known as a Bodhisattva's perfect wisdom, that he does not take hold of form, etc., and that he does not enter Nirvana midway, before he has realized the ten powers of a Tathagata, his four grounds of self-confidence, and the eighteen dharmas peculiar to a Buddha. Therefore this too should be known as a Bodhisattva's perfect wisdom. [10] Further, a Bodhisattva who courses in perfect wisdom and develops it, should consider and meditate on what that perfect wisdom is, on him who has it, and on this perfect wisdom as a dharma which does not exist, which cannot be apprehended. When these considerations do not make him afraid, then he is to be known as a Bodhisattva who possesses perfect wisdom.

Sariputra: How can a Bodhisattva be known as possessing perfect wisdom, when the very form does not possess the own-being of form, etc.; when perfect wisdom does not possess the own-being of perfect wisdom; when the very all-knowledge does not possess the own-being of all-knowledge?

Subhuti: It is so, Sariputra. Form itself does not possess the own-being of form, etc. Perfect wisdom does not possess the mark (of being) 'perfect wisdom.' A mark does not possess the own-being of a mark. The marked does not possess the own-being of being marked, and own-being does not possess the mark of [being] own-being. [11]

Sariputra: Nevertheless, the Bodhisattva who trains in this will go forth to all-knowledge?

Subhuti: He will. Because all dharmas are unborn, and do not go forth. When he courses thus, a Bodhisattva comes near to all-knowledge. To the extent that he comes near to all-knowledge, his body, thought and marks shall become perfectly pure, for the sake of maturing beings, and he shall meet with the Buddhas. It is thus that a Bodhisattva who courses in perfect wisdom comes near to all-knowledge.

Subhuti said further concerning the Bodhisattva: He courses in a sign when he courses in form, etc., or in the sign of form, etc., or in the idea that 'form is a sign,' or in the production of form, or in the stopping or destruction of form, or in the idea that 'form is empty,' or 'I course,' or 'I am a Bodhisattva.' For he actually courses in the idea 'I am a Bodhisattva' as a basis. [12] Or, when it occurs to him 'he who courses thus, courses in perfect wisdom and develops it,'—he courses only in a sign. Such a Bodhisattva should be known as unskilled in means.

Sariputra: How then must a Bodhisattva course if he is to course in perfect wisdom?

Subhuti: He should not course in the skandhas, nor in their sign, nor in the idea that 'the skandhas are signs,' nor in the production of the skandhas, in their stopping or destruction, nor in the idea that 'the skandhas are empty,' or 'I course,' or 'I am a Bodhisattva.' And [13] it should not occur to him, 'he who courses thus, courses in perfect wisdom and develops it.' He courses but he does not entertain such ideas as 'I course,' 'I do not course,' 'I course and I do not course,' 'I neither course nor do I not course,' and the same [four] with 'I will course.' He does not go near any dharma at all, because all dharmas are unapproachable and unappropriable. The Bodhisattva then has the concentrated insight 'Not grasping at any dharma' by name, vast, noble, unlimited and steady, not shared by any of the Disciples or Pratyekabuddhas. When he dwells in this concentrated insight, a Bodhisattva will quickly win the full enlightenment which the Tathagatas of the past have predicted for him. But when he dwells in that concentration, he does not review it, nor think 'I am collected,' 'I will enter into concentration,' 'I am entering into concentration,' 'I have entered into concentration.' All that in each and every way does not exist for him. [14]

Sariputra: Can one show forth that concentration?

Subhuti: No, Sariputra. Because that son of good family neither knows nor perceives it.

Sariputra: You say that he neither knows nor perceives it?

Subhuti: I do, for that concentration does not exist.

The Lord: Well said, Subhuti. And thus should a Bodhisattva train therein, because then he trains in perfect wisdom.

Sariputra: When he thus trains, he trains in perfect wisdom?

The Lord: When he thus trains, he trains in perfect wisdom.

Sariputra: When he thus trains, which dharmas does he train in?

The Lord: He does not train in any dharma at all. [15] Because the dharmas do not exist in such a way as foolish untaught, common people are accustomed to suppose.

Sariputra: How then do they exist?

The Lord: As they do not exist, so they exist. And so, since they do not exist [*avidyamāna*], they are called [the result of] ignorance [*avidyā*]. Foolish, untaught, common people have settled down in them. Although they do not exist, they have constructed all the dharmas. Having constructed them, attached to the two extremes, they do not know or see those dharmas [in their true reality]. So they construct all dharmas which yet do not exist. Having constructed them, they settle down in the two extremes. They then depend on that link as a basic fact, and construct past, future and present dharmas. After they have constructed, they settle down in name and form. They have constructed all dharmas which yet do not exist. But while they construct all dharmas which yet do not exist, they neither know nor see the path which is that which truly is. In consequence they do not go forth from the triple world, and do not wake up to the reality-limit. For that reason they come to be styled 'fools.' They have no faith in the true dharma. But a Bodhisattva does not settle down in any dharma.

Sariputra: When he trains thus, is a Bodhisattva trained in all-knowledge?

The Lord: When he thus trains himself, a Bodhisattva is not even trained in all-knowledge, and yet he is trained in all dharmas. [16] When he thus trains himself, a Bodhisattva is trained in all-knowledge, comes near to it, goes forth to it.

Subhuti: If, O Lord, someone should ask,—'Will this illusory man be trained in all-knowledge, will he come near it, will he go forth to it?'—How should one explain it?

The Lord: I will ask you a counter-question which you may answer as best you can.

Subhuti: Well said, O Lord. And the Venerable Subhuti listened to the Lord.

The Lord: What do you think, Subhuti, is form, etc., one thing, and illusion another?

Subhuti: No Lord. Because it is not so that illusion is one thing, and form, etc., another; the very form is illusion, the very illusion is form.

The Lord: What do you think, Subhuti, is that notion 'Bodhisattva,' that denomination, that concept, that conventional expression,—in the five grasping skandhas?

Subhuti: Yes, it is. Because a Bodhisattva who trains himself in perfect wisdom should train himself like an illusory man for full enlightenment. [17] For one should bear in mind that the five grasping aggregates are like an illusory man. Because the Lord has said that form is like an illusion. And what is true of form, is true also of the six sense organs, and of the five [grasping] aggregates.

Subhuti: Will not Bodhisattvas who have newly set out in the vehicle tremble when they hear this exposition?

The Lord: They will tremble if they get into the hands of bad friends, but not if they get into the hands of good friends.

Subhuti: Who then are a Bodhisattva's good friends?

The Lord: Those who instruct and admonish him in the perfections. Those who point out to him the deeds of Mara, saying 'this is how the faults and deeds of Mara should be recognized. These are the faults and deeds of Mara. You should get rid of them after you have recognized them.' These should be known as the good friends of a Bodhisattva, a great being, who is armed with the great armour, who has set out in the great vehicle, who has mounted on the great vehicle. [18]

3. THE MEANING OF 'BODHISATTVA'

Subhuti: With regard to what the Lord has said, in speaking of 'Bodhisattva,'—what is meant by the word 'Bodhisattva'?

The Lord: Nothing real is meant by the word 'Bodhisattva.' Because a Bodhisattva trains himself in non-attachment to all dharmas. For the Bodhisattva, the great being, awakes in non-attachment to full enlightenment in the sense that he understands all dharmas. Because he has enlightenment as his aim, an 'enlightenment-being' [Bodhisattva], a great being, is so called.

4. THE MEANING OF 'GREAT BEING'

Subhuti: Again, when the Lord speaks of a Bodhisattva as 'a great being,'—for what reason is a Bodhisattva called a 'great being'?

The Lord: A Bodhisattva is called 'a great being' in the sense that he will cause a great mass and collection of beings to achieve the highest.

Sariputra: It is clear also to me in what sense a Bodhisattva is called a 'great being.' [19]

The Lord: Then make it clear what you think now!

Sariputra: A Bodhisattva is called a 'great being' in the sense that he will demonstrate dharma so that the great errors should be forsaken,—such erroneous views as the assumption of a self, a being, a living soul, a person, of becoming, of not-becoming, of annihilation, of eternity, of individuality, etc.

Subhuti: It is clear also to me in what sense a Bodhisattva is called a 'great being.'

The Lord: Then make it clear what you think now!

Subhuti: A Bodhisattva is called a 'great being,' if he remains unattached to, and uninvolved in, the thought of enlightenment, the thought of all-knowledge, the thought without outflows, the unequalled thought, the thought which equals the unequalled, unshared by any of the Disciples or Pratyekabuddhas. Because that thought of all-knowledge is [itself] without outflows, and unincluded [in the empirical world]. And in respect of that thought of all-knowledge, which is without outflows and unincluded, he remains unattached and uninvolved. In that sense does a Bodhisattva come to be styled a 'great being.'

Sariputra: For what reason is he unattached even to that thought, and uninvolved in it?

Subhuti: Because it is no thought.

Sariputra: Is that thought, which is no thought, something which is?
[20]

Subhuti: Does there exist, or can one apprehend, in this state of absence of thought either a 'there is' or a 'there is not'?

Sariputra: No, not that.

Subhuti: How then can the Venerable Sariputra say, 'is that thought, which is no thought, something which is'?

Sariputra: Well do you expound this, you whom the Lord has announced as the foremost of those who dwell in Peace.

Thereupon the Venerable *Purna*, son of Maitrayani, said to the Lord: 'Great being,' one who is so called, armed with the great armour is that being, he sets out in the great vehicle, is mounted on the great vehicle. That is why he comes to be styled a 'great being.'

Subhuti: How great is that which entitles him to be called 'armed with the great armour'?

The Lord: Here the Bodhisattva, the great being, thinks thus: 'countless beings should I lead to Nirvana and yet there are none who lead to Nirvana, or who should be led to it.' However many beings he may lead to Nirvana, yet there is not any being that has been led to Nirvana, nor that has led others to it. For such is the true nature of dharmas, seeing that their nature is illusory. [21] Just as if, Subhuti, a clever magician, or magician's apprentice, were to conjure up at the crossroads a great crowd of people, and then make them vanish again. What do you think, Subhuti, was anyone killed by anyone, or murdered, or destroyed, or made to vanish?

Subhuti: No indeed, Lord.

The Lord: Even so a Bodhisattva, a great being, leads countless beings to Nirvana, and yet there is not any being that has been led to Nirvana, nor that has led others to it. To hear this exposition without fear, that is the great thing which entitles the Bodhisattva to be known as 'armed with the great armour.'

Subhuti: As I understand the meaning of the Lord's teaching, as certainly not armed with an armour should this Bodhisattva, this great being, be known.

The Lord: So it is. For all-knowledge is not made, not unmade, not effected. Those beings also for whose sake he is armed with the great armour are not made, not unmade, not effected.

Subhuti: So it is. For form, etc., [22] is neither bound nor freed. And that is true also of the Suchness of form, the Suchness of feeling, etc.

Purna: But what then is that form of which you say that it is neither bound nor freed, and what is that Suchness of form, etc.?

Subhuti: The form of an illusory man is neither bound nor freed. The Suchness of the form of an illusory man is neither bound nor freed. [23]

Because in reality it is not there at all, because it is isolated, because it is unproduced. This is the great armour, the great non-armour of a Bodhisattva, a great being, who is armed with the great armour, who has set out in the great vehicle, who has mounted on the great vehicle.

After these words the Venerable Purna was silent.

5. THE MEANING OF 'GREAT VEHICLE'

Subhuti: It is thus, O Lord, that a Bodhisattva, a great being is armed with the great armour, and becomes one who has set out in the great vehicle, who has mounted on the great vehicle. But what is that great vehicle? How should one know the one who has set out in it? From whence will it go forth and whither? Who has set out in it? Where will it stand? Who will go forth by means of this great vehicle?

The Lord: 'Great vehicle,' that is a synonym of immeasurableness. 'Immeasureable' means infinitude. By means of the perfections has a Bodhisattva set out in it. From the triple world it will go forth. It has set out to where there is no objective support. It will be a Bodhisattva, a great being who will go forth,—but he will not go forth to anywhere. Nor has anyone set out in it. It will not stand anywhere, but it will stand on all-knowledge, by way of taking its stand nowhere. [And finally], by means of this great vehicle no one goes forth, no one has gone forth, no one will go forth. [24] Because neither of these dharmas,—he who would go forth, and that by which he would go forth—exist, nor can they be got at. Since all dharmas do not exist, what dharma could go forth by what dharma? It is thus, Subhuti, that a Bodhisattva, a great being, is armed with the great armour, and has mounted on the great vehicle.

Subhuti: The Lord speaks of the 'great vehicle.' Surpassing the world with its Gods, men and Asuras that vehicle will go forth. For it is the same as space, and exceedingly great. As in space, so in this vehicle there is room for immeasurable and incalculable beings. So is this the great vehicle of the Bodhisattvas, the great beings. One cannot see its coming, or going, and its abiding does not exist. Thus one cannot get at the beginning of this great vehicle, nor at its end, nor at its middle. But it is self-identical everywhere. Therefore one speaks of a 'great vehicle.'

The Lord: Well said, Subhuti. So it is. It is thus that this is the great vehicle of the Bodhisattvas, the great beings. Trained therein, Bodhisattvas do reach all-knowledge, have reached it, will reach it.

Purna: This Elder Subhuti, when asked about perfect wisdom, fancies that the great vehicle is something that can be pointed out. [25]

Subhuti: Have I, O Lord, spoken of the great vehicle without transgressing against perfect wisdom?

The Lord: You have. In agreement with perfect wisdom you point out the great vehicle.

6. ATTAINMENT

Subhuti: Through the Buddha's might, O Lord. Moreover, O Lord, a Bodhisattva [who sets out on his journey] does not approach [the goal of full Bodhisattvahood] from where it begins, nor where it ends, nor in the middle either. Because a Bodhisattva is as boundless as form, etc., is boundless. He does not approach the idea that 'a Bodhisattva is form,' etc. That also does not exist, and is not apprehended. Thus in each and every way I do not get at any of the dharmas which constitute a Bodhisattva. I do not see that dharma which the word 'Bodhisattva' denotes. Perfect wisdom also I neither see nor get at. All-knowledge also I neither see nor get at. Since in each and every way I neither apprehend nor see that dharma,—what dharma should I instruct and admonish through what dharma in what dharma? 'Buddha,' 'Bodhisattva,' 'perfect wisdom,' all these are mere words. And what they denote is something uncreated. It is as with the self. [26] Although we speak of a 'self,' yet absolutely the self is something uncreated. Since therefore all dharmas are without own-being, what is that form, etc., which cannot be seized, and which is something uncreated? Thus the fact that all dharmas are without own-being is the same as the fact that they are uncreated. But the non-creation of all dharmas differs from those dharmas [themselves]. How shall I instruct and admonish a non-creation in a perfect wisdom which is also a non-creation? And yet, one cannot apprehend as other than uncreated all the dharmas, be they those which constitute a Buddha, or a Bodhisattva, or him who marches to enlightenment. If a Bodhisattva, when this is being taught, is not afraid, then one should know that 'this Bodhisattva, this great being, courses in perfect wisdom, develops it, investigates it, and meditates on it.' Because at the time a Bodhisattva investigates these dharmas in perfect wisdom, at that time he does not approach form, etc., nor go to it. Nor does he review the production of form, etc., nor its stopping. For the non-production of form, etc., is not form, etc. [27] The non-passing-away of form, etc., is not form, etc. Non-production and form are therefore not two, nor divided. Not-passing-away and form, etc., are therefore not two, nor divided. Inasmuch as one calls it 'form,' etc., one makes a count of what is not two. Thus the Bodhisattva investigates in perfect wisdom all dharmas in all their modes, and at that time he does [28] not approach form, etc.

Sariputra: As I understand the teaching of the Venerable Subhuti, a

Bodhisattva also is a non-production. But if a Bodhisattva is a non-production, how then does he go on the difficult pilgrimage, and how can he possibly endure the experience of those sufferings [which he is said to undergo] for the sake of beings?

Subhuti: I do not look for a Bodhisattva who goes on the difficult pilgrimage. In any case, one who courses in the perception of difficulties is not a Bodhisattva. Because one who has generated a perception of difficulties is unable to work the weal of countless beings. On the contrary, he forms the notion of ease, he forms the notion that all beings, whether men or women, are his parents and children, and thus he goes on the pilgrimage of a Bodhisattva. A Bodhisattva should therefore identify all beings with his parents or children, yes, even with his own self, like this: 'As I myself want to be quite free from all sufferings, just so all beings want to be quite free from all sufferings.' In addition with regard to all beings one should form the notion: 'I ought not to desert all these beings. I ought to set them free from the quite measureless heap of sufferings! And I should not produce towards them a thought of hate, even though I might be dismembered a hundred times!' It is thus that a Bodhisattva should lift up his heart. When he dwells as one whose heart is such, then he will neither course nor dwell as one who perceives difficulties. [29] And further a Bodhisattva should produce the thought that 'as in each and every way a self does not exist, and is not got at, so in each and every way all dharmas do not exist, and are not got at.' He should apply this notion to all dharmas, inside and outside. When he dwells as one whose heart is such, then he will neither course, nor dwell, as one who perceives difficulties. But when the Venerable Sariputra said that 'a non-production is the Bodhisattva,' indeed, it is so, 'a non-production is the Bodhisattva.'

Sariputra: Further, is just a Bodhisattva a non-production, or the dharmas also which constitute him?

Subhuti: The dharmas which constitute a Bodhisattva are also a non-production.

Sariputra: Are just the dharmas which constitute a Bodhisattva a non-production, or also the state of all-knowledge?

Subhuti: The state of all-knowledge is also a non-production.

Sariputra: Is just the state of all-knowlege a non-production, or also the dharmas which constitute it?

Subhuti: The dharmas which constitute all-knowledge are also a non-production.

Sariputra: Are just the dharmas which constitute all-knowledge a non-production, or also the common people?

Subhuti: The common people are also a non-production.

Sariputra: Are just the common people a non-production, or also the dharmas which constitute them?

Subhuti: The dharmas which constitute the common people are also a non-production. [30]

Sariputra: If, venerable Subhuti, the Bodhisattva is a non-production and also the dharmas which constitute him, and also the state of all-knowledge, and also the dharmas which constitute it, and also the common people, and also the dharmas which constitute them,—then, surely, the state of all-knowledge is reached by a Bodhisattva without any exertion?

Subhuti: I do not wish for the attainment of an unproduced dharma, nor for reunion with one. Further, does one attain an unproduced attainment through an unproduced dharma?

Sariputra: Is then an unproduced attainment attained through an unproduced dharma, or through a produced dharma?

Subhuti: Is then an unproduced dharma produced, or is it unproduced?

Sariputra: Is then production a dharma which is a non-production, or is non-production a dharma which is production?

Subhuti: To talk of a production-dharma as a non-production-dharma is not intelligible.

Sariputra: To talk of non-production is also not intelligible.

Subhuti: Non-production is just talk. Non-production just appears before the mind's eye. Non-production is just a flash in the mind. Absolutely it is nothing more than that.

Sariputra: In the first rank of the preachers of dharma should the Venerable Subhuti be placed. [31] For in whatever way he may be questioned, he finds a way out; he does not swerve from [the correct teaching about] the true nature of Dharma, and he does not contradict that true nature of Dharma.

Subhuti: This is the Lord's Absolute, the essence of the Disciples who are without any support, so that, in whatever way they are questioned, they find a way out, do not contradict the true nature of dharmas, nor depart from it. And that because they do not rely on any dharmas.

Sariputra: Well said, Subhuti. And what is that perfection of the Bodhisattvas which [allows them not to] lean on any dharmas?

Subhuti: The perfection of wisdom, beneficial to all the [three] vehicles, is also the perfection which [allows them not to] lean on any dharma, because [it shows that] all dharmas have no support [and can therefore give none]. For if a Bodhisattva, when this deep perfection of wisdom is being taught, remains unafraid, then one should know that he has adjusted himself to the perfection of wisdom, and that he is not lacking in this attention [to the true facts about dharmas].

Sariputra: How is it that a Bodhisattva does not lack in attention when he is adjusted to perfect wisdom? [32] For if a Bodhisattva is not lacking in attention, then he should [automatically] lack in adjustment to the perfection of wisdom. And if he does not lack in adjustment to the perfection of wisdom, then he would be lacking in attention. But if [in] a Bodhisattva the two facts that he is not lacking in attention, and that he is not lacking in dwelling in the perfection of wisdom, belong together, then all beings also will not be lacking in dwelling in the perfection of wisdom. Because they also dwell not lacking in attention.

Subhuti: Well said, and yet I must reprove you, although the Venerable Sariputra has taken hold of the matter correctly as far as the words are concerned. Because one should know that attention is without own-being in the same way in which beings are without own-being; that attention has no real existence in the same way in which beings have no real existence; that attention is isolated in the same way in which beings are isolated; that attention is unthinkable in the same way in which beings are unthinkable; that acts of mental attention do not undergo the process which leads to enlightenment in the same way in which beings do not undergo that process; that acts of attention do not in any real sense undergo the process which leads to enlightenment, any more than beings do. It is through an attention of such a character that I wish that a Bodhisattva, a great being, may dwell in this dwelling.

Chapter II

SAKRA

1. PREAMBLE

At that time again, many Gods came to that assembly, and took their seats: Sakra, Chief of Gods, with forty thousand Gods of the Thirty-three; the four world-guardians, with twenty thousand Gods belonging to the retinue of the four Great Kings; Brahma, ruler of this world system, with ten thousand Gods belonging to the company of Brahma; and five thousand Gods of the Pure Abode. But the might of the Buddha, his majesty and authority surpassed even the splendour of the Gods, a reward for the deeds they had done in the past.

Sakra: These many thousands of Gods, Subhuti, have come to this assembly, and taken their seats, because they want to hear about perfect wisdom from the Holy Subhuti, and to listen to his advice to the Bodhisattvas, to his instruction and admonition. How then should a Bodhisattva stand in perfect wisdom, how train in it, how devote himself to it?

Subhuti: Let me then explain it to you, through the Buddha's might, majesty and authority. Those Gods, who have not yet aspired to full enlightenment should do so. Those, however, who are certain that they have got safely out of this world [i.e., the Arhats who have reached their last birth, and think they have done with it all] are unfit for full enlightenment [because they are not willing to go, from compassion, back into birth-and-death]. And why? The flood of birth-and-death hems them in. [34] Incapable of repeated rebirths, they are unable to aspire to full enlightenment. And yet, if they also will aspire to full enlightenment, I confirm them also. I shall not obstruct their wholesome root. For one should uphold the most distinguished dharmas above all others.

The Lord: Well said, Subhuti. You do well to encourage the Bodhisattvas.

Subhuti then said to the Lord: We should be grateful to the Lord, and not ungrateful. For in the past the Lord has, in the presence of the Tathagatas of the past, led, for our sake, the holy life with enlightenment as his aim. Even after he had definitely become a Bodhisattva [a being dedicated to enlightenment], disciples still instructed and admonished him in the perfections, and by his coursing therein he has produced the utmost cognition. Even so also we should help, champion, aid and sustain the Bodhisattvas. Because the Bodhisattvas, if we help, champion, aid and sustain them, will soon know full enlightenment.

2. HOW TO STAND IN EMPTINESS,
OR THE PERFECTION OF WISDOM

Subhuti then said to Sakra: Now, Kausika, listen and attend well. I will teach you how a Bodhisattva should stand in perfect wisdom. Through standing in emptiness should he stand in perfect wisdom. [35] Armed with the great armour, the Bodhisattva should so develop that he does not take his stand on any of these: not on form, feeling, perception, impulses, consciousness; not on eye, ear, nose, tongue, body, mind; not on forms, sounds, smells, tastes, touchables, mind-objects; not on eye-consciousness, etc., until we come to: not on mind-consciousness, etc., until we come to: not on the elements, i.e., earth, water, fire, wind, ether, consciousness: not on the pillars of mindfulness, right efforts, roads to psychic power, faculties, powers, limbs of enlightenment, limbs of the Path; not on the fruits of Streamwinner, Once-Returner, Never-Returner, or Arhatship; not on Pratyekabuddhahood, nor on Buddhahood. He should not take his stand on the idea that 'this is form,' 'this is feeling,' etc., to: 'this is Buddhahood.' He should not take his stand on the ideas that 'form, etc., is permanent, [or] impermanent'; [36] that 'form is ease or ill'; that 'form is the self, or not the self,' that 'form is lovely or repulsive,' that 'form is empty, or apprehended as something.' He should not take his stand on the notion that the fruits of the holy life derive their dignity from the Unconditioned. Or that a Streamwinner is worthy of gifts, and will be reborn seven times at the most. Or that a Once-Returner is worthy of gifts, and will, as he has not yet quite won through to the end, make an end of ill after he has once more come into this world. Or that a Never-Returner is worthy of gifts, and will, without once more returning to this world, win Nirvana elsewhere. Or that an Arhat is worthy of gifts, and will just here in this very existence win Nirvana in the realm of Nirvana that leaves nothing behind. Or that a Pratyekabuddha is worthy of gifts, and will win Nirvana after rising above the level of a Disciple, but without having attained the level of a Buddha. That a Buddha is worthy of gifts, and will win Nirvana in the Buddha-Nirvana, in the realm of Nirvana that leaves nothing behind, after he has risen above the levels of a common man, of a Disciple, and of a Pratyekabuddha, wrought the weal of countless beings, led to Nirvana countless hundreds of thousands of *niyutas* of *kotis* of beings, assured countless beings [37] of Discipleship, Pratyekabuddhahood and full Buddhahood, stood on the stage of a Buddha and done a Buddha's work,—even thereon a Bodhisattva should not take his stand.

Thereupon the Venerable *Sariputra* thought to himself: If even thereon one should not take one's stand, how then should one stand, and train oneself? The Venerable *Subhuti*, through the Buddha's might, read his thoughts and said: What do you think, Sariputra, where did the Tathagata stand?

Sariputra: Nowhere did the Tathagata stand, because his mind sought no support. He stood neither in what is conditioned, nor in what is unconditioned, nor did he emerge from them.

Subhuti: Even so should a Bodhisattva stand and train himself. He should decide that 'as the Tathagata does not stand anywhere, nor not stand, [38] nor stand apart, nor not stand apart, so will I stand.' Just so should he train himself 'as the Tathagata is stationed, so will I stand, and train myself.' Just so should he train himself. 'As the Tathagata is stationed, so will I stand, well placed because without a place to stand on.' Even so should a Bodhisattva stand and train himself. When he trains thus, he adjusts himself to perfect wisdom, and will never cease from taking it to heart.

3. THE SAINTS AND THEIR GOAL ARE ILLUSIONS

Thereupon the thought came to some of the *Gods* in that assembly: What the fairies talk and murmur, that we understand though mumbled. What Subhuti has just told us, that we do not understand. *Subhuti* read their thoughts, and said: There is nothing to understand, nothing at all to understand. For nothing in particular has been indicated, nothing in particular has been explained.

Thereupon the *Gods* thought: May the Holy Subhuti enlarge on this! May the Holy Subhuti enlarge on this! What the Holy Subhuti here explores, demonstrates and teaches, that is remoter than the remote, subtler than the subtle, deeper than the deep. *Subhuti* read their thoughts, and said: No one can attain any of the fruits of the holy life, or keep it,—from the Streamwinner's fruit to full enlightenment—[39] unless he patiently accepts this elusiveness of the dharma.

Then those *Gods* thought: What should one wish those to be like who are worthy to listen to the doctrine from the Holy Subhuti? *Subhuti* read their thoughts, and said: Those who learn the doctrine from me one should wish to be like an illusory magical creation, for they will neither hear my words, nor experience the facts which they express.

Gods: Beings that are like a magical illusion, are they not just an illusion?

Subhuti: Like a magical illusion are those beings, like a dream. For not two different things are magical illusion and beings, are dreams and beings. All objective facts also are like a magical illusion, like a dream. The various classes of saints, from Streamwinner to Buddhahood, also are like a magical illusion, like a dream. [40]

Gods: A fully enlightened Buddha also, you say, is like a magical illusions, is like a dream? Buddhahood also, you say, is like a magical illusion, is like a dream?

Subhuti: Even Nirvana, I say, is like a magical illusion, is like a dream. How much more so anything else!

Gods: Even Nirvana, Holy Subhuti, you say, is like an illusion, is like a dream?

Subhuti: Even if perchance there could be anything more distinguished, of that too I would say that it is like an illusion, like a dream. For not two different things are illusion and Nirvana, are dreams and Nirvana.

Thereupon the Venerable Sariputra, the Venerable Purna, son of Maitrayani, the Venerable Mahakoshthila, the Venerable Mahakatyayana, the Venerable Mahakashyapa, and the other *Great Disciples*, together with many thousands of *Bodhisattvas*, said: Who, Subhuti, will be those who grasp this perfect wisdom as here explained?

Thereupon the Venerable *Ananda* said to those Elders: Bodhisattvas who cannot fall back will grasp it, or persons who have reached sound views, or Arhats in whom the outflows have dried up.

Subhuti: No one will grasp this perfect wisdom as here explained [i.e. explained in such a way that there is really no explanation at all]. [41] For no dharma at all has been indicated, lit up, or communicated. So there will be no one who can grasp it.

4. SAKRA'S FLOWERS

Thereupon the thought came to *Sakra*: Let me now, in order to do worship to this discourse on dharma which is being taught by the Holy Subhuti, conjure up some flowers, and scatter them over the Holy Subhuti. Sakra then conjured up flowers, and scattered them over the Venerable Subhuti. The Venerable *Subhuti* thought to himself by way of reply: These flowers which [now] appear among the Gods of the Thirty-three I had not noticed before. These flowers, which Sakra has scattered, are magical creations. They have not issued from trees, shrubs or creepers. These flowers which Sakra has scattered are mind-made. *Sakra* replied: These flowers did not issue forth at all. For there are really no flowers, whether they issue forth from mind, or from trees, shrubs or creepers. *Subhuti* then said to him: As you say, Kausika, 'these flowers did not issue forth at all, [42] neither from mind, nor from trees shrubs or creepers'—because that which has never issued forth is not a flower.

5. TRAINING IN PERFECT WISDOM

Then the thought came to *Sakra*, Chief of Gods: Profoundly wise, surely, is the Holy Subhuti, in that he explains this merely nominal existence [of all separate things], does not bring it into conflict [with the norm of truth], but enlarges on it and simply expounds it. He then said to the Venerable Subhuti: So it is. The Bodhisattva should so train himself therein [in this insight] as the Holy Subhuti points out.

Subhuti: So he should. When he thus trains himself, he does not train himself in the fruit of a Streamwinner, nor in the other fruits of the holy life, up to Buddhahood. When one trains oneself on those stages, one trains oneself in Buddhahood, or the state of all-knowledge; and thereby in the immeasurable and incalculable Buddha-dharmas. Thereby one trains oneself neither for the increase of form, feeling, etc., nor yet for their decrease; [43] neither to appropriate form, etc., nor to let them go. Nor does one train oneself to get hold of any other dharma, even of all-knowledge, nor to produce one, or make one disappear. When he trains thus, a Bodhisattva trains in all-knowledge, and he shall go forth to all-knowledge.

Sakra: Will a Bodhisattva go forth to all-knowledge, even though he does not train himself to get hold of any dharma,—even of all-knowledge,—nor to produce one, or make one disappear?

Subhuti: He will. [44]

Sakra then said to Sariputra: Where should a Bodhisattva search for perfect wisdom?

Sariputra: In the exposition of the Venerable Subhuti.

Sakra: Through whose might, and on whose authority, does the Holy Subhuti teach perfect wisdom?

Sariputra: Through the Tathagata's might, and on his authority.

Subhuti: It is indeed the Tathagata's might, Sakra, by which I teach perfect wisdom. And when you ask, 'Where should a Bodhisattva search for perfect wisdom?', the answer is: He should not search for it in form, nor in any other skandha; nor in that which is other than form, or other than any other skandha. Because perfect wisdom is not one of the skandhas, nor yet other than they. [45]

6. THE INFINITUDE OF PERFECT WISDOM

Sakra: This perfection of wisdom, Subhuti, is a great perfection, unlimited, measureless, infinite.

Subhuti: So it is. And why? Perfect wisdom is great, unlimited, measureless and infinite because form, feelings, etc., are so. Hence one does not settle down in the conviction that this is a 'great perfection,' an 'unlimited perfection,' a 'measureless perfection,' and 'infinite perfection.' That is why perfect wisdom is a great perfection, unlimited, measureless and infinite. [46] Perfect wisdom is an infinite perfection because objects as well as [individual] beings are infinite. Perfect wisdom is an infinite perfection because one cannot get at the beginning, middle, or end of any objective fact [since as a dharma it has no own-being]. Moreover, perfect wisdom is an infinite perfection because all objective facts are endless and boundless, and their beginning, middle, or end are not apprehended. For one cannot apprehend the beginning, middle and end of form, etc. In that way perfect wisdom is an infinite perfection by reason of the infinitude of objects. And further again, a being is endless and boundless because one cannot get at its beginning, middle or end. Therefore perfect wisdom is an infinite perfection by reason of the infinitude of beings.

Sakra: How is it, Holy Subhuti, that perfect wisdom is an infinite perfection by reason of the infinitude of beings?

Subhuti: It is not so because of their exceedingly great number and abundance.

Sakra: How then, Holy Subhuti, *is* perfect wisdom an infinite perfection by reason of the infinitude of beings? [47]

Subhuti: What factual entity does the word 'being' denote?

Sakra: The word 'being' denotes no dharma or non-dharma. It is a term that has been added on [to what is really there] as something adventitious, groundless, as nothing in itself, unfounded in objective fact.

Subhuti: Has thereby [i.e., by uttering the word 'being'] any being been shown up [as an ultimate fact]?

Sakra: No indeed, Holy Subhuti!

Subhuti: When no being at all has been shown up, how can there be an infinitude of them? If a Tathagata, with his voice of infinite range, with the deep thunder of his voice, should pronounce, for aeons countless as the sands of the Ganges, the word 'being,' 'being,'—would he thereby produce, or stop, any being whatsoever, either in the past, future or present?

Sakra: No indeed, Holy Subhuti! Because a being is pure from the very beginning, perfectly pure.

Subhuti: In this way also perfect wisdom is an infinite perfection by reason of the infinitude of beings. In this manner also the infinitude of perfect wisdom should be known from the infinitude of beings. [48]

7. CONFIRMATION

Thereupon the *Gods* around Indra, Brahma and Prajapati, and the hosts of men and women around the Rishis thrice shouted forth in triumph: Hail the Dharma! Hail the Dharma! Hail the Dharmahood of Dharma! And they added: Beautifully has Subhuti the Elder just now indicated, demonstrated, shown and clarified how a Tathagata comes to be manifest. As a potential Tathagata we shall henceforth regard that Bodhisattva who possesses the fullness of this perfection of wisdom and who dwells in it.

The Lord then said: So it is, O Gods! So did I, when I met the Tathagata Dipankara in the bazaar of Dipavati, the royal city, possess the fulness of this perfection of wisdom, so that Dipankara, the Tathagata, predicted that one day I should be fully enlightened, and said to me: "You, young Brahmin, shall in a future period, after incalculable aeons, become a Tathagata, Sakyamuni by name,—endowed with knowledge and virtue, Well-Gone, a world-knower, unsurpassed, tamer of men to be tamed, teacher of Gods and men, a Buddha, a Blessed Lord!"

The Gods replied: It is wonderful, O Lord, it is exceedingly wonderful, O Well-Gone, how much all-knowledge is nourished and promoted in the Bodhisattvas, the great beings, by this perfection of wisdom!

Chapter III

REVERENCE FOR THE RECEPTACLE OF THE PERFECTIONS, WHICH HOLDS IMMEASURABLE GOOD QUALITIES

1. WORDLY ADVANTAGES OF PERFECT WISDOM

The *Lord* saw that the Gods were assembled and seated, and that the monks, nuns, laymen and laywomen were assembled and seated, and he spoke thus to the Gods: Mara and his hosts will be unable to harm those who take up this perfection of wisdom, who bear it in mind, preach, study and spread it. Men and ghosts alike will be unable to harm them. Nor will they die an untimely death. Those deities who have set out for full enlightenment, but who have not yet got hold of this perfection of wisdom, will approach a person who has [50] done so, listen to him, and will also take up, etc., this perfection of wisdom. A person who is devoted to this perfection of wisdom will certainly experience no fear, he will certainly never be stiff with fright,—whether he be in a forest, at the foot of a tree, or in an empty shed, or an open place, or a road, or a highway, or the woods, or on the ocean.

The Four Great Kings: It is wonderful, O Lord, that those who take up, etc., this perfection of wisdom should discipline beings in the three vehicles, and yet not perceive any being. We, O Lord, will protect such a person. [51]

Sakra, Brahman and other Gods likewise promised to protect the follower of perfect wisdom.

Sakra: It is wonderful, O Lord, that by taking up, etc., this perfection of wisdom, one should gain so many advantages even here and now. Does one, when taking up the perfection of wisdom, take up all the six perfections?

The Lord: Yes. And further, by taking up, etc., the perfection of wisdom, one gains advantages even here and now. Listen attentively, and I will teach you which ones they are.

So be it, Lord, replied the *Gods*.

The Lord: The quarrels, contentions and contradictions of those who oppose my dharma will simply vanish away; the intentions of the opponents will remain unfulfilled. [52] Because it is a fact that for the followers of perfect wisdom those disputes will simply vanish away, and will not abide. This is one advantage even here and now. There is an herb, Maghi by name, a cure for all poison. Suppose a viper, famished, were to see a creature, and pursue it, following the scent, in order to eat it; but if that creature went to a patch of that herb and stood there, then the smell of that herb would cause the snake to turn back. Because the healing quality of that herb is so powerful that it overpowers the viper's poison. Just so will the quarrels, contentions and contradictions to which the follower of perfect wisdom is exposed, be stilled, be appeased, [53] through the piercing flame of perfect wisdom, through its power, its strength, through impregnation with its power. They will vanish, and not grow, nor abide. And why? Because it is perfect wisdom which appeases all evil,—from [ordinary] greed to seizing on Nirvana—and does not increase it. And the Gods and all the Buddhas, and all the Bodhisattvas, will protect this follower of perfect wisdom. This will be an advantage even here and now. And further, the speech of the follower of perfect wisdom will become acceptable, soft, measured and adequate. Wrath and conceit will not overpower him. Because perfect wisdom tames and transforms him. Wrath and conceit he does not increase. Neither enmity nor ill will take hold of him, not even a tendency towards them. [54] He will be mindful and friendly. He reflects: 'If I foster ill will in myself, my faculties will go to pieces, my features will be consumed, and it is, in any case, quite illogical that I, who have set out for full enlightenment, and who want to train myself for it, should come under the sway of wrath.' In this way he will quickly regain his mindfulness. This will be another advantage even here and now.

Sakra: It is wonderful how this perfection of wisdom has been set up for the control and training of the Bodhisattvas.

The Lord: And further, Kausika, if a follower of perfect wisdom were to go into battle, to the very front of it, he could not possibly lose his life in it. It is impossible that he should lose his life from the attack of somebody else. [55] If someone strikes at him,—with sword, or stick, or clod of earth, or anything else—his body cannot be hit. Because a great lore is this, the perfection of wisdom; a lore without measure, a quite measureless lore, an unsurpassed lore, a lore which equals the unequalled is this, the perfection of wisdom. Because when one trains oneself in this lore, then one is intent neither on disturbing one's own peace, nor that of others. The Bodhisattva, the great being who is trained in this lore, will reach full enlightenment, will gain the gnosis of the all-knowing. Once fully enlightened he will read the thoughts of all beings. Because to the Bodhisattvas, the great beings who are trained in this lore, nothing remains unattained, unknown, unrealized. That is why one speaks of the gnosis of the all-knowing. This is another advantage even here and now. [56]

Further, where this perfection of wisdom has been written down in a book, and has been put up and worshipped, where it has been taken up, etc., there men and ghosts can do no harm, except as a punishment for past deeds. This is another advantage even here and now.

Just, Kausika, as those men and ghosts who have gone to the terrace of enlightenment, or to its neighbourhood, or its interior, or to the foot of the tree of enlightenment, cannot be hurt by men or ghosts, or be injured by them, or taken possession of, even with the help of evil animal beings, except as a punishment for former deeds. Because in it the past, future and present Tathagatas win their enlightenment, they who promote in all beings and who reveal to them fearlessness, lack of hostility, lack of fright. Just so, Kausika, the place in which one takes up, etc., this perfection of wisdom, in it beings cannot be hurt by men or ghosts. [57] Because this perfection of wisdom makes the spot of earth where it is into a true shrine for beings,—worthy of being worshipped and adored,—into a shelter for beings who come to it, a refuge, a place of rest and final relief. This is another advantage even here and now.

2. THE CULT OF PERFECT WISDOM COMPARED WITH THE CULT OF THE BUDDHAS

Sakra: Suppose that there are two persons. One of the two, a son or daughter of good family, has written down this perfection of wisdom, made a copy of it; he would then put it up, and would honour, revere, worship, and adore it with heavenly flowers, incense, perfumes, wreaths, unguents, aromatic powders, strips of cloth, parasols, banners, bells, flags, with rows of lamps all round, and with manifold kinds of worship. The other would deposit in Stupas the relics of the Tathagata who has gone to Parinirvana; he would take hold of them and preserve them; he would honor, worship and adore them with heavenly flowers, incense, etc., as before. Which one of the two, O Lord, would beget the greater merit?

The Lord: I will question you on this point, and you may answer to the best of your abilities. The Tathagata, when he had acquired and known full enlightenment or all-knowledge, in which practices did he train the all-knowledge-personality which he had brought forth? [58]

Sakra: It is because the Lord has trained himself in just this perfection of wisdom that the Tathagata has acquired and known full enlightenment or all-knowledge.

The Lord: Therefore the Tathagata does not derive his name from the fact that he has acquired this physical personality, but from the fact that he has acquired all-knowledge. And this all-knowledge of the Tathagata has come forth from the perfection of wisdom. The physical personality of the

Tathagata, on the other hand, is the result of the skill in means of the perfection of wisdom. And that becomes a sure foundation for the [acquisition of the] cognition of the all-knowing [by others]. Supported by this foundation the revelation of the cognition of the all-knowing takes place, the revelation of the Buddha-body, of the Dharma-body, of the Samgha-body. The acquisition of the physical personality is thus the cause of the cognition of the all-knowing. As the sure foundation of that cognition it has, for all beings, become a true shrine, worthy of being saluted respectfully, of being honoured, revered and adored. After I have gone to Parinirvana, my relics also will be worshipped. It is for this reason that the person who would copy and worship the perfection of wisdom would beget the greater merit. For, in doing so, he would worship the cognition of the all-knowing. [59] The son or daughter of good family who has made a copy of the perfection of wisdom, and who worships it, would beget the greater merit. For by worshipping the perfection of wisdom he worships the cognition of the all-knowing.

Sakra: How can it be that those men of Jambudvipa, who do not copy this perfection of wisdom, nor take it up, nor study it, nor worship it, do not know that the Lord has taught that the cult of the perfection of wisdom is greatly profitable! How is it that they are not aware that the Lord has taught that the cult of the perfection of wisdom brings great advantages, fruits and rewards! But they do not know this, they are not aware of this! They have no faith in it!

The Lord: What do you think, Kausika, how many of those men of Jambudvipa are endowed with perfect faith in the Buddha, the Dharma, the Samgha? [60]

Sakra: Only a few.

The Lord: So it is, Kausika. Only a few men of Jambudvipa are endowed with perfect faith in the Buddha, the Dharma and the Samgha. Fewer than those few are those who attain the fruits of a Streamwinner, and, after that, the fruit of a Once-Returner, or of a Never-Returner. Fewer still are those who attain Arhatship. Fewer still realise Pratyeka-buddha-enlightenment. Fewer still raise their thoughts to full enlightenment. Fewer still are those who, having raised their thoughts to full enlightenment, strengthen that thought. Fewer still those who, having raised their thoughts to full enlightenment, and strengthened that thought, in addition dwell with vigor exerted. Fewer still those who pursue meditation on the perfection of wisdom. Fewer still those who course in the perfection of wisdom. Fewer still those who, coursing and striving in the perfection of wisdom, abide on the irreversible Bodhisattva-stage. Fewer still, coursing and striving in the perfection of wisdom, will know full enlightenment. Fewer still, coursing and striving in the perfection of wisdom, do know full enlightenment. Now, those Bodhisattvas who have stood on the irreversible Bodhisattva-stage, and who have known full enlightenment, they expound the perfection of wisdom to other sons and daughters of good family [61] who are earnestly intent, who train themselves, and strive, in the perfection of wisdom. And they, in their turn, take up the perfection of wisdom, study and worship it. There are, on the other hand, countless beings who raise their thoughts to enlightenment, who strengthen that thought of enlightenment, who course towards enlightenment,— and perhaps just one or two of them can abide on the irreversible Bodhisattva-stage! For full enlightenment is hard to come up to if one has inferior vigour, is slothful, an inferior being, has inferior thoughts, notions, intentions and wisdom. So then, if someone wants quickly to know full enlightenment, he should indefatigably and continually hear and study this very perfection of wisdom. For he will understand that in the past, when he was a Bodhisattva, the Tathagata trained in the perfection of wisdom; that also he should train in it; that she is his Teacher. In any case, when the Tathagata has disappeared into final Nirvana, the Bodhisattvas should run back to this very perfection of wisdom. [62] Therefore then, Kausika, if someone would build, for the worship of the Tathagata who has disappeared into final Nirvana, many kotis of Stupas made of the seven precious things, enshrining therein the relics of the Tathagata, and all his life honor them with flowers, etc., would he then, on the strength of that, beget a great deal of merit?

Sakra: He would, O Lord.

The Lord: Greater would be the merit of someone who would truly believe in this perfection of wisdom; who would, trustingly, confiding in it, resolutely intent on it, serene in his faith, his thoughts raised to enlightenment, in earnest intent, hear it, learn it, bear it in mind, recite and study it, spread, demonstrate, explain, expound and repeat it, illuminate it in detail to others, uncover its meaning, investigate it with his mind; who, using his wisdom to the fullest extent, would thoroughly examine it; who would copy it, and preserve and store away the copy—so that the good dharma might last long, so that the guide of the Buddhas might not be annihilated, so that the good dharma might not disappear, so that the Bodhisattvas, the great beings might continue to be assisted, since their guide will not give out,—and who, finally, would honour and worship this perfection of wisdom. [63] Greater would be the merit of the devotee of the perfection of wisdom compared not only with that of a person who would build many kotis of Stupas made of the seven precious things, enshrining the relics of the Tathagata. It would be greater than the merit of one who would completely fill the entire Jambudvipa with such Stupas. [64] It would be greater than the merit produced by all beings in a four-continent world system if each single one of them were to build such a Stupa. [65] Or, equally, if all beings in a small chiliocosm, [66] or in a medium dichiliocosm, [67] or in a great trichiliocosm would do likewise. [68] Or, if, to put an imaginary case, all beings in a great trichiliocosm should simultaneously become human beings, and each one of them build such a Stupa; and if each one of them should build all those Stupas, and honor them for an aeon or the remainder of an aeon; [69] still the devotee of the perfection of wisdom would have greater merit than that which results from the effect of the meritorious deeds of all those beings who erect and worship those countless Stupas.

Sakra: So it is, O Lord. For the person who honours the perfection of wisdom, in an absolute sense he honours the past, future and present Buddhas in all the world systems, which can be comprehended only by the cognition of a Buddha. His merit will be greater even than that of all beings in great trichiliocosms countless like the sands of the Ganges, [70] if each single being in them would build a Stupa, and if each one of them would build all those Stupas, and honor them for an aeon or the remainder of an aeon.

3. PERFECT WISDOM, A GREAT SPELL

The Lord: So it is, Kausika. The merit of the devotee of the perfection of wisdom is greater than that; it is immeasurable, incalculable, [71] inconceivable, incomparable, illimitable. Because from the perfection of wisdom the all-knowledge of the Tathagatas has come forth; from all-knowledge has come forth the cult of the relics of the Tathagata. Therefore the accumulation of merit of the devotee of the perfection of wisdom bears no proportion at all to the accumulation of merit born from building Stupas, made of the seven precious things, enshrining the relics of the Tathagata. [72]

Thereupon those *forty thousand gods* in the assembly said to Sakra, the Chief of Gods: Sir! do take up the perfection of wisdom! The perfection of wisdom, Sir, should be taken up, recited, studied and explained!

The Lord: Kausika, do take up the perfection of wisdom, recite, study and explain it! For if the Asuras form the idea of having a fight with the Gods of the Thirty-three, and if you, Kausika, bring to mind and repeat this perfection of wisdom, then the Asuras will drop that idea again. [73]

Sakra: A great lore is this perfection of wisdom, a lore without measure, a quite measureless lore, an unsurpassed lore, an unequalled lore, a lore which equals the unequalled.

The Lord: So it is, Kausika. For thanks to this lore, i.e. the perfection of wisdom, the Buddhas of the past have known full enlightenment. Thanks to it the Buddhas of the future will know it. Thanks to it, the Buddhas of the present do know it. Thanks to it I have known it. [74] Thanks to just this lore do the ten wholesome ways of acting become manifest in the world, the four trances associated with the limbs of enlightenment, the four Unlimited associated with the limbs of enlightenment, the four formless attainments upheld by the limbs of enlightenment, the six super-knowledges associated with the limbs of enlightenment, the thirty-seven dharmas which constitute the limbs of enlightenment, in short the eighty-four thousand articles of dharma, the cognition of the Buddha, the cognition of the Self-existent, the inconceivable cognition. But when there are no Tathagatas in the world, then it is the Bodhisattvas,—endowed with skill in means as a result of hearing the outpouring of the perfection of wisdom in the past (when there were Buddhas), full of pity for beings, come into this world out of pity,—who foster in the world the ten wholesome ways of acting, the four trances as dissociated from the limbs of enlightenment, etc. to: the five super-knowledges as dissociated from the limbs of enlightenment. [75] Just as thanks to the disk of the moon all the herbs, stars and constellations are illuminated according to their power and strength, so, after the Tathagata has passed away and His good dharma has disappeared, in the absence of the Tathagatas, whatever righteous, upright, outstanding, or wholesome life is conceived and manifested in the world, all that has come forth from the Bodhisattva, has been brought forth by him, has spread from his skill in means. But the skill in means of the Bodhisattvas should be known as having come forth from the perfection of wisdom. Moreover, those who are devoted to the perfection of wisdom, should expect therefrom many advantages here and now.

Sakra: Which are those advantages?

The Lord: Those devotees will not die an untimely death, nor from poison, or sword, or fire, or water, or staff, or violence. When they bring to mind and repeat this perfection of wisdom, [76] the calamaties which threaten them from kings and princes, from king's counsellors and king's ministers, will not take place. If kings, etc., would try to do harm to those who again and again bring to mind and repeat the perfection of wisdom they will not succeed; because the perfection of wisdom upholds them. Although kings, etc., may approach them with harmful intent, they will instead decide to greet them, to converse with them, to be polite and friendly to them. For this perfection of wisdom entails an attitude of friendliness and compassion towards all beings. Therefore, even though the devotee of the perfection of wisdom may be in the middle of a wilderness infested with venomous vipers, neither men nor ghosts can harm them, except as a punishment for past deeds.

Thereupon one hundred Wanderers of other sects approached the Lord with hostile intent. *Sakra*, Chief of Gods, perceived those Wanderers from afar, and he reflected: Surely, those Wanderers of other sects are approaching the Lord with hostile intent. Let me then recall as much of this perfection of wisdom as I have learned from the Lord, [77] bring it to mind, repeat and spread it, so that those Wanderers cannot approach the Lord, and the preaching of this perfection of wisdom may not be interrupted.

Thereupon Sakra, Chief of Gods, recalled as much of this perfection of wisdom as he had learned from the Lord, brought it to mind, repeated and spread it. Those Wanderers of other sects thereupon reverently saluted the Lord from afar, and went off on their way.

Thereupon it occurred to the Venerable *Sariputra*: For what reason have those heretical Wanderers reverently saluted the Lord from afar, and then departed on their way?

The Lord: When Sakra, Chief of Gods, perceived the thoughts of those hostile Wanderers of other sects, he recalled this perfection of wisdom, brought it to mind, repeated it and spread it, with the object of turning back those Wanderers of other sects who wanted to quarrel, dispute and obstruct, and of preventing them from approaching the place where the perfection of wisdom is being taught. And I have granted permission to Indra, Chief of Gods. Because I saw not even one pure dharma in those Wanderers. [78] They all wanted to approach with hostile intent, with thoughts of enmity.

Thereupon it occurred to *Mara*, the Evil One: The four assemblies of the Tathagata are assembled, and seated face to face with the Tathagata. Face to face [with the Tathagata] those Gods of the realm of sense-desire and of the realm of form are sure to be predicted in that assembly as Bodhisattvas to full enlightenment. Let me now approach to blind them. — Thereupon Mara conjured up a fourfold army, and moved towards the place where the Lord was.

Thereupon it occurred to *Sakra*, chief of gods: Surely, this is Mara, the Evil One, who, having conjured up a fourfold army, moves towards the place where the Lord is. But the array of this army is not the array of King Bimbisara's army, not of King Prasenajit's army, not of the army of the Sakyas or of the Licchavins. For a long time Mara the Evil One has pursued the Lord, looking for a chance to enter, searching for a chance to enter, intent on hurting beings. I will now recall this perfection of wisdom, bring it to mind, repeat and spread it. Thereupon Sakra recalled just this perfection of wisdom, brought it to mind, repeated and spread it. [79] Immediately Mara, the Evil One, turned back again, and went on his way.

Thereupon the *Gods* of the Thirty-three conjured up heavenly Mandarava flowers, flew through the air, and scattered them over the Lord. And in triumph they cried: "For a long time surely has this perfection of wisdom come to the men of Jambudvipa!" Seizing more Mandarava flowers, they scattered and strewed them over the Lord, and said: "Mara and his host will have no chance to enter those beings who preach and develop the perfection of wisdom, or who course in it. Those beings who hear and study the perfection of wisdom will be endowed with no small wholesome root. Those who come to hear of this perfection of wisdom have fulfilled their duties under the Jinas of the past. How much more so those who will study and repeat it, who will be trained in Thusness, progress to it, make endeavours about it; they will be people who have honoured the Tathagatas. [80] For it is in this perfection of wisdom that one should search for all-knowledge. Just as all jewels are brought forth by the great ocean, and should be searched for through it, just so the great jewel of the all-knowledge of the Tathagatas should be searched for through the great ocean of the perfection of wisdom."

The Lord: So it is, Kausika. It is from the great ocean of the perfection of wisdom that the great jewel of the all-knowledge of the Tathagatas has come forth.

4. PERFECT WISDOM, AND THE OTHER PERFECTIONS

Ananda: The Lord does not praise the perfection of giving, nor any of the first five perfections; he does not proclaim their name. Only the perfection of wisdom does the Lord praise, its name alone he proclaims.

The Lord: So it is, Ananda. For the perfection of wisdom controls the five perfections. What do you think, Ananda, can giving undedicated to all-knowledge be called perfect giving?

Ananda: No, Lord.

The Lord: The same is true of the other perfections. [81] What do you think, Ananda, is that wisdom inconceivable which turns over the wholesome roots by dedicating them to all-knowledge?

Ananda: Yes, it is inconceivable, completely inconceivable.

The Lord: The perfection of wisdom therefore gets its name from its supreme excellence [*paramatvāt*]. Through it the wholesome roots, dedicated to all-knowledge, get the name of 'perfections.' It is therefore because it has dedicated the wholesome roots to all-knowledge that the perfection of wisdom controls, guides and leads the five perfections. The five perfections are in this manner contained in the perfection of wisdom, and the term 'perfection of wisdom' is just a synonym for the fulfilment of the six perfections. In consequence, when the perfection of wisdom is proclaimed, all the six perfections are proclaimed. Just as gems, scattered about in the great earth, grow when all conditions are favourable; and the great earth is their support, and they grow supported by the great earth; even so, embodied in the perfection of wisdom, the five perfections rest in all-knowledge, they grow supported by the perfection of wisdom; and as upheld by the perfection of wisdom do they get the name of 'perfections.' [82] So it is just the perfection of Wisdom that controls, guides and leads the five perfections.

5. FURTHER ADVANTAGES FROM PERFECT WISDOM

Sakra: So far the Tathagata has not proclaimed all the qualities of the perfection of wisdom, qualities which one acquires by learning, studying and repeating the perfection of wisdom. For how else could the limited amount of the perfection of wisdom, which I had learned from the Lord, have spread [when just now the heretics and Mara were turned away]!

The Lord: So it is, Kausika. Moreover, not only one who has learned, studied and repeated the perfection of wisdom, will have those qualities, but also one who worships a copy of it, he also, I teach, will have those advantages here and now. [83]

Sakra: I also will protect one who worships a copy of the perfection of wisdom, and still more so one who in addition learns, studies and repeats it.

The Lord: Well said, Kausika. Moreover, when someone repeats this perfection of wisdom, many hundreds of Gods will come near, many thousands, many hundreds of thousands of Gods, so as to listen to the dharma. And, when they hear the dharma, those Gods will want to induce a readiness to speak in that preacher of dharma. Even when he is not willing to talk, the Gods still expect that, through their respect for dharma, a readiness to speak will be induced in him, and that he will feel urged to teach. [84] This again is another quality which someone acquires just here and now when learning, studying, and repeating the perfection of wisdom. Moreover, the minds of those who teach this perfection of wisdom will remain uncowed in front of the four assemblies. They will have no fear of being plied with questions by hostile persons. For the perfection of wisdom protects them. Immersed in the perfection of wisdom one does not see the hostility, nor those who act with hostility, nor those who want to be hostile. In that way, upheld by the perfection of wisdom, one

remains unaffected by censure and fear. These qualities also someone ac-
quires just here and now when learning, studying and repeating the perfec-
tion of wisdom. In addition, he will be dear to his mother and father, to
friends, relatives and kinsmen, to Sramanas and Brahmanas. Competent he
will be and capable of refuting, in accordance with dharma, any counter-
arguments that may arise, and able to deal with counter-questions. These
qualities also someone acquires just here and now when learning, studying
and repeating the perfection of wisdom. [85] Moreover, Kausika, among
the Gods of the Four Great Kings those Gods who have set out for full
enlightenment will make up their minds to come to the place where some-
one has put up a copy of the perfection of wisdom, and worships it. They
will come, look upon the copy of this perfection of wisdom, salute it
respectfully, pay homage to it, learn, study and repeat it. Then they will
depart again. And that applies to all the Gods, up to the Highest Gods.
[88] And that son or daughter of a good family should wish that the
Gods, Nagas, Yakshas, Gandharvas, Asuras, Garudas, Kinnaras, Mahoragas,
men and ghosts, in the ten directions in countless world systems, should,
with the help of this book, see the perfection of wisdom, salute it respect-
fully, pay homage to it, learn, study and repeat it; that then they should
return to their respective worlds; and that he should be able to give them
just this gift of dharma. You should not however think, Kausika, that only
in this four-continent world the Gods of the realm of sense-desire and of
the realm of form, who have set out for full enlightenment, will decide to
come to that place. Not so, Kausika, should you view it! No, all the Gods
in the great trichiliocosm, who have set out for full enlightenment, will
decide to come to that place. They will come, look upon the copy of this
perfection of wisdom, salute it respectfully, pay homage to it, learn, study
and repeat it. Moreover, the house, room or palace of the devotee of the
perfection of wisdom will be well guarded. No one will harm him, except
as a punishment for past deeds. This is another quality which one acquires
just here and now. [89] For very powerful Gods, and other supernatural
beings, will decide to come to that place.

Sakra: How does one know that Gods, or other supernatural beings,
have come to that place to hear, etc., the perfection of wisdom?

The Lord: When one perceives somewhere a sublime radiance or
smells a superhuman odour not smelled before, then one should know for
certain that a God, or other supernatural being, has come, has come near.
Further, clean and pure habits will attract those Gods, etc., and will make
them enraptured, overjoyed, full of zest and gladness. But the divinities of
minor power, who had before occupied that place, they will decide to
leave it. For they cannot endure the splendour, majesty and dignity of

those very powerful Gods, etc. And as those very powerful Gods, etc., will decide to come to him repeatedly, that devotee of the perfection of wisdom will gain an abundance of serene faith. This is another quality which that son or daughter of a good family will acquire just here and now. Further on, one should not form any unclean or impure habits within the circumference of that abode of the guide to Dharma; otherwise one's deep respect for it would remain incomplete. Moreover, the devotee of the perfection of wisdom will not be fatigued in either body or mind. At ease he lies down, at ease he walks about. In his sleep he will see no evil dreams. When he sees anything in his dreams, [91] he will just see the Tathagatas, or Stupas, or Bodhisattvas, or Disciples of the Tathagata. When he hears sounds, he will hear the sound of the perfections and of the wings to enlightenment. He will just see the trees of enlightenment; and underneath them the Tathagatas, while they wake up to full enlightenment. And likewise he will see how the fully Enlightened turn the wheel of dharma. And many Bodhisattvas he will see, chanting just this perfection of wisdom, delighted by its chorus, which proclaims how all-knowledge should be gained, how the Buddha-field should be purified. He is shown the skill in means. He hears the sublime sound of the full enlightenment of the Buddhas, the Lords: 'In this direction, in this part of the world, in this world system, under this name, a Tathagata demonstrates dharma, surrounded and accompanied by many thousands of Bodhisattvas and Disciples, nay by many hundreds of thousands of niyutas of kotis of Bodhisattvas and Disciples.' When he has such dreams, he will sleep at ease, he will wake up at ease. Even when food is thrown into it, his body will still feel at ease, and exceedingly light. No trend of thought will arise in him from excessive eagerness for food. He will take only a mild interest in food. [92] A devotee of the perfection of wisdom has no strong desire for food, and only a mild interest in it, even as a monk, who practices Yoga, and who has emerged from trance,—because his thoughts overflow with other interests. For to the extent that he has given himself up to devotion to the development of the perfection of wisdom, to that extent heavenly beings will provide him with heavenly food. These qualities also does one acquire even here and now. But again, Kausika, if someone has made a copy of the perfection of wisdom, and worships it, but does not learn, study and repeat it; and if someone else truly believes in the perfection of wisdom, trustingly confides in it, and, resolutely intent on it, serene in his faith, his thoughts raised to enlightenment, in earnest intent, hears it, learns it, bears it in mind, recites and studies it, spreads, demonstrates, explains, expounds and repeats it, illuminates it in detail for others, uncovers its meaning, investigates it with his mind, and, using his wisdom to the fullest, thoroughly examines it; copies it, and preserves and stores away the copy, so that the good dharma might last long, so that the guide of the Tathagatas might not be annihilated, so that the good dharma might not disappear, so that the Bodhisattvas, the great beings, might continue to be assisted, since their guide will not fail,—and finally, honours and worships this perfection of wisdom; then the latter begets the greater merit. [93] He should be imitated by those who want to acquire these distinguished qualities here and now, and they should truly believe in the perfection of wisdom, etc., to: because their guide will not fail. He will resolve to share it with those who desire it. So the great eye of the Guide of the Buddhas will not fail, either for him, or for others who are in quest of virtue. In addition the perfection of wisdom should at all times be honoured and worshipped.

Chapter IV

THE PROCLAMATION OF QUALITIES

1. RELATIVE VALUE OF TATHAGATA-RELICS AND OF PERFECT WISDOM

The Lord: If, Kausika, on the one hand you were given this Jambud-vipa filled up to the top with relics of the Tathagatas; and if, on the other hand, you could share in a written copy of this perfection of wisdom; and if now you had to choose between the two, which one would you take?

Sakra: Just this perfection of wisdom. Because of my esteem for the Guide of the Tathagatas. Because in a true sense this is the body of the Tathagatas. As the Lord has said: "The Dharma-bodies are the Buddhas, the Lords. But, monks, you should not think that this individual body is my body. Monks, you should see Me from the accomplishment of the Dharma-body." But that Taghagata-body should be seen as brought about by the reality-limit, i.e. by the perfection of wisdom. It is not, O Lord, that I lack in respect for the relics of the Tathagata. On the contrary, I have a real respect for them. As come forth from this perfection of wisdom are the relics of the Tathagata worshipped, and therefore, when one worships just this perfection of wisdom, then also the worship of the relics of the Tathagata is brought to fulfilment. For the relics of the Tathagata have come forth from the perfection of wisdom. It is as with my own godly seat in Sudharmā, the hall of the Gods. When I am seated on it, [95] the Gods come to wait on me. But when I am not, the Gods, out of respect for me, pay their respect to my seat, circumambulate it, and go away again. For they recall that, seated on this seat, Sakra, the Chief of Gods, demon-strates Dharma to the Gods of the Thirty-three. In the same way, the perfection of wisdom is the real eminent cause and condition which feeds the all-knowledge of the Tathagata. The relics of the Tathagata, on the other hand, are true deposits of all-knowledge, but they are not true conditions, or reasons, for the production of that cognition. As the cause of the cognition of the all-knowing the perfection of wisdom is also wor-shipped through the relics of the Tathagata. For this reason, of the two lots mentioned before, I would choose just his perfection of wisdom. But it is not because I lack in respect for the relics of the Tathagata. [In choosing thus] I have real respect for them, for those relics are worshipped because pervaded by the perfection of wisdom. And, if I had to choose between a copy of the perfection of wisdom on the one side, and even a great trichiliocosm filled to the top with relics of the Tathagata on the other, [96] I would still choose just this perfection of wisdom, for the same reasons. For the relics of the Tathagata are true deposits of the cognition of the all-knowing, but that cognition itself has come forth from the perfection of wisdom. Therefore then, of those two lots I would choose just this perfection of wisdom. But it is not that I lack in respect for the relics of the Tathagata. [In choosing thus] I have real respect for them. They, however, are worshipped because they have come forth from this perfection of wisdom, and are pervaded by it.

2. SIMILE OF THE WISHING JEWEL

It is like a priceless jewel which has the property of preventing men and ghosts from entering the place where it is put. If someone were possessed by a ghost, one would only have to introduce this jewel, and that ghost would depart. If someone were oppressed by the wind, and would apply this jewel when his body is inflated, he would hold back that wind, would prevent it from getting worse, would appease it. It would have a similar effect when applied to a body burning with bile, choked with phlegm, or painful as a result of a disease arising from a disorder of the humours. [97] It would illuminate the blackest darkness of night. In the heat it would cool the spot of earth where it is placed. In the cold it would warm it. Its presence drives vipers and other noxious animals from districts which they have infested. If a woman or man were bitten by a viper, one need only show them that jewel; and its sight will counteract that poison, and make it depart. Such are the qualities of this jewel. If one had a boil in the eye, or clouded eyesight, or a disease in the eye, or a cataract, one need only place that jewel on the eyes, and its mere presence will remove and appease those afflictions. Such are its qualities. Placed in water, it dyes the water all through with its own colour. Wrapped in a white cloth, and thrown into water, it makes the water white. Equally, when wrapped or bound in a black-blue, or yellow, or red, or crimson cloth, or into cloth of any other colour, it would dye that water into which it were thrown with the colour of the cloth. It would also clear up any turbidity there might be in the water. Endowed with such qualities would that jewel be. [98]

Ananda: Do these jewels, Kausika, belong to the world of the Gods, or to the men of Jambudvipa?

Sakra: They are found among the Gods. The jewels found among the men of Jambudvipa, on the other hand, are rather coarse and small, and not endowed with such qualities. They are infinitely inferior to those heavenly jewels. But those among the Gods are fine and full of all possible qualities. If that jewel were now put into a basket, or placed upon it, then that basket would still be desirable after the jewel had again been taken out. The basket, through the qualities of the jewel, would become an object of supreme longing. In the same way, O Lord, the qualities of the cognition of the all-knowing are derived from the perfection of wisdom. On account of it the relics of the Tathagata who has gone to Parinirvana are worshipped. For they are the true repositories of the cognition of the all-knowing. And as the demonstration of dharma by the Buddhas and Lords in all world systems should be worshipped because it has come forth from the perfection of wisdom, so also the dharma-preacher's demonstration of dharma. As a king should be worshipped, because his royal might gives courage to a great body of people, [99] so also the preacher of dharma, because, through the might of the Dharma-body, he gives courage to a great body of people. But the relics of the Tathagata are worshipped for the same reason that one worships the demonstration of dharma, and the preacher of dharma.

3. SUPREME VALUE OF THE PERFECTION OF WISDOM

Therefore then, O Lord, if there were two lots; and if not only this great trichiliocosm, but if all the world systems, countless as the sands of the Ganges, filled with the relics of the Tathagata, were put down as the first lot; and a copy of the perfection of wisdom as the second. If I were invited to choose either, and to take it, I would take just this perfection of wisdom. It is not, O Lord, that I lack respect for the relics of the Tathagata. My respect for them is a real one. But it is the perfection of wisdom which pervades all-knowledge, and the relics of the Tathagata are worshipped because they have come forth from all-knowledge. In consequence the worship of the perfection of wisdom is in effect a worship of the Buddhas and Lords, past, future and present. Moreover, O Lord, someone who wants to see, in accordance with dharma, the Buddhas and Lords who just now exist in immeasurable and incalculable world systems, should course in the perfection of wisdom, make endeavours in it, develop it. [100]

The Lord: So it is, Kausika. All the Tathagatas owe their enlightenment to just this perfection of wisdom,—whether they live in the past, future or present. I also, Kausika, just now a Tathagata, owe my enlightenment to just this perfection of wisdom.

Sakra: A great perfection is this perfection of wisdom. For it allows the Tathagata to rightly know and behold the thoughts and doings of all beings.

The Lord: So it is, Kausika. It is because a Bodhisattva courses for a long time in this perfection of wisdom that he rightly knows and beholds the thoughts and doings of all beings.

Sakra: Does a Bodhisattva course only in the perfection of wisdom, and not in the other perfections?

The Lord: He courses in all the six perfections. But it is the perfection of wisdom [101] which controls the Bodhisattva when he gives a gift, or guards morality, or perfects himself in patience, or exerts vigour, or enters into trance, or has insight into dharmas. One cannot get at a distinction or difference between these six perfections,—all of them upheld by skill in means, dedicated to the perfection of wisdom, dedicated to all-knowledge. Just as no distinction or difference is conceived between the shadows cast by different trees in Jambudvipa,—though their colours may differ, and their shapes, and their leaves, flowers and fruits, and their height and circumference—but they are all just called 'shadows'; even so one cannot get at a distinction or difference between these six perfections,—all of them upheld by skill in means, dedicated to the perfection of wisdom, dedicated to all-knowledge.

Sakra: Endowed with great qualities is this perfection of wisdom, with immeasurable qualities, with boundless qualities!

Chapter V

THE REVOLUTION OF MERIT

1. THE PERFECTION OF WISDOM A SOURCE OF GREAT MERIT

Sakra: Let us again consider two people. The one truly believes in the perfection of wisdom, trustingly confides in it, etc., to: since their guide will not fail [as p. 62]. And when he has heard this exposition, he will resolve that he will never abandon this perfection of wisdom,—surely so greatly profitable, so great an advantage, so great a fruit, so great a reward, endowed with so great qualities!—that he will guard and preserve it, because it is exceedingly hard to get. And he himself would honour, worship and adore it. The other person would first venerate it, and then give a copy of it to another son or daughter of a good family, who, desirous of it and eager, asks for it. [103] Which one of these two persons begets the greater merit, the one who intends to give it away, or the one who does not?

The Lord: I will question you on this point, and you may answer to the best of your abilities. If one person by himself were to honour the relics of the Tathagata after his Parinirvana, minister to them and preserve them; and if another were not only himself to honour the relics of the Tathagata, minister to them and revere them, but in addition reveal them to others, give them away, and share them, in the hope that the worship of the relics would become widespread, from pity for beings; then which one of these two persons would beget the greater merit: The one who, while worshipping them himself, reveals, gives and shares with others, or the one who by himself, singly, worships them?

Sakra: The one who shares with others. [104]

The Lord: So it is, Kausika. The person who would give this perfection of wisdom to others, who helps others, who intends to give it away, he would on the strength of that beget the greater merit. If in addition he would go to where there are persons who have become fit vessels for this perfection of wisdom, and would share it with them, then he would beget still more merit. Moreover, Kausika, great would be the merit of someone who would instigate all beings in Jambudvipa to observe the ten ways of wholesome action, and would establish them in them?

Sakra: Great it would be.

The Lord: Greater would be the merit of someone who would make a copy of this perfection of wisdom, would believe in it and have faith in it, faith serene and firm; who would raise his thought to enlightenment, and with earnest intention would give this perfection of wisdom to another Bodhisattva who had raised his thought to enlightenment; would first of all perfect himself by tireless writing and reciting; then after much zealous labour, he would persuade the other Bodhisattva, explain this perfection of wisdom to him, instigate to it, fill with enthusiasm for it, [105] make him rejoice in it, would, by his words, lead him to it, educate him in it, illuminate its benefits to him, cleanse his thought and remove his doubts; and who would address him as follows: "Come here, son of a good family, do train yourself in just this Path of the Bodhisattvas, for as a result of this training, this coursing, this struggling you will surely quickly awake to full enlightenment. After that you will educate an infinite number of beings in the complete extinction of the substratum of rebirth, in other words, in the revelation of the reality-limit." Because he intends to give away, therefore his merit is the greater. And this is true even if it is compared with the merit of someone who establishes in the observation of the ten wholesome ways of acting all the beings in world systems of any size, [106] even in all the world systems that there are, numerous as the sands of the Ganges River. [107] Or if it is compared with that of someone who would establish others in the four trances, the four Unlimited, the four formless attainments, the five superknowledges, in any number of world systems. [112] In each case a person who would not only write this perfection of wisdom and recite it by himself, but would write it for others and give it away to them, would easily beget the greater merit. Moreover, Kausika, someone would also beget a greater merit if they were conversant with the meaning when reciting this perfection of wisdom; and having written it for others, would give it away, expound and light it up, both the meaning and the letter.

2. THE COUNTERFEIT PERFECTION OF WISDOM

Sakra: Can one then expound this perfection of wisdom?

The Lord: Yes, one should expound it to someone who does not understand it. For in the future a counterfeit of the perfection of wisdom will arise. When he hears it, a person who does not understand should beware of making obeisance to it, if he wants to win full enlightenment.

Sakra: How should he recognize in the future if and when the counterfeit perfection of wisdom is expounded? [113]

The Lord: In the future there will be some monks whose bodies are undeveloped, whose moral conduct, thought and wisdom are undeveloped, who are stupid, dumb like sheep, without wisdom. When they announce that they will expound the perfection of wisdom, they will actually expound its counterfeit. They will expound the counterfeit perfection of wisdom by teaching that the impermanence of form, etc., is to be interpreted as the destruction of form, etc. To strive for that insight, that, according to them, will be the coursing in the perfection of wisdom. But on the contrary, one should not view the impermanence of form, etc., as the destruction of form, etc. For to view things in that way means to course in the counterfeit perfection of wisdom. For that reason, Kausika, should one expound the meaning of the perfection of wisdom. By expounding it one would beget the greater merit.

3. THE PERFECTION OF WISDOM GREATER THAN ANY OTHER SPIRITUAL GIFT

And that merit would be greater than if one were to establish beings in any number of world systems in the fruit of a Streamwinner. [116] And that holds good also of the fruit of a Once-Returner, of a Never-Returner, and of an Arhat. For it is the perfection of wisdom which brings about the fruit of a Once-Returner, of a Never-Returner, and of an Arhat. [125] And the Bodhisattva will increase his endurance by the reflection that by training himself in the perfection of wisdom, he will by and by become one who obtains the dharmas which constitute a Buddha, and will get near to full enlightenment. For he knows that by training himself in this training, coursing in it, struggling in it, he will bring forth all the fruits of the holy life, from that of a Streamwinner to Buddhahood. The merit of the person who shares the perfection of wisdom will also be greater than that of one who establishes in Pratyekabuddhahood any number of beings in any number of world systems. [128] Moreover, Kausika, if someone were to raise to full enlightenment the hearts of as many beings as there are in Jambudvipa; and if someone else were not only to raise their hearts to full enlightenment, but would also in addition give them a copy of this perfection of wisdom; or, if he would present a copy of this perfection of wisdom to an irreversible Bodhisattva, in the hope that he will let himself be trained in it, [129] make endeavours about it, develop it, and as a result of the growth, increase, and abundance of the perfection of wisdom, fulfil the Buddha-dharmas; then, compared with that former person, he will beget the greater merit, for certainly he will, once he has awoken to full enlightenment, end the sufferings of beings. And his merit will be greater, even if the other person raises to full enlightenment the hearts of any number of beings in any number of world systems. [130] Or, let us again compare two persons: The first would present a copy of this perfection of wisdom to any number of beings in any number of world systems who have become irreversible from full enlightenment, who have definitely set out for it; the second would in addition expound it to them, according to the meaning and according to the letter. Would he not on the strength of that beget much merit? [131]

Sakra: His merit would indeed be great. One could not easily even calculate that heap of merit, or count it, or find anything that it is similar to, that it resembles, or that it can be compared with.

The Lord: Still greater would be the merit of someone who in addition would instruct and admonish in this perfection of wisdom those irreversible Bodhisattvas who want more quickly to win full enlightenment. [133] And further, still another Bodhisattva would arise, who would say that he would win full enlightenment more quickly than they. If someone would instruct and admonish in the perfection of wisdom that Bodhisattva of quicker understanding, he would beget a still greater merit.

Sakra: To the extent that a Bodhisattva comes nearer to full enlightenment, to that extent he should be instructed and admonished in the perfection of wisdom, for that brings him nearer and nearer to Suchness. When he comes nearer to Suchness, he confers many fruits and advantages on those who have done him services, i.e. on those through whom he enjoys his robes, alms-bowl, lodging, and medicinal appliances for sickness. His merit now becomes still greater, in consequence of the fact that he comes nearer to full enlightenment. [134]

Subhuti: Well said, Kausika. You fortify those who belong to the Bodhisattva-vehicle, help them, stand by them. Even so should you act. A holy disciple who wants to give help to all beings, he fortifies the Bodhisattvas in their attitude to full enlightenment, helps them, stands by them. It is so that one should act. For begotten from the perfection of wisdom is the full enlightenment of the Bodhisattvas. Because, if the Bodhisattvas would not produce that thought of enlightenment, they would not train themselves in full enlightenment, nor in the six perfections, and in consequence they would not awake to full enlightenment. But because the Bodhisattvas train themselves in the Bodhisattva-training, in these six perfections, therefore do they produce this thought of enlightenment, therefore do they awake to full enlightenment.

Chapter VI

DEDICATION AND JUBILATION

1. SUPREME MERIT OF DEDICATION AND JUBILATION

Maitreya: On the one side we have, on the part of a Bodhisattva, the meritorious work which is founded on his rejoicing at the merit of others, and on his dedication of that merit to the utmost enlightenment of all beings; on the other side there is, on the part of all beings, the meritorious work founded on giving, on morality, on meditational development. Among these the meritorious work of a Bodhisattva founded on jubilation and dedication is declared to be the best, the most excellent and sublime, the highest and supreme, with none above it, unequalled, equalling the unequalled.

2. THE RANGE OF JUBILATION

Subhuti: A Bodhisattva, a great being, considers the world with its ten directions, in every direction, extending everywhere. He considers the world systems, quite immeasurable, quite beyond reckoning, quite measureless, quite inconceivable, infinite and boundless.

He considers in the past period, in each single direction, in each single world system, the Tathagatas, quite immeasurable, quite beyond reckoning, quite measureless, quite inconceivable, infinite and boundless, who have won final Nirvana in the realm of Nirvana which leaves nothing behind,— [136] their tracks cut off, their course cut off, their obstacles annulled, guides through [the world of] becoming, their tears dried up, with all their impediments crushed, their own burdens laid down, with their own weal reached, in whom the fetters of becoming are extinguished, whose thoughts are well freed by right understanding, and who have attained to the highest perfection in the control of their entire hearts.

He considers them, from where they began with the production of the thought of enlightenment, proceeding to the time when they won full enlightenment, until they finally entered Nirvana in the realm of Nirvana which leaves nothing behind, and the whole span of time up to the vanishing of the good Dharma [as preached by each one of these Tathagatas].

He considers the mass of morality, the mass of concentration, the mass of wisdom, the mass of emancipation, the mass of the vision and cognition of emancipation of those Buddhas and Lords.

In addition he considers the store of merit associated with the six perfections, with the achievement of the qualities of a Buddha, and with the perfections of self-confidence and of the powers; and also those associated with the perfection of the superknowledges, of comprehension, of the vows; and the store of merit associated with the accomplishment of the cognition of the all-knowing, with the solicitude for beings, the great friendliness and the great compassion, and the immeasurable and incalculable Buddha-qualities.

And he also considers the full enlightenment and its happiness, and the perfection of the sovereignty over all dharmas, and the accomplishment of the measureless and unconquered supreme wonderworking power which has conquered all, and the power of the Tathagata's cognition of what is truly real, which is without covering, attachment or obstruction, unequalled, equal to the unequalled, incomparable, without measure, and the power of the Buddha-cognition preeminent among the powers, and the vision and cognition of a Buddha, the perfection of the ten powers, the obtainment of that supreme ease which results from the four grounds of self-confidence, [137] and the obtainment of Dharma through the realization of the ultimate reality of all dharmas.

He also considers the turning of the wheel of Dharma, the carrying of the torch of Dharma, the beating of the drum of Dharma, the filling up of the conch shell of Dharma, the wielding of the sword of Dharma, the pouring down of the rain of Dharma, and the refreshment of all beings through the gift of Dharma, through its presentation to them. He further considers the store of merit of all those who are educated and trained by those demonstrations of Dharma,— whether they concern the dharmas of Buddhas, or those of Pratyekabuddhas, or of Disciples,—who believe in them, who are fixed on them, who are bound to end up in full enlightenment.

He also considers the store of merit, associated with the six perfections, of all those Bodhisattvas of whom those Buddhas and Lords have predicted full enlightenment. He considers the store of merit of all those persons who belong to the Pratyekabuddha vehicle, and of whom the enlightenment of a Pratyekabuddha has been predicted. He considers the meritorious work founded on giving, morality and meditational development, of the four assemblies of those Buddhas and Lords, i.e. of the monks and nuns, the laymen and laywomen. He considers the roots of good planted during all that time by Gods, Nagas, Yakshas, Gandharvas, Asuras, Garudas, Kinnaras and Mahoragas, by men and ghosts, and also by animals, at the time when those Buddhas and Lords demonstrated the Dharma, and when they entered Parinirvana, and when they had entered

Parinirvana [138]—thanks to the Buddha, the Lord, thanks to the Dhar-
ma, thanks to the Samgha, and thanks to persons of right mind-culture.
[In his meditation the Bodhisattva] piles up the roots of good of all those,
all that quantity of merit without exception or remainder, rolls it into one
lump, weighs it, and rejoices over it with the most excellent and sublime
jubilation, the highest and utmost jubilation, with none above it, une-
qualled, equalling the unequalled. Having thus rejoiced, he utters the re-
mark: "I turn over into full enlightenment the meritorious work founded
on jubilation. May it feed the full enlightenment [of myself and of all
beings]!"

3. A METAPHYSICAL PROBLEM

Now, as concerns these foundations through which the person belong-
ing to the Bodhisattva-vehicle has rejoiced, concerning those objective sup-
ports and points of view, through which he has raised that thought,—
would those foundations, objective supports and points of view be appre-
hended in such a way that they would be treated as signs?

Maitreya: No, they would not. [139]

Subhuti: If he treated as an objective support or as a sign that founda-
tion which does not exist, and that objective support which does not exist,
would he then not have a perverted perception, perverted thought, per-
verted views? For in a greedy person also, when he has discriminated a
nonexisting entity [foundation] and pondered on it—thinking that there is
permanence in the impermanent, ease in suffering, the self in what is not
the self, loveliness in what is repulsive—there arises a perverted perception,
perverted thought, perverted view. And as the foundation [entity], the
objective support, the point of view [are non-existent], so is enlighten-
ment, so is the thought [of enlightenment] and so all dharmas, all ele-
ments. But then on which foundations, by which objective supports, or
points of view does he turn over what thought into full enlightenment, or
what meritorious work founded on jubilation does he turn over into what
utmost, right and perfect enlightenment?

Maitreya: This should not be taught or expounded in front of a
Bodhisattva who has newly set out in the vehicle. For he would lose that
little faith, which is his, that little affection, serenity and respect which are
his. In front of an irreversible Bodhisattva should this be taught and ex-
pounded. Alternatively, a Bodhisattva who is propped up by a good friend
would thereby not be cowed, nor become stolid, nor cast down, nor
depressed, would not turn his mind away from it, nor have his back
broken, nor tremble, be frightened, be terrified. [140] And thus should

the Bodhisattva turn over into all-knowledge the meritorious work founded on jubilation.

Subhuti: The thought by which one has rejoiced and turned over, or dedicated that [wholesome root connected with jubilation],—that thought of [rejoicing] is [at the time of turning over] extinct, stopped, departed, reversed. Therefore, what is that thought by which one turns over to full enlightenment? Or what is that thought which turns over into full enlightenment the meritorious work founded on jubilation? Or, if no two thoughts can ever meet, how can one by thought turn over, or dedicate, thought? Nor is it possible to turn over [or to overturn, to transform] that thought as far as its own being is concerned.

Sakra: The Bodhisattvas who have newly set out in the vehicle should beware of being afraid when they have heard this exposition. How then should a Bodhisattva turn that meritorious work founded on jubilation over into full enlightenment? And how does someone who takes hold of the meritorious work founded on jubilation succeed in taking hold of that thought connected with jubilation, and how does one who turns over the thought connected with jubilation succeed in turning it over?

Thereupon the Venerable *Subhuti* turned his mind to the Bodhisattva Maitreya, concentrated his mind on him, and spoke thus [141]: Here the Bodhisattva considers the merit connected with the past Buddhas and Lords, in the way we described before [i.e. 135-38]. He piles up the wholesome roots of all those, all that quantity of wholesome roots without exception and remainder, rolls it into one lump, weighs it, and rejoices over it. He then turns the meritorious work founded on jubilation over to full enlightenment. [142] How can the Bodhisattva when he turns over, be without perverted perception, perverted thought, perverted view?

4. HOW PERVERTED VIEWS CAN BE AVOIDED

Maitreya: The Bodhisattva must not, as a result of the thought by which he turns that over, become one who perceives a thought. It is thus that the meritorious work founded on jubilation becomes something which is turned over into full enlightenment. If he does not perceive that thought, [identifying it] as 'this is that thought,' then a Bodhisattva has no perverted perception, thought or view. But if he perceives the thought by which he turns that over, [identifying it] as 'this is that thought,' then he becomes one who perceives thought. As a result he has a perverted perception, thought and view. But a Bodhisattva turns over rightly, not wrongly, when he perceives and brings to mind the thought which turns over [143] in such a way that he regards it as 'just extinct, extinct,' as 'stopped, departed, reversed'; and when he reflects that what is extinct that cannot be turned over; and that this [extinctness, etc.] is the very dharmic nature also of that thought by which one turns over, and also of the dharmas through which one turns over, as well as of the dharmas to which one turns over. It is thus that the Bodhisattva should turn over. He should [in 145-49] consider the future Buddhas, the present Buddhas, the past, future and present Buddhas in the same way in which he considered the past Buddhas. Under which circumstances is he without perverted perception, thought or views? If, while he turns over, he brings to mind those dharmas as extinct, stopped, departed, reversed, and that dharma into which it is turned over as inextinguishable, then it [the wholesome root] becomes something which has been turned over into full enlightenment. For he does not settle down in that process of dedication. If further he considers that no dharma can be turned over into a dharma, then also it becomes something which has been turned over into full enlightenment. It is thus that the Bodhisattva who turns over is without perverted perception, thought or view. For he does not settle down in that process of dedication. If further he perceives that thought cannot cognize thought, nor can dharma cognize dharma, then also it becomes something which has been turned over into full enlightenment. This is the supreme maturity of the Bodhisattva. But if, on the other hand, a Bodhisattva perceives that accumulation of merit, then he cannot turn it over into full enlightenment. Because he settles down in that process of dedication. If further he reflects that also this accumulation of merit is isolated and quietly calm, that also the meritorious work founded on jubilation [150] is isolated and quietly calm, then he turns over into full enlightenment. If in addition he does not even perceive that all conditioned events are calmly quiet and isolated, then that is the perfection of wisdom of that Bodhisattva. But he does not turn over into full enlightenment if he perceives that this here is the wholesome root of the Buddhas, the Lords who have gone to Parinirvana; that that wholesome root is just as [illusory] as that process of dedication; and that also that [thought] by which it is turned over is of the same kind, has the same mark, belongs to the same class, has the same own-being. For the Buddhas and Lords do not allow a dedication to take place through a sign. He does not bring to mind nor turn over [that wholesome root] to full enlightenment if he brings about a sign by reflecting that what is past is extinct, stopped, departed, reversed; that what is future has not yet arrived; and that of the present no stability is got at, and that that which is not got at has no sign or range. On the other hand he also does not turn over to full enlightenment if he fails to bring about a sign or to bring to mind as a result of sheer inattentiveness, if he fails to attend as a result of lack of mindfulness, or of lack of understanding. But that wholesome root becomes something which has been turned over into full enlightenment on condition that he brings to mind that sign, but does not treat it as a sign. It is thus that the Bodhisattva should train himself therein. This should be known as his skill in means. When, through that skill in means, he turns over a wholesome root, then he is near to all-knowledge. The Bodhisattva who wants to train himself in this skill in means should, however, constantly hear just this perfection of wisdom, study it and ask questions about it. [151] For without the help of the perfection of wisdom one untaught cannot enter on the work of dedication by means of the perfection of wisdom. But one should not make a statement to the effect that thanks to the perfection of wisdom it is possible to transform that meritorious work into full enlightenment. For stopped are those personal lives, stopped are those karma-formations, calmly quiet, isolated, lacking in basis. Moreover, that person has brought about a sign, and made a discrimination, he perceives what is truly real in what is not truly real as if it were truly real, and he would transform a basis into what is without basis. The Buddhas, the Lords do not allow his wholesome roots to become something which is in this way transformed into full enlightenment. For they become to him a great basis. Even the Parinirvana of the Buddhas, the Lords he treats as a sign and discriminates, he gets at Nirvana from a viewpoint, and it is not the dedication carried out by one who perceives a basis which the Tathagatas have called a source of great welfare. For this process of dedication is not without poison, not without thorn. It is just as with food that seems excellent, but is really poisonous. Its colour, smell, taste and touch seem desirable, but nevertheless, as poisonous it should be shunned and not eaten by circumspect people. Although fools and stupid people might think that it should be eaten. The colour, smell, taste and touch of that food promise happiness, but its transformation in a man who would eat it would lead to a painful conclusion. As a result he would incur death, or deadly pain. Just so some [perceivers of a basis] who seize badly the meaning of what is well taught, badly distinguish it, badly master it, and misunderstand it, not understanding the meaning as it really is, they will instruct [152] and admonish others to consider the mass of merit of the past, future and present Buddhas and Lords, in the way described before [pp. 135-38], to rejoice at it, and to turn over into full enlightenment the meritorious work founded on jubilation. Thus that turning over, since it is being carried out by means of a sign, is turned into poisonousness. It is just like the poisonous food mentioned before. There can be no turning over for someone who perceives a basis. For a basis is poisonous [has a range]. [153] Therefore a person who belongs to the vehicle of the

Bodhisattvas should not train himself thus. How then should he train himself? How should he take hold of the wholesome root of the past, future and present Buddhas and Lords? And how does that which is taken hold of become something which is successfully taken hold of? How should he turn over? And how does it become something which has been successfully turned over into the supreme enlightenment? Here the son or daughter of a good family who belongs to the vehicle of the Bodhisattvas, and who does not want to calumniate the Tathagata, should thus rejoice over all that wholesome root, should thus turn it over: "I rejoice in that wholesome root considered as the Tathagatas with their Buddha-cognition and their Buddha-eye know and see it,—its kind such as it is, its class such as it is, its quality such as it is, its own-being such as it is, its mark such as it is, and its mode of existence such as it is. And I turn it over in such a way that those Tathagatas can allow that wholesome root to be turned over into full enlightenment." When he thus rejoices, thus turns over, a Bodhisattva becomes free from guilt. The righteousness of the Buddhas, the Lords, is rejoiced in. That wholesome root becomes something that has been turned over into full enlightenment. And he does not calumniate those Tathagatas. In this way his turning over becomes a non-poisonous turning over, a great turning over, a turning over into the dharma-element; it becomes perfect, quite perfect, through the earnest intention and the resolve of him who turns over. Moreover, someone who belongs to the vehicle of the Bodhisattvas should turn over with the understanding that all morality, concentration, wisdom, emancipation, vision and cognition of emancipation, are unincluded in the world of sense-desire, the world of form, the formless world, and that they are not past, future, or present. For everything that is in the three periods of time or [154] in the triple world is unincluded [in ultimate reality]. In consequence the turning over is also unincluded, and so is the dharma [i.e. Buddahood] into which that process of transformation is being turned,—if only he firmly believes that. When a Bodhisattva turns over in such a way, he can never again lose the turning over, and it becomes unincluded, non-poisonous, a great turning over, a turning over of the dharma-element, perfect, quite perfect. But, on the other hand, when he settles down in what he turns over, and treats it as a sign, then he turns it over wrongly. A Bodhisattva, however, turns over with the idea that it is through this turning it over into the dharma-element, as the Buddhas, the Lords know and permit it, that that wholesome root becomes something which has been turned over into full enlightenment, successfully turned over. This is the right method of turning it over. And in this way it becomes something that has been turned over into supreme enlightenment, successfully turned over.

The Lord: Well said, Subhuti, well said. You perform the office of the Teacher when you demonstrate Dharma to the Bodhisattvas. For it is this turning over, which is the turning over of the dharma-element, that is the turning over of a Bodhisattva. He thinks: "As the Buddhas and Lords know and see that wholesome root in this dharmahood,—its kind such as it is, its class such as it is, its quality such as it is, its own-being such as it is, its mark such as it is, its mode of existence such as it is,—so I rejoice in it. And as they grant permission, so I turn it over." [155]

5. CONSIDERATIONS OF MERIT

This heap of merit of a Bodhisattva, which is born from his turning over of the Dharma-element, that is declared to be superior to the accumulation of merit on the part of someone who would instigate to, and establish in the ten wholesome ways of action all the beings in the great trichiliocosms which are countless as the sands of the Ganges. And it remains superior also if those beings would all gain the four trances, or the four Unlimited, or the four formless attainments, or [156] the five superknowledges; or equally if they would become Streamwinnners, etc., to: Pratyekabuddhas. This is not all. [157] If all beings in all world systems had set out for the supreme enlightenment; and if, Subhuti, each single Bodhisattva were to furnish, for aeons countless like the sands of the Ganges, all those beings in the various great trichiliocosms, countless as the sands of the Ganges, with all they might need; but they would give that gift while perceiving a basis. And if, proceeding in this manner, we imagine that all those beings are a single one, and if each single Bodhisattva would for aeons countless as the sands of the Ganges furnish all those Bodhisattvas with all they might need, and treat them with respect; if thus each single one of all those Bodhisattvas, if they all together would give that gift, would now those Bodhisattvas on the strength of that beget a great deal of merit?

Subhuti: A great deal indeed, O Lord. That heap of merit would even defy calculation. If it were a material thing, it could not find room in even the great trichiliocosms countless as the sands of the Ganges.

The Lord: So it is, Subhuti. And yet, this accumulation of merit, due to giving on the part of the Bodhisattvas who perceive a basis, is infinitesimal compared with the merit begotten by someone who belongs to the vehicle of the Bodhisattvas, and who, taken hold of by perfection of wisdom and by skill in means, turns that wholesome root over into full enlightenment by means of this turning over of the dharma-element. [158] For although the basis-perceiving Bodhisattvas have given a good many gifts, they have also reckoned them up as 'a good many.'

Thereupon twenty thousand Gods of the Four Great Kings, with folded hands paid homage to the Lord, and said: "This transformation into all-knowledge of wholesome roots by those who have been taken hold of by the perfection of wisdom and by skill in means, is a great transformation of the Bodhisattvas. Because it surpasses the accumulation of merit, derived from giving, of those Bodhisattvas who are based on something, however great it may be."

Thereupon again one hundred thousand Gods of the Thirty-three rained down on the Lord heavenly flowers, incense, perfumes, wreaths, ointments, aromatic powders, jewels and garments. They worshipped the Lord with heavenly parasols, banners, bells, flags, and with rows of lamps all around, and with manifold kinds of worship. They played on heavenly musical instruments [in honour of the Lord] and they said: [159] "This transformation of the dharma-element is surely a great transformation of the Bodhisattva. Because it surpasses the heap of accumulated merit resulting from the gifts of the Bodhisattvas who have a basis in something, just because that great transformation has been taken hold of by the perfection of wisdom and by skill in means."

All the other classes of Gods appeared on the scene, worshipped the Lord, and raised their voices. They said: "It is wonderful, O Lord, to what an extent this transformation of a wholesome root by the Bodhisattvas who have been taken hold of by the perfection of wisdom and by skill in means surpasses the heap of merit of those Bodhisattvas who have a basis in something, although it has accumulated for such a long time, and was procured by such manifold exertions."

Thereupon the Lord said to those Gods, from the gods belonging to the Pure Abode downwards: "Let us leave the case of the accumulation of the merit of all beings in countless world systems who have definitely set out for full enlightenment, and who have given gifts for the sake of gaining full enlightenment. [160] Let us, in the same manner, consider the case of all beings in countless world systems who, having made a vow to gain full enlightenment, and having raised their thoughts to enlightenment, would give gifts on the extensive scale described before [i.e. p. 157]. On the other hand we consider a Bodhisattva, taken hold of by the perfection of wisdom and by skill in means, who takes hold of the wholesome roots of all the Buddhas, Bodhisattvas, Pratyekabuddhas and Disciples, and of all other beings also the wholesome roots which have been planted, will be planted, and are being planted, and who rejoices over them all in the way described above. Then infinitesimal will be the accumulation of merit on the part of the former Bodhisattvas who give gifts while perceiving a basis—just because they perceive a basis. [161]

Subhuti: The Lord has described the jubilation over the wholesome roots of all beings as a most excellent jubilation. For what reason is this jubilation a most excellent one?

The Lord: If a person who belongs to the vehicle of the Bodhisattvas does not seize on past, future and present dharmas, does not mind them, does not get at them, does not construct, nor discriminate them, does not see nor review them [162], if he considers them with the conviction that all dharmas are fabricated by thought construction, unborn, not come forth, not come, not gone, and that no dharma is ever produced or stopped in the past, future or present; if he considers those dharmas in such a way, then his jubilation is in accordance with the true nature of those dharmas, and so is his transformation [of the merit] into full enlightenment. This is the first reason why the jubilation of the Bodhisattva is a most excellent one. The meritorious work founded on giving on the part of Bodhisattvas who perceive a basis, who have a basis in view, is infinitesimal compared with the transformation of the wholesome root by that Bodhisattva. Moreover, Subhuti, someone who belongs to the vehicle of the Bodhisattvas, and who wants to rejoice in the wholesome roots of all the Buddhas and Lords, should rejoice in such a way: As emancipation [is unoriginated, since the obstacles from defilements and from the cognizable have ceased], so the gift; so the morality, etc.; so the jubilation, so the meritorious work founded on jubilation; [163] as the emancipation, so the transformation, so the Buddhas and Lords, and the Pratyekabuddhas, and the Disciples who have entered Parinirvana; as the emancipation, so are the dharmas which are past, or stopped; and likewise the dharmas which are future, or not yet produced; and the dharmas which are present, or proceeding just now; as the emancipation so are all the past, future and present Buddhas and Lords. Thus, I rejoice with the most excellent jubilation in the true nature of those dharmas, which are unbound, unfreed, unattached. Thereafter I turn that meritorious work founded on jubilation over into full enlightenment; but really no turning over takes place, because nothing is passed on, nothing destroyed. This is the second reason why the jubilation of the Bodhisattva is a most excellent one. [164]

But to return to the question of merit. Let us now consider the case where all the beings in countless world systems have definitely set out for full enlightenment, and where, in order to advance to full enlightenment, they would for countless aeons undertake the obligation of observing morality, i.e. good conduct of body, speech and mind,—but while perceiving a basis. Nevertheless their accumulation of merit is infinitesimal compared with that of a Bodhisattva's merit derived from jubilation,—just because they perceive a basis. [165] And the same would be true, if all those beings would for countless aeons practise patience, although they were ever so much abused, struck and reviled; [166] or if they would practise vigour, and under no circumstances would be cast down, or conquered by sloth and torpor; [168] or, finally, if they would enter the trances. As long as they carry out those practices while perceiving a basis, their merit will be infinitesimal compared with that of a Bodhisattva who rejoices over the wholesome roots of all beings with the most excellent jubilation, and transforms this wholesome root into the supreme enlightenment.

Chapter VII

HELL

1. HYMN TO THE PERFECTION OF WISDOM

Sariputra: The perfection of wisdom, O Lord, is the accomplishment of the cognition of the all-knowing. The perfection of wisdom is the state of all-knowledge.

The Lord: So it is, Sariputra, as you say.

Sariputra: The perfection of wisdom gives light, O Lord. I pay homage to the perfection of wisdom! She is worthy of homage. She is unstained, the entire world cannot stain her. She is a source of light, and from everyone in the triple world she removes darkness, and she leads away from the blinding darkness caused by the defilements and by wrong views. In her we can find shelter. Most excellent are her works. She makes us seek the safety of the wings of enlightenment. She brings light to the blind, she brings light so that all fear and distress may be forsaken. She has gained the five eyes, and she shows the path to all beings. She herself is an organ of vision. She disperses the gloom and darkness of delusion. [171] She does nothing about all dharmas. She guides to the path those who have strayed on to a bad road. She is identical with all-knowledge. She never produces any dharma, because she has forsaken the residues relating to both kinds of coverings, those produced by defilement and those produced by the cognizable. She does not stop any dharma. Herself unstopped and unproduced is the perfection of wisdom. She is the mother of the Bodhi-sattvas, on account of the emptiness of own marks. As the donor of the jewel of all the Buddha-dharmas she brings about the ten powers (of a Buddha). She cannot be crushed. She protects the unprotected, with the help of the four grounds of self-confidence. She is the antidote to birth-and-death. She has a clear knowledge of the own-being of all dharmas, for she does not stray away from it. The perfection of wisdom of the Buddhas, the Lords, sets in motion the wheel of the Dharma.

2. PREDOMINANCE OF PERFECT WISDOM OVER THE OTHER PERFECTIONS

How should a Bodhisattva stand in the perfection of wisdom, how attend and pay homage to it?

The Lord: In every way the perfection of wisdom should be treated like the Teacher himself.

Sakra then asked Sariputra: Wherefrom, and for what reason has this question of the holy Sariputra arisen? [172]

Sariputra: It arose because I heard it said that "a Bodhisattva who, taken hold of by perfection of wisdom and skill in means, transforms into all-knowledge the meritorious work founded on jubilation, surpasses the entire meritorious work founded on giving, morality, patience, vigour, and trance of all the Bodhisattvas who observe a basis." It is just the perfection of wisdom which directs the five perfections in their ascent on the path to all-knowledge. Just as, Kausika, people born blind, one hundred, or one thousand, or one hundred thousand of them, cannot, without a leader, go along a path and get to a village, town or city; just so, Giving, Morality, Patience, Vigour and Trance cannot by themselves be called 'perfections,' for without the perfection of wisdom they are as if born blind, without their leader unable to ascend the path to all-knowledge, and still less can they reach all-knowledge. When, however, Giving, Morality, Patience, Vigour and Trance are taken hold of by the perfection of wisdom, then they are termed 'perfections,' for then [173] these five perfections acquire an organ of vision which allows them to ascend the path to all-knowledge, and to reach all-knowledge.

3. NOTHING PROCURED BY PERFECT WISDOM

Sariputra said to the Lord: How should a Bodhisattva consummate the perfection of wisdom?

The Lord: He should view the non-consummation of form, etc. The non-consummation of the five skandhas, that is called the 'consummation of the perfection of wisdom.' In this way, because nothing is effected, the consummation of the five skandhas is called the consummation of the perfection of wisdom.

Sariputra: When the perfection of wisdom has been consummated by such a consummation, what dharma does it procure?

The Lord: When consummated in such a way, the perfection of wisdom does not procure any dharma, and in consequence of that fact she comes to be styled 'perfection of wisdom.'

Sakra: Then, O Lord, this perfection of wisdom does not even procure all-knowledge?

The Lord: It does not procure it as if it were a basis, or a mental process, or a volitional act. [174]

Sakra: How then does it procure?

The Lord: In so far as it does not procure, to that extent it procures.

Sakra: It is wonderful, O Lord, to see the extent to which this perfection of wisdom neither produces nor stops any dharma. For the purpose of the non-production and of the non-stopping of all dharmas has the perfection of wisdom been set up, without, however, being really present.

Subhuti: If a Bodhisattva should perceive this also, then he will keep far away from this perfection of wisdom, treat it as worthless and insignificant, and fail to act on it.

The Lord: This is quite true. For where the perfection of wisdom is lit up, there form does not become lit up, nor the other skandhas, nor the fruits of the holy life, up to Buddhahood.

Subhuti: This perfection of wisdom is a great perfection, O Lord! [175]

4. WHY THE PERFECTION OF WISDOM IS GREAT

The Lord: What do you think, Subhuti, in what manner is this perfection of wisdom a great perfection?

Subhuti: It does not make form, etc., greater or smaller, and it does not assemble nor disperse form, etc. It also does not strengthen or weaken the powers of a Tathagata, nor does it assemble or disperse them. It does not even make that all-knowledge greater or smaller, nor does it assemble or disperse it. For all-knowledge is unassembled [uncollected] and undispersed [undisturbed]. If the Bodhisattva perceives even this, then he courses not in the perfection of wisdom, how much more so if he forms the notion: 'Thus will I, endowed with the cognition of the all-knowing, demonstrate dharma to beings, thus will I lead those beings to final Nirvana.' For this apprehension of beings as a basic fact, when he says, "I will lead those beings to final Nirvana," cannot be an outcome of the perfection of wisdom. This would indeed be a great basis of apprehension on his part. For the absence of own-being in beings should be known as belonging to the very essence of the perfection of wisdom. One should know that the perfection of wisdom is without own-being because [or: in the same way in which] beings are without own-being; that the perfection of wisdom is isolated because beings are isolated; that the perfection of wisdom is unthinkable, because beings are; [176] that the perfection of wisdom has an indestructible nature because beings have; that the perfection of wisdom does not actually undergo the process which leads to enlightenment because beings do not; that the perfection of wisdom taken as it really is, does not undergo the process which leads to enlightenment because beings, as they really are, do not undergo that process; that the way in which the Tathagata arrives at the full possession of his powers should be understood after the way in which beings arrive at the full possession of their power. It is in this manner that the perfection of wisdom is a great perfection.

5. CAUSES OF BELIEF IN THE PERFECTION OF WISDOM

Sariputra: Bodhisattvas who are reborn here, and who will here resolutely believe in this deep perfection of wisdom, without hesitation, doubt or stupefaction, where have they deceased and for how long have they practised, they who will follow the doctrine of this perfection of wisdom, understand its meaning, and instruct others in it both by the method which shows the meaning and by the method which shows the doctrine?

The Lord: One should know that such a Bodhisattva is reborn here after he has deceased in other world systems where he has honoured and questioned the Buddhas, the Lords. Any Bodhisattva who, after he has deceased in other world systems where he has honoured and questioned the Buddhas, the Lords, is reborn here, would, when he hears this deep perfection of wisdom being taught, identify this perfection of wisdom with the Teacher, [177] and be convinced that he is face to face with the Teacher, that he has seen the Teacher. When the perfection of wisdom is being taught, he listens attentively, pays respect to it before he hears it, and does not cut the story short. Such a Bodhisattva should be known as one who has practised for long, who has honoured many Buddhas.

Subhuti: Is it at all possible to hear the perfection of wisdom, to distinguish and consider her, to make statements and to reflect about her? Can one explain, or learn, that because of certain attributes, tokens or signs this is the perfection of wisdom, or that here this is the perfection of wisdom, or that there that is the perfection of wisdom?

The Lord: No indeed, Subhuti. This perfection of wisdom cannot be expounded, or learned, or distinguished, or considered, or stated, or reflected upon by means of the skandhas, or by means of the elements, or by means of the sense-fields. This is a consequence of the fact that all dharmas are isolated, absolutely isolated. Nor can the perfection of wisdom be understood otherwise than by the skandhas, elements or sense-fields. For just the very skandhas, elements and sense-fields are empty, isolated and calmly quiet. It is thus that the perfection of wisdom and the skandhas, elements and sense-fields are not two, nor divided. As a result of their emptiness, isolatedness and quietude they cannot be apprehended. The lack of a basis of apprehension in all dharmas, *that* is called 'perfect wisdom.' Where there is no perception, appellation, conception or conventional expression, there one speaks of 'perfection of wisdom.' [178]

Subhuti: As one who has practised for how long should that Bodhisattva be known who makes endeavours about this deep perfection of wisdom?

The Lord: One must make a distinction in this, owing to the unequal endowment of different Bodhisattvas.

6. CAUSES AND CONSEQUENCES OF DISBELIEF

It is quite possible that some Bodhisattvas, although they have seen many hundreds, many thousands, many hundreds of thousands of Buddhas, and have led the holy life in their presence, might nevertheless have no faith in the perfection of wisdom. The reason is that in the past also they have had no respect for this deep perfection of wisdom when, in the presence of those Buddhas and Lords, it was taught. Because they lacked in respect for it, they had no desire to learn more about it, did not honour it, were unwilling to ask questions, and lacked in faith. Lacking in faith they thereupon walked out of the assemblies. It is because in the past they have produced, accumulated, piled up and collected karma conducive to the ruin of dharma that also at present they walk out when this deep perfection of wisdom is being taught. From lack of respect without faith and firm belief in the perfection of wisdom, they have no concord either in their bodies or in their thoughts. Devoid of concord they do not know, see, recognise or make known this perfection of wisdom. First they do not believe, then they do not hear, then they do not see, then they do not recognise it, and thus they produce, accumulate, pile up and collect karma conducive to the ruin of dharma. [179] This in its turn will bring about karma conducive to weakness in wisdom. That in its turn will make them refuse, reject and revile this perfection of wisdom when it is being taught, and, having rejected it, they will walk out. But by rejecting this perfection of wisdom they reject the all-knowledge of the Buddhas and Lords, past, future and present. Not content with having vitiated their own continuities, they will, as if all aflame, deter, dissuade, turn away others also,— persons of small intelligence, wisdom, merit and wholesome roots, endowed with but a little faith, affection, serenity, and desire-to-do, beginners, essentially unqualified,—trying to take away even that little faith, affection, serenity and desire-to-do. They will say that one should not train in it, they will declare that it is not the Buddha's word. They first vitiate and estrange their own continuities, and then those of others. Thereby they will calumniate the perfection of wisdom. To calumniate the perfection of wisdom means to calumniate all-knowledge, and therewith the past, future and present Buddhas. They will be removed from the presence of the Buddhas and Lords, deprived of the Dharma, expelled from the Samgha. In each and every way they will be shut out from the

Triple Jewel. Their activities cut down the welfare and happiness of beings, and they will collect from them karma conducive to the great hells. [180] Because they have raised these karma-formations, they will be reborn in the great hells, for many hundreds of years, etc. to: for many hundreds of thousands of niyutas of kotis of aeons. From one great hell they will pass on to another. After a good long time their world will be consumed by fire. They will then be hurled into the great hells in another world system, where again they will pass on from great hell to great hell. When also that world is consumed by fire, they will again be hurled into the great hells in another world system, where again they will pass on from great hell to great hell. When also that world is consumed by fire, this karma of theirs will still be unexhausted, will still have some residue of efficacy and, deceased there, they will again be hurled into this world system. Here again they will be reborn in the great hells, and experience great sufferings in them, until the time when this world is once more consumed by fire. [181] They will therefore, as we see, experience a karma which involves many painful feelings. And why? Because their teachings are so bad.

Sariputra: Even the aftereffect of the five deadly sins bears no proportion to this misconduct of mind and speech?

The Lord: It does not. All those who oppose this perfection of wisdom and dissuade others from it are persons to whom I do not grant any vision. How can one become intimate with them, how can they gain wealth, honour and position? As a matter of fact they should be regarded as defamers of dharma, as mere rubbish, as blackguards, as mere vipers. [182] They are persons who bring misfortune, they will ruin those who listen to them. For those who defame the perfection of wisdom should be regarded as persons who defame Dharma.

Sariputra: The Lord has not told us about the length of time such a person must spend in the great hells.

The Lord: Leave that alone, Sariputra. If this were announced those who hear it would have to beware lest hot blood spurt out of their mouths, lest they incur death or deadly pain, lest harsh oppression weigh them down, lest the dart of grief enter their hearts, lest they drop down with a big fall, lest they shrivel up and wither away, lest they be overpowered by a great fright. —So the Lord refused to answer the Venerable Sariputra's question. For a second time, for a third time the Venerable *Sariputra* spoke thus to the Lord: Tell me, O Lord, the length of that person's sojourn in hell, as a guidance for future generations.

The Lord: Because he has brought about, accumulated, piled up and collected this karma of mind and speech he must sojourn for a long while in the great hells. Just so much guidance will be given to future generations, that he will, in consequence of the unwholesome karma-formations of this misconduct of speech and mind, experience pain for just so long. The mere announcement of the measurelessness and magnitude of his pain will be a sufficient source of anxiety to virtuous sons and daughters of good family. [183] It will turn them away from activities conducive to the ruin of dharma, they will cause the formation of merit, and they will not reject the good dharma, even to save their lives, for they do not wish to meet with such pains.

Subhuti: Such a person should become well-restrained in the deeds of his body, speech or mind. For so great a heap of demerit is begotten by such false teachings. Which, O Lord, is the deed that begets so great a heap of demerit?

The Lord: Such false teachings do. Just here there will be deluded men, persons who have left the world for the well-taught Dharma-Vinaya, who will decide to defame, to reject, to oppose this deep perfection of wisdom. But to oppose the perfection of wisdom is to oppose the enlightenment of the Buddhas and Lords. And that means that one opposes the all-knowledge of the Buddhas and Lords in past, future and present. To oppose all-knowledge means to oppose the good dharma. To oppose the good dharma means to oppose the community of the Disciples of the Tathagata. And when one opposes also the community of the Disciples of the Tathagata, then one is shut out in each and every way from the Triple Jewel. One has then managed to acquire an unwholesome karma-formation which is greater than immeasurable and incalculable.

Subhuti: For what reason [184] do those people believe that they should oppose this perfection of wisdom?

The Lord: Such a person is beset by Mara. His karma is conducive to weakness in wisdom, and so he has no faith or serene confidence in deep dharmas. Endowed with those two evil dharmas he will oppose this perfection of wisdom. Moreover, Subhuti, that person will be one who is in the hands of bad friends; or he may be one who has not practised; or one who has settled down in the skandhas; or one who exalts himself and deprecates others, looking out for faults. Endowed also with these four attributes will be that person who believes that this perfection of wisdom should be opposed when it is being taught.

Chapter VIII

PURITY

1. DEPTH AND PURITY OF PERFECT WISDOM

Subhuti: It is hard to gain confidence in the perfection of wisdom if one is unpractised, lacks in wholesome roots and is in the hands of a bad friend.

The Lord: So it is, Subhuti. It is hard to gain confidence in the perfection of wisdom if one is unpractised, has only diminutive wholesome roots, is dull-witted, does not care, has learned little, has an inferior kind of wisdom, relies on bad friends, is not eager to learn, unwilling to ask questions and unpractised in wholesome dharmas.

Subhuti: How deep then is this perfection of wisdom, since it is so hard to gain confidence in it?

The Lord: Form is neither bound nor freed, because form has no own-being. The past starting point of a material process [=form] is neither bound nor freed, because the past starting point of a material process is without own-being. The end of a material process, in the future, is neither bound nor freed, because the future end of a material process is without own-being. A present material process is without own-being, because the fact of being present is not a part of the own-being of a present form. [186] And so for the remaining skandhas.

Subhuti: It is hard, it is exceedingly hard to gain confidence in the perfection of wisdom, if one is unpractised, has planted no wholesome roots, is in the hands of a bad friend, has come under the sway of Mara, is lazy, of small vigour, robbed of mindfulness and stupid.

The Lord: So it is, Subhuti. Because the purity of form is identical with the purity of the fruit, and the purity of the fruit is identical with the purity of form. It is thus that the purity of form and the purity of the fruit are not two, nor divided, are not broken apart, nor cut apart. It is thus that the purity of form comes from the purity of the fruit, and the purity of the fruit from the purity of form. [187] And the same identity exists between the purity of form and the purity of all-knowledge. The same applies to the other skandhas.

Sariputra: Deep, O Lord, is the perfection of wisdom!

The Lord: From purity.

Sariputra: A source of illumination is the perfection of wisdom.

The Lord: From purity.

Sariputra: A light is perfect wisdom.

The Lord: From purity.

Sariputra: Not subject to rebirth is perfect wisdom.

The Lord: From purity.

Sariputra: Free from defilement is perfect wisdom.

The Lord: From purity.

Sariputra: There is no attainment or reunion in perfect wisdom.

The Lord: From purity.

Sariputra: Perfect wisdom does not reproduce herself.

The Lord: From purity. [188]

Sariputra: There is absolutely no rebirth of perfect wisdom, whether in the world of sense-desire, or in the world of form, or in the formless world.

The Lord: From purity.

Sariputra: Perfect wisdom neither knows nor perceives.

The Lord: From purity.

Sariputra: What then does perfect wisdom neither know nor perceive?

The Lord: Form, and the other skandhas. And why? From purity.

Sariputra: Perfect wisdom neither helps nor hinders all-knowledge.

The Lord: From purity.

Sariputra: Perfect wisdom neither gains nor abandons any dharma.

The Lord: From purity.

Subhuti: The purity of form, etc., is due to the purity of self.

The Lord: Because it is absolutely pure. [189]

Subhuti: The purity of the fruit, and the purity of all-knowledge, are due to the purity of self.

The Lord: Because of its absolute purity.

Subhuti: The absence of attainment and reunion is due to the purity of self.

The Lord: Because of its absolute purity.

Subhuti: The boundlessness of form, etc., is due to the boundlessness of self.

The Lord: Because of its absolute purity.

Subhuti: A Bodhisattva who understands it thus, he has perfect wisdom.

The Lord: Because of his absolute purity.

Subhuti: Moreover, this perfection of wisdom does not stand on the shore this side, nor on the shore beyond, nor athwart the two.

The Lord: Because of its absolute purity. [190]

Subhuti: A Bodhisattva who treats even that [insight] as an object of perception, will thereby part from this perfection of wisdom, and get far away from it.

2. ATTACHMENTS

The Lord: Well said, Subhuti. For also names and signs are sources of attachment.

Subhuti: It is wonderful, O Lord, to see the extent to which this perfection of wisdom has been well taught, well explained, well rounded off. The Lord even announces these sources of attachment.

Sariputra: Which, Subhuti, are these attachments?

Subhuti: It is an attachment if one perceives that the skandhas are empty, that past dharmas are past dharmas, future dharmas are future dharmas, and present dharmas are present dharmas. It is an attachment if one forms the notion that someone who belongs to the vehicle of the Bodhisattvas begets so great a heap of merit through his first production of the thought of enlightenment.

Sakra: In which manner, holy Subhuti, does the thought of enlightenment become a source of attachment?

Subhuti: One becomes attached when one perceives this thought of enlightenment as 'this is the first thought of enlightenment,' and if one converts it into full enlightenment while conscious that one does so. For it is quite impossible to turn over the essential original nature of a thought. One should therefore keep in agreement with true reality when one makes others see the highest, and rouses them to win supreme enlightenment. [191] In that way one does not waste one's self away, and the manner in which one rouses others to win the highest has the sanction of the Buddhas. And one succeeds in abandoning all those points of attachment.

The Lord: Well said, Subhuti, you who make the Bodhisattvas aware of these points of attachment. I will now announce other, more subtle, attachments. Listen to them well, and pay good attention. I will teach them to you.

"Well said, O Lord," and the Venerable *Subhuti* listened in silence.

The Lord: Here Subhuti, a son or daughter of good family, full of faith, attends to the Tathagata through a sign. But, so many signs, so many attachments. For from signs comes attachment. It is thus that he is conscious that he rejoices in all the dharmas without outflows of the Buddhas and Lords, past, future and present, and that, after rejoicing, he turns over into full enlightenment the wholesome root which is associated with his act of jubilation. As a matter of fact, however, the true nature of dharmas is not past, nor future, nor present; it lies quite outside the three periods of time; and for that reason it cannot possibly be converted, cannot be treated as a sign, or as an objective support, and it cannot be seen, nor heard, nor felt, nor known. [192]

3. NON-ATTACHMENT

Subhuti: Deep is the essential original nature of the dharmas.

The Lord: Because it is isolated.

Subhuti: Deep is the essential nature of perfect wisdom.

The Lord: Because its essential nature is pure and isolated, therefore has the perfection of wisdom a deep essential nature.

Subhuti: Isolated is the essential nature of perfect wisdom. I pay homage to the perfection of wisdom.

The Lord: Also all dharmas are isolated in their essential nature. And the isolatedness of the essential nature of all dharmas is identical with the perfection of wisdom. For the Tathagata has fully known all dharmas as not made.

Subhuti: Therefore all dharmas have the character of not having been fully known by the Tathagata?

The Lord: It is just through their essential nature that those dharmas are not a something. Their nature is no-nature, and their no-nature is their nature. Because all dharmas have one mark only, i.e. no mark. It is for this reason that all dharmas have the character of not having been fully known by the Tathagata. For there are no two natures of dharma, but just one single one is the nature of all dharmas. And the nature of all dharmas is no nature, and their no-nature is their nature. It is thus that all those points of attachment are abandoned. [193]

Subhuti: Deep, O Lord, is the perfection of wisdom.

The Lord: Through a depth like that of space.

Subhuti: Hard to understand, O Lord, is the perfection of wisdom.

The Lord: Because nothing is fully known by the enlightened.

Subhuti: Unthinkable, O Lord, is the perfection of wisdom.

The Lord: Because the perfection of wisdom is not something that thought ought to know, or that thought has access to.

Subhuti: Not something made is the perfection of wisdom, O Lord.

The Lord: Because no maker can be apprehended.

Subhuti: How then under these circumstances, should a Bodhisattva course in perfect wisdom?

The Lord: A Bodhisattva courses in perfect wisdom if, while coursing, he does not course in the skandhas; or if he does not course in the conviction that the skandhas are impermanent, or that they are empty, or that they are neither defective nor entire [194]. And if he does not even course in the conviction that form is not the defectiveness or entirety of form, and so for the other skandhas, then he courses in perfect wisdom.

Subhuti: It is wonderful, O Lord, how well the reasons for the attachment and non-attachment of the Bodhisattvas have been explained.

The Lord: One courses in perfect wisdom if one does not course in the idea that form is with attachment, or without attachment. And as for form, so for the other skandhas, the sight organ, etc., to feeling born from eye contact; so for the physical elements, the six perfections, the thirty-seven wings of enlightenment, the powers, the grounds of self-confidence, the analytical knowledges, the eighteen special Buddha-dharmas, and the fruits of the holy life, from the fruit of a Streamwinner to all-knowledge. [195] When he courses thus, a Bodhisattva does not generate attachment to anything, from form to all-knowledge. For all-knowledge is unattached, it is neither bound nor freed, and there is nothing that has risen above it. It is thus, Subhuti, that Bodhisattvas should course in perfect wisdom through rising completely above all attachments. [196]

4. LIKE SPACE OR AN ECHO

Subhuti: It is wonderful, O Lord, how deep is this dharma, I mean the perfection of wisdom. Demonstration does not diminish or increase it. Non-demonstration also does not diminish or increase it.

The Lord: Well said, Subhuti. It is just as if a Tathagata should, during his entire life, speak in praise of space, without thereby increasing the volume of space; and space would not diminish, either, while he was not speaking in praise of it. Or it is as with an illusory man. Praise does not penetrate into him or win him over. When there is no praise he is not affected, or frustrated. Just so the true nature of dharmas is just so much, whether it be demonstrated or not.

Subhuti: A doer of what is hard is the Bodhisattva who, while he courses in perfect wisdom, does not lose heart nor get elated; who persists in making endeavours about it and does not turn back. The development of perfect wisdom is like the development of space. Homage should be paid to those Bodhisattvas who are armed with this armour. For with space they want to be armed when, for the sake of beings, they put on the armour. Armed with the great armour is a Bodhisattva, a hero is a Bodhi-sattva, when he wants to be armed with an armour, and win full enlighten-ment, for the sake of beings who are like space, who are like the realm of dharma. He is one who wants to liberate space, he is one who wants to get rid of space, he is one who has won the armour of the great perfection of vigour [197], that Bodhisattva who is armed with the armour for the sake of beings who are like space, who are like the realm of Dharma.

Thereupon *a certain monk* saluted the Lord with folded hands and said to the Lord: I pay homage, O Lord, to the perfection of wisdom! For it neither produces nor stops any dharma.

Sakra: If someone, holy Subhuti, would make efforts about this perfection of wisdom, what would his efforts be about?

Subhuti: He would make efforts about space. And he would make his efforts about a mere vacuity if he would decide to train in perfect wisdom or to work on it.

Sakra: Please, O Lord, command me to shelter, defend and protect that son or daughter of good family who bears in mind this perfection of wisdom!

Subhuti: Sakra, can you see that dharma which you intend to shelter, defend and protect?

Sakra: Not so, holy Subhuti.

Subhuti: So when a Bodhisattva stands in the perfection of wisdom as it has been expounded, then just that will be his shelter, defence and protection. On the other hand, when he is lacking in perfect wisdom, [198] then those men and ghosts who look for entry will gain entrance into him. One would, however, want to arrange shelter, defence and protection for space if one would want to arrange shelter, defence and protection for a Bodhisattva who courses in perfect wisdom. What do you think, Kausika, are you able to arrange shelter, defence and protection for an echo?

Sakra: Not so, holy Subhuti.

Subhuti: Just so a Bodhisattva, who courses and dwells in perfect wisdom, comprehends that all dharmas are like an echo. He does not think about them, does not review, identify, or perceive them, and he knows that those dharmas do not exist, that their reality does not appear, cannot be found, cannot be got at. If he dwells thus, he courses in perfect wisdom.

5. CONCLUSION

Thereupon, through the Buddha's might the four Great Kings in the great trichiliocosm, and all the Sakras, Chiefs of Gods, and all the great Brahma Gods, and Sahapati, the great Brahma—all came to where the Lord was. They reverently saluted the Lord's feet with their heads, walked three times round the Lord, and stood on one side. Through the Buddha's might and through his miraculous power their minds were impressed by the sight of a thousand Buddhas. [199]

In these very words, by monks called Subhuti, etc., has this very perfection of wisdom been expounded, just this very chapter of the perfection of wisdom. With reference to it just the Sakras, Chiefs of Gods, ask questions and counter-questions. At this very spot of earth has just this perfection of wisdom been taught. Maitreya also, the Bodhisattva, the great being will, after he has won the supreme enlightenment, at this very spot of earth teach this very same perfection of wisdom.

Chapter IX

PRAISE

1. PERFECT WISDOM PERFECTLY PURE

Subhuti: To call it 'perfection of wisdom,' O Lord, that is merely giving it a name. And what that name corresponds to, that cannot be got at. One speaks of a 'name' with reference to a merely nominal entity. Even this perfection of wisdom cannot be found or got at. In so far as it is a word, in so far is it perfect wisdom; in so far as it is perfect wisdom, in so far is it a word. No duality of dharmas between those two can either be found or got at. For what reason then will Maitreya, the Bodhisattva, the great being, after he has won the supreme enlightenment, preach just this very same perfection of wisdom at this very spot of earth in just these same words?

The Lord: The reason is that Maitreya will be fully enlightened as to the fact that the skandhas are neither permanent nor impermanent, that they are neither bound nor freed, that they are absolutely pure.

Subhuti: Perfectly pure indeed is the perfection of wisdom. [201]

The Lord: Perfect wisdom is perfectly pure because the skandhas are pure, and because their non-production is perfectly pure, their non-stopping, their non-defilement and their non-purification. It is pure because space is pure and because the skandhas are stainless, and the defiling forces cannot take hold of them. Perfect wisdom is perfectly pure because, like space or an echo, it is unutterable, incommunicable, and offers no basis for apprehension. It is perfectly pure because it is not covered by any dharma, stained or stainless.

2. EFFECTS OF PERFECT WISDOM

Subhuti: It is indeed a great gain to these sons and daughters of good family that they should even come to hear of this perfection of wisdom. How much greater the gain if they take it up, bear it in mind, recite, study, spread, teach, explain and master it. Their eyes, ears, nose, tongues and bodies will be free from disease, and their minds free from stupefaction. They will not die a violent death. Many thousands of Gods will follow closely behind them. [202] Wherever, on the eighth, fourteenth and fifteenth day, when he preaches dharma, a son or daughter of good family teaches the perfection of wisdom, there he will beget a great deal of merit.

The Lord: So it is, Subhuti. Many thousands of Gods, Subhuti, will follow closely behind that son or daughter of good family, and many thousands of Gods will come to where perfect wisdom is being taught. Desirous of hearing dharma, they will all of them protect the preacher of dharma who teaches this perfection of wisdom. For perfect wisdom is the most precious thing in the world with its Gods, men and Asuras. That also is a reason why such a person will beget a great deal of merit. On the other hand, there will be many obstacles to this deep perfection of wisdom being written, taken up, borne in mind, recited, studied, spread, explained and repeated. For very precious things provoke much hostility. The more excellent they are, the more violent the hostility. But this is the most precious thing in the entire world, this perfection of wisdom, which has been set up and undertaken for the benefit and happiness of the world, by showing that all dharmas have not been produced nor destroyed, are neither defiled nor purified. [203] But perfect wisdom does not cling to any dharma, nor defile any dharma, nor take hold of any dharma. For all these dharmas neither exist nor are they got at. Because it has not been apprehended is the perfection of wisdom without any stain. 'To be free from stains,' that is the same thing as perfect wisdom. And it is because the skandhas are free from stains that perfect wisdom is without any stain. A Bodhisattva courses in perfect wisdom if he does not perceive even that. Moreover, this perfection of wisdom does not enter or place itself into any dharma, it does not reveal or define any dharma, it does not bring in any dharma nor carry one away.

3. THE SECOND TURNING OF THE WHEEL OF DHARMA

Thereupon a great many thousands of Gods in the intermediate realm called out aloud with cries of joy, waved their garments, and said: We now, indeed, see the second turning of the wheel of dharma taking place in Jambudvipa!

The Lord: This, Subhuti, is not the second turning of the wheel of dharma. No dharma can be turned forwards or backwards. Just this is a Bodhisattva's perfection of wisdom. [204]

Subhuti: Great is this perfection of a Bodhisattva who, unattached to all dharmas, wants to know full enlightenment, and who yet is not enlightened about any dharma, or who will turn the wheel of dharma and who yet will not show up any dharma. For no dharma is here got at, no dharma is indicated, no dharma will move on any dharma. Because absolutely, reproduction is alien to all dharmas. Nor will any dharma turn back any other dharma. Because from the very beginning all dharmas have not been reproduced, since their essential nature is isolated.

The Lord: So it is, Subhuti. For emptiness does not proceed nor recede, and that holds good also for the Signless and the Wishless. To demonstrate that is to demonstrate all dharmas. But no one has demonstrated it, no one has heard it, no one has received it, and no one realizes it, in the past, present or future. Nor by this demonstration of dharma does anyone ever go to Nirvana. Nor by this demonstration of dharma has anyone ever been made worthy of gifts. [205]

4. MODES AND QUALITIES OF PERFECT WISDOM

Subhuti: This is a perfection of what is not, because space is not something that is. This is a perfection which equals the unequalled, because all dharmas are not apprehended. This is an isolated perfection, on account of absolute emptiness. This perfection cannot be crushed, because all dharmas are not apprehended. This is a trackless perfection, because both body and mind are absent. This is a perfection which has no own-being, because it neither comes nor goes. This perfection is inexpressible, because all dharmas are not discriminated. This perfection is nameless, because the skandhas are not apprehended. This perfection does not go away, because no dharma ever goes away. One cannot partake of this perfection, because no dharma can be seized. This perfection is inexhaustible, as linked to the inexhaustible dharma. This perfection has had no genesis, because no dharma has really come about. This is a perfection which does nothing, because no doer can be apprehended. This perfection does not generate [cognize] anything, because all dharmas are without self. This perfection does not pass on, because there is no genesis of decease and rebirth. This perfection does not discipline, because the past, future and present periods are not apprehended. This is the perfection of a dream, an echo, a reflected image, a mirage, or an illusion, because it informs about non-production. This perfection is free from defilement, because greed, hate and delusion have no own-being. This perfection knows no purification, because no possible receptacle [which might have to be purified] can be apprehended. This perfection is spotless, because space is spotless. [206] This perfection is free from impediments, because it rises completely above all mental attitudes to dharmas. This perfection has no mental attitude, because it is imperturbable. This perfection is unshakeable, in consequence of the stability of the realm of dharma. This perfection has turned away from greed, because there is no falseness in dharmas. This perfection does not rise up, because there is no discrimination in dharmas. This perfection is quieted, because no sign is apprehended in all dharmas. This perfection is faultless, as the perfection of all virtues. This perfection is undefiled, because imagination is something that is not. No living being is found in this perfection, because of the reality-limit. This perfection is unlimited, because the manifestation of all dharmas does not rise up. This perfection does not follow after the duality of opposites, because it does not settle down in all dharmas. This perfection is undifferentiated, because all dharmas are. This perfection is untarnished, because it is free from any longing for the level of Disciples and Pratyekabuddhas. This perfection is undiscriminated, because of the basic identity of all that is discriminated. This perfection is infinite, because the nature of dharma is unlimited. This perfection is unattached, because of its non-attachment to all dharmas. Impermanent is this perfection, because all dharmas are unconditioned. Ill is this perfection, because the nature of dharma is the same as space. Empty is this perfection, because all dharmas are not apprehended. Not-self is this perfection, because there is no settling down in all dharmas. Markless is this perfection, because there is no reproduction in dharmas. [207] This is a perfection of all emptiness, because endless and boundless. This is a perfection of the wings of enlightenment, such as the pillars of mindfulness, etc., because they cannot be apprehended. This is a perfection of Emptiness, of the Signless, of the Wishless, because the three doors to deliverance cannot be apprehended. This is a perfection of the eight deliverances, because they cannot be apprehended. This is a perfection of the nine successive stations, because the first trance, etc., cannot be apprehended. This is a perfection of the four Truths, because ill, etc., cannot be apprehended. This is a perfection of the ten perfections, because giving, etc., cannot be apprehended. This is a perfection of the ten powers, because it cannot be crushed. This is a perfection of the four grounds of self-confidence, because absolutely it cannot be cowed. This is a perfection of the analytical knowledges, because it is unobstructed when unattached to all-knowledge. This is a perfection of all the special Buddha-dharmas, because they have transcended all counting. This is a perfection of the Suchness of the Tathagata, because there is no falseness in all dharmas. This is a perfection of the Self-existent, because all dharmas have no own-being. This perfection of wisdom is a perfection of the cognition of the all-knowing, because it comprehends all the modes of the own-being of all dharmas.

Chapter X

PROCLAMATION OF THE QUALITIES OF BEARING IN MIND

1. PAST DEEDS, AND THE PRESENT ATTITUDE TO PERFECT WISDOM

Thereupon it occurred to *Sakra,* Chief of Gods: Those who come to hear of this perfection of wisdom must be people who have fulfilled their duties under the former Jinas, who have planted wholesome roots under many Buddhas, who have been taken hold of by good friends. How much more so those who take up this perfection of wisdom, bear it in mind, study, spread and explain it, and who, in addition, train in Thusness, progress to Thusness, make efforts about Thusness. They are endowed with more than trifling wholesome roots. They will be people who have honoured many Buddhas, and who have again and again questioned them. It was just this perfection of wisdom which they have heard in the past in the presence of former Tathagatas. They have planted wholesome roots under many Buddhas, [209] those sons and daughters of good family who, when just this perfection of wisdom is being taught, explained and repeated, will not become cowed nor stolid, will not become cast down nor depressed, will not turn their minds away from it nor have their backs broken, will not tremble, be frightened, be terrified.

Sariputra read Sakra's thoughts, and said: Like an irreversible Bodhisattva should one regard that person who, when just this deep perfection of wisdom is being taught and explained, has faith in it, and, trusting, firmly believing, his heart full of serene faith, raises a thought directed towards enlightenment, takes up, etc., this perfection of wisdom, trains in Thusness, progresses to Thusness, makes efforts about Thusness. For this perfection of wisdom is deep, O Lord, and therefore someone with diminutive wholesome roots, who, unwilling to ask questions, has learned nothing when face to face with the Buddhas and Lords in the past, and who has not practised in the past, cannot just here believe in this so deep perfection of wisdom. And as to those who neither believe in it nor understand it, and who decide to reject it, [210] in the past also they have rejected this deep perfection of wisdom when it was taught, and that in consequence of the inadequacy of their wholesome roots. For those who have not practised in the past cannot believe in this perfection of wisdom. When they reject it now, they have also rejected it in the past. And that is the reason why, when this deep perfection of wisdom is being taught, they have no faith, or patience, or pleasure, or desire-to-do, or vigour, or vigilance, or resolve. And in the past also they have questioned neither the Buddhas, the Lords, nor their disciples.

Sakra: Deep, O holy Sariputra, is the perfection of wisdom. It is not at all astonishing that, when it is being taught, a Bodhisattva would not believe in it, if he had not practised in the past.

Sakra then said to the Lord: I pay homage, O Lord, to the perfection of wisdom! One pays homage to the cognition of the all-knowing when one pays homage to the perfection of wisdom.

The Lord: So it is. For from it has come forth the all-knowledge of the Buddhas, the Lords, [211] and, conversely, the perfection of wisdom is brought about as something that has come forth from the cognition of the all-knowing. That is why one should course, stand, progress, and make efforts in this perfection of wisdom.

Sakra: How does a Bodhisattva, who courses in perfect wisdom, become one who has stood in the perfection of wisdom? How does he make efforts about the perfection of wisdom?

The Lord: Well said, well said, Kausika. Well said, again, well said, Kausika, since you have decided to question the Tathagata about this matter. In that you have been inspired by the Buddha's might. Here, Kausika, a Bodhisattva who courses in perfect wisdom does not stand in form, etc., does not stand in the notion that 'this is form,' and that means that he makes efforts about form, etc. He does not apply himself to the notion that 'this is form, etc.' Insofar as he does not apply himself to the notion that 'this is form, etc.,' he does not stand in the notion that 'this is form, etc.' [212] Thus he becomes one who has stood in perfect wisdom, thus he makes efforts.

Sariputra: Deep, O Lord, is the perfection of wisdom. Hard to fathom is the perfection of wisdom. Hard to grasp is the perfection of wisdom. Unlimited is the perfection of wisdom.

The Lord: So it is, Sariputra. He does not stand in the notion that 'form, etc., is deep.' Insofar as he does not stand in this notion he makes efforts about form, etc. He does not make efforts about the notion that 'form, etc., is deep.' In so far as he makes no efforts about this notion he does not stand in the notion that 'form, etc., is deep.'

2. QUALIFICATIONS OF A BODHISATTVA
WHO OBTAINS PERFECT WISDOM

Sariputra: In front of an irreversible Bodhisattva, of a Bodhisattva predestined to enlightenment, should the deep perfection of wisdom be taught. For he will not hesitate, not doubt, not be stupefied, not dispute it. [213]

Sakra: What would be the fault in teaching this perfection of wisdom in front of an unpredestined Bodhisattva?

Sariputra: If Kausika, unpredestined, a Bodhisattva obtains this perfection of wisdom, for vision, praise, worship and hearing, and if he remains unafraid when he hears it, one can be sure that he has come from afar, has set out for long in the vehicle, and that his wholesome roots are well matured. It will not be long from now onwards until he receives the prediction to supreme enlightenment. One can be sure that that prediction will be near, and will come to him before he has passed by one, two or three Tathagatas. And, of course, he will please the Tathagatas whom he passes by, will please them permanently, and he will see to it that the vision of those Tathagatas will bear the fruit of the prediction, that it will lead him to the prediction to supreme enlightenment [itself]. Come from afar, O Lord, set out for long in the great vehicle, with wholesome roots well matured is that Bodhisattva who obtains this perfection of wisdom for vision, praise, worship and hearing. How much more so if he would not only hear it, but also take it up, [214] bear it in mind, preach, study, spread, explain and repeat it.

The Lord: So it is, Sariputra, as you have said.

3. FIVE SIMILES TO ILLUSTRATE NEARNESS TO FULL ENLIGHTENMENT

Sariputra: A simile or example flashes into my mind, O Lord. Just as we can be sure that a person belonging to the vehicle of the Bodhisattvas, when he dreams that he sits on the terrace of enlightenment, is actually near to supreme enlightenment; just so we can be sure that a person who fulfils the conditions just outlined has come from afar, has set out for long in the vehicle of the Bodhisattvas, and is near his prediction to enlightenment. We can be sure that the Buddhas, the Lords, will predict [215] that this Bodhisattva shall win full enlightenment. For a Bodhisattva has set out for long in the vehicle, and his wholesome roots are mature, if he gets to this deep perfection of wisdom, even if he gets no further than hearing it. How much more so if he would also bear it in mind, etc., to: repeat it. For the thoughts of beings who are not without an abundance of accumulations of karma conducive to the ruin of dharma will become averse to this deep perfection of wisdom, will sway away from it. Through the abundance of that karma beings who have not collected wholesome roots will find no satisfaction nor faith in this reality-limit. But those who find satisfaction and faith in it are people who have collected wholesome roots, well collected them.

A man coming out of a huge wild forest, one hundred miles big, up to a thousand miles big, might see certain signs which indicate a town, or other inhabited place,—such as cowherds, or cattle keepers, or boundary lines, or gardens, or groves. [216] From those signs he will infer the nearness of an inhabited place. He feels happier, and robbers no longer worry him. Just so a Bodhisattva for whom this deep perfection of wisdom turns up should know that he is quite near to supreme enlightenment, that before long he will receive the prediction to it. He should also no longer be afraid of the level of the Disciples and Pratyekabuddhas. For this sign has appeared to him, i.e., that he has received this deep perfection of wisdom for vision, praise, worship, and hearing.

The Lord: So it is, Sariputra. May you make clear also this section. For what you say, and what you will say, is due to the Buddha's might.

Sariputra: A man, desirous of seeing the great ocean, might travel to it. As long as on his travels he sees a tree, or the sign of a tree, a mountain, or the sign of a mountain, he knows that the great ocean is still far away. But when he no longer sees either tree or mountain, then he knows that the great ocean is quite near from there. For this great ocean gradually slopes away, and within it there is neither tree nor mountain. [217] And although he may not yet see the great ocean directly before his eyes, he nevertheless can be quite certain that the ocean is quite near, not much farther away from there. Similar is the case of the Bodhisattva who has heard this deep perfection of wisdom. He knows that, although he has not yet, face to face with these Tathagatas, been predicted to supreme enlightenment, nevertheless he is quite near that prediction. For he has received this deep perfection of wisdom, for vision, praise, worship and hearing.

In spring, O Lord, when last year's leaves have withered away, one can see sproutings on many trees. The men of Jambudvipa will then be glad, because when they have seen these symptoms in the woods, they know that soon also flowers and fruits will come out. For they have seen these signs on the trees. Just so, O Lord, one can be sure that a Bodhisattva, when he receives this deep perfection of wisdom, when it turns up for him, that he has matured his wholesome roots for a long time. It is just because of the existence of these wholesome roots in him that this deep perfection of wisdom has bent over to him. Then those divinities who have seen the Buddhas of the past are delighted, overjoyed and enchanted, because they feel that surely it will not be long before this Bodhisattva will receive his prediction to full enlightenment, since also with the Bodhisattvas of the past these were the symptoms of their coming prediction to full enlightenment. [218]

A woman, pregnant with a heavy womb, is twisted, and all weary, she does not walk about a great deal, takes little food, finds little rest, speaks little, has little strength but many pains, often cries out aloud and abstains from habitual cohabitation. She realises that she experiences all these unpleasant feelings in her body as a result of indulging in unwise attention in the past, practising it, developing it, making much of it. When these symptoms are seen in her, one can be sure that before long she will give birth to a child. Just so, when for a Bodhisattva this deep perfection of wisdom turns up for the sake of vision, praise, worship, and hearing, and if, when he hears it, his thought delights in it, and he becomes desirous of it, then one can be sure that before long he will receive the prediction to full enlightenment.

4. WHY BODHISATTVAS ARE WELL FAVOURED BY THE BUDDHAS

Subhuti: It is wonderful to see the extent to which the Tathagata has well taken hold of the Bodhisattvas, has well encompassed and favoured them. [219]

The Lord: It is because these Bodhisattvas have practised for the weal and happiness of the many, out of pity for the world. Out of pity for Gods and men, for the benefit, the weal and happiness of a great mass of people do they want to win the supreme enlightenment, and thereafter to demonstrate the supreme dharma.

5. RIGHT ATTITUDE TO PERFECT WISDOM

Subhuti: How does the development of perfect wisdom, on the part of a Bodhisattva who courses in perfect wisdom, become increasingly perfect?

The Lord: A Bodhisattva courses in perfect wisdom when he reviews neither the growth nor the diminution of form, etc., when he does not review either dharma or no-dharma. It is thus that his development of perfect wisdom becomes increasingly perfect.

Subhuti: This explanation is surely unthinkable.

The Lord: Because form is unthinkable, and so are the other skandhas. When he does not even perceive that form, etc., are unthinkable, then he courses in perfect wisdom. [220]

Sariputra: Who will zealously believe in this so deep perfection of wisdom?

The Lord: A Bodhisattva who is practised in perfect wisdom.

Sariputra: How does a Bodhisattva become practised, and what is the meaning of the word 'practised'?

The Lord: Here a Bodhisattva does not construct the powers, nor the grounds of self-confidence, nor the Buddha-dharmas, nor even the state of all-knowledge. Because the powers are unthinkable, and so are the grounds of self-confidence, so are the Buddha-dharmas, so is the state of all-knowledge, and so are all dharmas. When, thus practised, a Bodhisattva does not course anywhere, then he courses in perfect wisdom. For that reason is he called 'practised,' and that is the meaning of the word 'practised.'

6. OBSTACLES TO PERFECT WISDOM

Subhuti: Deep, O Lord, is perfect wisdom. It is a heap of treasure. It is a pure heap, as pure as space. It would not be surprising if many obstacles should arise to someone who takes up, etc., this perfection of wisdom. [221]

The Lord: There will be many obstacles to the study of this perfection of wisdom. For Mara, the Evil One, will make great efforts to cause difficulties. Therefore one should hurry up with one's task of copying it out. If one has one month to do it in, or two months, or three months, one should just carry on with the writing. If one has a year or more, even then one should just carry on with writing this perfection of wisdom [since after, or even during, that time one may be prevented by all kinds of interruptions]. Because it is a fact that in respect of very precious things many difficulties are wont to arise.

Subhuti: Here, O Lord, when the perfection of wisdom is being studied, Mara, the Evil One, will in many ways show zeal, and exert himself to cause difficulties.

The Lord: In spite of that [222] he is powerless to cause really effective obstacles to a Bodhisattva who gives his undivided attention to his task.

7. THE BODHISATTVA SUSTAINED BY THE BUDDHAS

Sariputra: If, O Lord, Mara, the Evil One, is determined to cause obstacles to the study of this perfection of wisdom, how can just now people actually study it, and through whose might can they do so?

The Lord: It is through the might of the Buddhas and Lords, of the Tathagatas, that they study it, and that they make progress in training in Thusness. For it is in the nature of things that the Buddhas, the Lords, who stand, hold and maintain themselves in immeasurable and incalculable world-systems, should bring to mind and uphold everyone who teaches [223] and studies this perfection of wisdom. The Buddhas will bring him to mind and assist him. And it is quite impossible to cause an obstacle to someone who has been brought to mind and upheld by the Buddhas.

Sariputra: It is through the Buddha's might, sustaining power and grace that Bodhisattvas study this deep perfection of wisdom, and progressively train in Thusness? [224]

The Lord: So it is, Sariputra. They are known to the Tathagata, they are sustained and seen by the Tathagata, and the Tathagata beholds them with his Buddha-eye. And those Bodhisattvas who study this perfection of wisdom, and who are progressively training in Thusness, they are near to the Thusness of the supreme enlightenment, and they stand poised in their decision to win full enlightenment. If they only just study this perfection of wisdom, without progressively training in Thusness, [225] they will not stand poised in Suchness in the supreme enlightenment; but nevertheless they also are known to the Tathagata, sustained and seen by the Tathagata, and the Tathagata beholds them with his Buddha-eye. That continual study of the perfection of wisdom, and the mental excitation about it, will be greatly profitable to them, a great advantage, fruit and reward. For, as aiming at ultimate reality, the perfection of wisdom has been set up for the penetration by all beings into what dharmas truly are.

8. PREDICTION ABOUT SPREAD OF PERFECT WISDOM

Moreover, these Sutras associated with the six perfections will, after the passing away of the Tathagata, appear in the South. From the South they will spread to the East, and from there to the North—from the time when the Dharma-Vinaya is like freshly made cream right into the period when the good law disappears. Those who at that time study and preserve this perfection of wisdom will be brought to mind by the Tathagata; the Tathagata will know, sustain and see them, and behold them with his Buddha-eye.

Sariputra: Will even this so deep perfection of wisdom in the last time, in the last period, be widespread in the northern direction, in the northern part of the world?

The Lord: Those who, in the North, will make efforts in this deep perfection of wisdom after they have heard it, [226] they will make it widespread. As set out for long in the vehicle should the Bodhisattvas be known who will study this perfection of wisdom then.

9. DESCRIPTION OF BODHISATTVAS WHO
   WILL STUDY PERFECT WISDOM

Sariputra: Those Bodhisattvas who in the North will study this deep perfection of wisdom, will they be many or few?

The Lord: There will be many, a good many Bodhisattvas in the North. But there will be only a few among them who will study this deep perfection of wisdom, and who, when it is being taught, will not become demoralized by it. As set out for long in the vehicle should they be known. [227] In the past already they have pursued, questioned and worshipped the Tathagatas. They will become morally perfect, and they will promote the welfare of many people, i.e. starting from just this my supreme enlightenment. For it is just for them that I have preached just the sermons associated with the state of all-knowledge. In them, even after they have passed through this present birth, just these ideas associated with the state of all-knowledge and with the perfection of wisdom, will persist by force of habit. And just this sermon will they both preach and delight in, i.e. concerning the supreme enlightenment. And they will be well established in this perfection of wisdom and concentrate on it. They cannot be diverted from it even by Mara, how much less by other beings, whether they use willpower or mantras. Because of their firm and irresistible drive towards full enlightenment. From hearing this perfection of wisdom those sons and daughters of good family will gain an uncommon degree of zest, elation and serene faith. For many people they will plant wholesome roots, i.e. in supreme enlightenment. Because in my presence, face to face with me, they have uttered the vow: "We, coursing in the practices of a Bodhisattva, shall set going on their way to full enlightenment many hundreds of living beings, yea, many [228] niyutas of kotis of living beings. We shall hold up perfect enlightenment to them, instigate, encourage and excite them to win it, help it to come forth, help them to get established in it, help them to become irreversible." And when I had surveyed their thought with my thought, I rejoiced in those sons and daughters of good family who belong to the vehicle of the Bodhisattvas and who had made this vow. In consequence they will become so much confirmed in their faith that they will seek rebirth in other Buddha-fields, and also there will come face to face with the Tathagatas there, who demonstrate dharma, and from whom they will hear in detail just this deep perfection of wisdom. In those Buddha-fields also they will set countless living beings going on their way to the supreme enlightenment, and will help them in their quest for full enlightenment. [229]

Sariputra: It is wonderful to think that in past, future and present dharmas there is nothing that the Tathagata has not seen, not heard, not felt, and of which he is unaware. There is no dharma that he has not cognized, there is no conduct of any being that he is unaware of. He has cognized even the future conduct of those Bodhisattvas who are zealous for enlightenment, who are full of earnest intentions, who have exerted vigour. But among those sons and daughters of good family who in the future will study this deep perfection of wisdom, who have exerted themselves on behalf of these six perfections and of the welfare of all beings, and who seek, search and strive to obtain this deep perfection of wisdom, some will not obtain it, while others will obtain it without striving to get it. What, O Lord, is the reason for that?

The Lord: So it is, Sariputra. There is nothing in past, future or present dharmas that the Tathagata has not seen, heard and felt, or of which he is unaware. It is further true that at that time in that period, some Bodhisattvas who hunt and [230] search for this perfection of wisdom will not get it. Others will get it without hunting and searching for it. They will be Bodhisattvas who in the past have persistently hunted and searched for this perfection of wisdom. It is through the impetus of this former wholesome root that they will get this perfection of wisdom, in spite of the fact that they do not now hunt and search for it. And also the Sutras different from this one, which welcome just this perfection of wisdom, will of their own accord come to them. For it is a rule, Sariputra, that, if a Bodhisattva persistently hunts and searches for this perfection of wisdom, he will, after one or two births, get it, and also the other Sutras associated with perfect wisdom will then come to him on their own.

Sariputra: Will only just these Sutras associated with the six perfections come to him, and no others?

The Lord: There will be also other very deep Sutras which will come to this son or daughter of good family of their own accord. For it is a rule, Sariputra, that, if Bodhisattvas set others going on their way to full enlightenment, and help them in their quest for it, [231] help them to become irreversible, and if they also themselves train in that, then, after they have passed through this present birth, of their own account these very deep Sutras will come to them, Sutras associated with the non-apprehension of a basis, associated with emptiness, associated with the six perfections.

Chapter XI

MARA'S DEEDS

1. VARIOUS DEEDS OF MARA

Subhuti: The Lord has proclaimed these virtues of those sons and daughters of good family. Are there again any obstacles which will arise to them?

The Lord: Many will be the deeds of Mara that will cause obstructions to them.

Subhuti: Of what kind are they?

The Lord: The Bodhisattvas who teach the perfection of wisdom will understand it only after a long time. Or, after understanding has been generated, it will immediately again be disturbed. Or they will write yawning, laughing and sneering. Or they will study it with their thoughts disturbed. Or they will write with their minds on other things. Or they will not gain mindfulness. Or they will write while deriding one another, or while sneering at one another, or with distracted eyes. [233] Or their writing will be in mutual discord. "We gain no firm footing in it, we derive no enjoyment from it," with these words they will get up from their seats and take their leave. Their thoughts devoid of serene faith they will think 'we are not predestined for this perfection of wisdom,' will get up from their seats and leave. Or, because this book does not name the place where they were born, does not mention their own name and clan, nor that of their mother and father, nor that of their family, they may decide not to listen to the perfection of wisdom, and take their leave. And each time they take their leave, they will again and again have to take to birth-and-death for as many aeons as they have had productions of thought, and during those aeons they will have to make new efforts. For what reason? Because Bodhisattvas who refuse to listen to this perfection of wisdom cannot go forth to the spiritual dharmas, be they worldly or supramundane.

2. THE PERFECTION OF WISDOM AND THE SUTRAS OF THE DISCIPLES

In addition, persons who belong to the vehicle of the Bodhisattvas may give up and abandon this perfection of wisdom which nourishes the cognition of the all-knowing, and decide to look for Sutras which do not nourish it. Furthermore, those do not train themselves in this perfection of wisdom who do not want to train in worldly and supramundane spiritual dharmas, nor to go forth to them. [234] As they do not train in perfect wisdom, they cannot go forth to worldly and supramundane spiritual dharmas. Those people of limited intelligence get rid of and abandon the perfection of wisdom, which is the root of the comprehension of worldly and supramundane spiritual dharmas, as they really are, and instead decide to look for support in what are mere branches. Just as if a dog would spurn a morsel of food given to him by his master, and prefer to take a mouthful of water from a servant; just so, in the future, some persons belonging to the vehicle of the Bodhisattvas will spurn this perfection of wisdom, which is the root of the cognition of the all-knowing, and decide to look for the core, for growth, for Buddhahood, in the vehicle of the Disciples and Pratyekabuddhas, which really corresponds to branches, leaves and foliage. This also should be known as done to them by Mara. For those people of small intelligence will not cognize that the perfection of wisdom alone nourishes the cognition of the all-knowing. They get rid of, abandon and spurn the perfection of wisdom, and decide to study, as superior to it, other Sutras, those which welcome the level of a Disciple or Pratyekabuddha. They should be compared to branches, leaves and foliage. For a Bodhisattva should not train in the same way in which persons belonging to the vehicle of the Disciples or Pratyekabuddhas are trained. How then are the Disciples and Pratyekabuddhas trained? They make up their minds that "one single self we shall tame, one single self we shall pacify, one single self we shall lead to final Nirvana." Thus they undertake exercises which are intended to bring about wholesome roots for the sake of taming themselves, pacifying themselves, leading themselves to Nirvana. A Bodhisattva should certainly not in such way train himself. On the contrary, he should train himself thus: [235] "My own self I will place in Suchness, and, so that all the world might be helped, I will place all beings into Suchness, and I will lead to Nirvana the whole immeasurable world of beings." With that intention should a Bodhisattva undertake all the exercises which bring about all the wholesome roots. But he should not boast about them. Imagine a man who, unable to see an elephant, would try to determine his colour and shape. In the darkness he would touch and examine the foot of the elephant, and decide that the colour and shape of the elephant should be inferred from his foot. Would that be an intelligent thing to do?

Subhuti: No, Lord!

The Lord: The same is true of those persons who belong to the vehicle of the Bodhisattvas, who do not understand this perfection of wisdom and ask no questions about it, but, while desirous of full enlightenment, spurn it and prefer to look for the Sutras which welcome the level of a Disciple or of a Pratyekabuddha. Also this has been done to them by Mara. Just as if a person who desires jewels would not look for them in the great ocean, but in a puddle in a cow's footprint, and would thus in effect equate the great ocean with the water in a cow's footprint. Would he be a very intelligent person?

Subhuti: No, Lord!

The Lord: The same applies to persons who belong to the vehicle of the Bodhisattvas if, though they have got this perfection of wisdom, they nevertheless cut themselves off from it, [236] without plunging or probing into it. And who prefer the Sutras which welcome the level of Disciples or Pratyekabuddhas, through advocating a dwelling in unconcerned inactivity, and which do not recommend the vehicle of the Bodhisattvas, but only the taming, appeasing, Nirvana of one single self. The decision to win seclusion, to win the fruits of a holy life, from the fruit of a Streamwinner to Pratyekabuddhahood, to enter Parinirvana after one has, in this very life, freed thought, without further clinging, from the outflows,—that means to be "associated with the level of a Disciple or Pratyekabuddha." Not to that should Bodhisattvas raise their thoughts. For when they have set out in the great vehicle Bodhisattvas put on the great armour. Their thoughts should not be raised to any unconcernedness whatsoever. For they are real men, leaders of the world, promoters of the world's weal. Therefore they should constantly and always be trained in the six perfections. But those persons who belong to the vehicle of the Bodhisattvas, and who, without knowing and understanding the Sutras associated with the six perfections, spurn this perfection of wisdom, and prefer the Sutras which welcome the level of Disciple or Pratyekabuddha,—their wholesome root is immature, their intelligence limited and poor, their resoluteness but weak. They resemble a mason, or mason's apprentice, who would want to build a palace of the size of the Vaijayanta palace, and who would take its measure from measuring the car of sun or moon. [237] A similar procedure is adopted by those who reject the perfection of wisdom and try to find all-knowledge through Sutras associated with the level of Disciples and Pratyekabuddhas, Sutras which recommend the taming, appeasing, and Nirvana of nothing more than one self only. If they would look for such Sutras and train with this intention, would these Bodhisattvas be very intelligent?

Subhuti: No, Lord!

The Lord: This also has been done to them by Mara. Suppose a person who first sees the universal monarch, and determines from the signs of what he sees his complexion, shape, beauty and majesty. He would then do the same with the commander of a fort. If he were unable to make a distinction, if he were to say of the commander of a fort, "just like that is the universal monarch in complexion, shape, beauty and majesty," [238] if he would, in other words, equate a universal monarch with the commander of a fort, would that be an intelligent thing to do?

Subhuti: No, Lord!

The Lord: The same applies to persons who belong to the Bodhisattva-vehicle and who in the future will reject this perfection of wisdom, and seek for all-knowledge through sutras associated with the level of Disciple or Pratyekabuddha. This also has been done to them by Mara. On the contrary, I certainly do not say that Bodhisattvas should seek for all-knowledge through the Sutras associated with the level of Disciple or Pratyekabuddha. Bodhisattvas can certainly not go forth to supreme enlightenment unless they are trained in what the Tathagata has announced in the perfection of wisdom as the skill in means of a Bodhisattva. For the full knowledge of a Bodhisattva is stupid in other Sutras. Therefore then, Subhuti, the Tathagata, seeing this advantage in the perfection of wisdom, by manifold methods shows it to the Bodhisattvas, instigates and introduces to it, fills them with enthusiasm about it, makes them rejoice at it, entrusts them with it, in the hope that thus the Bodhisattva may become irreversible to full enlightenment. Subhuti, do those Bodhisattvas appear to be very intelligent who, having obtained and met with the irreversible, the great vehicle, will again abandon it, turn away from it, and prefer an inferior vehicle?

Subhuti: No, Lord! [239]

The Lord: If a starving man would refuse superior and excellent food, and prefer to eat inferior and stale food, would he be very intelligent?

Subhuti: No, Lord!

The Lord: Just so, Subhuti, in the future some Bodhisattvas will refuse this perfection of wisdom, will prefer the Sutras associated with the level of Disciple or Pratyekabuddha, and will seek for all-knowledge through the Sutras which welcome the level of Disciple or Pratyekabuddha. Would these Bodhisattvas be very intelligent?

Subhuti: No, Lord!

The Lord: Also this has been done to them by Mara. A man who had got a priceless gem and who considered it equal to a gem of inferior value and quality, would he be an intelligent person?

Subhuti: No, Lord! [240]

The Lord: Just so there will be in the future some persons belonging to the vehicle of the Bodhisattvas who, though they have got this deep and brightly shining gem of perfect wisdom, will nevertheless think that it should be considered equal with the vehicle of Disciples and Pratyekabuddhas, and will decide to seek for all-knowledge and for skill in means on the level of Disciple or Pratyekabuddha. Would they be very intelligent?

Subhuti: No, Lord!

The Lord: This also has been done to them by Mara.

3. VARIOUS DEEDS OF MARA

Moreover, Subhuti, when this perfection of wisdom is being taught, demonstrated, explained, learned, recited, repeated, or even merely written down, many flashes of insight will come up in bewildering multitude, and they will make for confusion of thought. This also has been done by Mara to these Bodhisattvas.

Subhuti: Is it at all possible to write down the perfection of wisdom?

The Lord: No, Subhuti. It is also a deed of Mara if after one has written down the perfection of wisdom, one should either think that it is the perfection of wisdom which is written down, or that it is not the perfection of wisdom which is written down, or if one should adhere to the perfection of wisdom either in the letters, or as something not in the letters. —Moreover, Subhuti, while they write down the perfection of wisdom, their minds are on all sorts of things: places, villages, towns, cities, country districts, nations, royal cities, pleasure groves, preceptors, [241] tales, robbers, bathing places, streets, palanquins, occasions for happiness, occasions for fear, women, men, neuters, unsuitable situations, mother and father, brothers and sisters, friends, maternal relatives, kinsmen, chief wives, sons and daughters, houses, food and drink, clothes, beds, seats, livelihood, obligations, occasions of greed, hate and delusion, on right times, lucky times, unlucky times, on songs, music, dances, poems, plays, treatises, business, jokes, musical shows, sorrows, troubles, and themselves. These and other acts of attention Mara, the Evil One, will arrange when this perfection of wisdom is being taught, studied, or merely written down, and thus he will cause obstacles and confusion of thought to the Bodhisattvas. A Bodhisattva should recognize this as a deed of Mara, and avoid it. [242] In addition, his thoughts may also be on kings, royal princes, elephants, horses, chariots and troops of soldiers. Also that has been done to him by Mara. In addition, his thoughts may be on fire, temptations, money, corn and affluence. This also Mara has done to him. Moreover, difficulties will arise about gain, honour, robes, alms-bowl, lodging, and medicinal appliances for use in sickness, or alternatively, thoughts relishing gain, honour and fame may torment the Bodhisattvas who teach, explain, repeat, or merely write this perfection of wisdom. This also Mara does to them. They should recognize and avoid these deeds of Mara. Furthermore, Mara, the Evil One, will come to where Bodhisattvas teach, etc., this perfection of wisdom, and he will bring along the very deep Sutras which are associated with the level of Disciples and Pratyekabuddhas. He will advise them that they should "train in this, write, expound, and repeat this, for from it all-knowledge will be created." [243] But a Bodhisattva who is skilled in means should not long for those Sutras. For although they teach Emptiness, the Signless and the Wishless, nevertheless they do not announce the skill in means of the Bodhisattvas. A Bodhisattva who remains without the higher knowledge of the distinction of the cognition of skill in means spurns this deep perfection of wisdom, and seeks instead for skill in means in the Sutras associated with the level of Disciples and Pratyekabuddhas. This also should be known as Mara's deed to a Bodhisattva.

4. SOURCES OF DISCORD BETWEEN TEACHER AND PUPIL

Then again there are the deeds of Mara which wreck the chances of cooperation between teacher and pupil. First of all, it may be that the pupil is zealous, and desires to learn perfect wisdom, but that the teacher is indolent, and has no desire to demonstrate dharma. Or, the teacher may be untiring, and desire to give perfect wisdom, while the pupil is tired or too busy. Secondly, it may be that the pupil is zealous, and desires to learn the perfection of wisdom, to bear it in mind, preach, study, spread, or merely to write it, that he is clever, intelligent and has a good memory; but the teacher may move into a different district, or he may be unacquainted with the main points, unacquainted with the details, without the higher knowledge. [244] Or, the teacher may be untiring, in possession of the higher knowledge, willing to give and preach this perfection of wisdom; but the pupil has set out for another district, or is unacquainted with the main points, unacquainted with the details, without the higher knowledge. Further, the teacher may be a person who attaches weight to fleshly things, to gain, honour and robes, while the pupil is a man of few wishes, easily contented, and quite detached. Or he may be a person who is unwilling to give away anything of value. This also would cause discord, when it is a question of training in perfect wisdom, or of copying it. On the other hand, a pupil may be full of faith, desirous of hearing this perfection of wisdom and of understanding its meaning, liberal and generous; but the teacher has no faith, is too easily satisfied, and does not desire to teach. Or, the pupil may be full of faith, and desire to hear and to

understand the meaning; but it may be that the teacher, because some
obstacle hinders his access to dharma, does not have these Sutras at his
disposal, and cannot fathom them; a pupil would obviously be out of
touch with a teacher who has not attained them. [245] Or again, a teacher
may desire to teach, when a pupil is not zealous to hear. Further, it may
be that the pupil does not want to listen because he is weighed down by
sloth, weighed down by bodily fatigue, but the teacher is willing to teach;
conversely, a teacher may, although the pupil will want to listen, not
desire to teach because he is weighed down by sloth or physical fatigue.
This discord will also make writing, preaching and study difficult.

5. MISDIRECTION OF AIM

Moreover, when people write, or teach the perfection of wisdom, or
train in it, someone will come along and disparage life in the hells, in the
animal world, among the Pretas and Asuras, saying "so ill are all these
forms of life, so ill are all conditioned things; do make an end to just this
ill, and leave those beings to their fate." This also is a work of Mara. [246]
Or again, someone may come along and praise life among the Gods: "So
happy are the Gods, so happy is life in the heavens. One should therefore
tend sense-desires in the world of sense-desires, enter into the well-known
trances in the world of form, and enter into the well-known attainments in
the formless world." Considered by wisdom all this is, however, nothing
but rebirth in suffering. Because the Lord has said: "I do not praise any
kind of rebirth in becoming, because it lasts no longer than a finger-snap.
For everything that is conditioned is impermanent. Anything that may
cause fear is ill. All that is in the triple world is empty. All dharmas are
without self. When the wise have understood that all this is thus devoid of
eternity, impermanent, ill, doomed to reversal, then just here they should
attain the fruits of the holy life, from the fruit of a Streamwinner to
Arhatship. Let them beware of meeting any further with those attain-
ments, which are really failures, and which abound in suffering." But
nevertheless, to some Bodhisattvas this will be a source of anxiety [be-
cause they will feel deterred from the quest for full enlightenment by a
desire for rebirth among the Gods]. This also Mara does to them.

6. MORE DISCORD BETWEEN TEACHER AND PUPIL

Furthermore, the teacher may be a monk who is fond of solitude
while the pupils prefer a communal life. He will tell them that he will give
this perfection of wisdom to those who come to where he is, but not to

those who do not. In their desire and zeal for the dharma which they value they go to where the teacher is, and still he gives them no opportunity to learn anything. He is one who is eager for trifling bits of fleshly things, but they do not want to give him anything that he values. [247] Wherever he goes he will be short of food, surrounded by troubles, and in danger of his life. And his pupils will hear from others that that place is short of food, full of troubles and dangers to life. And that teacher will say to those sons of good family: "This place is short of food. Of course, sons of good family, you may come here if you wish. But I am afraid that you will regret having come." This is a subtle device by which he rejects them. In disgust they will interpret these remarks as signs of refusal, not as signs of a desire to give. Convinced that he does not want to give, they will not go to where he is. Moreover, the teacher may have set out for a spot where there is danger from vermin, from beasts of prey, from ghosts. And he will move from there to a wild place with beasts of prey, snakes and robbers, marked by drought and famine. To those prospective pupils he will say: "You are aware, I suppose, that in this spot for which we have set out there are many dangers, from vermin, beasts of prey, flesh-eating ghosts, that it is swarming with snakes and robbers, that it has neither food nor water. So you must be able to experience a great deal of suffering." Thus he will reject them through a subtle device. Disgusted, they will not go with him, and turn back. [248] Finally, the teacher may be one of the monks who attach weight to their relations with the friendly families who feed them. All the time he goes to see them, he is kept very busy that way, and refuses those prospective pupils on the ground that, "first of all, there is someone I must go and see." This also will be a source of discord when this perfection of wisdom is being written and studied. This also is Mara's work. In such ways Mara will bestir himself to prevent people from learning, studying, teaching and writing this perfection of wisdom. Therefore then, Subhuti, all the factors which prevent cooperation between teacher and pupil should be recognized as Mara's deeds, and one should try to avoid them.

7. MARA DISSUADES FROM PERFECT WISDOM

Subhuti: What then, O Lord, is the reason why Mara makes great efforts and bestirs himself to prevent, by this or that device, people from learning and studying this perfection of wisdom? [249]

The Lord: Perfect wisdom is the source of the all-knowledge of the Buddhas, the Lords. And that in its turn is the source of the religion of the Tathagatas, which leads immeasurable and incalculable beings to forsake their defilements. But to those who have forsaken the defilements, Mara cannot gain entry, and that makes him distressed and dispirited, and the dart of sorrow vexes him. In consequence, when this perfection of wisdom is being written and studied, he makes in his great tribulation a great effort and bestirs himself, with this or that device, to prevent the study of this perfection of wisdom. Mara, the Evil One, will, moreover, come along in the guise of a Shramana, and cause dissension. In order to dissuade the sons of good family who have but recently set out in the vehicle he will say: "Not is that the perfection of wisdom which your Honours listen to. As it has been handed down in my Sutras, as it is included in my Sutras, that is the perfection of wisdom." Thus he will sow doubts in the minds of Bodhisattvas who have but recently set out in the vehicle, whose intelligence is small, sluggish and limited, who are blind, and whose future enlightenment has not yet been predicted. Seized by doubt they will not learn, study or write this perfection of wisdom. [250] This also Mara does to them. Moreover, Mara may come along in the guise of a Buddha, with magically created monks around him, and maintain that a Bodhisattva who courses in deep dharmas is one who realises the reality-limit, who becomes a Disciple, and not a Bodhisattva, as this Bodhisattva. This also is one of Mara's deeds. Subhuti, when this perfection of wisdom is being written and studied, Mara, the Evil One, produces these deeds, which I have mentioned, and many others also. They all should be recognized by a Bodhisattva, and avoided, not cultivated. The Bodhisattva should reply to them with vigour, mindfulness and self-possession.

8. ANTAGONISM BETWEEN MARA AND BUDDHA

Subhuti: So it is, O Lord. Whatever is very precious, that provokes much hostility. Because it is so superior, being hard to get, and of great value. One should therefore expect that as a rule many obstacles will arise to this perfection of wisdom. When, overawed by these obstacles, someone becomes lazy, one should know that those who decide not to learn, study and write this perfection of wisdom are people who are beset by Mara, have but recently set out in the vehicle, their intelligence is small, sluggish, limited and perverted, [251] and their thought refuses to function in these very sublime dharmas.

The Lord: So it is, Subhuti. And while it is true that these deeds of Mara are bound to arise, a great many agencies will arise in their turn that oppose the faults of Mara. Those who decide to learn, study and write this perfection of wisdom have been swayed by the Buddha's might, by his sustaining power, by his grace. [252] For whereas Mara, the Evil One, will make great efforts to cause obstacles, the Tathagata in his turn will send help.

Chapter XII

SHOWING THE WORLD

1. PERFECT WISDOM THE MOTHER OF THE BUDDHAS

The Lord: It is as with a mother who has many children,—five, or ten, or twenty, or thirty, or forty, or fifty, or one hundred, or one thousand. If she fell ill, they would all exert themselves to prevent their mother from dying, to keep her alive as long as possible, to keep pain and unpleasantness away from her body. Because they are aware that to her they owe their existence, that in great pain she has brought them into the world, that she has instructed them in the ways of the world. They would therefore look well after her, give her everything that can make her happy, protect her well, make much of her, and they will hope that she be free from pain—derived from contact with eye, ear, nose, tongue, body or mind, or coming from wind, bile, phlegm, or a disorder of the humours, or from stinging insects, mosquitoes, or crawling animals, from men or from ghosts, from anything falling upon her, or tearing her asunder, or from a disastrous crash. [254] In this way those sons honour their mother by giving her all that can make her happy, make much of her, cherish and protect her, because they are aware that she is their mother and begetter, that, in great pain, she brought them into the world, that she instructed them in the ways of the world. In just this same way the Tathagatas bring this perfection of wisdom to mind, and it is through their might, sustaining power and grace that people write, learn, study, spread and repeat it. And also the Tathagatas who dwell in other world systems just now,—for the weal and happiness of the many, out of pity for the many, for the weal and happiness of a great body of people, from pity for Gods, men and all beings—they also all bring this perfection of wisdom to mind, and they put forth zeal so that this perfection of wisdom may last long, so that it may not be destroyed, so that Mara and his host may not prevent this perfection of wisdom from being taught, written, and practised. So fond are the Tathagatas of this perfection of wisdom, so much do they cherish and protect it. For she is their mother and begetter, she showed them this all-knowledge, she instructed them in the ways of the world. From her have the Tathagatas come forth. For she has begotten and shown that cognition of the all-knowing, she has shown them the world for what it really is. [255] The all-knowledge of the Tathagatas has come forth from her. All the Tathagatas, past, future, and present, win full enlightenment thanks to this very perfection of wisdom. It is in this sense that the perfection of wisdom generates the Tathagatas, and instructs them in this world.

2. HOW THE TATHAGATA KNOWS THE WORLD

Subhuti: How does perfect wisdom instruct the Tathagatas in this world, and what is it that the Tathagatas call 'world'? [256]

The Lord: The five skandhas have by the Tathagata have declared as 'world' [*loka*]. Which five? Form, feeling, perceptions, impulses, and consciousness.

Subhuti: How have the five skandhas been shown up by the perfection of wisdom of the Tathagatas, or what has been shown up by her?

The Lord: The perfect wisdom of the Tathagatas has pointed out the five skandhas as 'the world' [*loka*], because they do not crumble, nor crumble away [*lujyante, pralujyante*]. For the five skandhas have emptiness for own-being, and, as devoid of own-being, emptiness cannot crumble nor crumble away. It is in this sense that perfect wisdom instructs the Tathagatas in this world. And as emptiness does not crumble, nor crumble away, so also the Signless, the Wishless, the Uneffected, the Unproduced, Non-existence, and the Realm of Dharma.

3. HOW THE TATHAGATA KNOWS THE THOUGHTS OF BEINGS *

Moreover, Subhuti, thanks to this perfection of wisdom the Tathagata wisely knows immeasurable and incalculable beings as they really are. And that through the absence of own-being in beings. [257] The Tathagata also knows wisely the thoughts and doings of immeasurable and incalculable beings, since beings have no real existence [as separate individualities]. Moreover, the Tathagata, thanks to the perfection of wisdom, wisely knows as they really are the *collected* thoughts of countless beings as 'collected thoughts.' And how does the Tathagata know them? He wisely sees that collectedness is equivalent to extinction [of the individual thought which, empirically speaking, has ceased to exist, being merged into the absolute]. And also that that extinction is [if we consider its true reality], just non-extinction. Furthermore the Tathagata wisely knows the *distracted* thoughts of beings for what they are. For he wisely knows that

---

* The following disquisition is quite unintelligible as it stands. I have therefore freely interpolated the comments of Haribhadra's commentary.

thoughts are distracted [by the objects of the external world because no attention is paid to] the realm of Dharma. On the other hand he knows that those thoughts, as they really are in ultimate reality, are without marks, do not get extinguished [from moment to moment], that their continuity is not interrupted, and that they are not really distracted [because they cannot, in actual fact, be directed on external objects]. [258] The Tathagata knows the *infinite and inexhaustible* minds of beings. For the Tathagata in his great compassion, has willed a mind by which he wisely knows as it really is that "in the likeness of the immeasurable inextinction of space should the immeasurable inextinction of the minds of all beings be understood." And that mind of the Buddha is never stopped, it was never produced, it has no duration in between production and stopping, it gives no support, it is infinite, since it cannot be measured, and it is inexhaustible, like the realm of Dharma itself. The Tathagata knows the *polluted* minds of beings for what they are. For he knows that the minds of ordinary people are not actually polluted by the polluting forces of perverted views, which, being nothing but wrong ideas, do not really find a place in them. [259] The Tathagata knows *unpolluted* thoughts for what they are. For he knows that those minds are transparently luminous in their essential original nature. The Tathagata knows *slack* thoughts for what they really are. For he knows that those thoughts are in reality unable to slouch on any resting place. The Tathagata knows *tensely active* thoughts for what they really are. For he knows that thoughts are exerted so as to win dispassion, and that they can no longer be exerted when there is nothing left that can be seized upon. The Tathagata knows [260] thoughts *with outflows* for what they really are. For he knows that those thoughts are without own-being, that they are just a false representation of what is not. The Tathagata knows thoughts *without outflows* for what they really are. For he knows that these thoughts lead to the non-existence [of the outflows] and that [when a continuity is quite pure], there is nothing they can be directed to. The Tathagata knows *greedy* thoughts for what they really are. For he knows that a greedy mind is not a mind as it really is, and that a mind as it really is is not a greedy mind. [261] The Tathagata knows minds *free from greed* for what they really are. For he knows that a mind from which greed departs is not a greedy mind, and that the true reality of a mind which forsakes greed is not a greedy mind, because it gets detached from greed. And as the Tathagata wisely knows the minds that are greedy and free from greed, so he knows, in the same manner, the minds that are *with hate* and that are *without hate,* that are *with delusion,* and that are *without delusion.* [263] The Tathagata also knows the *scant* thoughts of beings for what they really are. For he knows that those thoughts are not joined up with the world of appearance, that they are not included in the world of appearance. The Tathagata knows *extensive* or *abundant* thoughts for what they really are. For he knows that those thoughts do neither diminish nor increase; that those thoughts do not depart, because they cannot possibly do so [as they are essentially identical with the realm of Dharma, and have nowhere outside that to go to]. The Tathagata knows thoughts which have *not gone great* for what they really are. For he knows that those thoughts have not come, that they do not go away, and that their reality is not included in the present, either. [264] The Tathagata knows thoughts that have *gone great* for what they really are. For he knows that those thoughts are all the same in ultimate Sameness, and that, in addition, they are all the same in their own-being [i.e. mere illusion]. The Tathagata knows thoughts that have become *unlimited* for what they really are. For he knows that those thoughts have become unlimited because they have ceased to lean on anything. The Tathagata knows thoughts *with perceptible attributes* for what they really are. For he knows that all those thoughts look at the same thing, and that in their own-being they are all thoughts [265]. The Tathagata knows thoughts *without perceptible attributes* for what they really are. For he knows that that thought, since it is itself without marks, and isolated from its object, is imperceptible, and does not come within the range of the three, or even all the five, kinds of vision. The Tathagata knows *reacting* thoughts for what they really are. For he knows that those thoughts represent what is not really there, that they are empty, devoid of objective support. The Tathagata knows *non-reacting* thoughts for what they really are. For he knows that those thoughts are non-dual, [266] and that, ultimately unreal, they only seem to arrive at some reality. The Tathagata knows *lower* thoughts for what they really are. For he knows that in the true reality of lower thoughts there is no self-conceited imagining. The Tathagata knows *supreme* thoughts for what they really are. For he knows that those thoughts are unimpeded, because not even the least thought has been apprehended. The Tathagata knows *unconcentrated* thoughts for what they really are. [267] For he knows that those thoughts are the same in that they take hold of differences; [directed toward a faulty presentation of a world of separate things they are distracted, and] they do not achieve a synthesis; in that sense they are unconcentrated. The Tathagata knows *concentrated* thoughts for what they really are. For he knows that those thoughts are the same in the self-identical realm of dharma, and that, by undoing all distractions, they do achieve synthesis, and that it is in this sense that they are concentrated thoughts, the same as space. The Tathagata knows *unemancipated* thoughts for what they really are. For he knows that those thoughts are, in their own-being, already now emancipated, for they have non-existence for own-being. [268] The Tathagata knows *emancipated* thoughts for what they really are. For the Tathagata has not apprehended any thought as past, as future, or as present, because thought is not really there. The Tathagata knows *imperceptible* thoughts for what they really are. For he knows with regard to that thought that, because it is not really there, it cannot be perceived; that, because it has no reality, it cannot be discerned; that, because it falls short of the perfect reality, it cannot be grasped,—not by the eye of wisdom, not by the heavenly eye, and how much less by the fleshly eye, since it does not come within the range of any of them. Furthermore, the Tathagata wisely knows, for what they really are, the *tendencies* of countless beings *to make positive and negative statements about objects.* For he knows [269] that all these ideas arise in dependence on form, and the other skandhas. How has he discerned the dependence on the skandhas of those positive and negative statements? If we take such statements as—'The Tathagata continues to exist after death,' 'The Tathagata does not continue to exist after death,' 'The Tathagata does and does not continue to exist after death,' 'The Tathagata neither does nor does not continue to exist after death'—then these statements refer to the skandhas only [and they have no basis in the true reality of the Tathagata]. The same holds good of similar statements, i.e. when one says: 'Eternal are self and the world,—just that is the truth, everything else is delusion.' And so if one maintains that self and the world are non-eternal, both eternal and non-eternal, neither eternal nor non-eternal. [270] Or, similarly, if one maintains that self and the world are finite, or not finite, or both finite and not finite, or neither finite nor not finite. Or, finally, if one says 'that which is the soul, that is the body,' or 'one thing is the soul, another the body,' all these statements refer only to the skandhas. It is thanks to the perfection of wisdom that the Tathagata knows those positive and negative statements for what they really are. [271] The Tathagata cognizes the skandhas as identical with Suchness. That is why He knows, thanks to perfect wisdom, those positive and negative statements for what they really are. It is thus that the Tathagata makes known Suchness through the Suchness of the Tathagata, through the Suchness of the skandhas, through the Suchness of the positive and negative statements. And just that Suchness of the skandhas, that is also the Suchness of the world. For it has been said by the Tathagata that "the five skandhas are reckoned as the 'world.' " Therefore then, Subhuti, that which is the Suchness of the skandhas, that is the Suchness of the world; that which is the Suchness of the world, that is the Suchness of all dharmas; that which is the Suchness of all dharmas that is the Suchness of the fruit of a Streamwinner, and so on, up to: that is the Suchness of Pratyekabuddhahood, that is the Suchness of the Tathagata. In consequence all this Suchness,—the Suchness of the Tathagata, of the skandhas, of all dharmas, of all holy Disciples and Pratyekabuddhas—is just one single Suchness, is without any trace of the variety of positivity and negativity, as being one, non-different, inextinguishable, unaffected, non-dual, without cause for duality. [272] That is this Suchness which the Tathagata has, thanks to the perfection of wisdom, fully known. It is thus that perfect wisdom instructs the Tathagata in this world. It is thus that the Tathagata shows up the world to this infatuated world for what it really is. And thus a vision of this world takes place. It is thus that perfect wisdom is the mother of the Tathagatas, who has generated them. It is thus that the Tathagata, after he has been enlightened as to Suchness, cognizes the Suchness of the world, its Non-falseness, its unaltered Suchness. And in consequence, just because he has been enlightened about Suchness [*tathatā*] is the Tathagata called a 'Tathagata.'

Subhuti: Deep, O Lord, is Suchness. The enlightenment of the Buddhas, the Lords, is brought about and revealed through it. Who else could firmly believe in it, except an irreversible Bodhisattva, or an Arhat whose intentions are fulfilled, or a person who has achieved right views? These extremely deep stations were therefore described by the Tathagata after he had been enlightened to them.

The Lord: So it is, Subhuti. For this Suchness which the Tathagata has fully known, is inexhaustible, and he has described it as inexhaustible after he had fully known it.

4. DEEP MARKS, AND HOW THEY ARE FASTENED

Thereupon, headed by Sakra, Chief of Gods, the Gods of the realm of sense-desire and of the realm of form and twenty thousand of the Gods of the realm of Brahma came to where the Lord was, saluted his feet with their heads, stood on one side, and said: Deep dharmas are being revealed, O Lord. How, O Lord, are the marks fixed onto them? [273]

The Lord: The marks are fixed on to the fact that they are empty, signless, wishless, not brought together, not produced, not stopped, not defiled, not purified, that they are non-existence, Nirvana, the realm of Dharma, and Suchness. For those marks are not supported by anything. They are like unto space. Those marks are not fixed on by the Tathagata, they cannot be reckoned among the skandhas, they are not dependent on the skandhas, they are not fixed on by Gods, Nagas or men, and they cannot be shaken off by the world with its Gods, men and Asuras. For also this world with its Gods, men and Asuras has just that mark. No hand has fixed on those marks. Would it be correct to say that this space is fixed on by something?

The Gods: No, Lord, because it is unconditioned.

The Lord: So it is, O Gods. Independent of whether Tathagatas are produced or not, [274] those marks stand out just as such. In accordance with what stands out just as such has the Tathagata described their reality, after he had fully known it. Therefore is the Tathagata called a 'Tathagata.'

Subhuti: Deep, O Lord, are these marks which the Tathagata has fully known. But this perfection of wisdom is the unattached cognition of the Tathagatas. As a field of unattached cognition is the perfection of wisdom the range of the Tathagatas.

5. THE WORLD SHOWN AS EMPTY

The Lord: So it is, Subhuti. It is thus that the perfection of wisdom instructs the Tathagatas in this world. To the extent that the Tathagatas dwell in intimate dependence on this dharma, the perfection of wisdom, to that extent are those dharmas, which stand out for ever, fully known by the Tathagatas, through their taking their stand nowhere. Thereby they dwell in close and intimate dependence on just the Dharma. They treat the Dharma with respect, revere, worship and adore it, for they know that this essential nature of dharmas is just the perfection of wisdom. For the all-knowledge of the Tathagatas has been brought about from this perfection of wisdom, and for that the Tathagatas are grateful and thankful to her. With justice can the Tathagata be called 'grateful and thankful' [*kritajña kritavedin*]. In gratitude and thankfulness the Tathagata [275] favours and cherishes the vehicle on which he has come, and the path by which he has won full enlightenment. That one should know as the gratitude and thankfulness of the Tathagata. In addition, the Tathagata has fully known all dharmas as not made [*akrita*], as not unmade, as not brought together. This also one should know as the gratitude and thankfulness of the Tathagata. For it is thanks to the perfection of wisdom that the cognition of the Tathagata has thus proceeded in all dharmas. That is another aspect of the fact that perfect wisdom instructs the Tathagatas in this world.

Subhuti: But how can perfect wisdom instruct the Tathagatas in this world if all dharmas are unknowable and imperceptible?

The Lord: It is good, Subhuti, that you should have decided to question the Tathagata about this matter. All dharmas are indeed unknowable and imperceptible. Because they are empty, and do not lean on anything. It is thus that all those dharmas have, thanks to perfect wisdom, been fully known by the Tathagatas. For another reason also the perfection of wisdom can be regarded as the instructress of the Tathagatas in this world, i.e. because none of the skandhas has been viewed. [276]

Subhuti: How can there be a non-viewing of form, etc.?

The Lord: Where there arises an act of consciousness which has none of the skandhas for objective support, there the non-viewing of form, etc., takes place. But just this non-viewing of the skandhas is the viewing of the world. That is the way in which the world is viewed by the Tathagata. It is thus that perfect wisdom acts as an instructress in the world to the Tathagatas. And how does perfect wisdom show up the world for what it is? She shows that the world is empty, unthinkable, calmly quiet. As purified of itself she shows up the world, she makes it known, she indicates it.

Chapter XIII

UNTHINKABLE

1. FIVE ATTRIBUTES OF PERFECT WISDOM

Subhuti: Deep, O Lord, is perfect wisdom. Certainly as a great enterprise has this perfection of wisdom been set up, as an unthinkable, incomparable, immeasurable, incalculable enterprise, as an enterprise which equals the unequalled.

The Lord: So it is, Subhuti. And why is it an unthinkable enterprise? Because unthinkable are Tathagatahood, Buddhahood, Self-existence, and the state of all-knowledge. And on these one cannot reflect with one's thought, since they cannot be an object of thought, or of volition, or of any of the dharmas which constitute thought. And why is it an incomparable enterprise? Because one cannot reflect on Tathagatahood, etc., nor compare it. And why is it immeasurable? [278] Because Tathagatahood, etc., is immeasurable. And why is it incalculable? Because Tathagatahood, etc., is incalculable. And why is it an enterprise which equals the unequalled? Because nothing can be equal to the Tathagata, to the fully Enlightened One, to the Self-existent, to the All-knowing, how much less can anything be superior to him?

Subhuti: Do these five attributes apply only to Tathagatahood, etc., or also to the skandhas, and to all dharmas?

The Lord: They apply to them also. Also the skandhas, and also all dharmas are unthinkable. For with regard to the true essential nature of form, etc., there is no thought, nor volition, nor any of the dharmas which constitute thought, nor any comparing. For that reason the skandhas and all dharmas are [279] also unthinkable and incomparable. They are also immeasurable, because one cannot conceive of a measure of form, etc., since such a measure does not exist, in consequence of the infinitude of all dharmas. They are also incalculable, because they have risen above all possibility of counting. They are also equal to the unequalled, because all dharmas are the same as space. What do you think, Subhuti, does there exist with reference to space any sameness, or counting or measure, or comparison, or thought, or a dharma which constitutes thought?

Subhuti: No, Lord. [280]

The Lord: In like manner also all dharmas are unthinkable, incomparable, immeasurable, incalculable, equal to the unequalled. For they are Tathagata-dharmas. But those Tathagata-dharmas are unthinkable because all thought has ceased, and incomparable because they have completely risen above all comparison. By the words 'unthinkable' and 'incomparable' are denoted all the objects which belong to consciousness. And so with 'immeasurable,' 'incalculable' and 'equal to the unequalled.' Because all measure, calculation and sameness have ceased are the Tathagata-dharmas immeasurable, incalculable, equal to the unequalled. They are immeasurable, incalculable, equal to the unequalled because their immeasurableness and incalculability is the same as that of space. These dharmas are incomparable in the same sense in which space is incomparable. These dharmas can certainly not be placed side by side, and that is why they cannot be compared. These dharmas are unthinkable, incomparable, immeasurable, incalculable, equal to the unequalled in the same sense that space has these attributes.

2. SPIRITUAL REBIRTH RESULTING FROM THIS KNOWLEDGE

When this doctrine of unthinkability, etc., was being taught, the minds of five hundred monks were freed, without further clinging, from the outflows, and so were the minds of two thousand nuns. Six thousand lay brethren and three thousand lay sisters obtained the pure, dispassionate, unstained eye of dharma. Twenty thousand Bodhisattvas won the patient acceptance of dharmas which fail to be produced. And the Lord has predicted that they shall win enlightenment in this very Bhadrakalpa. And as to the lay brethren and lay sisters, whose dharma-eye was purified, they also have been predestined by the Lord, and they also will be freed, without further clinging, from the outflows. [281]

3. NOTHING TO TAKE HOLD OF

Subhuti: Deep, O Lord, is perfect wisdom. Certainly as a great enterprise it has been set up.

The Lord: So it is, Subhuti. For all-knowledge has been entrusted to it, and so has the level of a Pratyekabuddha and the level of all the Disciples. An anointed king, a Kshatriya, who feels strong and secure in his kingdom, entrusts all his business concerning his kingly office, and the city and the kingdom to his minister, and he himself has few cares and his burden is light. Just so, whatever dharmas of Buddhas, Pratyekabuddhas, or Disciples there may be, they are all entrusted to the perfection of wisdom. It is the perfection of wisdom which in them does the work. It is in this manner that perfect wisdom has been set up for a great enterprise, i.e. so that one should not take hold of form, etc., nor settle down in it. And as for the skandhas, so also for the fruits of the holy life, from the fruit of a Streamwinner to the state of all-knowledge.

Subhuti: In what way has perfect wisdom been set up so that one should not take hold of the state of all-knowledge, nor settle down in it? [282]

The Lord: Do you view Arhatship as a real dharma which you could take hold of, or settle down in?

Subhuti: No, Lord!

The Lord: So it is, Subhuti. I also do not view Tathagatahood as real, and therefore I do not take hold of it, do not settle down in it. For that reason all-knowledge also is a state in which one neither takes hold of anything, nor settles down in anything.

Subhuti: Bodhisattvas who have but newly set out in the vehicle, and whose wholesome roots are but small, must beware that they do not tremble when they hear this exposition. On the other hand, Bodhisattvas will, on hearing this deep perfection of wisdom, firmly believe in it if they are suitable for Buddhahood, have fulfilled their duties under the Jinas of the past, and have planted wholesome roots for a long time.

The Lord: So it is, Subhuti.

4. REACTION OF THE GODS

Thereupon the *Gods* of the realm of sense-desire and of the realm of form said to the Lord: Deep, O Lord, is the perfection of wisdom, hard to see, hard to understand. [283] Bodhisattvas who resolutely believe in this so deep perfection of wisdom must have fulfilled their duties under the Jinas of the past, must have planted wholesome roots for a long time. If, O Lord, all the beings in this great trichiliocosm should, for an aeon or the remainder of an aeon, course on the stage of a Faith-follower; and if, on the other hand, someone should, for one day only, find pleasure in the patient acceptance of this deep perfection of wisdom, and should search for it, reflect on it, weigh it up, investigate it and meditate on it, then this latter will be better than all those beings.

The Lord: If someone would hear, O Gods, this deep perfection of wisdom, etc., then one would expect his Nirvana to take place more quickly than that of those who course on the stage of a faith-follower for an aeon, or for the remainder of an aeon.

The Gods: A great perfection is this perfection of wisdom! —After these words, they saluted the Lord's feet with their heads, thrice walked round the Lord, decided to go away from the presence of the Lord, took friendly leave of him, and moved away. Before they had gone far, they disappeared from sight, and the Gods of the realm of sense-desire departed for the world of sense-desire, and the Gods of the realm of form departed for the Brahma-world.

Chapter XIV

SIMILES

1. FUTURE AND PAST REBIRTHS

Subhuti: If a Bodhisattva, on merely hearing it, immediately believes in this deep perfection of wisdom, does not become cowed, stolid, paralysed or stupefied, does not doubt or hesitate, but delights in perfect wisdom,—where has he deceased, where is he reborn?

The Lord: If a Bodhisattva reacts in such a way to the perfection of wisdom, if he delights in seeing and hearing it, bears it in mind and develops it, keeps his mind fixed on it without diverting it elsewhere, feels an urge to take it up, bear it in mind, preach, study and spread it, if, once he has heard of perfect wisdom, he follows and pursues the reciter of dharma and does not let him go, until he knows this perfection of wisdom by heart or has got it in the form of a book, just as a cow does not abandon her young calf,—then this Bodhisattva has deceased among men and will be reborn among men. [285]

Subhuti: Could a Bodhisattva, who is endowed with just these qualities have deceased in other Buddha-fields before he was reborn here?

The Lord: It is quite possible that a Bodhisattva who is endowed with these qualities, has, before he was reborn here, deceased in other Buddha-fields, where he has honoured and questioned the Buddhas and Lords. Or he may also have deceased among the Tushita Gods. It may be that he has honoured Maitreya, the Bodhisattva, and persistently questioned him concerning this perfection of wisdom.

2. PAST DEEDS OF A BODHISATTVA WHO FAILS IN PERFECT WISDOM

On the other hand, if a Bodhisattva in the past has heard this deep perfection of wisdom but has asked no questions about it, and if later on, when he is reborn among men and hears this deep perfection of wisdom being taught, he hesitates and is stupefied and cowed, then one can be sure that in the past also he was one of those who were unwilling to ask questions. Another Bodhisattva, again, may in the past have had the right attitude to this deep perfection of wisdom, for one, two, three, four or five days, and now only for a certain time he has faith in it, but afterwards it is withdrawn again and he no longer feels like asking questions about it. For it is a fact that if [286] a Bodhisattva has in the past not all the time asked questions about this deep perfection of wisdom, and has not pursued it all the time, then later on he would at some time feel urged to pursue the hearing of this deep perfection of wisdom, but not so at other times; he would again fall from his faith, become disheartened, and his intelligence would become unsteady, and like cotton wool. One can be sure that such a Bodhisattva has but lately set out in the vehicle. Come but lately to the vehicle, he will lose his faith in it, his serene confidence in it, his urge for it, in other words he will no further take up this deep perfection of wisdom, and pursue it. One must expect that he will move on either of two levels, on the level of a Disciple, or on the level of a Pratyekabuddha.

3. FOUR SIMILES

When a ship is wrecked in the middle of the ocean, people will die in the water without getting to the shore, if they do not find support on a log, or plank, or other solid body. But those who manage to gain such a support will not die in the water; safely and unhindered they will cross over to the shore beyond, and stand, unhurt and uninjured, on firm ground. In the same way, a Bodhisattva who is endowed with but a little faith, just a little serene confidence, just a little affection, just a little desire-to-do, and who does not gain the support of perfect wisdom, is bound to incur a fall in the middle of a bad road, and, without having attained to the state of all-knowledge, he will stand in Discipleship or Pratyekabuddhahood. Different is the case of a Bodhisattva [287] who has faith in it, accepts it patiently, has a taste for it, has desire-to-do, vigour, vigilance, resolve, earnest intention, renunciation, a title to be respected, joyous zest, elation, serene confidence, affection for it, and persistence in trying to win full enlightenment, and who also gains the support of the perfection of wisdom; having attained the perfection of wisdom, he will stand in all-knowledge. If one would use a badly baked jar to carry water in, that jar would not last long, and would actually quickly fall to pieces and melt away. For in its unbaked condition it would actually soon come to an end on the ground. Just so, although a Bodhisattva may have all the qualities enumerated above, from faith to a persistent desire to win enlightenment, as long as he is not taken hold of by perfect wisdom and skill in means, he is bound to come to a bad fall in the middle of a bad road, in other words, he will fall on the level of a Disciple or Pratyekabuddha. But if someone would carry water, from a river, or lake, or pond, or well, or any other water-bearing place, in a well-baked jar, then that jar will with the water [288] get safely and uninjured to the house.

just because of the well-baked condition of that jar. Just so a Bodhi-
sattva, who has not only the qualities enumerated above, but who in
addition also has been taken hold of by perfect wisdom and skill in means,
will not in the middle of a bad road incur a fall, and, unhurt and unin-
jured, he will stand in all-knowledge. A stupid man would launch into the
water a seafaring vessel which was not caulked or repaired, and had been
tied to its moorings for a long time, would overload it with goods, and
mount on it, and set out in it. His ship is doomed to collapse before it has
conveyed the goods across the water. When his ship has burst asunder, that
stupid merchant, who is unskilled in means, will have lost a huge fortune, a
great source of wealth. Just so a Bodhisattva who has all the qualities
enumerated above, but who lacks in perfect wisdom and skill in means,
[289] without having gained the wealth of all-knowledge he is bound to
collapse midway, to incur a fall; he has lost a great deal of his own wealth,
and he has also lost a great deal of the wealth of others, because he has lost
all-knowledge, which is like a huge fortune and a great source of wealth;
not to mention his collapse in the middle of the bad road, his fall unto the
level of Disciple or Pratyekabuddha. An intelligent merchant, on the other
hand, would construct a solid ship, would launch it with proper care into
the water, load it with goods and distribute them evenly, and with a
favourable wind his vessel would gradually sail to the country which is the
goal of his voyage. His ship will not collapse in the water, it will go to
where it is meant to go, and the merchant will win great wealth in the
shape of worldly jewels. Likewise, a Bodhisattva who has faith, and the
other qualities enumerated above, and who in addition has been taken
hold of by perfect wisdom and does not lack in skill in means, it is certain
that he will not collapse in the middle of a bad road, that he will not incur
a fall, that he will stand in supreme enlightenment. For it is a fact that
[290] if a Bodhisattva has faith, and the other qualities enumerated above,
and if, in addition, these dharmas of his have been taken hold of by
perfect wisdom, and are not lacking in skill in means, then they will not
hasten towards the level of a Disciple or Pratyekabuddha, but on the
contrary these dharmas will face in the direction of all-knowledge, and
they will set out for it, and they will conduce to the winning of full
enlightenment. If a person were very aged, advanced in years, decrepit, say
one hundred and twenty years old, and if he would fall ill in his body,
could he rise from his bed without being taken hold of by others?

    Subhuti: No, Lord!

    The Lord: And even if he could rise from his bed, he would certainly
not have the strength to walk about for half a mile. Wasted away by both
old age and illness he could not walk about for any length of time, even if

he could rise from his bed. Likewise, even if a Bodhisattva has all the qualities enumerated above, if he has not been taken hold of by perfect wisdom, and is lacking in skill in means, then, although he may have set out for full enlightenment, he is nevertheless bound to collapse in the middle of a bad road, he is bound to incur a fall, in other words, he will stand on the level of Disciple or Pratyekabuddha. [291] This is a necessary consequence of the fact that he has not been taken hold of by perfect wisdom, and that he lacks in skill in means. But it may be that two strong men take hold of that old and sick man, and carefully lift him up, and promise him that he may go wherever he wishes, and as far as he wishes, because they will assist him, and he need not fear to fall on the way which takes him to the place which he has to go to. In the same way, a Bodhisattva who has faith, etc., and who is assisted by perfect wisdom, and endowed with skill in means, he is certain not to collapse in the middle of a bad road, he will not incur a fall, he is able to reach this station, i.e. the station of full enlightenment.

Chapter XV

GODS

1. THE BEGINNER'S TASK

Subhuti: How should a Bodhisattva who is only just beginning stand in perfect wisdom, how train himself?

The Lord: Such a Bodhisattva should tend, love and honour the good friends. His good friends are those who will instruct and admonish him in perfect wisdom, and who will expound to him its meaning. They will expound it as follows: "Come here, son of good family, make endeavours in the six perfections. Whatever you may have achieved by way of giving a gift, guarding morality, perfecting yourself in patience, exertion of vigour, entering into concentration, [293] or mastery in wisdom,—all that turn over into full enlightenment. But do not misconstrue full enlightenment as form, or any other skandha. For intangible is all-knowledge. And do not long for the level of Disciple or Pratyekabuddha. It is thus that a Bodhisattva who is just beginning should gradually, through the good friends, enter into perfect wisdom."

2. HOW A BODHISATTVA HELPS BEINGS

Subhuti: Doers of what is hard are the Bodhisattvas who have set out to win full enlightenment. Thanks to the practice of the six perfections, as described above, they do not wish to attain release in a private Nirvana of their own. They survey the highly painful world of beings. They want to win full enlightenment, and yet they do not tremble at birth-and-death.

The Lord: So it is. Doers of what is hard are the Bodhisattvas who have set out for the benefit and happiness of the world, out of pity for it. "We will become a shelter for the world, a refuge, the place of rest, the final relief, islands, lights and leaders of the world. We will win full enlightenment, and become the resort of the world,"—with these words they make a vigorous effort to win such a full enlightenment. [294]

1. How then do the Bodhisattvas awakened to full enlightenment become the world's *shelter*? They protect from all the sufferings which belong to birth-and-death, they struggle and make efforts to rid the world of them.

2. How do they become the world's *refuge*? They set free from birth, decay, illness, death, sorrow, lamentation, pain, sadness and despair those

beings who are doomed to undergo these conditions.

3. How do they become the world's *resting place*? The Tathagatas demonstrate Dharma to beings so that they may learn not to embrace anything.

Subhuti: How does that non-embracing come about?

The Lord: The non-embracing of form, etc., is the same as its non-connection, and as its non-production and non-stopping. [295] One thus learns not to embrace anything as a result of the cognition and vision that all dharmas are non-embracing, non-connected.

4. How do they become the world's *final relief*? The state beyond form is not form; and yet, as the Beyond, so form, etc., and all dharmas.

Subhuti: If form, etc., and all dharmas are the Beyond, then surely the Bodhisattvas must fully know all dharmas. Because there is no discrimination between them.

The Lord: So it is. In that Beyond there is no discrimination. Through their non-discrimination do all dharmas become fully known to the Bodhisattvas. This also is most hard for the Bodhisattvas that they meditate on all dharmas, but neither realize [296], nor become cowed, and that they meditate thus: "In this way should all these dharmas be fully known; and thus, awakened to full enlightenment, will we demonstrate these dharmas, and reveal them."

5. How do they become the world's *islands*? 'Islands' are pieces of land limited by water, in rivers or great lakes. Just so form, etc., is limited at its beginning and end, and so are all dharmas. But the limitation of all dharmas is the same as the Calm Quiet, the Sublime, as Nirvana, as the Really Existing, the Unperverted.

6. How do they become the world's *lights*? Here the Bodhisattvas win full enlightenment, and then take away all the darkness and gloom of the un-cognition from beings who for long are enveloped in the membrane of the eggshell of ignorance, and overcome by darkness, and they illuminate them through wisdom. [297]

7. How do they become the world's *leaders*? When they have become enlightened, the Bodhisattvas demonstrate dharma in order to reveal the absence of production and stopping in the essential nature of form, etc., and in the dharmas which constitute and distinguish ordinary people, Disciples, Pratyekabuddhas, Bodhisattvas and Buddhas, and in all dharmas in general.

8. How are they the world's *resort*? When they have become enlightened, the Bodhisattvas demonstrate dharma by teaching that form, etc., is situated in the world's space. All dharmas are situated in space, they have not come, they have not gone, they are the same as space. Space has not

come, nor gone, it is not made, nor unmade, nor effected; it has not stood up, does not last, nor endure; it is neither produced nor stopped. The same is true of all dharmas which are, after the fashion of space, undiscriminate. [298] Because the emptiness of form, etc., neither comes nor goes. Nor does the emptiness of all dharmas. For all dharmas are situated in emptiness, and from that situation they do not depart. They are situated in the signless, the wishless, the ineffective, in non-production, no-birth, in the absence of positivity, in dream and self, in the boundless, in the calm quiet, in Nirvana, in the Unrecoverable; they have not come, nor gone, situated in immobility; they are situated in form, etc., [299] and in the full enlightenment of Arhats and Pratyekabuddhas.

3. DESCRIPTION OF PERFECT WISDOM

Subhuti: Who can understand this perfection of wisdom?

The Lord: Bodhisattvas who have coursed under Tathagatas in the past, and who have matured their wholesome roots.

Subhuti: What is their own-being?

The Lord: Their own-being is isolated from the need for discipline.

Subhuti: Will these Bodhisattvas be so situated that, after they have fully known this resort, they demonstrate it to all beings? Is it in this sense that they will become the resort of all beings? [300]

The Lord: So it is, Subhuti. It is in this sense that a Bodhisattva will, after he has known full enlightenment, become the resort of countless beings.

Subhuti: A doer of what is hard is the Bodhisattva who has armed himself with this armour: "Immeasurable and incalculable beings I shall lead to Nirvana."

The Lord: The armour of such a Bodhisattva is, however, not connected with form, etc., nor is it put on for the sake of form, etc. It is not connected with the level of a Disciple, or a Pratyekabuddha, or a Buddha, nor put on for their sake. For surely unconnected with all dharmas is that armour of a Bodhisattva who is armed with the great armour.

Subhuti: Three standpoints one should not desire for a Bodhisattva who is armed with the great armour and who courses thus in deep wisdom. Which three? The level of a Disciple, or of a Pratyekabuddha, or of a Buddha. [301]

The Lord: For what reason do you say that? It is, of course, impossible, it cannot be, that such a Bodhisattva should belong to the vehicle of the Disciples or Pratyekabuddhas. But, since he put on his armour for the sake of all beings, surely he should desire the level of a Buddha.

Subhuti: Deep, O Lord, is perfect wisdom. It cannot be developed by anything, nor by anyone, nor is there anything or anyone to be developed. For in perfect wisdom nothing at all has been brought to perfection. The development of perfect wisdom is like the development of space, or of all dharmas, or of non-attachment, of the infinite, of what is not, of not-taking-hold-of.

The Lord: So it is [302]. Because of what you said a Bodhisattva, who adjusts himself to deep and perfect wisdom, is to be regarded as irreversible from full enlightenment. For then a Bodhisattva does not settle down in this deep and perfect wisdom, nor in the declarations or counsels of others; he does not go by someone else whom he puts his trust in. When this deep perfection of wisdom is being taught, he does not become cowed, or stolid, nor does he turn his back on it; he will not tremble, be frightened, or terrified; he does not hesitate, or doubt, or get stupefied, but he plunges right into it, becomes resolutely intent on it, and delights in its vision and hearing. One should know that in a former life already he has explored the perfection of wisdom. Because now, when this deep and perfect wisdom is being taught, he does not tremble, is not frightened, nor terrified.

Subhuti: By means of what mode does a Bodhisattva who does not tremble when this deep perfection of wisdom is being taught apperceive perfect wisdom?

The Lord: This Bodhisattva apperceives perfect wisdom through a series [of thoughts] which are inclined to all-knowledge.

Subhuti: How does one apperceive such a series of thoughts? [303]

The Lord: Through a series of thoughts inclined towards space, prone to space, sloping towards space. This apperception is won through a series of thoughts inclined to all-knowledge. And why? Because all-knowledge is immeasurable and unlimited. What is immeasurable and unlimited, that is not form, or any other skandha. That is not attainment, or reunion, or getting there; not the path or its fruit; not cognition, or consciousness; not genesis, or destruction, or production, or passing away, or stopping, or development, or annihilation. It has not been made by anything, it has not come from anywhere, it does not go to anywhere, it does not stand in any place or spot. On the contrary, it comes to be styled 'immeasurable, unlimited.' From the immeasurableness of space is the immeasurableness of all-knowledge. But what is immeasurableness that does not lend itself to being fully known by anything, be it form, or any skandha, or any of the six perfections. Because form is all-knowledge, and so are the other skandhas, and the six perfections.

Thereupon *Sakra* approached [304] and said: Deep, O Lord, is perfect wisdom. It is hard to fathom, hard to see, hard to understand. The thought of a Tathagata who considers this depth of dharma, and who, seated on the terrace of enlightenment, has just won full enlightenment, is inclined to carefree non-action, and not to demonstration of dharma.

The Lord: So it is. Deep certainly is this dharma I have fully known. Nothing has been, or will be, or is being fully known, and that is the depth of this dharma. This dharma which I have fully known is deep through the depth of space, the depth of the self, the depth of the not-coming of all dharmas, and of their not going. [305]

Sakra: It is wonderful, O Lord, it is astonishing, O Well-Gone! As contrary to the ways of the whole world is this dharma demonstrated, —it teaches you not to seize upon dharmas, but the world is wont to grasp at anything.

Chapter XVI

SUCHNESS

1. TATHAGATA-SUCHNESS

Subhuti: As the non-observation of all dharmas, to be sure, is this dharma taught. Nowhere is this dharma obstructed. Through its identity with space this dharma is, to be sure, marked with non-obstruction, since no traces of it are noticed. It has no counterpart, because it is without a second. It has no opponent, because it has gone beyond all opposites. It is without a trace, because it has not been caused to become. It is unproduced, because there is no occasion for rebirth. It is pathless, because no path is noticed.

Sakra and the Gods: Born after the image of the Lord is this Disciple, the holy Subhuti, the Elder. For, whichever dharma he demonstrates, he always starts from emptiness. [307]

Subhuti: Because he is not born is Subhuti, the Elder, born after the image of the Tathagata. He is born after the image of the Tathagata's Suchness. As that has neither come nor gone, so also the Suchness of Subhuti has neither come nor gone. From the very beginning Subhuti the Elder has been born after the image of the Tathagata's Suchness. Because the Suchness of the Tathagata and the Suchness of all dharmas are the same thing, and they are both the Suchness of Subhuti the Elder. Born after the image of that Suchness is Subhuti the Elder; hence born after the image of the Tathagata. But that Suchness is also no Suchness, and after the image of that Suchness has he been born. It is in that sense that the Elder Subhuti is born after the image of the Tathagata, and that as a result of the established order of the Suchness of the Tathagata. Subhuti's Suchness is immutable and unchangeable, undiscriminated and undifferentiated, just as the Suchness of the Tathagata. It is thus that Subhuti the Elder, immutable, unchangeable, undiscriminated, undifferentiated, through that Suchness, is born after the image of the Tathagata. And just as the Suchness of the Tathagata, which is immutable and undifferentiated, is nowhere obstructed, so also the Suchness of all dharmas, which is also immutable and undifferentiated. For the Suchness of the Tathagata, and the Suchness of all dharmas, they are both one single Suchness, not two, not divided. A non-dual Suchness, however, is nowhere, is from nowhere, belongs to nowhere. It is because it is a Suchness which belongs nowhere that it is non-dual. It is therefore through an unmade Suchness that the Elder Subhuti is born after the image of the Tathagata. An un-

made Suchness, however, is at no time not Suchness [308] and therefore
it is non-dual. It is in this sense that the Elder Subhuti is born after the
image of the Tathagata. Just as the Suchness of the Tathagata is undiscrim-
inated and undifferentiated, at all times and in all dharmas, so also the
Suchness of Subhuti. And for that reason, although we seem to have a
duality when Subhuti has been conjured up from the Suchness of the
Tathagata, nevertheless nothing real has been lopped off that Suchness,
which remains unbroken, because one cannot apprehend an actually real
agent that could break it apart. In that sense is Subhuti the Elder born
after the image of the Tathagata. As the Suchness of the Tathagata is not
outside the Suchness of all dharmas, so also the Suchness of Subhuti. But
what is not outside the Suchness of all dharmas, that is not of anything
not the Suchness. The Suchness of Subhuti is therefore just the same as the
Suchness of all dharmas. Subhuti the Elder has undergone the experience
of that Suchness by imitating in himself the unaltered Suchness, but in
actual fact no one has anywhere undergone a process of imitation. It is in
this sense that Subhuti the Elder is born after the image of the Tathagata.
As the Suchness of the Tathagata is neither past, nor future, nor present, so
also the Suchness of all dharmas. As born in the image of that Suchness is
Subhuti called "born after the image of the Tathagata." Because it is also
through the Suchness of the Tathagata [and not only his own] that he has
conformed to Suchness. It is just through the Suchness of the Tathagata
that he has conformed to past Suchness, and it is just through past Such-
ness that he has conformed to the Suchness of the Tathagata. And so with
the future and the present. It is through the Suchness of the Tathagata
that he has conformed to past, future and present Suchness, and it is
through past, future and present Suchness that he has conformed to the
Suchness of the Tathagata. In this sense the Suchness of Subhuti, and past,
future and present Suchness, and the Suchness of the Tathagata, are not
two, nor divided. The Suchness of all dharmas and the Suchness of Subhu-
ti are therefore not two, nor divided. [309] And also, the Suchness of the
Lord when he was a Bodhisattva that is the Suchness of the Lord when he
had won full enlightenment. And that is the Suchness through which a
Bodhisattva, when he has definitely won full enlightenment, comes to be
called a 'Tathagata.'

2. THE EARTH SHAKES, AND MANY ARE SAVED

When this disquisition of the Suchness of the Tathagata had taken
place, the great earth shook in six ways, stirred, quaked, was agitated,
resounded and tumbled, as it did when the Tathagata won full enlighten-
ment.

Subhuti: It is thus, O Gods, that Subhuti the Elder is born after the image of the Tathagata. But he is not born after the image of form, or of any of the fruits of a holy life, from the fruit of a Streamwinner to Buddhahood. For those dharmas, which might be born after the image of something, or in the image of which he would be born, they do not exist, they are not got at. It is thus that Subhuti the Elder is born in the image of the Tathagata.

Sariputra: This Suchness, O Lord, courses in the deep!

The Lord: So it is, Sariputra.

But when this disquisition of Suchness was expounded, the minds of three hundred monks were freed from the outflows, without any further clinging. Five hundred nuns obtained the pure, dispassionate and unstained dharma-eye. [310] Five thousand Gods, who in the past had made the necessary preparations, acquired the patient acceptance of dharmas which fail to be produced. And the minds of six thousand Bodhisattvas were free from the outflows, without any further clinging.

3. PERFECT WISDOM AND SKILL IN MEANS

Sariputra knew that the thoughts of those Bodhisattvas were freed from the outflows, without any further clinging, and he asked the Lord for the reason, or cause, of that.

The Lord: Those Bodhisattvas have honoured five hundred Buddhas, and during all that time they have given gifts, guarded their morality, perfected their patience, exerted their vigour, and produced trance. But they were not upheld by perfect wisdom and lacked in skill in means. And so, although they had gained the path of emptiness, had coursed in the Signless, had put their minds to work on the Wishless, as wanting skill in means they had realised the reality limit, and come forth on the level of Disciple or Pratyekabuddha, and not on the level of a Buddha. Suppose there is a very huge bird, one hundred, or up to five hundred miles large, but without any wings, or with crippled or damaged wings. That bird would want to fly down to Jambudvipa from the Heaven of the Gods of the Thirty-three. If in the intermediate space, in the middle of its journey [311] to Jambudvipa, it would want to return to the Gods of the Thirty-three, would it be able to do so?

Sariputra: No, Lord.

The Lord: And could it hope to come down on Jambudvipa without damage or injury?

Sariputra: No, Lord. It is bound to get damaged and injured, and when it drops down on Jambudvipa it will incur death or deadly pain.

Because of the fact that, whereas its body is huge, the strength of its wings
is insufficient, and it just drops down from above.

The Lord: So it is, Sariputra. Even if a Bodhisattva, after he has raised
his mind to full enlightenment, would, for countless aeons, give gifts,
guard his morality, perfect his patience, exert his vigour, and enter the
trances, how ever great may be his setting forth and the thought which he
raises to full enlightenment,—if he is not upheld by perfect wisdom and
lacks in skill in means, he is bound to fall on the level of Disciple or
Pratyekabuddha. Furthermore, Sariputra, it may be that a Bodhisattva
brings to mind, and retains in his mind, [312] of the Buddhas and Lords,
past, future and present, the morality, the concentration, the wisdom, the
emancipation, the vision and cognition of emancipation, —but all that
after the manner of a sign. He then neither knows nor sees the morality of
the Tathagatas, nor their concentration, or wisdom, or emancipation, or
their vision and cognition of emancipation. Ignorant of them, blind to
them, he hears the word 'emptiness,' treats that as a sign, and wishes to
covert [that mass of merit] into a full enlightenment [which he regards as
emptiness]. In consequence he will remain on the level of a Disciple or
Pratyekabuddha, —because of the fact that he is not upheld by perfect
wisdom, that he lacks in skill in means.

Sariputra: As I understand the meaning of the Lord's teaching, al-
though a Bodhisattva may be joined to a huge equipment of merit, as long
as he is not upheld by perfect wisdom and is without skill in means, he
lacks the good friend, and his attainment of full enlightenment is uncer-
tain. A Bodhisattva who wants to win full enlightenment should therefore
develop the perfection of wisdom, and become skilled in means.

The Lord: So it is, Sariputra. [313]

Sakra and the Gods: Deep, O Lord, is perfect wisdom! Hard to win,
exceedingly hard to win is full enlightenment!

The Lord: So it is, O Gods. Deep is this perfection of wisdom. Hard to
win, exceedingly hard to win is full enlightenment, if one is weak in
wisdom, below the mark in vigour and resolve, unskilled in means, and if
one serves the bad friends.

4. ENLIGHTENMENT AND EMPTINESS

Subhuti: How can the Lord say that full enlightenment is hard to win,
exceedingly hard to win, when there is no one who can win enlighten-
ment? For, owing to the emptiness of all dharmas, no dharma exists that
would be able to win enlightenment. All dharmas are empty. That dharma
also for the forsaking of which dharma is demonstrated, that dharma does

not exist. And also that dharma which [314] would be enlightened in full enlightenment, and that which should be enlightened, and that which would cognize [the enlightenment], and that which should cognize it, —all these dharmas are empty. In this manner I am inclined to think that full enlightenment is easy to win, not hard to win.

The Lord: Because it cannot possibly come about is full enlightenment hard to win, because in reality it is not there, because it cannot be discriminated, because it has not been fabricated [as a false appearance].

Sariputra: Also because it is empty is it hard to win, O Subhuti. For it does not occur to space that it will win full enlightenment. As such, i.e. as without own-being, should these dharmas be known in enlightenment. For all dharmas are the same as space. And, Subhuti, if full enlightenment were easy to win, then countless Bodhisattvas would not turn away from it. But as countless Bodhisattvas do turn away from it, therefore one can discern [315] that full enlightenment is hard to win, exceedingly hard to win.

Subhuti: But, Sariputra, does form, etc., turn away from full enlightenment?

Sariputra: No, Subhuti.

Subhuti: Is then the dharma which turns away from full enlightenment other than form, etc.?

Sariputra: No, Subhuti.

Subhuti: Does the Suchness of form, etc., turn away?

Sariputra: No, Subhuti. [316]

Subhuti: Is the dharma which turns away from full enlightenment other than the Suchness of form, etc.?

Sariputra: No, Subhuti.

Subhuti: Does form, etc., know full enlightenment?

Sariputra: No, Subhuti.

Subhuti: Is the dharma which knows full enlightenment other than form, etc.?

Sariputra: No, Subhuti.

Subhuti: Does the Suchness of form, etc., know full enlightenment?

Sariputra: No, Subhuti. [317]

Subhuti: Is the dharma which knows full enlightenment other than the Suchness of form, etc.?

Sariputra: No, Subhuti.

Subhuti: Should form, etc., be known in full enlightenment, or a dharma other than form, etc. [318] or the Suchness of form, etc., or a dharma other than the Suchness of form, etc.?

Sariputra: No, Subhuti.

Subhuti: Does Suchness turn away from full enlightenment?

Sariputra: No, Subhuti.

Subhuti: Is that dharma which turns away from full enlightenment in Suchness?

Sariputra: No, Subhuti. [319]

Subhuti: What then, Sariputra, is this dharma which turns away from full enlightenment, when we consider it as it stands in this nature of dharmas, which is just emptiness, after the manner of taking no stand on any dharma? Or what dharma, is that Suchness? Is it perhaps Suchness which is turned away?

Sariputra: No, Subhuti.

Subhuti: Since thus, in ultimate truth and as things stand, no dharma can be apprehended as real, what is that dharma which is turned away from full enlightenment?

Sariputra: When one adopts the method of considering dharmas in their ultimate reality, which Subhuti the Elder uses in this exposition, then indeed there is no dharma which turns away from full enlightenment. But then, Venerable Subhuti, there is no longer any ground for the distinction of those who have set their hearts on enlightenment into three kinds of persons, as described by the Tathagata, who differ with respect to the vehicle which they have chosen. According to the exposition of the Venerable Subhuti there should be only one vehicle [for those whose hearts are set on enlightenment], i.e. the Buddha-vehicle, the Bodhisattva-vehicle, the great vehicle.

Purna: First of all the Venerable Sariputra must ask the Venerable Subhuti the Elder whether he admits even one single kind of being whose heart is set on enlightenment, and who uses either the vehicle of the Disciples, or that of the Pratyekabuddhas, or the great vehicle.

Sariputra: Subhuti, do you admit even one single kind of being whose heart is set on enlightenment, and who uses either the vehicle of the Disciples, or that of the Bodhisattvas, or the great vehicle? [320]

Subhuti: Sariputra, do you see in the Suchness of Suchness even one single being whose heart is set on enlightenment [i.e. as a real entity], be he one who uses the vehicle of the Disciples, or that of the Pratyekabuddhas, or the great vehicle?

Sariputra: Not so, Subhuti. Suchness, first of all, is not apprehended as of three kinds, how much less the being whose heart is set on enlightenment.

Subhuti: Is then Suchness apprehended as of one kind even?

Sariputra: Not so, Subhuti.

Subhuti: Do you then perhaps see in Suchness even one single dharma which would constitute a being whose heart is set on enlightenment?

Sariputra: Not so, Subhuti.

Subhuti: Since thus, in ultimate truth and as things stand, such a dharma which could constitute a being whose heart is set on enlightenment cannot be apprehended, where do you get the idea that "this one belongs to the vehicle of the Disciples, that one to the vehicle of the Pratyekabuddhas, that one to the great vehicle"? If a Bodhisattva who hears this absence of difference, distinction or differentiation between the three kinds of persons who have set their hearts on enlightenment, in so far as they are encompassed by the same Suchness, does not become cowed or stolid in mind, does not turn back, then one should know that he will go forth to enlightenment. [321]

The Lord: Well said, Subhuti. Through the might and sustaining power of the Tathagata have you been inspired to say this.

Sariputra: To which enlightenment, O Lord, will that Bodhisattva go forth?

The Lord: To the full and supreme enlightenment.

5. REQUISITES OF GOING FORTH TO ENLIGHTENMENT

Subhuti: How should a Bodhisattva behave, how should he train, if he wants to go forth to the full and supreme enlightenment?

The Lord: The Bodhisattva should adopt the same attitude towards all beings, his mind should be even towards all beings, he should not handle others with an uneven mind, but with a mind which is friendly, well disposed, helpful, free from aversion, avoiding harm and hurt, he should handle others as if they were his mother, father, son or daughter. [322] As a saviour of all beings should a Bodhisattva behave towards all beings, should he train himself, if he wants to know the full and supreme enlightenment. He should, himself, stand in the abstention from all evil, he should give gifts, guard his morality, perfect himself in patience, exert vigour, enter into the trances, achieve mastery over wisdom, survey conditioned coproduction, both in direct and in reverse order; and also others he should instigate to do the same, incite and encourage them. In the same way he should stand in everything from the meditation on the truths to the stage when he reaches the certainty that it is as a Bodhisattva that he will be saved, and when he matures beings, and also others he should instigate to do the same, incite and encourage them. When he longs eagerly for all that and trains himself in it, then everything will be uncovered to him, from form to the established order of dharma.

Chapter XVII

ATTRIBUTES, TOKENS AND SIGNS OF IRREVERSIBILITY

1. VARIOUS TOKENS OF IRREVERSIBILITY

Subhuti: What, O Lord, are the attributes, tokens and signs of an irreversible Bodhisattva, and how can we know that a Bodhisattva is irreversible?

The Lord: The level of the common people, the level of the Disciples, the level of the Pratyekabuddhas, the level of the Buddhas—they are all called the "Level of Suchness." With the thought that all these are, through Suchness, not two, nor divided, not discriminated, undiscriminate, he enters on this Suchness, this nature of Dharma. After he has stood firmly in Suchness, he neither imagines nor discriminates it. In that sense does he enter into it. When he has thus entered on it, even when he has gone away from the assembly where he has heard about Suchness, he does not hesitate, does not become perplexed, does not doubt, and he is not stupefied by the thought [concerning form, etc.] that 'it is not thus.' On the contrary, he firmly believes that 'it is just thus, just Suchness,' and like that he plunges into it. But he does not prattle away about everything that comes into his head. He only speaks when it is profitable [to others], and not when it is not profitable. He does not look down on what others have done or have not done. Endowed with these attributes, tokens and signs a Bodhisattva should be borne in mind as irreversible from full enlightenment. Furthermore, an irreversible Bodhisattva does not pander to Shramanas and Brahmins of other schools, telling them that they know what is worth knowing, that they see what is worth seeing. [324] He pays no homage to strange Gods, offers them no flowers, incense, etc., does not put his trust in them. He is no more reborn in the places of woe, nor does he ever again become a woman. Furthermore, Subhuti, an irreversible Bodhisattva undertakes to observe the ten avenues [ways] of wholesome action. He himself observes, and he instigates others to observe, abstention from taking life, abstention from taking what is not given, abstention from wrong conduct as regards sensuous pleasures, abstention from intoxicants as tending to cloud the mind, abstention from lying speech, abstention from malicious speech, abstention from harsh speech, abstention from indistinct prattling, abstention from covetousness, abstention from ill will, abstention from wrong views. [325] It is quite certain that an irreversible

Bodhisattva observes the ten ways of wholesome action, and instigates others to observe them, incites and encourages them to do so, establishes and confirms others in them. Even in his dreams he never commits offenses against those ten precepts, and he does not nurse such offences in his mind. Even in his dreams an irreversible Bodhisattva keeps the ten wholesome paths of action present in his mind. Furthermore, when an irreversible Bodhisattva masters a text of dharma, and offers it to others, he has in mind the welfare and happiness of all beings, and he offers that gift of dharma in common to all beings, without distinction. [326] Furthermore, when deep dharmas are being taught, a Bodhisattva does not hesitate, does not become perplexed, does not doubt, does not get stupefied. He only says what is beneficial, he speaks gently and in moderation. He has little sloth and torpor, and he loses all the latent biases to evil. Whether he goes out or comes back, his mind does not wander, but his mindfullness is fixed before him. When he steps on the ground he knows what he does, and when he lifts up or puts down his feet he neither loiters nor hurries but remains at ease. His robe is free from lice, his habits are clean, he is rarely ill, and his afflictions are few. In his body the eighty thousand families of worms which are present in the bodies of other beings cannot at all develop, because his wholesome roots have elevated him above the whole world. And as those wholesome roots of his go on increasing, in due course he will gain the perfect purity of body, speech and thought. [327]

Subhuti: What should be known as perfect purity of thought on the part of this Bodhisattva?

The Lord: As those wholesome roots of his go on increasing, in due course he will gain a state of mind where he has few cares, and is free from treachery, deceit, crookedness and craftiness. In addition his perfect purity of thought also consists in that he has transcended the level of Disciples and Pratyekabuddhas. Furthermore, an irreversible Bodhisattva is not one to attach weight to gain, honour, or fame, or to robes, alms bowl, lodging or medicinal appliances for use in sickness. He is not one who is full of envy and meanness. And, when deep dharmas are being taught, he does not lose heart; but his intelligence becomes steady, his intelligence goes deep. With respect he hears the Dharma from others. All the dharmas which he hears from others he unites with the perfection of wisdom, and also all worldly arts and professions he unites, thanks to the perfection of wisdom, with the nature of dharma. There is not any dharma which he does not see as yoked to the nature of dharmas, and each dharma he sees simply as engaged in that effort. [328]

2. MARA'S DEEDS

Furthermore, Mara, the Evil One, conjures up a vision of the eight great hells, with many hundreds, many thousands, many hundreds of thousands of Bodhisattvas in them, and he says to the irreversible Bodhisattva: "Those Bodhisattvas, described by the Tathagata as irreversible, have been reborn in the great hells. Just so you also, since you have been described as irreversible, will fall into the great hells. Confess that that thought of enlightenment was an error! Abandon it! What is Buddhahood to you? In that way you will avoid rebirth in the hells. If you act thus you will be one who goes to heaven." If even then the mind of the Bodhisattva does not waver, is not put out, if he is certain in his knowledge that an irreversible Bodhisattva cannot possibly be reborn against his will in the hells, then this is another token of his irreversibility. Furthermore, Mara, the Evil One, may come along in the guise of a Shramana, and say: "Give up what you have heard up to now, abandon what you have gained so far! And if you follow this advice, we will again and again approach you, and say to you: 'What you have heard just now, that is not the word of the Buddha. It is poetry, the work of poets. But what I here teach to you, that is the teaching of the Buddha, that is the word of the Buddha.' " If, on hearing that, a Bodhisattva wavers and is put out, then one should know that he has not been predicted by the Tathagata, that he is not fixed on full enlightenment, [329] that he does not stand firmly in the element of irreversibility. But if, even when he has heard these words of Mara, he does not waver, but flees back to the nature of dharma, to Non-production, to Non-stopping, to the Uneffected, then he is not one of those who put their trust in others. An Arhat, a monk whose outflows are dried up, does not go by someone else whom he puts his trust in, but he has placed the nature of dharma directly before his own eyes, and Mara has no access to him. Just so an irreversible Bodhisattva cannot be crushed by persons who belong to the vehicle of the Disciples and Pratyekabuddhas, he cannot, by his very nature, backslide into the level of Disciple or Pratyekabuddha, he is fixed on all-knowledge, and ends up in perfect enlightenment. It is quite certain that a Bodhisattva who stands firmly in the element of irreversibility cannot possibly be led astray by others. Furthermore, someone will come to the irreversible Bodhisattva and say: "A journey in birth-and-death is this coursing in perfect wisdom, and not the journey of someone who is in quest of enlightenment. Put an end to all suffering in this very life! You will then no longer experience all the sufferings and disappointments which are bound up with the plane of birth-and-death. Aye surely, in this very life already will this personality of yours be finished, why do you

think of taking upon yourself another one [for the sake of other beings]?"
If even then the Bodhisattva neither wavers nor is put out, then Mara
himself will say to him: "Just have a look at those Bodhisattvas who for
countless aeons have presented the necessities of life [330] to the Bud-
dhas, the Lords, who have led holy lives in the presence of countless
Buddhas, who have honoured countless Buddhas and Lords, have ques-
tioned them about just this vehicle of the Bodhisattvas, have asked them
how a Bodhisattva should stand, have heard the answer of the Tathagatas,
and have acted on it! In spite of the fact that they have stood, coursed and
exerted themselves as they should, —to this very day they have not yet
known full enlightenment! They stand firm in their instructions, they train
themselves as they should, —but they have not reached all-knowledge!
How then will you reach full enlightenment ever?" If even then he does
not waver and is not put out, then Mara, the Evil One, will conjure up some
monks in that place, and say: "Those monks have become Arhats, with
their outflows dried up. They who have set out for enlightenment, in the
meantime have reached Arhatship, and become established in it. How will
you ever reach full enlightenment?" It is quite certain that a Bodhisattva
must be irreversible from full enlightenment if, when this is being said and
expounded, his mind does not waver and is not put out. If the mind of a
Bodhisattva who has heard from a stranger these discouraging remarks is
not excluded from the true nature of dharma, if he does not go back on it,
if he does not change his mind, if he recognizes those deeds of Mara for
what they are, then it is quite impossible that he who courses correctly in
the perfections should not reach all-knowledge. Mara, the Evil One, cannot
possibly gain entry to a Bodhisattva who not only courses but also trains
himself correctly, who does not lack in the practices described by the
Tathagatas, who is completely adjusted to this mental activity which is
associated with the perfections. [331] If a Bodhisattva recognizes the
deeds of Mara, if, when he hears discouraging remarks from strangers, he
does not desist, nor slide back, nor change his mind, if he perceives those
deeds of Mara for what they are, then this is another token of irreversibil-
ity.

Furthermore, an irreversible Bodhisattva does not piece together a
perception of form, etc., nor produce one. For the irreversible Bodhisattva
who has through dharmas which are empty of their own marks definitely
entered on the certainty that he will win salvation as a Bodhisattva does
not apprehend even that dharma, and so he cannot piece it together, or
produce it. One says therefore that "a Bodhisattva is irreversible if he
patiently accepts the cognition of non-production." This is another token
of irreversibility. Furthermore, Mara, the Evil One, comes along in the

guise of a monk and tries to deter the Bodhisattva with the words: "The same as space is this all-knowledge. It is a dharma which is not, it is non-existent. Who can anoint himself for it, who fully know it? There is no one who could go forth to it, there is no one who could fully know it, nothing that should be fully known, there is no one who would understand, there is nothing that should be understood. At all times those dharmas are the same as space, it is useless for you to resist, revealed as a deed of Mara is this doctrine that 'one should know full enlightenment,' it is not the Buddha's teaching." A son or daughter of good family should then cognize, realize and know that [332] this kind of critical examination is just a deed of Mara. After he has made this reflection, he should make his mind firm, unshakeable, irrestible. This is another token of irreversibility.

3. MORE TOKENS OF IRREVERSIBILITY

Furthermore, an irreversible Bodhisattva is one who has turned away from the level of Disciples and Pratyekabuddhas, and who has proceeded in the direction of all-knowledge. According to plan he enters into the first, second, third and fourth trance, and he dwells in those four trances. He becomes a complete master over the trances, i.e. he enters into the trances, but his future rebirth is not determined by their influence. It is on the dharmas of the sphere of sense-desire that he bases his rebirth. This also should be known as a mark of irreversibility in an irreversible Bodhisattva. Furthermore, an irreversible Bodhisattva does not attach weight to a name, nor to renown, title or fame. He does not get attached to a [particular] name [which in any case is absent in emptiness]. His mind remains undismayed, and interested only in the welfare of all beings. Whether he goes out or comes back, his mind does not wander, and he remains ever mindful. When he lives the life of a householder, he has no great love for pleasant things, and he does not want them too much. With fear and disgust he possesses all pleasant things. Situated in a wilderness infested with robbers one would eat one's meals in fear, and with the constant thought [333] of getting away, of getting out of this wilderness, and not with repose. Just so an irreversible Bodhisattva who lives the life of a householder, possesses any pleasant things he may have simply without caring for them, without eagerness, without attachment. He is not one of those people who care for dear and pleasant forms. Those who live the lives of householders and who are involved in the five kinds of sensuous pleasures do not earn their living in an irregular way, but in the right way. Neither do they incur death in a state of sin, nor do they inflict injuries on others. For they have incited all beings to win the supreme happiness,

—those worthy men, those great men, supermen, excellent men, splendid men, bulls of men, sublime men, valiant men, heroes of men, leaders of men, waterlilies of men, lotuses of men, thoroughbred men, Nagas of men, lions of men, trainers of men! It is in this spirit that Bodhisattvas live the life of householders, inasmuch as they have been impregnated with the power of the perfection of wisdom, —and that is another token of their irreversibility. Furthermore, Vajrapani, the great Yaksha, constantly follows behind the irreversible Bodhisattva. Unassailable, the Bodhisattva cannot be defeated by either men or ghosts. All beings find it hard to conquer him, and his mind is not disturbed [by their attacks]. His faculties are all complete, and he is not deficient in any. He possesses the organs of a virile man, [334] not those of an impotent man. He does not in any way embark on those spells, mutterings, herbs, magical formulae, medical incantations, etc., which are the work of women. He earns his livelihood in a clean way, not in a wrong way. His character is neither quarrelsome nor disputatious. His views are upright, he does not exalt himself nor deprecate others. With these and other similar qualities he is endowed. He does not predict to women or men that they will have a son or a daughter. Such faulty ways of making himself acceptable will not be his. All this is another token of irreversibility. Furthermore, Subhuti, I will demonstrate the attributes, tokens and signs of an irreversible Bodhisattva. Endowed with them he would be known as irreversible from full enlightenment. Again, which are they? The following: He does not give himself over to occupation and preoccupation with the skandhas, the sense-fields, the elements, and with conditioned coproduction. He is not preoccupied with the kind of talk one is fond of in society, with talk about kings, and robbers, about armies and battles; about villages, [335] cities, market towns, countries, kingdoms, and capitals; about himself, about ministers and prime ministers; about women, men and neuters; about journeys, parks, monasteries, palaces, pools, lakes, ponds, lotus ponds, woods, gardens and mountains; about Yakshas, Rakshasas, Pretas, Pishacas, Kataputana-demons and Kumbhanda-demons; about food, drink, dresses, ornaments, perfumes, garlands and ointments; about roads, crossroads, streets, markets, palanquins and people; about songs, dances, tales, actors, dancers, and wandering singers; about the ocean, about rivers, about islands. They do not devote themselves to talk which obstructs dharma, to the kind of talk which delights the common people, but to talk on the perfection of wisdom, and they become people who do not lack in the mental activities which are associated with all-knowledge. But talk about fightings and strife, about quarrels and disputes they avoid. They are willing for what is right, and not willing for what is wrong. They praise without causing dissension, and not in order to cause dissension. They want friendship, and not its opposite. They preach dharma, and not its opposite. They plan to gain a vision of those Tathagatas who dwell in other world systems, and thus they produce a thought which leads them to rebirth in their presence. According to plan they are reborn near them, and so they do not lack in the vision of the Tathagatas, [336] nor in opportunities for honouring and serving them. Furthermore, when an irreversible Bodhisattva has definitely terminated his existence among the Gods, — whether they belong to the sphere of sense-desire, or the sphere of form, or the formless sphere, —he is reborn in just this middle region, in Jambudvipa. For in the border countries there are only a few beings with a good knowledge of the arts, of poetry, of mantras, of secret lore, of the standard treatises, of portents and of the meaning of religion, but in the middle region they are reborn in abundance. But those who are reborn in the border regions are at least reborn in the big towns. This is another mark of irreversibility. Furthermore, to an irreversible Bodhisattva it does not occur to ask himself whether he is irreversible or not. No doubt about it arises in him, he has no uncertainty about the stage he has made his own, and he does not sink down below it. Just as a Streamwinner has no hesitations or doubts about the fruit of a Streamwinner, if that is the stage which is his by right, just so an irreversible Bodhisattva has no hesitations or doubts about being on the stage of a Bodhisattva, when that stage is his by right, he has no uncertainties about the stage which is his by right, nor does he sink below it. And he quickly sees through any deed of Mara that may have arisen, and does not come under his sway. [337] A man who has committed one of the deadly sins will never again, until his death, lose the thought of that action, he cannot get rid of it or remove it, but it follows after him until the time of his death. Just so the irreversible mind of an irreversible Bodhisattva has learned to stand firm on the irreversible stage which is his by right, and even the whole world, with its Gods, men and Asuras, cannot deflect, divert or diverge him from it. He recognizes any deeds of Mara that may have arisen for what they are, and does not come under their sway. He is free from hesitations and doubts about the stage which is his by right, and even after he has passed through this present life the thoughts which are characteristic of Disciples and Pratyekabuddhas will not arise in him. But when he has passed through this present life he will think: "It is not the case that I shall not win full enlightenment. I am sure to win full enlightenment, I who have stood firm on the stage which is mine by right." He can no longer be led astray by others, and on the stage which is his by right he cannot be crushed. For, as he has stood firm on it, his mind becomes insuperable, his cognition becomes insuperable. Suppose

that Mara, the Evil One, in the guise of the Buddha himself were to come
to him, and say: "Realize Arhatship in this very life! You are not pre-
destined to full enlightenment. You have not the attributes, tokens and
signs with which a Bodhisattva must be endowed in order to win full
enlightenment. Why then should you course in this?" If the Bodhisattva
then experiences a change of heart, one should know that he has not been
predicted to full enlightenment by the Tathagatas in the past. [338] If, on
the other hand, he considers that "this, surely, is Mara, the Evil One, who
has come along after he has, by magical means, adopted the disguise of the
Buddha, I am beset by Mara, this is one of Mara's magical creations, but
not the Tathagata. The Tathagata has spoken to the effect that one should
not realize Arhatship, and not otherwise," if he sees and understands that
"this, surely, is Mara, the Evil One, who has manufactured a magical double
of the appearance of the Buddha, and who wants to estrange me from
supreme enlightenment," and if Mara, after that, turns back, then this
Bodhisattva has certainly in the past been predicted to full enlightenment
by the Tathagatas, and he has stood firmly on the irreversible Bodhisattva-
stage. Where these attributes, tokens and signs are found in a Bodhisattva,
there one can be certain, beyond any shadow of a doubt, that, as he has
those qualities, he has been predicted by the Tathagatas in the past, and
has stood firm on the irreversible Bodhisattva-stage. For he has the attrib-
utes, tokens and signs of an irreversible Bodhisattva. This is another token
of irreversibility. Furthermore, an irreversible Bodhisattva tries to gain the
good dharma even if it costs him his life and all his belongings. Therefore
he makes a supreme effort to gain the good dharma, through his affection
and respect for the Buddhas and Lords, past, future and present. In the
conviction that "the Dharma-bodies are the Buddhas, the Lords" [339] he
wins the good dharma through his affection and respect for Dharma. He
gains the good dharma not only of the past Buddhas and Lords, but also of
the present and future Buddhas and Lords. He becomes convinced that he
also has joined the ranks of those who are reckoned as future Buddhas and
Lords, that he also has been predicted to that supreme enlightenment, that
also he will gain just this good dharma. Also these considerations he bears
in mind when, in his efforts to gain the good dharma, he renounces even
his life and all his belongings, when he does not lose heart, or becomes
indolent. This is another token of irreversibility. Moreover, when the
Tathagata demonstrates dharma, an irreversible Bodhisattva does not hesi-
tate or doubt.

Subhuti: Does he also not hesitate or doubt when a Disciple demon-
strates dharma?

The Lord: No, he does not. For a Bodhisattva who has acquired the patient acceptance of dharmas which fail to be produced does not hesitate or doubt when he hears about the unobstructed true nature of all dharmas. Endowed with these virtues a Bodhisattva becomes irreversible. [340] These also should be known as the attributes, tokens and signs of a Bodhisattva who is irreversible from full enlightenment.

Chapter XVIII

EMPTINESS

1. DEEP STATIONS

Subhuti: It is wonderful, O Lord, with how great, with what unlimited and measureless qualities a Bodhisattva is endowed!

The Lord: So it is, Subhuti. For an irreversible Bodhisattva has gained a cognition which is endless and boundless, and to which Disciples and Pratyekabuddhas have no claim.

Subhuti: For aeons on end the Lord could go on expounding the attributes, tokens and signs of an irreversible Bodhisattva. Hence he now might indicate the very deep positions of a Bodhisattva which are connected with perfect wisdom.

The Lord: Well said, Subhuti. You obviously bring up the very deep positions because you want me to change the subject. "Deep," Subhuti, of Emptiness that is a synonym, of the Signless, the Wishless, the Uneffected, the Unproduced, of No-birth, Non-existence, Dispassion, Cessation, Nirvana and Departing. [342]

Subhuti: Is it a synonym only of these, or of all dharmas?

The Lord: It is a synonym of all dharmas. For form, etc., is deep. How is form, etc., deep? As deep as Suchness, so deep is form, etc. As deep as the Suchness of form, etc., so deep is form, etc. Where there is no form, etc., that is the depth of form, etc.

Subhuti: It is wonderful, O Lord, how a subtle device has opened up [or: impeded] form, etc., and indicated Nirvana at the same time.

2. HOW TO ATTEND TO PERFECT WISDOM

The Lord: When a Bodhisattva reflects, ponders and meditates on these very deep positions which are connected with perfect wisdom, and strives to stand, train and progress as it is ordained, described and explained in the perfection of wisdom, [343] then, if he does so for one day only, how great is the deed he does during that one day! If a man, moved by considerations of greed, had made a date with a handsome, attractive and good-looking woman, and if now that woman were held back by someone else and could not leave her house, what do you think, Subhuti, with what would that man's preoccupations be connected?

Subhuti: With the woman, of course. He thinks about her coming,

about the things they will do together, and about the joy, fun and delight
he will have with her.

The Lord: Will he have many such ideas in the course of a day?

Subhuti: Many indeed, O Lord.

The Lord: As many such ideas as he has in the course of a day, for so
many aeons a Bodhisattva spurns birth-and-death, turns his back on it,
seeks to end it.

3. MERIT

When he stands, trains, progresses, meditates and strives as it is or-
dained, described and explained in this perfection of wisdom, he gets rid
also of those faults which cause him to turn away from full enlightenment.
[344] If now one Bodhisattva gives himself up to devotion to perfect
wisdom, and does deeds for one day only while dwelling completely in
mental activities connected with perfect wisdom; and if another Bodhi-
sattva lacks in perfect wisdom, but gives gifts for countless aeons; superior
to him is the Bodhisattva who, for one day only, makes endeavours about
perfect wisdom. A Bodhisattva who for one day only makes endeavours
about perfect wisdom begets greater merit than another Bodhisattva who
for countless aeons gives and bestows gifts on all the classes of holy per-
sons, —from Streamwinners to Tathagatas—but lacks in perfect wisdom. If
that other Bodhisattva should not only bestow gifts as indicated, but in
addition observe the moral precepts, but lack in perfect wisdom, then this
Bodhisattva, a dweller in perfect wisdom, would beget the greater merit if,
after he had emerged from his mental work on perfect wisdom, he would
demonstrate dharma. And that would remain true [345] even if the other
Bodhisattva in addition were endowed with patience. Even if in addition
he would exert vigour, would make endeavours about the trances and
wings of enlightenment, but were still lacking in perfect wisdom; a Bodhi-
sattva who, after he had given the gift of dharma, as said before, would
turn it over to full enlightenment, would beget a merit greater than his.
Greater still would be the merit of a Bodhisattva who not only gave the
gift of dharma, not only turned it over into full enlightenment, but em-
ployed the kind of turning over which has been taught in the perfection of
wisdom. But if a Bodhisattva, after he has done all that, makes no further
efforts about it in meditative seclusion, [346] then his merit is less than
that of one who also makes efforts about it in meditative seclusion and
who, taken hold of by perfect wisdom, causes that meditative seclusion to
be not devoid of perfect wisdom. The latter begets the greater merit.

4. IMMEASURABLE, EMPTY AND TALK

Subhuti: How can one say that he begets the greater merit since the Lord has described all accumulations as the result of false discrimination?

The Lord: In that case also the accumulation of merit on the part of a Bodhisattva who courses in perfect wisdom must be described as just empty, worthless, insignificant and unsubstantial. To the extent that a Bodhisattva goes on contemplating all dharmas in this manner, to that extent he becomes one who does not lack in perfect wisdom. And to the extent that he does not lack in perfect wisdom, to that extent he begets an immeasurable and incalculable heap of merit.

Subhuti: Is there any distinction or difference between immeasurable and incalculable?

The Lord: It is 'immeasurable' because in it all measurements must cease. It is 'incalculable' because it exhausts all efforts to count it.

Subhuti: Would there be a reason to assume that the skandhas are immeasurable?

The Lord: Yes, there would be. [347]

Subhuti: Of what is that term 'immeasurable' a synonym?

The Lord: Of Emptiness, of the Signless, of the Wishless.

Subhuti: Is it a synonym only of those and not of the other dharmas?

The Lord: Have I not described all dharmas as 'empty'?

Subhuti: As simply empty has the Tathagata described all dharmas.

The Lord: And, being empty, they are also inexhaustible. And what is emptiness, that is also immeasurableness. Therefore then, according to ultimate reality, no distinction or difference can be apprehended between these dharmas. As talk have they been described by the Tathagata. One just talks when one speaks of 'immeasurable,' or 'incalculable,' or 'inexhaustible,' or of 'empty,' or 'signless,' or 'wishless,' or 'the Uneffected,' or 'Non-production,' 'no-birth,' 'non-existence,' 'dispassion,' 'cessation,' 'Nirvana.' This exposition has by the Tathagata been described as the consummation of his demonstrations. [348]

Subhuti: It is wonderful to see the extent to which the Tathagata has demonstrated the true nature of all these dharmas, and yet one cannot properly talk about the true nature of all these dharmas, [in the sense of predicating distinctive attributes to separate real entities]. As I understand the meaning of the Tathagata's teaching, even all dharmas cannot be talked about, in any proper sense?

The Lord: So it is, for one cannot properly express the emptiness of all dharmas in words.

5. NO GROWTH OR DIMINUTION

Subhuti: Can something have growth, or diminution, if it is beyond all distinctive words?

The Lord: No, Subhuti.

Subhuti: But if there is no growth or diminution of an entity which is beyond all distinctive words, then there can be no growth or diminution of the six perfections. And how then could a Bodhisattva win full enlightenment through the force of these six perfections, if they do not grow, and how could he come close to full enlightenment, since, without fulfilling the perfections, he cannot come close to full enlightenment? [349]

The Lord: So it is, Subhuti. There is certainly no growth or diminution of a perfection-entity. A Bodhisattva who courses in perfect wisdom, who develops perfect wisdom, and who is skilled in means, does obviously not think that "this perfection of giving grows, this perfection of giving diminishes." But he knows that "this perfection of giving is a mere word." When he gives a gift he turns over to full enlightenment the mental activities, the productions of thought, the roots of good which are involved in that act of giving. But he turns them over in such a way that he respects the actual reality of full enlightenment. And he proceeds in the same way when he takes upon himself the moral obligations, when he perfects himself in patience, [350] when he exerts vigour, enters into the trances, courses in perfect wisdom, develops perfect wisdom.

Subhuti: What then is this supreme enlightenment? [351]

The Lord: It is Suchness. But Suchness neither grows nor diminishes. A Bodhisattva who repeatedly and often dwells in mental activities connected with that Suchness comes near to the supreme enlightenment, and he does not lose those mental activities again. It is certain that there can be no growth or diminution of an entity which is beyond all words, and that therefore neither the perfections, nor all dharmas, can grow or diminish. It is thus that, when he dwells in mental activities of this kind, a Bodhisattva becomes one who is near to perfect enlightenment.

Chapter XIX

THE GODDESS OF THE GANGES

1. CONDITIONED COPRODUCTION

Subhuti: If a Bodhisattva wins full enlightenment, is that due to the production of the first thought of enlightenment, or due to the last thought of enlightenment? Those two acts of thought can nowhere be synthesized [and therefore they cannot cooperate in producing a result]. How can an accumulation of a Bodhisattva's wholesome roots take place?

The Lord: What do you think, Subhuti, is the wick of a burning oil lamp burned up by the first incidence of the flame, or by the last incidence of the flame?

Subhuti: Not so, O Lord! It is not burned up by the first incidence of the flame, nor independent of it, and it is also not burned up by the incidence of the last flame, nor independent of it.

The Lord: Has then this wick been definitely burned up?

Subhuti: Yes, Lord.

The Lord: In the same way, it is neither through the first nor through the last thought of enlightenment, nor independent of them [353] that a Bodhisattva wins full enlightenment. He does not win it through these productions of thought, nor otherwise than through them. And yet he does win full enlightenment.

2. NO DEVELOPMENT

Subhuti: Deep is this conditioned coproduction!

The Lord: Subhuti, will that [first] thought which has stopped [after its momentary appearance] be again produced [at the time of the second thought]?

Subhuti: No Lord.

The Lord: That thought which has [in the past] been produced, is that by its very nature doomed to stop?

Subhuti: Yes it is, O Lord.

The Lord: If something is by its very nature doomed to stop, will that be destroyed?

Subhuti: No, Lord. [354]

The Lord: That thought which has [not yet] been produced, is that by its very nature doomed to stop?

Subhuti: No, Lord [because something which has not been produced cannot be stopped].

The Lord: But when it comes to the point when by its own nature it is doomed to stop, will it then be destroyed?

Subhuti: No, Lord.

The Lord: If the essential nature of that thought involves neither production nor stopping, will that then be stopped?

Subhuti: No, Lord.

The Lord: If a dharma is, by its essential original nature, stopped already in its own-being, will that dharma be stopped?

Subhuti: No, Lord.

The Lord: Will the true nature of dharmas be stopped?

Subhuti: No, Lord.

The Lord: Will the Bodhisattva stand firm in the same way in which Suchness stands firm?

Subhuti: Yes, he will. [355]

The Lord: WIll then that Suchness not be in danger of being changed away from its overtowering immobility?

Subhuti: No, Lord.

The Lord: Deep is Suchness.

Subhuti: It is deep, O Lord.

The Lord: Is thought in Suchness?

Subhuti: No, Lord.

The Lord: Is thought [identical with] Suchness?

Subhuti: No, Lord.

The Lord: Is thought other than Suchness?

Subhuti: No, Lord.

The Lord: Can you see a Suchness?

Subhuti: No, Lord.

The Lord: One who courses like unto Suchness, he courses in the deep?

Subhuti: He courses nowhere at all. For any ideas as to his own performance habitually neither proceed in him, nor befall him.

The Lord: Where does a Bodhisattva course when he courses in perfect wisdom? [356]

Subhuti: In ultimate reality.

The Lord: When coursing in ultimate reality does he course in a sign?

Subhuti: No, Lord.

The Lord: Is then the sign to him something which he has not undone by meditational development?

Subhuti: No, Lord.

The Lord: Does then the sign become to the Bodhisattva who courses in perfect wisdom, something which he has undone by his meditational development?

Subhuti: That Bodhisattva does not make any efforts, while he courses in the course of a Bodhisattva, to reach in this present birth the state in which all signs are forsaken. If he were to reach that state before all Buddha-dharmas are complete in him, he would automatically become a Disciple. The skill in means of a Bodhisattva consists in this, that he cognizes that sign, both its mark and cause, and yet he surrenders himself completely to the Signless [realm of dharma, in which no sign has ever arisen].

Sariputra: Does a Bodhisattva's perfect wisdom increase when in his dreams he develops the three doors to deliverance, i.e. the Empty, the Signless and the Wishless?

Subhuti: If it increases through development by day, then it also increases in one who dreams [about it]. For the Lord has said that dream and waking are indiscriminate, [essentially the same]. If [357] a Bodhisattva who has received perfect wisdom, day by day courses in perfect wisdom, then he also in his dreams remains quite close to perfect wisdom, and develops it even then in abundance.

Sariputra: If someone in his dreams does a deed, wholesome or unwholesome, will that be added on to the heap or collection of his karma?

Subhuti: In so far as the Lord has taught that ultimately all dharmas are like a dream, in so far [i.e. from the standpoint of ultimate reality] that deed will not be added to his heap or collection of karma. But on the other hand [from the standpoint of empirical reality], that deed will be added to the heap and collection of his karma if, after the man has woken up, he thinks the dream over, and consciously forms the notion that he wants to kill someone. How does he do that? During his dream he may have taken life, and after he has woken up, he thinks it over like this: "it is good that he was killed! It is right that he was killed! It was just that he was killed! It was I who killed him." Such thoughts are equivalent to the conscious notion that he wants to kill someone.

3. NO OBJECTIVE SUPPORTS AND NO OWN-BEING

Sariputra: If as a result of such conscious reflections the deed of that man is added on to his collection of karma, then the deed of the Buddha, the Lord, when he, thinking to himself, consciously forms the notion that he wants to enter extinction, [358] will also be added to the Buddha's heap and collection of karma?

Subhuti: No, indeed not, Sariputra. For the Tathagata is one who has forsaken all reflections and discriminations. Space on its own cannot raise a deed or a thought without the help of an objective support. A deed can arise only with an objective support, not without one. A thought can arise only with an objective support, not without one. Intellectual acts must refer to dharmas which are seen, heard, felt, or known. In respect of some objects intellectual acts take defilement upon themselves, in respect of others purification. Acts of will and deeds can therefore arise only with objective support, not without.

Sariputra: Since the Lord has described all objective supports as isolated [without an inherent relation to a subject], how can an act of will arise only with objective support, and not without?

Subhuti: An act of will is raised only with an objective support, and not without, in the sense that one treats an actually non-existent objective support as a sign, as an objective support. In fact also the act of will is isolated, and also the sign. And so are Karma-formations which are conditioned by ignorance, and so all the links of conditioned co-production, up to decay and death conditioned by birth. Even so objective supports are isolated. The act of will is isolated from the sign [which seems to cause it], and it arises only in reference to the conventional expressions current in the world.

Sariputra: If in his dreams a Bodhisattva gives a gift, and dedicates it to full enlightenment, can that gift be called effectively dedicated? [359]

Subhuti: We are face to face with Maitreya, the Bodhisattva, the great being. The Tathagata has predicted his supreme enlightenment. He is a direct eyewitness of this matter, he will dispose of this matter.

Sariputra: Subhuti the Elder, Maitreya, has said: "There is Maitreya, the Bodhisattva, the great being! He will dispose of this matter." Dispose of this matter, Venerable Ajita!

Maitreya: With reference to what the Venerable Subhuti has said, what corresponds to those words "Maitreya" and "he will dispose of this matter"? Will my form reply? Or my feeling, perception, impulses, or consciousness? Will my outward appearance reply, or my shape? Or will the emptiness of form reply, or the emptiness of feeling, perception, impulses, or consciousness? Obviously the emptiness of form, etc., does not have the capacity to reply. [360] Nor do I see any dharma which could reply, or which should reply, or by which one could reply, or any dharma which has been predicted to the supreme enlightenment.

Sariputra: Maitreya, have you then perhaps really witnessed those dharmas in the way in which you teach?

Maitreya: I have not. Even I do not know those dharmas, do not apprehend, do not see them, in the way in which my words express, and my thoughts reflect on them. But certainly the body could not touch them, speech could not express them, mind could not consider them. That is the own-being of all dharmas, because they are without any own-being.

Sariputra thought: Deeply wise, indeed, is this Bodhisattva Maitreya the great being. How he expounds the perfection of wisdom in which he has coursed for such a long time!

The Lord: Why did that thought occur to you? Can you, Sariputra, see that dharma endowed with which you have been made into an Arhat?

Sariputra: No, Lord. [361]

The Lord: In the same way it does not occur to a Bodhisattva who courses in perfect wisdom, that "this dharma has been predestined to full enlightenment, that dharma will be predestined, that dharma is being predestined, that dharma will know full enlightenment." When he courses in such a way, then he courses in perfect wisdom.

4. FIVE PLACES WHICH INSPIRE FEAR

While he courses thus, he is not afraid. He is impregnated with the strength that he has gained [in his coursings in the baseless], and that enables him to persist in his endeavours and to think: "It is not the case that I shall not be fully enlightened." If he courses thus, then he courses in perfect wisdom. Moreover a Bodhisattva is not afraid when he gets into a wilderness infested with wild beasts. For it is his duty to renounce everything for the sake of all beings. Therefore he should react with the thought: "If these wild beasts should devour me, then just that will be my gift to them. The perfection of giving will become more perfect in me, and I will come nearer to full enlightenment. And after I have won full enlightenment I will take steps so that in my Buddha-field there will be no animals at all, that one will have even no conception of them, but that all beings in it will live on heavenly food." Moreover, a Bodhisattva should not be afraid if he finds himself in a wilderness infested by robbers. For Bodhisattvas take pleasure in the wholesome practice of renouncing all their belongings. A Bodhisattva must cast away even his body, and he must renounce all that is necessary to life. He should react to the danger with the thought [362]: "If those beings take away from me everything that is necessary to life, then let that be my gift to them. If someone should rob me of my life, I should feel no ill will, anger or fury on account of that. Even against them I should take no offensive action, either by body, voice, or mind. This will be an occasion to bring the perfections of giving, morality and patience to greater perfection, and I will get nearer to full enlightenment. After I have won full enlightenment, I will act and behave in such a manner that in my Buddha-field wildernesses infested with robbers will in no way whatsoever either be, or even be conceivable. And my exertions to bring about perfect purity in that Buddha-field will be so great that in it neither these nor other faults will exist, or even be conceivable." Furthermore, in a waterless waste also a Bodhisattva should not be afraid. For his character is such that he is not alarmed or terrified. He should resolve that his own training might result in removing all thirst from all beings. He should not tremble when he thinks that, if he dies from thirst, he will be reborn as a Preta. On the contrary, he should direct a thought of great compassion unto all beings, and think [363]: "Alas, certainly those beings must be of small merit if in their world such deserts are conceivable. After I have won enlightenment, I will see to it that in my Buddha-field no such deserts exist, or are even conceivable. And I will bestow on all beings so much merit that they shall have the most excellent water. Thus will I exert firm vigour on behalf of all beings, so that on that occasion also the perfection of vigour shall become more perfect in me." Furthermore, in a foodless waste also a Bodhisattva should not be afraid. He should arm himself with the thought: "I will exert firm vigour, I will purify my own Buddha-field in such a way that, after I have won enlightenment, in that Buddha-field there will be no foodless wastes, and none will be even conceivable. The beings in that field shall be entirely happy, filled with happiness, possessed of all happiness. And thus will I act that all the intentions and plans of those beings shall be realised. Just as with the Gods of the Thirty-three an idea in their minds is sufficient to produce anything they may desire, so I will exert firm vigour so that those beings can realize and produce everything by merely thinking of it in their minds. In order that their legitimate intentions should be fulfilled, in order that all beings, everywhere and anywhere, should not go short of the requirements of life, [364] I will so struggle for perfect purity in my own thought, for the sake of all beings, that on that occasion also the perfection of concentration will become more perfect in me. Furthermore, a Bodhisattva will not be afraid in a district infested by epidemics. But he should consider, reflect and deliberate that 'there is no dharma here which sickness could oppress, nor is that which is called 'sickness' a dharma." In that manner he should contemplate emptiness, and he should not be afraid. But he should not think that "it will be an excessively long time before I shall win full enlightenment," and he should not tremble at such a thought. For that thought-moment [which in reality has not been produced] is the extreme limit of something which has no beginning; in other words, it is the absence of a limit. A Bodhisattva should therefore avoid dwelling in his mind on difficulties, and he should think that "great and long is this limit which has no beginning, for it is connected with one single thought-moment, in other words, it is the absence of a limit." This will prevent a Bodhisattva from trembling at the thought that it will be long before he will win full enlightenment. Moreover, Subhuti, if these and other fears and terrors, be they seen, heard, felt or known, do not cause a Bodhisattva to tremble, then one should know that "this son or daughter of good family is capable of knowing full enlightenment." A Bodhisattva should therefore put on the great armour of the thought [365]: "Thus will I act, thus will I exert firm vigour that, after I have won full enlightenment, all beings in my Buddha-field shall not suffer from sickness, and shall not even know what it is. I will act in such a way that I shall preach what the Tathagatas have taught, and that I will do what I have preached. And I will so master the perfection of wisdom, for the sake of all beings, that on that occasion also the perfection of wisdom will in me come to fulfillment."

5. PREDICTION OF THE GODDESS OF THE GANGES

Thereupon a certain *woman* came to that assembly, and sat down in it. She rose from her seat, put her upper robe over one shoulder, saluted the Lord with folded hands, and said: 'I, O Lord, when placed in those positions, will not be afraid, and, without fear, I shall demonstrate dharma to all beings.'

Thereupon the Lord at that time smiled a golden smile. Its lustre irradiated endless and boundless world systems, it rose up to the Brahma-world, returned from there, circulated three times round the Lord, and disappeared again in the head of the Lord. When she saw that smile, that woman seized golden flowers, and scattered them over the Lord. Without being fixed anywhere, they remained suspended in the air. [366]

Ananda: What is the reason, O Lord, of this smile? It is not without reason that the Tathagatas manifest a smile.

The Lord: This Goddess of the Ganges, Ananda, will, in a future period, become a Tathagata, "Golden Flower" by name, —an Arhat, fully Enlightened, proficient in knowledge and conduct, Well-Gone, a knower of the world, unsurpassed, a tamer of men to be tamed, a teacher of Gods and men, a Buddha, a Lord. In the starlike aeon he will appear in the world and know full enlightenment. When she has deceased here she will cease to be a woman, she will become a man. He will be reborn in Abhirati, the Buddha-field of the Tathagata Akshobhya, in whose presence he will lead the holy life. After his decease there he will pass from Buddha-field to Buddha-field, never deprived of the sight of the Tathagata. He will go on passing from Buddha-field to Buddha-field, from here to there, always choosing those in which he is not without the Buddhas, the Lords. A universal monarch can pass from palace to palace, and the soles of his feet never, during his entire life, tread upon the surface of the earth, [367] and he dies without ever, up to the time of his death, having trodden with his feet on the ground. Just so the Ganges Goddess will pass from Buddha-field to Buddha-field, and she will never at any time be deprived of the Buddhas and Lords, until the time of her full enlightenment.

Ananda thought: Those Bodhisattvas who will be with the Tathagata Akshobhya must actually be considered as the congregation of the Tathagata.

The Lord read Ananda's thoughts, and said: So it is, Ananda. Those Bodhisattvas who lead the holy life in the Buddha-field of Akshobhya, the Tathagata, should be known as having emerged from the mud, as having approached to the accomplishment of enlightenment. In addition, Ananda, the community of the disciples of the Tathagata "Golden Flower" will not be bound by any measure. For his disciples will be so many that there will be no measure to them. They will, on the contrary, have to be styled "immeasurable, incalculable." In addition, Ananda, at that time, on that occasion there will be in that Buddha-field no wildernesses infested with wild beasts, or with robbers, and no waterless wastes, and no districts infested by epidemics, and no foodless wastes. [368] All these, and all other disagreeable places will in that Buddha-field, in no way whatsoever either be, or be conceived. It is quite certain that, after the Tathagata "Golden Flower" has known full enlightenment, all these kinds of places which inspire fear and terror will then no longer exist, or be even conceivable.

Ananda: Who was the Tathagata in whose presence this Goddess of the Ganges has planted the wholesome root of the first thought of enlightenment, and turned it over to supreme enlightenment?

The Lord: That was under the Tathagata Dipankara. And she actually scattered golden flowers over the Tathagata when she requested of him [the prediction to] the supreme enlightenment. It was when I strewed the five lotus flowers over Dipankara, the Tathagata, and I acquired the patient acceptance of dharmas which fail to be produced, and then Dipankara predicted my future enlightenment with the words: "You, young man, will in a future period become a Tathagata, Shakyamuni by name!" Thereupon, when she had heard my prediction, that Goddess produced a thought to the effect that [369]: "Oh, certainly, like that young man I also would like to be predicted to full enlightenment!" And in that way,

Ananda, in the presence of the Tathagata Dipankara, that Goddess planted the wholesome root of the first thought of enlightenment, [and turned it over to] full enlightenment.

Ananda: Certainly, as one who has made the necessary preparations, as one who has made the grade has this Goddess of the Ganges been predicted to full enlightenment.

The Lord: So it is, Ananda, as you say.

Chapter XX

DISCUSSION OF SKILL IN MEANS

1. EMPTINESS AND REALITY-LIMIT

Subhuti: How should a Bodhisattva, who courses in perfect wisdom, achieve the complete conquest of emptiness, or how should he enter into the concentration on emptiness?

The Lord: He should contemplate form, etc., as empty. But he should contemplate that with an undisturbed series of thoughts in such a way that, when he contemplates the fact that "form, etc., is empty," he does not regard that true nature of dharmas [i.e. emptiness] as something which, as a result of its own true nature [i.e. emptiness] is a real entity. But when he does not regard that true nature of dharmas as a real thing, then he cannot realise the reality-limit.

Subhuti: With reference to the Lord having said that "a Bodhisattva should not realise emptiness," how does a Bodhisattva who has stood [firmly in the repeated practice of] this concentration [on emptiness] not realize emptiness?

The Lord: It is because a Bodhisattva contemplates that emptiness which is possessed of the best of all modes [i.e. of the six perfections]. He does, however, not contemplate that "I shall realize," or "I should realize," but he contemplates that "this is the time for complete conquest, and not for realization." [371] Without losing himself in the concentration, he ties his thought to an objective support [for his compassion] and he determines that he will take hold of perfect wisdom [which is essentially skill in means], and that he will not realize [emptiness, because its realization is not the final goal]. Meanwhile, however, the Bodhisattva does not lose the dharmas which act as the wings to enlightenment. He does not effect the extinction of the outflows [which would prevent renewed rebirths], but over that also he achieves complete conquest. At the time when a Bodhisattva dwells in the concentration on emptiness—which is one of the doors to deliverance—he should also dwell in the concentration on the Signless, but without realizing the Signless. For, endowed with the dharma of the wholesome root which has thus come about, he contemplates that "this is the time for maturing beings, and not for realization." Taken hold of by perfect wisdom he does not realize the reality limit.

2. THREE SIMILES

The Lord: Suppose, Subhuti, that there were a most excellent hero, very vigorous, of high social position, handsome, attractive and most fair to behold, of many virtues, in possession of all the finest virtues, of those virtues which spring from the very height of sovereignty, morality, learning, renunciation and so on. He is judicious, able to express himself, to formulate his views clearly, to substantiate his claims; one who always knows the suitable time, place and situation for everything. In archery he has gone as far as one can go, he is successful in warding off all manner of attack, most skilled in all arts, and foremost, through his fine achievements, in all crafts. He has a good memory, is intelligent, clever, steady and prudent, versed in all the treatises, has many friends, is wealthy, strong of body, with large limbs, with all his faculties complete, [372] generous to all, dear and pleasant to many. Any work he might undertake he manages to complete, he speaks methodically, shares his great riches with the many, honours what should be honoured, reveres what should be revered, worships what should be worshipped. Would such a person, Subhuti, feel ever increasing joy and zest?

Subhuti: He would, O Lord.

The Lord: Now suppose, further, that this person, so greatly accomplished, should have taken his family with him on a journey, his mother and father, his sons and daughters. By some circumstances, they find themselves in a great, wild forest. The foolish ones among them would feel fright, terror and hair-raising fear. He, however, would fearlessly say to his family: "Do not be afraid! I shall soon take you safely and securely out of this terrible and frightening forest. I shall soon set you free!" If then more and more hostile and inimical forces should rise up against him in that forest, would this heroic man decide to abandon his family, and to take himself alone out of that terrible and frightening forest—he who is not one to draw back, who is endowed with all the force of firmness and vigour, who is wise, exceedingly tender and compassionate, courageous and a master of many resources? [373]

Subhuti: No, O Lord. For that person, who does not abandon his family, has at his disposal powerful resources, both within and without. On his side forces will arise in that wild forest which are quite a match for the hostile and inimical forces, and they will stand up for him and protect him. Those enemies and adversaries of his, who look for a weak spot, who seek for a weak spot, will not gain any hold over him. He is competent to deal with the situation, and is able, unhurt and uninjured, soon to take out of that forest both his family and himself, and securely and safely they will reach a village, city or market-town.

The Lord: Just so, Subhuti, is it with a Bodhisattva who is full of pity and concerned with the welfare of all beings, who dwells in friendliness, compassion, sympathetic joy and impartiality, who has been taken hold of by skill in means and perfect wisdom, who has correctly turned over his wholesome roots, employing the kind of transformation which has the Buddha's sanction. Although he enters into the concentrations which are the doors to deliverance, i.e. the concentrations on emptiness, the signless and the wishless, —he nevertheless just does not realise the reality-limit, i.e. neither on the level of a Disciple, nor on that of a Pratyekabuddha. For he has at his disposal very strong and powerful helpers, in perfect wisdom and skill in means. Since he has not abandoned all beings, he is thus able to win full enlightenment, safely and securely. At the time when a Bodhisattva has made all beings into an objective support for his thought of friendliness, and with the highest friendliness ties himself to them, at that time he rises above the factiousness of the defilements and of Mara, he rises above the level of Disciple and Pratyekabuddha, [374] and he abides in that concentration [on friendliness]. But he is not one who has attained the extinction of the outflows, he achieves a complete conquest of emptiness, which [in his case] is endowed with the highest perfections. At the time when a Bodhisattva dwells in the concentration on emptiness, which is one door to freedom, at that time he does not dwell in the concentration on the Signless, nor does he realise the concentration on the Signless. It is just like a bird who on its wings courses in the air. It neither falls onto the ground, nor does it stand anywhere on any support. It dwells in space, just in the air, without being either supported or settled therein. Just so a Bodhisattva dwells in the dwelling of emptiness, achieves complete conquest over emptiness. Just so he dwells in the dwelling of the Signless and Wishless, and achieves complete conquest over the Signless and Wishless. But he does not fall into emptiness, or into the Signless, or into the Wishless, with his Buddha-dharmas remaining incomplete. It is as with a master of archery, strong, well trained, perfectly trained in archery. He first would shoot one arrow upwards. He would then send after that another arrow which would check the fall of the first. By a regular succession of arrows he would not permit that first arrow to fall to the ground, and that arrow would be kept up in the air until he should decide that it should fall to the ground. In the same way a Bodhisattva who courses in perfect wisdom and who is upheld by skill in means, does not realise that farthest reality-limit until his wholesome roots are matured, well matured in full enlightenment. Only when his wholesome roots are matured, well matured in full enlightenment, [375] only then does he realise that farthest reality-limit. A Bodhisattva who courses in perfect wisdom, who develops perfect wisdom, should therefore contemplate and meditate on the deep true nature of those dharmas, but he should not realise it.

3. DOORS TO DELIVERANCE AND VOWS ABOUT BEINGS

Subhuti: A doer of what is hard is the Bodhisattva, a doer of what is most hard, if he courses and dwells in emptiness, if he enters into the concentration on emptiness, and yet does not realise the reality-limit! Exceedingly wonderful is this, O Well-Gone!

The Lord: So it is, Subhuti. For the Bodhisattva has not abandoned all beings. He has made the special vows to set free all those beings. If the mind of a Bodhisattva forms the aspiration not to abandon all beings but to set them free, and if in addition he aspires for the concentration on emptiness, the Signless, the Wishless, i.e. for the three doors to deliverance, then that Bodhisattva should be known as one who is endowed with skill in means, and he will not realise the reality-limit midway, before his Buddha-dharmas have become complete. For it is this skill in means which protects him. His thought of enlightenment [376] consists in just that fact that he does not want to leave all beings behind. When he is thus endowed with the thought of enlightenment and with skill in means, then he does not midway realise the reality-limit. Moreover, while a Bodhisattva either actually contemplates those deep stations, i.e. the three doors to deliverance, or becomes desirous of contemplating them, he should in his mind form the following aspiration: "For a long time those beings, because they have the notion of existence, course in the apprehension of a basis. After I have won full enlightenment I shall demonstrate dharma to those beings so that they may forsake the erroneous views about a basis." As a free agent he then enters into the concentrations on emptiness, on the Signless, on the Wishless. A Bodhisattva who is thus endowed with this thought of enlightenment and with skill in means does not midway realise the reality-limit. On the contrary, he does not lose his concentration on friendliness, compassion, sympathetic joy and impartiality. For, upheld by skill in means, he increases his pure dharmas more and more. His faith, etc., becomes keener and keener, and he acquires the powers, the limbs of enlightenment, and the path. [377] Moreover, a Bodhisattva reflects that "for a long time those beings, because they perceive dharmas, course in the apprehension of a basis," and he develops this aspiration as he did the former one, entering the concentration on emptiness. Furthermore, he reflects that by perceiving a sign, those beings have, for a long time, coursed in the sign, and he deals with this aspiration as before, entering the concentration on the

Signless. Furthermore, a Bodhisattva reflects: "For a long time have these beings been perverted by the perceptions of permanence, of happiness, of the self, of loveliness. I will act in such a way that, after my full enlightenment, I shall demonstrate dharma in order that they may forsake the perverted views of the perception of permanence, of happiness, of the self, of loveliness, and in order that they may learn that 'impermanent is all this, not permanent; ill is all this, not happiness; without self is all this, not with a self; repulsive is all this, not lovely.' " Endowed with this thought of enlightenment, [378] and with the previously described skill in means, taken hold of by perfect wisdom, he does not realize the reality-limit midway, before all his Buddha-dharmas are complete. He dwells thus, and he has entered on the concentration on the Wishless, but he does not lose his concentration on friendliness, etc. For, upheld by skill in means, he increases more and more his pure dharmas. His faith, etc., becomes keener and keener, and he acquires the powers, the limbs of enlightenment, and the path. If a Bodhisattva raises the following thought: "These beings also have for a long time been in the habit of coursing in the apprehension of a basis, and even just now they do so. They have for a long time been in the habit of coursing in the apprehension of a basis, and even just now they do so. They have for a long time been in the habit of coursing in the perception of signs, in perverted views, in perceptions of material objects, in perceptions of unreal objects, in wrong views, and even now they continue to do so. Thus will I act that these faults in each and every way may cease to be in them, that they will be inconceivable in them"; if a Bodhisattva brings all beings to mind in such a way, if he is endowed with this recollection of all beings, with this production of thought, and with skill in means, if he is taken hold of by perfect wisdom, and if, endowed with all these qualities, he thus contemplates the true nature of those deep dharmas— through their emptiness, or Signlessness, or Wishlessness, or through their being uneffected, unproduced, without birth, [379] without any positivity—then it is quite impossible that such a Bodhisattva, who is endowed with such a cognition, could either fall into the Uneffected, or become intimate with what belongs to the triple world. That cannot possibly be.

4. IRREVERSIBILITY

Suppose that a Bodhisattva is asked by another Bodhisattva who wants to win full enlightenment: "Over which dharmas should one achieve complete conquest? What kind of aspiration should one form in one's mind, aspirations which enable a Bodhisattva not to realise emptiness, or the Signless, or the Wishless, or the Uneffected, or non-production, or non-positivity, but to go on developing the perfection of wisdom?" If the Bodhisattva answers that just emptiness should be attended to, just the Signless, just the Wishless, just the Uneffected, just non-production, just no-birth, just non-positivity, and if he should not make manifest this production of the thought of the non-abandonment of all beings, or if he should not include skill in means in his answer, then one must know that this Bodhisattva has not in irreversibility been predicted to full enlightenment by the Tathagatas of the past. For he does not indicate this special dharma of an irreversible Bodhisattva [i.e. the non-abandonment of all beings], does not make much of it, does not make it manifest, does not wisely know it, does not include it in his answer, and he does not induce others to enter into that stage [of skill in means] which is the true stage of an irreversible Bodhisattva. [380]

Subhuti: And how can a Bodhisattva, in regard to this question, be regarded as irreversible?

The Lord: He should be known as an irreversible Bodhisattva if, whether he has heard this perfection of wisdom or not, he hits upon the correct answer.

Subhuti: There are many who course towards enlightenment, but a few only could give the correct answer.

The Lord: Because few only are the Bodhisattvas who have been predicted to the irreversible stage on which this cognition becomes possible. But those who have been predestined for it, they will give the correct answer. One can be sure that they have planted splendid wholesome roots in the past, and the whole world, with its Gods, men and Asuras, cannot overwhelm them.

5. DREAM EXPERIENCES AND THE MARK OF IRREVERSIBILITY

Furthermore, if a Bodhisattva even in his dreams beholds that "all dharmas are like a dream," but does not realize [that experience, regarding it as final] then also that should be known as the irreversible mark of an irreversible Bodhisattva. It is another mark if, even in his dreams, neither the level of Disciple or Pratyekabuddha, nor anything that belongs to the triple world, becomes an object of his longing, or appears advantageous to him. It is another mark if, even in his dreams, he sees himself as a Tathagata, —in the middle of an assembly of many hundreds of thousands of niyutas of kotis of persons, [381] seated in a circular hall with a peaked roof, surrounded by a community of monks, revered by the community of Bodhisattvas, demonstrating dharma. It is another mark, if, even in his dreams, he rises into the air and demonstrates dharma to beings, if he perceives the halo round the Buddha, if he conjures up monks who go into the different directions to fulfil the functions of Buddhas in other world systems and demonstrate dharma there. Even when he dreams he has such perceptions. It is another mark if, when he dreams, he remains unafraid when a village, town, city, or kingdom is sacked; or when he sees a huge conflagration spreading; or when he sees wild beasts or other offensive animals; or when his head is about to be cut off, or when he is subjected to other great fears and terrors, and when he sees the fears and terrors to which other beings are subjected. In no case do fear and terror arise in him, and he remains unafraid. And immediately after he has woken up from his dream, he reflects that "like a dream is all this which belongs to the triple world. And in that sense should I demonstrate dharmas after I have won enlightenment, as one who demonstrates dharma correctly." It is again another mark of irreversibility if a Bodhisattva, on seeing in his dreams [382] the beings that are in the hells, reflects that "Thus will I act that in my Buddha-field, after I have won full enlightenment, there shall be no states of woe at all!" This also should be known as a mark which shows that an irreversible Bodhisattva has become so pure that he can never again be reborn [against his will] in the states of woe. And how could one know that there would be no states of woe in the Buddha-field of that Bodhisattva? If a Bodhisattva, on seeing in his dream the beings reborn in the hells, as animals, or as Pretas, sets up mindfulness and determines to bring about a Buddha-field without such states of woe, then that should be known as the mark which shows that he has become so pure that he can never again be reborn in the states of woe. Furthermore, a Bodhisattva may dream [a prophetic dream] to the effect that a town or village is on fire. After he has woken up, he considers thus: "I have the attributes, tokens and signs which I have seen, in my dream, as the attributes, tokens and signs by which an irreversible Bodhisattva should be borne in mind. Because of this Truth, because of my utterance of this Truth, let this town fire or village fire, which is taking place there, be appeased, cooled, extinguished." If that fire is then extinguished, one should know [383] that that Bodhisattva has been predicted to full enlightenment by the Tathagatas in the past; if it is not extinguished, one should know that he has not been so predicted. If again, Subhuti, instead of being appeased, this conflagration passes beyond all bounds and spreads from house to house, from road to road, then one should know that this Bodhisattva has in the past collected karma consisting in the refusal of dharma, conducive to weakness in wisdom. From that results the karma of his which led him to this experience in his present life [i.e. to his distress at being unable to control that fire], which is just a result of karma left over from his refusal of dharma [in the past]. For, as you know, a Bodhisattva's past lives condition the [absence or presence of the] mark of irreversibility later on. A Bodhisattva who succeeds in controlling the fire should, on the other hand, be borne in mind as irreversible from full enlightenment.

6. IRREVERSIBILITY AND THE MAGICAL POWER OF VERACITY

And once more, Subhuti, I will demonstrate the attributes, tokens and signs by which an irreversible Bodhisattva should be borne in mind. Listen well and attentively. I will teach you.

Subhuti: So be it, O Lord.

The Lord: If a person, —man or woman, boy or girl, —were seized or possessed by a ghost, then a Bodhisattva, who has come across him, should perform the Act of Truth, and say: "If it is true that I have been predicted to full enlightenment by the Tathagatas of the past, [384] and if it is true that my intention to win full enlightenment is perfectly pure, —to the extent that I want to win full enlightenment and that my attention to it is perfectly pure, to that extent I have left behind the thoughts of Disciples and Pratyekabuddhas. It is my duty to win full enlightenment. Not shall I not win full enlightenment! But I shall win just full enlightenment! There is nothing that the Buddhas and Lords who reside in countless world systems have not cognized, seen, felt and fully known. Those Buddhas and Lords know my earnest intention that also I want to win full enlightenment. —Because this is the truth, because this is an utterance of the Truth, may he depart who seized and possessed that person with his ghostly seizure!" If, as a result of these words of the Bodhisattva that ghost does not depart, one should know that the Bodhisattva has not had his prediction; but if he departs one should know that he has had his prediction to full enlightenment.

Chapter XXI

MARA'S DEEDS

1. PRIDE AND THE MAGICAL POWER OF VERACITY

The Bodhisattva, as we saw, has said: "I have been predicted to full enlightenment by the Tathagatas of the past. Because that is the Truth, because of my utterance of that Truth, let that ghost depart!" Mara in his turn tries, at that time, to induce the ghost to depart. And his efforts will be particularly strong and energetic when he has to deal with a Bodhisattva who has but recently set out in the vehicle. It will then be the magical power of Mara which has driven the ghost away. But the Bodhisattva thinks that it was his might which drove him away, and he does not know that it was Mara's might. He will then slacken in his efforts. But as a result of his [apparent] victory over the ghost he thinks that he has had his prediction in the past, and he despises other Bodhisattvas, sneers at them, ironically compliments, contemns and deprecates them. His pride will go on increasing, will become quite firm and rigid. That pride, arrogance, hauteur, false pride, conceit keep him away from all-knowledge, from the supreme cognition of a Buddha, from the cognition of the Self-Existent, [386], from the cognition of the all-knowing, from supreme enlightenment. When he meets with Bodhisattvas who could be his good friends, —virtuous in character, resolutely intent on the sublime, earnestly intent, skilled in means, endowed with the irreversible dharma, —in his conceit he despises them, does not tend, love and honour them. So he will tighten the bond of Mara still further. One would expect him to belong to one of the two levels, either that of a Disciple, or that of a Pratyekabuddha. In this way, in connection with the magical power of the enunciation of a Truth, Mara the Evil One may cause an obstacle to full enlightenment in a Bodhisattva who has but recently set out in the vehicle, who has little faith, has learned little, lacks in the good friend, is not upheld by perfect wisdom, and lacks in skill in means. This also should be known as Mara's deed to a Bodhisattva.

2. PRIDE IN CONNECTION WITH THE ANNUNCIATION OF THE NAME

Moreover, Subhuti, the deeds of Mara will operate also in connection with the annunciation of a Bodhisattva's name. And how? Mara uses even the annunciation of the name, and of the other details connected with it, to tempt a Bodhisattva. He comes to him in all kinds of disguises, and says to him: "You have had your prediction from the Tathagatas in the past. The proof is that this is the name you will have as a Buddha, and these are the names of your mother, your father, your brother, your sister, your friends, maternal relatives, kinsmen and relations." He proclaims these names backwards through seven generations. He tells you that you were born in this region, this country, this village, town or marketplace. [387] If you have any particular quality, he will tell you that you have had that same quality also in the past. Whether the Bodhisattva be dull by nature, or keen in his faculties, Mara will tell him that he was the same in the past. Or take other qualities which he has in this present life: He is, say, a forest dweller, or one who begs for his food from door to door without accepting invitations, or he wears clothes made of rags taken from a dust heap, or he never eats any food after midday or he eats his meal in one sitting, or he sleeps at night wherever he may happen to be, or he possesses no more than three robes, or he lives in and frequents cemeteries, or he dwells at the foot of a tree, or even in his sleep he remains in a sitting posture, or he lives in an open, unsheltered place, or he wears a garment made of felt, or he has few wishes, is easily contented, detached, frugal, soft in speech, or a man of few words, —in each case Mara will announce to him that also in the past he has been endowed with this same quality, and that for certain the Tathagatas of the past must have predicted him to full enlightenment and to the stage of an irreversible Bodhisattva, for he now has the just mentioned qualities of an austere ascetic, and he must therefore in all certainty also have been endowed with them in the past. It may be that then a Bodhisattva feels conceit when he thinks of the annunciation of his names and circumstances in the past, and of his present austere penances as a rigid ascetic. He may actually think that he has had his prediction in the past because now he has those qualities of a rigid ascetic. And Mara will confirm him in this view. [388] In the guise of a monk, or nun, or lay brother, or lay sister, or Brahmin, or householder, or mother, father, brother, sister, friend or relative Mara will come to the Bodhisattva and tell him that he has had his prediction in the past to full enlightenment and to the irreversible stage of a Bodhisattva for the simple reason that now he has those qualities of a rigid ascetic, which, according to him, are the qualities of an irreversible Bodhisattva. But the Bodhisattva has not got the attributes, tokens and signs of an irreversible Bodhisattva which I have described. He is surely a man beset by Mara, unlike those other Bodhisattvas [who could be his good friends]. For he has not got the attributes, tokens and signs which are actually characteristic of an irreversible Bodhisattva. And as a result of the annunciation of the circumstances of his past he feels conceit. In his conceit, overcome by great and rigid conceit, defeated by the magical power of Mara, he despises his fellow-Bodhisattvas, sneers at them and deprecates them. One should recognize this as a deed of Mara, who makes use of the annunciation of the past circumstances of a Bodhisattva. [389] Furthermore, Subhuti, Mara also operates in connection with the prediction of the name which a Bodhisattva will have as a Buddha. In the guise of a monk he comes to a Bodhisattva and predicts to him that "this will be your name when you have won full enlightenment." And Mara will predict that name which the Bodhisattva had already guessed for himself when he had pondered over the name he would bear after his full enlightenment. If the Bodhisattva is weak in wisdom, and without skill in means, he reflects that the name which that monk has mentioned is the same which he had guessed himself. He compares the name which he had thought out by himself with the name proclaimed by that monk, who is either beset by Mara, or was conjured up by Mara or his host, he finds that the two agree, and he concludes that he has in the past been predicted to full enlightenment by the Tathagatas by name. But he has not got the attributes, tokens and signs of an irreversible Bodhisattva which I have described. Since he lacks in them, he feels conceit as a result of that prediction of his name. In his conceit [390] he despises his fellow-Bodhisattvas, and thinks that, while he has had his prediction, they have not had it. That pride, arrogance and conceit which makes him despise those other Bodhisattvas keep him far away from all-knowledge and the cognition of a Buddha. Not upheld by perfect wisdom, lacking in skill in means and the good friend, taken hold of by the bad friend, he would, we must expect, belong to one of the two levels, that of a Disciple, or that of a Pratyekabuddha. But even if, after he has spent a long time, a good long time in erring about and in wandering about [in birth-and-death], he would again become one who wants to know full enlightenment by resorting to just this perfection of wisdom; and if he were to go to the good friends and regularly approach them; and if, in his newfound outlook on life he would, first of all, censure his former ideas, vomit them up, abhor them, throw them back, see their error,—even then it will be hard for him to get to the Buddha-level. So serious is the offence of conceitedness. Among the monks who belong to the vehicle or level of the Disciples four unforgivable offences are so serious that, if someone has been guilty of one of them, he ceases to be a monk, a Shramana, a son of the Shakya. More serious than those four unforgivable offences is this production of a proud thought, when, on the occasion of the prediction of his name, a Bodhisattva has despised other Bodhisattvas, and produced a thought which is very unwholesome, which is more serious than the four unforgivable offences. Not only that, but it is more serious even than the five deadly sins, this production of a thought connected with pride, [391] produced on the occasion when a Bodhisattva's future name [as a Buddha] is announced. That thought is more serious even than the five deadly sins. In this way, even through the annunciation of a Bodhisattva's name very subtle deeds of Mara may arise. They should be recognized for what they are, and avoided, both by the Bodhisattva himself, and by others.

3. FAULTS IN CONNECTION WITH DETACHMENT

Furthermore, Mara the Evil One may come to the Bodhisattva and exhort and inform him in connection with the quality of detachment that the Tathagata has praised detachment, and that that means that one should dwell in the remote forest, in a jungle, in mountain clefts, burial grounds, or on heaps of straw, etc. But that is not what I teach as the detachment of a Bodhisattva, that he should live in a forest, remote, lonely and isolated, or in jungle, mountain clefts, burial grounds, on heaps of straw, etc.

Subhuti: If that is not the detachment of the Bodhisattva, what then is it?

The Lord: A Bodhisattva dwells detached when he becomes detached from the mental activities associated with the Disciples and Pratyekabuddhas [392]. For, if he is taken hold of by perfection of wisdom and skill in means, and if he dwells in the dwelling of friendliness and of great compassion towards all beings, then he dwells detached even when he dwells in the neighborhood of a village. It is I who have ordained this detachment from the mental activities associated with the Disciples and Pratyekabuddhas. A Bodhisattva dwells detached if he passes day and night dwelling in this detachment. If a Bodhisattva dwells in this dwelling while he lives in remote dwelling places, in the remote forest, in the jungle, in mountain clefts or burial grounds, then he dwells detached. But as to the detachment recommended by Mara, the Evil One, —i.e. the dwelling in remote forests, jungles, mountain clefts and burial grounds, —if that detachment is actually contaminated by the mental activities associated with Disciples and Pratyekabuddhas, then, as he does not practise the perfection of wisdom, he does not fulfil the conditions necessary to win all-knowledge. He dwells in a contaminated dwelling, in a mental activity which is not quite pure, and in consequence his deeds of body, voice and mind cannot be quite pure. In consequence of that he despises other Bodhisattvas who dwell in villages, but who are uncontaminated by mental activities associated with Disciples and Pratyekabuddhas, who dwell in the dwelling of wisdom with its many devices, and with its great compassion. Since his deeds of body, voice and mind are not quite pure, he is just a dweller in contamination, not a dweller in detachment, although he may dwell in the remote forest. At first he despises those who live in the neighborhood of a village, though they dwell in the dwelling of wisdom, with its devices and great compassion, though they are habitually quite pure in what they do with their body, voice or mind, though they are detached from mental activities associated with Disciples and Pratyekabuddhas, uncontaminated by them [393]; after that he finds that he cannot gain the Trances, Concentrations, Attainments, Emancipations and Superknowledges, and that they do not reach their fulfilment in him. The reason is that he is without skill in means. Even though a Bodhisattva may dwell in deserted forests hundreds of miles wide, with no other company than beasts of prey, antelopes, flocks of birds, uninfested even by the smaller wild animals, by Yakshas and Rakshasas, and untroubled by the fear of robbers, and even though he may settle there for one year, or for one hundred years, or even for hundreds of thousands of niyutas of kotis of years, or for more than that; —if he does not know the detachment which I have explained, and through which a Bodhisattva dwells as one who has set out with earnest intention, who has achieved earnest intention; then even one completely devoted to life in the remote forest fails to gladden my heart, if he does not know this [detachment], if he is without skill in means, if he leans on that detachment of his, clings to it, is bent on it, indulges in it. For the detachment of a Bodhisattva which I have described does not appear in his detachment. But from a place high up in the air Mara will say to the dweller in the remote forest that he does well, that his detachment is the one which the Tathagata has described, that he should go on dwelling in just this detachment, and that in consequence of it he will quickly win full enlightenment. [394] When he leaves that isolated place in the forest, and comes back to a village, he despises the Bodhisattvas there, monks who are well behaved, chaste, lovely in character, uncontaminated by mental activities associated with Disciples and Pratyekabuddhas, and living lives quite pure, in body, voice and mind. He tells them that they surely do not dwell in a detached dwelling, but in a contaminated and crowded one. Those Bodhisattvas there, who dwell in a detached dwelling, he warns against contaminated and crowded dwellings. He tries to commit them to a detached dwelling [as he conceives it]. He claims their respect for his isolated residence, he becomes proud, and tells them: "Superhuman beings have exhorted me, superhuman beings have come to inform me! This [isolated place in the forest], Subhuti, is the dwelling in which I dwell. What dweller in a village has ever been exhorted and informed by superhuman beings?" In this kind of way he despises the persons who belong to the vehicle of the Bodhisattva. He should be known as a Candala of a Bodhisattva, as a defamer of Bodhisattvas, as a mere fake of a Bodhisattva, as a counterfeit Bodhisattva, as filth of a Bodhisattva, as a robber in the guise of a Shramana, a robber of persons belonging to the vehicle of the Bodhisattvas, a robber of the world with its Gods. Such a one should surely not be tended, loved or honoured. For such persons have fallen into conceit. [395] They will even succeed in corrupting other kindred spirits, weaklings who have but recently set out in the vehicle. They should be regarded as impure by nature, as devoid of proper teachers, devoid of the qualities of holiness. But a Bodhisattva should not tend such persons, nor love or honour them, if he is one who has neither abandoned all beings, nor all-knowledge, nor full enlightenment, if he wants earnestly to win full enlightenment, and to bring about the weal of all beings. On the contrary, one who has raised himself to a height where he considers the weal of all beings, should, so that he may see through these and other deeds of Mara, always have a mind which is anxious to expound the path to beings who have not yet got it, a mind which does not tremble and which is not submerged in the wanderings through the triple world; he has first of all an attitude of friendliness, and an attitude of compassion, he has produced the great compassion and is moved by pity, he has a thought of joy in sympathy with the beings who progress in the right direction, he is impartial because the true nature of dharmas is such that it cannot be apprehended; [with all this in mind] he should form the resolution: "Thus will I act that in future all the faults of Mara's deeds shall in no way whatsoever either be, or be produced; or, if produced, that they shall at once pass away again. Thus will I train myself!" This should also be known as a Bodhisattva's courageous advance towards his own higher knowledge. So much for what a Bodhisattva should know about Mara's deeds in connection with the quality of detachment.

Chapter XXII

THE GOOD FRIEND

1. THE GOOD FRIENDS

A Bodhisattva who has set out with earnest intention and wants to win full enlightenment should from the very beginning tend, love and honour the good friends.

Subhuti: Who are those good friends of a Bodhisattva?

The Lord: The Buddhas and Lords, and also the irreversible Bodhisattvas who are skilful in the Bodhisattva-course, and who instruct and admonish him in the perfections, who demonstrate and expound the perfection of wisdom. The perfection of wisdom in particular should be regarded as a Bodhisattva's good friend. All the six perfections, in fact, are the good friends of a Bodhisattva. They are his Teacher, his path, his light, his torch, his illumination, his shelter, his refuge, his place of rest, his final relief, [397] his island, his mother, his father, and they lead him to cognition, to understanding, to full enlightenment. For it is in these six perfections that the perfection of wisdom is accomplished. Simply from the six perfections has come forth the all-knowledge of the Tathagatas who, in the past period, have won full enlightenment and then entered Nirvana. And so has the all-knowledge of the Tathagatas who in a future period will win enlightenment, and of the Tathagatas who just now reside in incalculable, immeasurable, infinite, inconceivable world systems. I also, Subhuti, am a Tathagata who has in this present period won full enlightenment, and my all-knowledge also has come forth from the six perfections. For the six perfections contain the thirty-seven dharmas which act as wings to enlightenment, they contain the four Brahma-dwellings, the four means of conversion, and any Buddha-dharma there may be, any Buddha-cognition, cognition of the Self-Existent, any unthinkable, incomparable, immeasurable, incalculable, unequalled cognition, any cognition which equals the unequalled, any cognition of the all-knowing. Therefore, Subhuti, simply the six perfections of a Bodhisattva [398] should be known as his good friends. They are his Teacher, etc., to: they lead him to cognition, to understanding, to full enlightenment. In addition, a Bodhisattva who trains in the six perfections becomes a true benefactor to all beings who are in need of one. But if he wants to train in the six perfections, a Bodhisattva must above all hear this perfection of wisdom, take it up, bear it in mind, recite, study, spread, demonstrate, expound, explain and write it, and investigate its meaning, content and method, meditate on it, and ask questions about it. For this perfection of wisdom directs the six perfections, guides, leads, instructs and advises them, is their genetrix and nurse. Because, if they are deprived of the perfection of wisdom, the first five perfections do not come under the concept of perfections, and they do not deserve to be called 'perfections.' A Bodhisattva should therefore train in just this perfection of wisdom if he wishes to get to a state where he cannot be led astray by others, and to stand firmly in it.

2. EMPTINESS, DEFILEMENTS AND PURIFICATION

Subhuti: How is perfect wisdom marked? [399]

The Lord: It has non-attachment for mark.

Subhuti: Would it be feasible to say that that same mark of non-attachment, which exists in perfect wisdom, exists also in all dharmas?

The Lord: So it is, Subhuti. For all dharmas are isolated and empty. Therefore that same mark of non-attachment, which makes perfect wisdom isolated and empty, also makes all dharmas isolated and empty.

Subhuti: If all dharmas are isolated and empty, how is the defilement and purification of beings conceivable? For what is isolated cannot be defiled or purified, what is empty cannot be defiled or purified, and what is isolated and empty cannot know full enlightenment. Nor can one get at any dharma outside emptiness which has known full enlightenment, which will know it, or which does know it. How then shall we understand the meaning of this teaching? Show us, O Lord, show us, O Sugata!

The Lord: What do you think, Subhuti. Do beings course for a long time in I-making and mine-making? [400]

Subhuti: So it is, Lord.

The Lord: Are also I-making and mine-making empty?

Subhuti: They are, O Lord.

The Lord: Is it just because of their I-making and mine-making that beings wander about in birth-and-death?

Subhuti: So it is, Lord.

The Lord: It is in that sense that the defilement of beings becomes conceivable. To the extent that beings take hold of things and settle down in them, to that extent is there defilement. But no one is thereby defiled. And to the extent that one does not take hold of things and does not settle down in them, to that extent can one conceive of the absence of I-making and mine-making. In that sense can one form the concept of the purification of beings, i.e. to the extent that they do not take hold of things and do not settle down in them, to that extent there is purification.

But no one is therein purified. When a Bodhisattva courses thus, he courses in perfect wisdom. It is in this sense that one can form the concept of the defilement and purification of beings in spite of the fact that all dharmas are isolated and empty.

Subhuti: This is truly wonderful! And a Bodhisattva who courses thus, he courses in perfect wisdom. Because he then does not course in form, or the other skandhas. When he courses thus, [401] a Bodhisattva cannot be crushed by the whole world with its Gods, men and Asuras. When he courses thus, a Bodhisattva surpasses the coursings of all the persons who belong to the vehicle of the Disciples and Pratyekabuddhas, and he gains an insuperable position. For Buddhahood is insuperable, and so is Tathagatahood, the state of the Self-Existent, the state of all-knowledge. A Bodhisattva, who day and night passes his time dwelling on these mental activities associated with perfect wisdom, is quite near full enlightenment and shall quickly know it.

3. ATTENTIONS TO PERFECT WISDOM, AND THE PEARL OF GREAT PRICE

The Lord: So it is, Subhuti. Suppose, Subhuti, that all beings in Jambudvipa should simultaneously acquire a human personality, should raise their thoughts to full enlightenment, abide in [402] that thought of enlightenment all their lives, and honour, revere and worship all the Tathagatas all their lives. If now [after all this preparation], they should give gifts to all beings, and turn [the merit from] that giving over into full enlightenment, —would those Bodhisattvas on the strength of that beget much merit?

Subhuti: They would, O Lord.

The Lord: Truly again, Subhuti, that son or daughter of good family begets a greater heap of merit, who, as a Bodhisattva, dwells for even one single day only in mental activities connected with the perfection of wisdom. For, as he goes on dwelling day and night in those mental activities, he becomes more and more worthy of the sacrificial gifts of all beings. Because no other being has a mind so full of friendliness as he has, except for the Buddhas, the Lords. And the Tathagatas, of course, are matchless, without a like, endowed with unthinkable dharmas. How then does that son or daughter of good family at first aspire to that merit? He becomes endowed with that kind of wise insight which allows him to see all beings as on the way to their slaughter. Great compassion on that occasion takes hold of him. [403] He surveys countless beings with his heavenly eye, and what he sees fills him with great agitation: so many carry the burden of a

karma which leads to immediate retribution in the hells, others have ac-
quired unfortunate rebirths [which keep them away from the Buddha and
his teachings], others are doomed to be killed, or they are enveloped in
the net of false views, or fail to find the path, while others who had gained
a fortunate rebirth have lost it again. And he attends to them with the
thought that: "I shall become a saviour to all those beings, I shall release
them from all their sufferings!" But he does not make either this, or
anything else, into a sign to which he becomes partial. This also is the great
light of a Bodhisattva's wisdom, which allows him to know full enlighten-
ment. For Bodhisattvas, when they dwell in this dwelling, become worthy
of the gifts of the whole world, and yet they do not turn back on full
enlightenment. They purify the gifts and offerings of those who give them
the requisites of life, when their thoughts are well supported by perfect
wisdom, and they are near to all-knowledge. Therefore a Bodhisattva
should dwell in this mental work associated with perfect wisdom, if he
does not want to consume his alms fruitlessly, if he wants to point out the
path to all beings, [404] to shed light over a wide range, to set free from
birth-and-death all the beings who are subject to it, and to cleanse the
organs of vision of all beings. If he wishes to dwell in mental activities
directed towards these goals, he should bring to mind mental activities
associated with the perfection of wisdom. For one who decides to bring
these to mind, his mind works on the welfare of all beings. But he should
give no room to other mental activities, such as lack in perfect wisdom. If
he acts so [as the mental work, which is essentially a loving concern for
beings, impels him], he spends his days and nights in mental activities
associated with the perfection of wisdom. Suppose a man, well versed in
jewelry and the different varieties of jewels, had newly acquired a very
precious gem. That would make him very glad and elated. If he again lost
this precious gem, he would be most sad and distressed. Constantly and
always mental activities associated with that jewel would proceed in him,
and he would regret to be parted from it. He would not forget about it,
until he had either regained this gem, or gained another one of like quality
and kind. Just so a Bodhisattva who has again lost the precious jewel of
perfect wisdom; [405] with a clear perception of the preciousness of
perfect wisdom, and convinced that he has not been definitely parted from
it, he should, with a thought that is not lacking in mental work on perfect
wisdom, and which is directed to the state of all-knowledge, search about
everywhere until he has regained this Sutra, or gained an equivalent one.
All that time he should be one who is not lacking in mental activities
associated with the acquisition of the precious jewel of the perfection of
wisdom, one who is not lacking in mental activities associated with the

acquisition of the great jewel of all-knowledge.

Subhuti: But, since the Lord has taught that all dharmas and all mental activities are lacking in own-being, and empty, —how then can a Bodhisattva become one who is not lacking in mental activities associated with perfect wisdom, or with all-knowledge?

The Lord: If the mind of a Bodhisattva works on the fact that all dharmas are through their own-being isolated and empty, and agrees that that is so, then he becomes one who is not lacking in mental activities associated with perfect wisdom and with all-knowledge. For perfect wisdom is empty, it neither increases nor decreases.

4. EMPTINESS AND GROWTH IN ENLIGHTENMENT

Subhuti: If that is so, how can a Bodhisattva arrive, without an increase in perfect wisdom, at the full attainment of enlightenment, how can he know full enlightenment?

The Lord: In actual fact a Bodhisattva who courses in perfect wisdom neither increases nor decreases. Just as perfect wisdom is empty, without increase or decrease, just so also a Bodhisattva is empty, without increase or decrease. It is because of this fact, —i.e. that just as perfect wisdom is empty, [406] without increase or decrease, so also the Bodhisattva is empty, without increase or decrease, —that a Bodhisattva arrives at the full attainment of enlightenment, and thus knows full enlightenment. If a Bodhisattva, when this is being taught, is not afraid nor loses heart, then he should be known as a Bodhisattva who courses in perfect wisdom.

Subhuti: Does then perfect wisdom course in perfect wisdom?

The Lord: No, Subhuti.

Subhuti: Does the emptiness of perfect wisdom course in perfect wisdom?

The Lord: No, Subhuti.

Subhuti: Can one then apprehend outside the emptiness of perfect wisdom any dharma which courses in perfect wisdom?

The Lord: No, Subhuti.

Subhuti: Does emptiness course in perfect wisdom? [407]

The Lord: No, Subhuti.

Subhuti: Can one apprehend in emptiness any dharma that courses in perfect wisdom?

The Lord: No, Subhuti.

Subhuti: Does emptiness course in emptiness?

The Lord: No, Subhuti.

Subhuti: Does form, etc., course in perfect wisdom?

The Lord: No, Subhuti.

Subhuti: Can one apprehend outside form, etc., any dharma which courses in perfect wisdom?

The Lord: No, Subhuti.

Subhuti: How then does a Bodhisattva course in perfect wisdom?

The Lord: Do you then, Subhuti, see a real dharma which courses in perfect wisdom?

Subhuti: No, Lord. [408]

The Lord: Do you see that perfect wisdom, in which the Bodhisattva courses, as a real thing?

Subhuti: No, Lord.

The Lord: Do you see as real that dharma which offers no basis for apprehension? Has that dharma by any chance been produced, or will it be produced, or is it being produced, has it been stopped, will it be stopped, or is it being stopped?

Subhuti: No, Lord.

The Lord: This insight gives a Bodhisattva the patient acceptance of dharmas which fail to be produced. When he is endowed with that, he is predestined to full enlightenment. He is bound to progress towards the self-confidence of a Tathagata. It is quite impossible that a Bodhisattva, who courses, strives and struggles in this way, and progresses in this direction, should not reach the supreme cognition of a Buddha, the cognition of the all-knowing, the cognition of the great Caravan Leader.

Subhuti: Can the true nature of all dharmas, which consists in the fact that they fail to be produced, can that be predestined to full enlightenment?

The Lord: No, Subhuti.

Subhuti: How then in that case does the prediction of this dharma to full enlightenment take place?

The Lord: Do you see as real that dharma which has a prediction to full enlightenment? [409]

Subhuti: No, Lord. I do not see any real dharma which is at any time predestined to full enlightenment. Nor do I see any real dharma which is known by the enlightened, which should be known to them, or by means of which they would have their full knowledge. It is because all dharmas cannot be apprehended, that it does not occur to me to think that "this dharma is known to the Enlightened, this dharma should be known to them, by means of this dharma they do have their full knowledge."

Chapter XXIII

SAKRA

1. THE SUPERIOR POSITION OF BODHISATTVAS

At that time *Sakra*, Chief of Gods, was seated amid that assembly, and said: To be sure, deep is this perfection of wisdom, hard to see, hard to understand!

The Lord: So it is, Kausika. With the depth of space is this perfect wisdom deep. As isolated it is hard to see, as empty it is hard to understand.

Sakra: Those beings who hear this perfection of wisdom, take it up, study, spread, and write it, must be endowed with more than a puny wholesome root!

The Lord: So it is. If all the beings in Jambudvipa were endowed [411] with [the ability to observe] the ten ways of wholesome action, would they on the strength of that beget much merit?

Sakra: They would, O Lord.

The Lord: A person who hears, studies, spreads and writes this perfection of wisdom begets greater merit than they. The just mentioned heap of merit, due to the morality of all beings in Jambudvipa, is infinitesimal compared with the heap of merit which is due to the wholesome root of someone who hears, studies, spreads and writes this deep perfection of wisdom.

Thereupon a *monk* said to Sakra, Chief of Gods: You have been surpassed, Kausika, by that person who hears, studies, spreads and writes this deep perfection of wisdom!

Sakra: I am even surpassed by that son or daughter of good family who has raised but one single thought to enlightenment: [412] how much more so if in addition they train in Thusness, progress to it, make endeavours about it; on their journey they surpass the whole world with its Gods, men and Asuras. On their journey they not only surpass the world with its Gods, men and Asuras, but also all the Streamwinners, Once-Returners, Never-Returners, Arhats and Pratyekabuddhas. They surpass also those Bodhisattvas who are great almsgivers but lack in perfect wisdom and skill in means; and equally those whose morality is perfectly pure, who possess a vast quantity of morality, whose observation of the moral rules is unbroken, flawless, unstained, complete, perfectly pure and unspotted, but who lack in perfect wisdom and skill in means; and equally those who have won patience and peaceful calm, [413] whose thoughts are free from hostility, who feel no thought of malice even when burned at the stake, but who lack in perfect wisdom and skill in means and equally those who have exerted vigour, who persist in trying, who are free from sloth, and remain uncowed in all they do with body, voice and mind, but who lack in perfect wisdom and skill in means; and equally those who are fond of the trances and delight in them, who are strong and powerful in the trances, who are established in the trances, who are masters of the trances, but who lack in perfect wisdom and skill in means. For, when he courses in the perfection of wisdom as it has been expounded, a Bodhisattva surpasses the world with its Gods, men and Asuras, surpasses all those who belong to the vehicle of the Disciples and Pratyekabuddhas, surpasses also the Bodhisattvas who are not skilled in means. And they cannot surpass him. For a Bodhisattva who courses in the perfection of wisdom as it has been expounded, who complies with it, has taken up his position so that the lineage of the all-knowing should not be interrupted, and he does not keep aloof from the Tathagatas. His journey will, when he progresses in this way, shortly bring him to the terrace of enlightenment; [414] he will, training himself in this way, rescue the beings who have sunk into the mud of the defilements. Training himself in this way, he trains in the training of a Bodhisattva, and not in the training of a Disciple or Pratyekabuddha.

2. REWARDS OF PERFECT WISDOM

And the four Great Kings, the World Guardians, will come to the Bodhisattva who trains in this way in the perfection of wisdom, and they will say to him: "Train yourself quickly in this course of a Bodhisattva, son of good family! Nimbly train yourself! Here are the four begging bowls which you shall receive when you are seated on the terrace of enlightenment, as one who then has won full enlightenment." Not only the four World Guardians will come to the Bodhisattva who trains in perfect wisdom as it has been expounded, but I also, not to mention the other Gods. Constantly also the Tathagatas will bring him to mind. All the worldly ills that might befall the Bodhisattva who courses in perfect wisdom, such as attacks from others, etc., shall be prevented from affecting him in any way. This also, O Lord, is a quality which a Bodhisattva who courses in perfect wisdom gains in this very life.

Ananda thereupon thought: Is this speech of Sakra, Chief of Gods, due to his own insight, or to the Buddha's might?

Sakra, through the Buddha's might, read his thoughts, and said: To the Buddha's might, Ananda, to the Buddha's sustaining power should this be attributed. For I myself [415] am quite incapable of uttering anything relevant on the subject of Bodhisattvas.

The Lord: So it is, Ananda. What Sakra, Chief of Gods, has said was due to the Tathagata's might, to his sustaining power.

Chapter XXIV

CONCEIT

1. CONDITIONS WHICH OPEN A BODHISATTVA TO MARA'S INFLUENCE

At the time when a Bodhisattva trains in perfect wisdom, makes endeavours about it and develops it, all the Evil Maras in the great trichiliocosm are in a state of uncertainty: "Will this Bodhisattva prematurely realize the reality-limit on the level of Disciple or Pratyekabuddha, or will he know full enlightenment?" Moreover, when a Bodhisattva dwells in the dwelling of perfect wisdom, the Evil Maras are pierced by the dart of sorrow. When a Bodhisattva courses in perfect wisdom, makes endeavours about it and develops it, the Evil Maras think how they can hurt him. They may, for instance, try to make him afraid by letting loose a shower of meteors in all directions, causing the impression that the horizon is all aflame. They hope that then the Bodhisattva will become cowed, that his hair will stand on end, so that at least one single thought directed on full enlightenment might get extinguished. [417] But Mara, the Evil One, does not attempt to hurt each and every Bodhisattva. Some he tries to hurt, and others not.

Ananda: What kind of a Bodhisattva does Mara try to hurt?

The Lord: Mara tries to hurt a Bodhisattva who in the past, when the perfection of wisdom was being taught, did not produce a thought of firm belief, and he gains entry to him. He tries to hurt Bodhisattvas who, when this deep perfection of wisdom is being taught, are seized by uncertainties, feel perplexed, and think that "perhaps this perfection of wisdom is so, perhaps it is not so"; or Bodhisattvas who lack the good friend, who have been taken hold of by bad friends, who, when the perfection of wisdom is being taught, do not hear about the very deep stations, remain in ignorance of them, and do not ask how the perfection of wisdom should be developed; or Bodhisattvas who cling to someone who upholds that which is not the true dharma, and say: "I am his adherent, and in all things he does not abandon me. [418] There are many other Bodhisattvas whom I might adhere to, but they do not suit me. I have taken this one as my fitting companion and he will suit me." Moreover, a Bodhisattva might, when this deep perfection of wisdom is being taught, say to another Bodhisattva: "Deep, indeed, is this perfection of wisdom! What point is there in your listening to it? For even when I apply myself to it in the way in which the Tathagata has taught in the other Sutrantas, even then I do not get to the bottom of it, nor derive any enjoyment from it. What is the point in your hearing and writing it? In that way he tries to estrange other Bodhisattvas. Mara comes also to such a Bodhisattva, tries to hurt him, and gains entry to him. Furthermore, Ananda, Mara becomes contented, elated and enraptured, he is overjoyed, exultant and glad, thrilled, delighted and jubilant, in case a Bodhisattva despises other Bodhisattvas, and thinks: "I dwell in the dwelling of detachment, but not so they; not theirs the dwelling in detachment." And Mara is so joyful because this Bodhisattva keeps far away from full enlightenment.

Furthermore, when a Bodhisattva takes on a name or clan, or when his ascetic qualities are proclaimed, he may regard that as a sufficient reason to despise other Bodhisattvas, well-behaved and lovely in character though they may be. [419] But he has not got the qualities of irreversible Bodhisattvas who course in perfect wisdom, nor their attributes, tokens or signs. Since he has not got the irreversible qualities, he gives rise to defilement, i.e. he exalts himself, deprecates others, and thinks that they are not equal to those dharmas, as he is. The Evil Maras then foresee that the realms of Mara will not remain empty, that the great hells, the animal kingdom, the world of the Pretas, and the assemblies of the Asuras will be overcrowded. And Mara, the Evil One, becomes still more determined, and thinks: "With this kind of start those Bodhisattvas will soon be smothered by gain and honour. They will become plausible talkers, and with their plausible talk they will catch hold of many people. Those people will decide to listen to them, will imitate what they have seen and heard, and in consequence will not train in Thusness, not progress into it, not make endeavours about it. Not training themselves in Suchness, not progressing in it, not making endeavours about it, they will still further increase their defilements. So it will come about that all the deeds—of body, voice or mind—which they may undertake with their perverted mentality shall lead them to a rebirth in conditions which are unserviceable, disagreeable, unpleasing, and unpleasant. In consequence the realms of Mara will become overcrowded, i.e. the great hells, the animal world, the world of the Pretas, and [420] the assemblies of the Asuras." When he considers this sequence of events, Mara the Evil One becomes contented, elated, enraptured, overjoyed, exultant and jubilant. Furthermore, Ananda, when a Bodhisattva fights with a person belonging to the vehicle of the Disciples, disputes and quarrels with him, abuses and reviles him, feels ill-will and hatred for him, then Mara thinks that "surely, this son of good family will keep away from all-knowledge, he will remain far away from it." Mara becomes still more jubilant if a person belonging to the vehicle of the Bodhisattvas fights with someone else who also belongs to the vehicle of the Bodhisattvas, for he thinks that "both these Bodhisattvas remain far from all-knowledge." But if a Bodhisattva who has had his prediction fights with another Bodhisattva who has also had his prediction, and cherishes malice for him — for a great many aeons he must, if he has such an attitude of mind, put on the armour [which enables him to struggle against it], —unless, of course, he has abandoned all-knowledge completely. [421]

2. THE BODHISATTVA'S RIGHT ATTITUDE TO OTHER BODHISATTVAS

Ananda: Can he escape from those attitudes of mind, or is he definitely condemned to go on putting on the armour for all that length of time?

The Lord: I have, Ananda, demonstrated a dharma which includes the possibility of escape, —for persons of the Disciple-vehicle, for persons of the Pratyekabuddha-vehicle, for persons of the Bodhisattva-vehicle. As to the person who belongs to the vehicle of the Bodhisattvas and who has quarrelled with someone else who also belongs to the vehicle of the Bodhisattvas, —if he does not confess his fault, does not promise restraint in future, harbours a latent bias towards hate, and dwells tied to that bias, —of that person I do not teach the escape [i.e. from the consequences of his action], but he is definitely condemned to go on putting on the armour for all that length of time. But I teach his escape if he confesses his fault, promises restraint in future, and reflects as follows: "I whose duty it is to drive away, to pacify and appease the quarrels, disputes and conflicts of all beings, yet I myself engage in disputes! It is indeed a loss to me, and not a gain, that I should answer back as I am spoken to. When I should be to all beings a bridge across the sea of birth-and-death, I nevertheless say to another, 'the same to you,' or return a harsh and rough answer. This is not the way in which I should speak. In fights, quarrels and disputes I should behave like a senseless idiot, or like a dumb sheep. When I hear someone using offensive, abusive, insulting words towards me, my heart should not cherish malice for others. It is not [422] meet and proper for me to perceive the faults of others, or to think that what is being said about the faults of others is worth listening to. For I, since I am earnestly intent [on full enlightenment], should not do harm to others. When I should make all beings happy by giving them everything that brings happiness, when I should lead them to Nirvana after having won full enlightenment, —yet nevertheless I bear ill will! I should not bear ill will even against those who have offended against me, and I must avoid getting into a rage, and I must make a firm effort in that direction. Even when my life is in danger I must not get into a rage, and no frown should appear on my face." Of such a Bodhisattva I teach the escape. This is the attitude which a Bodhisattva should adopt also towards persons who belong to the vehicle of the Disciples. Never to get angry with any being, that is the attitude of mind one should adopt towards all beings. What attitude then should a Bodhisattva have towards other persons belonging to the vehicle of the Bodhisattvas? The same as towards the Teacher. He should have the attitude that "these Bodhisattvas are my teachers." Surely, they have mounted on the same vehicle as I, have ascended by the same path, are of like intention with me, have set out in the same vehicle as I. Wherein they should be trained, that is the method by which I should be trained. But if some of them dwell in a dwelling contaminated [by the ideas of Disciples and Pratyekabuddhas], [423] then I should not do likewise. If, however they dwell in an uncontaminated dwelling, in mental activities associated with all-knowledge, then I also should train as they do. No obstacles to full enlightenment can arise to a Bodhisattva who trains himself in this way in all-knowledge, and he quickly knows full enlightenment.

Chapter XXV

TRAINING

1. HOW A BODHISATTVA IS TRAINED IN ALL KNOWLEDGE

Subhuti: Wherein, O Lord, must a Bodhisattva train to be trained in all-knowledge?

The Lord: He must train in Extinction, in Non-production, in Non-stopping, in No-birth, in the absence of positivity, in Isolatedness, in Dispassion, in Space, in the element of dharma, and Nirvana.

Subhuti: For what reason does that amount to a training in all-knowledge?

The Lord: What do you think, Subhuti, the Suchness of the Tathagata, which is the prime cause of the Tathagata being a Tathagata, does that become extinct?

Subhuti: No, Lord. For extinction cannot become extinct, extinction being inextinguishable. [425]

The Lord: The Suchness of the Tathagata, which is the prime cause of the Tathagata being a Tathagata, is that now produced, or stopped, or born; or does it become or cease to become; or does it become isolated; or impassioned or dispassionate; or does it become like space, or does it become of the nature of dharma?

Subhuti: No, Lord.

The Lord: Does that Suchness then enter Nirvana?

Subhuti: No, Lord.

The Lord: Therefore then, Subhuti, a Bodhisattva who trains himself thus, he trains in [the conviction that] "Suchness does not get extinct." When he trains thus, he will reach the perfection of all training. He cannot be crushed by Mara, or by Mara's associates or by Mara's host. Soon he shall reach the condition of irreversibility. Soon he shall sit on the terrace of enlightenment. He courses in his own range. [426] He is trained in the dharmas which make him into a saviour, in the great friendliness, the great compassion, the great sympathetic joy, the great impartiality. He trains for the turning of the wheel of dharma, with its three revolutions and twelve aspects. He trains so as to save no fewer beings than he should. He trains to ensure the non-interruption of the lineage of the Tathagatas. He trains in order to open the door of the deathless element. An inferior being is, however, incapable of this sublime training. For a weakling cannot be trained in this training. Because those who are trained in this training are the very cream of all beings, are persons who want to save all beings. They want to reach a state where they are elevated above all beings. A Bodhisattva who trains thus is not reborn in the hells, nor among animals, nor in the realms of the Pretas, nor among the Asuras, nor in outlying districts [among barbarous populations], nor in the families of outcasts or fowlers, of hunters, fishermen or butchers, nor in other low class families of that kind, in which one is addicted to low deeds. He does not become blind, deaf, or one-eyed; he is not a cripple, nor hunch-backed, nor a man with withered hand or arm, nor limping, or lame, or stunned, [427] not tremulous, quivering or shaky; his limbs are not puny, nor incomplete, nor abnormal: he is not weak, nor has he a bad complexion or shape; his faculties are not inferior nor incomplete, but they are in every way perfect; and he has a melodious voice. He does not become a person who takes life, or who takes what is not given, or who goes wrong about his sense-desires, or who speaks falsely, or maliciously, or harshly, or who prattles indistinctly, or who is covetous, or who harbours ill will in his heart, or who has wrong views, and he does not earn his livelihood in the wrong fashion. He is not reborn among the long-lived Gods, he does not take up bad moral practices, does not take hold of unreal dharmas, and he does not get reborn through the influence of his trances and [formless] attainments. For there is his skill in means, and endowed with that he does not get reborn among the long-lived Gods. But what is that skill in means of a Bodhisattva? It is just this perfection of wisdom. And he applies himself to this skill in means in such a way that, endowed with it, the Bodhisattva enters into the trances without being reborn through the influence of the trances. [428] When he trains thus, a Bodhisattva incurs the perfect purity of the powers, of the grounds of self-confidence, of the Buddha-dharmas. He reaches all that.

Subhuti: But if, O Lord, as we all know, all dharmas are by nature perfectly pure, then with regard to what dharma does a Bodhisattva incur and reach the perfect purity of the powers, the grounds of self-confidence and the Buddha-dharmas?

The Lord: So it is, Subhuti. For all dharmas are just by [their essential original] nature perfectly pure. When a Bodhisattva who trains in perfect wisdom does not lose heart and remains uncowed although all dharmas are by their nature perfectly pure, then that is his perfection of wisdom. But the foolish common people do not know nor see that these dharmas are really so constituted, and they neither know nor see the true nature of dharmas. On behalf of those beings the Bodhisattvas struggle on and exert vigour so that those who do not know may be enabled to know, so that those who do not see may be made to see. In this training they train, and therefore [in the world of appearance] a Bodhisattva reaches the powers, the grounds of self-confidence, and all Buddha-dharmas. When they train thus, Bodhisattvas wisely know the throbbing thoughts and actions of other beings, of other persons as they really are. And then they go beyond the knowledge of the thoughts and actions of others. [429]

2. FEWNESS OF BODHISATTVAS

On this earth, few are the places free from stones, few the spots where gold and silver are found. Much more numerous are saline deserts, arid deserts, places covered with grass, or thorns, or steep chasms. Just so, in the world of beings few Bodhisattvas exist who train in this training in all-knowledge, i.e. in the training in perfect wisdom. Much more numerous are those who train in the training characteristic of Disciples and Pratyeka-buddhas. Furthermore, Subhuti, in the world of beings few have done deeds which lead them to the authority of a universal monarch. Much more numerous are those who have done deeds which lead them to the authority of a commander of a fort. Just so, in the world of beings few are the Bodhisattvas who have mounted on this path of perfect wisdom, and who have resolved to know full enlightenment. Much more numerous are those who have mounted on the path of Disciples and Pratyekabuddhas. Furthermore, few only have done deeds which permit them to become Sakra, Chief of Gods. Much more numerous are those whose deeds lead them to the world of [the minor] Gods. Just so, few beings only are Bodhisattvas who train in this training in perfect wisdom. Much more numerous are the Bodhisattvas who train in the training of Disciples and Pratyekabuddhas. [430] Furthermore, few beings only have done deeds which permit them to become Brahma. Much more numerous are those whose deeds lead them to Brahma's assembly. Just so, few beings only are irreversible to full enlightenment. Much more numerous are those Bodhi-sattvas who turn away from full enlightenment. Therefore then, Subhuti, in the world of beings few beings exist who have set out for full enlight-enment. Fewer are those who progress in Thusness. Still fewer are those very few who make endeavours about perfect wisdom. Still fewer even are those very very few Bodhisattvas who are irreversible from full enlight-enment. A Bodhisattva who wants to be numbered among those very, very few irreversible Bodhisattvas should therefore train in just this perfection of wisdom, and make endeavours about it. Moreover, Subhuti, no harsh thought arises to a Bodhisattva who thus trains in perfect wisdom, nor a doubting thought, or an envious or mean thought, or an immoral thought, or a thought of ill will, or a lazy thought, or a distracted thought, or a stupid thought.

3. THE PERFECTION OF WISDOM
   COMPREHENDS ALL PERFECTIONS

It is thus that when a Bodhisattva trains in the perfection of wisdom, [431] all the perfections are automatically incorporated, taken up, followed after and included. The view of individuality includes all the sixty-two views, and even so, for a Bodhisattva who trains in the perfection of wisdom, all the perfections are included in that. As long as someone's life-faculty goes on, all the other faculties are included in it. Even so for a Bodhisattva who trains in perfect wisdom all the other wholesome dharmas are included in that. When someone's life-faculty is stopped, all the other faculties are also stopped. Even so, for a Bodhisattva who trains in perfect wisdom, all the other unwholesome dharmas are stopped when only non-cognition is stopped, and all the other perfections are included in that, and automatically taken hold of.

4. MERIT FROM PERFECT WISDOM

Therefore then, Subhuti, a Bodhisattva who wants to take hold of all perfections should train in the perfection of wisdom. When he trains in the perfection of wisdom, a Bodhisattva trains in that which is the highest possible degree of perfection for any being. For his merit is the greatest possible. Subhuti, if you consider all the beings in the great trichiliocosm, are they many?

Subhuti: Even in Jambudvipa alone there are many beings, how many more would there be in the great trichiliocosm?

The Lord: If one single Bodhisattva were, during his entire life, to furnish all those beings with robes, alms bowl, lodging, medicinal appliances for use in sickness, and all that brings them happiness, – [432] would such a Bodhisattva on the strength of that beget a great deal of merit?

Subhuti: He would, O Lord.

The Lord: A much greater merit still would that Bodhisattva beget who would develop this perfection of wisdom for even the duration of a finger-snap. So greatly profitable is the perfection of wisdom of the Bodhisattvas, because she feeds the supreme enlightenment. A Bodhisattva should therefore train in perfect wisdom if he wants to know full enlightenment, to arrive at the supreme position among all beings, to become a protector of the helpless, to reach the sphere of the Buddha, to emulate the manliness of the Buddha, to sport with a Buddha's sport, to roar a Buddha's lion roar, to reach the accomplishment of a Buddha, and to explain the dharma in the great trichiliocosm. When a Bodhisattva trains in the perfection of wisdom, I do not see the accomplishment in which he has not been trained.

5. BODHISATTVAS AND DISCIPLES

Subhuti: Is then a Bodhisattva also trained in the accomplishment of a Disciple?

The Lord: He should also be trained in that. But he does not train with the intention of always continuing with the accomplishment of a Disciple, or with the idea of making it in any way his own. [433] Not thus does he train. He also knows the qualities of the Disciples, but does not abide with them. He assimilates them, without opposing them. He trains with the intention that he should demonstrate and reveal also the virtues of the Disciples. When he trains thus, a Bodhisattva arrives at a condition where he is worthy of receiving gifts from the world with its Gods, men and Asuras. He surpasses all other people who are worthy of gifts, associated with Disciples or Pratyekabuddhas. And all-knowledge will be near to him. When he trains thus, a Bodhisattva does not part from the perfection of wisdom, but he courses in it, is not lacking in the dwelling of the perfection of wisdom. When he courses thus a Bodhisattva should be known as "unfailing, definitely unfailing" with regard to all-knowledge, and he keeps away from the level of a Disciple or Pratyekabuddha. He is near to full enlightenment. If, however, it occurs to him that "this is the perfection of wisdom which brings this all-knowledge,"—then one who has such a notion does not course in the perfection of wisdom. On the contrary he has no notion even of perfect wisdom, he does not perceive or review that "this is the perfection of wisdom," or "his is the perfection of wisdom," or "it shall feed all-knowledge." If he courses thus, a Bodhisattva courses in the perfection of wisdom.

Chapter XXVI

LIKE ILLUSION

1. SAKRA PRAISES THE BODHISATTVAS

Thereupon it occurred to *Sakra*, Chief of Gods: A Bodhisattva, even if he courses only just so far, surpasses all; how much more so when he has known full enlightenment! A great gain has accrued to those beings, a good life do they live when their thought strides in all-knowledge; how much more so when they have raised their thought to full enlightenment! To be envied are those beings, the very cream of all beings, who will know full enlightenment!

Thereupon *Sakra*, Chief of Gods, conjured up Mandarava flowers, saluted them reverently, scattered them over the Tathagata, and said: May those persons who belong to the vehicle of the Bodhisattvas, and who have raised their thoughts to full enlightenment, succeed in their resolve to know full enlightenment, and, after that, to transfer all beings who are borne along by the great flood of birth-and-death to the smooth yonder shore! May that thought of enlightenment which they have wished for, thought over and taken hold of, bring to fulfilment in them the dharmas of a Buddha, the dharmas associated with all-knowledge, the dharmas of the Self-Existent, the insuperable dharmas! I have not even the slightest suspicion that those Bodhisattvas, who are endowed with the great compassion, might turn away from full enlightenment, [435] or that those persons who belong to the vehicle of the Bodhisattvas and who have set out for full enlightenment might turn away from it. On the contrary, I am sure that this resolve to win full enlightenment will increase more and more in them, as they survey the ills which afflict beings on the plane of birth-and-death. For through their great compassion they desire the welfare of the world with its Gods, men and Asuras, desire to benefit it, are full of pity for it, they, who are endowed with this attitude of mind, dwell in the attitude of mind which is expressed in their resolution that "we have crossed over, we shall help beings to cross over! Freed we shall free them! Recovered we shall help them to recover! Gone to Nirvana we shall lead them to Nirvana!"

2. JUBILATION, TURNING OVER AND MERIT

The son or daughter of good family who rejoices at the productions of thought of those Bodhisattvas who have just begun to set out in the vehicle, as well as at the productions of thought of those who progress on the course, as well as at the irreversible nature of those who are irreversible, as well as at the nature of those who are bound to one more birth only, —to what extent is their merit a superior one?

The Lord: One might be able, Kausika, to grasp the measure of Sumeru, king of mountains, or of a world system, up to a great trichiliocosm, with the help of a tip of straw, but one could not possibly grasp the measure of the merit coming to that son or daughter of good family, or to a Bodhisattva, from the production of a thought connected with that jubilation. [436]

Sakra: Beset by Mara are those beings who do not come to hear of this immeasurable merit of that jubilation over the career of Bodhisattva—which begins with the first thought of enlightenment and which ends with full enlightenment — who do not know it, who do not see it, who do not bring that jubilation to mind. They are partisans of Mara, deceased in Mara's realms. For those who have brought to mind those thoughts, who have turned them over into the supreme enlightenment, have rejoiced at them, they have done so in order to shatter Mara's realm. One should, O Lord, rejoice at the various stages of the thought which the Bodhisattvas have raised to enlightenment. [437] Sons and daughters of good family who have not abandoned the Tathagata, and the Dharma, and the Community, they should rejoice in those stages of the thought of enlightenment!

The Lord: So it is, Kausika. And those sons or daughters of good family who have rejoiced in the stages of the thought of enlightenment, they shall—whether they belong to the vehicle of the Bodhisattvas, or that of the Pratyekabuddhas, or that of the Disciples — soon please the Tathagatas, and not displease them.

Sakra: So it is, O Lord. Therefore, wherever they may be reborn as a result of the wholesome roots [they have planted] when their hearts were filled with jubilation, there they shall be treated with respect, revered, worshipped and adored. They shall never see any unpleasant sights, nor hear any unpleasant sounds, nor smell any unpleasant smells, nor taste any unpleasant tastes, [438] nor come into contact with anything unpleasant to the touch. One must expect them to be reborn in the heavens, and not in the places of woe. For they have rejoiced in the wholesome roots of countless beings, roots which bring happiness to all beings. The thoughts of jubilation of those who, after they have produced an urge towards enlightenment, have rejoiced over the successive stages of the thought of enlightenment in persons who belong to the vehicle of the Bodhisattvas, shall, as they grow, become the nourishers of full enlightenment. After they have won full enlightenment, they also shall lead countless beings to Nirvana.

The Lord: So it is, Kausika, as you have said it, through the Tathagata's might. The wholesome roots of countless beings are rejoiced over, planted and consummated as a consequence of the action of a son or daughter of good family who has rejoiced over the successive stages of the thought of enlightenment in those persons who belong to the vehicle of the Bodhisattvas.

3. THE NATURE OF ILLUSION

Subhuti: But how can a thought which is like illusion know full enlightenment?

The Lord: Subhuti, so you see the thought which is like illusion as a separate real entity?

Subhuti: No, Lord.

The Lord: Do you see illusion as a separate real entity?

Subhuti: No, Lord. [439]

The Lord: When you see neither illusion, nor the thought which is like illusion, as a real separate entity, do you then perhaps see that dharma which knows full enlightenment as something other than illusion, or as something other than the thought which is like illusion?

Subhuti: No, Lord, I do not. In consequence, to what dharma could I point, and say that "it is" or "it is not"? But a dharma which is absolutely isolated, to that one cannot attribute that "it is" or that "it is not.' Also an absolutely isolated dharma does not know full enlightenment. Because a dharma which has no existence cannot know full enlightenment. Therefore then, O Lord, perfect wisdom is absolutely isolated. But a dharma which is absolutely isolated, that is not a dharma that should be developed, nor does it bring about or remove any dharma. How then can a Bodhisattva, by resorting to an absolutely isolated perfection of wisdom, know full enlightenment? Even full enlightenment is absolutely isolated. [440] If, O Lord, the perfection of wisdom is absolutely isolated, and if full enlightenment is absolutely isolated, how can the isolated become known through the isolated?

The Lord: So it is, Subhuti. It is just because the perfection of wisdom is absolutely isolated that the absolutely isolated full enlightenment is known [by it]. But if a Bodhisattva forms the notion that "the perfection of wisdom is absolutely isolated," then that is not the perfection of wisdom. It is thus certain that it is thanks to perfect wisdom that a Bodhisattva knows full enlightenment, and that he cannot know it without resorting to it. The isolated cannot be known by the isolated, and nevertheless a Bodhisattva knows full enlightenment, and he does not know it without resorting to the perfection of wisdom.

Subhuti: As I understand the meaning of the Lord's teaching, a Bodhisattva in this way courses in a deep object.

The Lord: A doer of what is hard is the Bodhisattva who courses in a deep object, and who yet does not realize that object [or: gain], i.e. on the level of Disciple or Pratyekabuddha.

Subhuti: As I understand the meaning of the Lord's teaching, there is in this way no Bodhisattva at all who is a doer of what is hard. [441] For that very dharma is not got at which could realize, nor that which could be realized, nor that by means of which one could realize. If, when this is being taught, a Bodhisattva does not despond, become cowed or stolid, does not turn back, and remains unafraid, then he courses in perfect wisdom. When he does not review it as a certain fact that he courses, then he courses in perfect wisdom. If he does not review it as a real fact that he is near to full enlightenment, then he courses in perfect wisdom. If it does not even occur to him that he has kept aloof from the level of Disciples and Pratyekabuddhas, then he courses in perfect wisdom. It does not occur to space that "I am near to this, or, I am far from that." For space does not make such discriminations. Just so it does not occur to a Bodhisattva who courses in perfect wisdom that "full enlightenment is near to me, the level of Disciple and Pratyekabuddha is far from me." For the perfection of wisdom does not make any discriminations. It is as with a man created by magical illusion to whom it does not occur that "the conjurer is near to me, but the assembled crowd of spectators is far from me." For illusory men make no such discriminations. [442] It is as with the reflection of an object in a mirror or in water, to whom it does not occur that "the object which produces the reflection is near to me, but those who come along in that mirror or bowl of water are far from me." For that reflection of an object makes no discriminations. Just as a Tathagata, because he has forsaken all constructions and discriminations, finds nothing dear or not dear, just so a Bodhisattva who courses in perfect wisdom. For there is no discrimination on the part of perfect wisdom. Just as the Tathagata is one who has forsaken all constructions and discriminations, even so perfect wisdom has forsaken all constructions and discriminations. It does not occur to a fictitious creature which the Tathagata has magically conjured up that "the level of Disciples and Pratyekabuddhas is far from me, full enlightenment is near to me." For that fictitious creature does not make any discriminations. In the same way a Bodhisattva who courses in perfect wisdom does not think that "the level of Disciples and Pratyeka-buddhas is far from me, full enlightenment is near to me." And that simply because of lack of all discrimination on the part of the perfection of wisdom. [443] A fictitious creature [who has been conjured up by the Tathagata] to do a certain work [in converting beings], performs that work, but remains without discrimination. Just because it is so constituted that it lacks all discrimination. Just so a Bodhisattva performs the work for the sake of which he develops the perfection of wisdom, but the perfection of wisdom remains without discrimination. Because it is so constituted that it lacks all discrimination. An expert mason, or mason's apprentice, might make of wood an automatic man or woman, a puppet which could be moved by pulling the strings. Whatever action it were made to perform, that action it would perform. And yet that wooden machine would have no discriminations. Because it is so constituted that it lacks all discrimination. Just so a Bodhisattva performs the work for the sake of which he develops the perfection of wisdom, but the perfection of wisdom remains without discrimination. Because that perfection of wisdom is so constituted that it lacks all discriminations.

Chapter XXVII

THE CORE

1. THE BODHISATTVA'S COURAGE IN DIFFICULTIES

Sariputra: In the core and substance of things verily courses a Bodhisattva who courses in perfect wisdom!

Subhuti: In something unsubstantial verily courses a Bodhisattva who courses in perfect wisdom.

Thereupon this occurred to many thousands of *Gods* of the realm of sense-desire: Homage is due to those beings who raise their thoughts to, and who consummate their thoughts in full enlightenment, who course in this deep perfection of wisdom, and who, when they course thus, do not realize the reality-limit, be it on the level of a Disciple or that of a Pratyekabuddha. In this way also should the Bodhisattvas be known as doers of what is hard, when they course in the true nature of dharma, but do not realize it.

Subhuti read their thoughts, and said to them: Not that is hard for those Bodhisattvas that they do not realize the reality-limit. This, however, is hard for them, this is most hard for them, [445] that they put on the armour of the resolution to lead countless beings to Nirvana, when absolutely those beings do not exist. And since they do not exist, they cannot be got at. Owing to the isolatedness of beings, those who should be disciplined do thus absolutely not exist. It is in this spirit that the Bodhisattvas have set out for full enlightenment, and have decided to discipline beings. One would decide to discipline space if one were to decide to discipline beings. For the isolatedness of beings should be known after the pattern of the isolatedness of space. In this way also Bodhisattvas are doers of what is hard, when they put on the armour for the sake of beings who do not exist, who cannot be got at. One would decide to put on space if one were to decide to put on the armour for the sake of beings. And yet this armour has been put on by the Bodhisattvas for the sake of beings. But that non-apprehension of beings, in [ultimate and] absolute reality, has been taught by the Tathagata. And this non-apprehension of beings can be inferred from their isolatedness, and from the isolatedness of those who should be disciplined should the isolatedness of a Bodhi-being be inferred. If a Bodhisattva, when this is being taught, does not lose heart, then one should know that he courses in the perfection of wisdom. For from the isolatedness of a being should be known the isolatedness of form, etc., and of all dharmas. [446] Thus should the isolatedness of all dharmas be viewed. When the isolatedness of all dharmas is thus being taught, a Bodhi-sattva does not lose heart, and because of that he courses in the perfection of wisdom.

The Lord: For what reason does a Bodhisattva not lose heart when the isolatedness of all dharmas is thus being taught?

Subhuti: Because of isolatedness no dharma can ever lose heart. For one cannot get at any dharma that would lose heart, nor at any dharma that would make a dharma lose heart.

The Lord: So it is, Subhuti. It is quite certain that a Bodhisattva courses in perfect wisdom if, when this is being taught, demonstrated, expounded and pointed out, he does not lose heart, is not cast down or depressed, does not become cowed or stolid, does not turn his mind away from it, does not have his back broken, and remains unafraid.

2. THE BODHISATTVA PROTECTED BY THE GODS, AND AGAINST MARA

Subhuti: So it is. If a Bodhisattva courses thus, then he courses in perfect wisdom. And the Gods round Indra, round Brahman, round Praja-pati, round Ishana, and the crowds of men and women round the Rishis will from a distance pay homage with folded hands to a Bodhisattva who courses thus. [447]

The Lord: And not only they, but also all the other Gods, up to the Akanishta Gods, shall pay homage to him. And with their Buddha-eye the Tathagatas who at present reside in countless world systems behold the Bodhisattva who thus courses in perfect wisdom, and they help him, and bring him to mind. It is quite certain, Subhuti, that the Bodhisattvas who course in perfect wisdom, and who are helped and brought to mind by the Tathagatas, should be borne in mind as irreversible from full enlighten-ment. No obstacle put up by Mara or anyone else can stop them. Even if all beings in the great trichiliocosm should become evil Maras, and if each one of them would conjure up just as many diabolic armies, [448] then even they all together would not have the strength to obstruct on his way to full enlightenment that Bodhisattva who is brought to mind by the Buddhas, and who courses in perfect wisdom. And that would remain true even if all the beings in all the countless trichiliocosms should become evil Maras, and if each one of them should conjure up just as many diabolic armies. The endowment with two dharmas safeguards a Bodhisattva against all attacks from the Maras, or their hosts: He does not abandon any being, and he surveys all dharmas from emptiness. Two other dharmas have the same effect: As he speaks so he acts, and he is brought to mind by the Buddhas, the Lords. When a Bodhisattva courses thus, the Gods also will decide to go up to him. They will decide to ask questions and counter-questions, [449] to honour him, and to strengthen his determination by saying to him: "Soon, son of good family, shall you know full enlightenment! Therefore go on dwelling in this dwelling of perfect wisdom! For thereby you shall become a saviour of the helpless, a defender of the defenceless, a refuge to those without refuge, a place of rest to those without resting place, the final relief of those who are without it, an island to those without one, a light to the blind, a guide to the guideless, a resort to those without one, and you shall guide to the path those who have lost it, and you shall become a support to those who are without support."

3. THE BUDDHAS PRAISE THE BODHISATTVA

For the Buddhas and Lords, who reside in the countless world-systems, and who, surrounded by the congregation of monks and attended by a multitude of Bodhisattvas, demonstrate dharma, will proclaim the name, clan, power, appearance and form of a Bodhisattva who courses and dwells in perfect wisdom, and who is endowed with the virtues of roaming in perfect wisdom. And they will, when they demonstrate Dharma, exult over that Bodhisattva, proclaiming his name, clan, power, colour and form. Just here and now I demonstrate dharma, and I proclaim the name, etc., of the Bodhisattva Ratnaketu, and of the Bodhisattva Sikhin. [450] I exult over them, and also over the other Bodhisattvas who just now lead the holy life with the Tathagata Akshobhya. In a similar way, the Buddhas in other Buddha-fields proclaim the name, etc., of those Bodhisattvas who just now lead the holy life here in my Buddha-field, and who dwell in the dwelling of perfect wisdom. And they exult over them.

Subhuti: Do the Buddhas honour all Bodhisattvas in such a manner?

The Lord: No, Subhuti. But only those who are irreversible and free from all attachment.

Subhuti: Are there, apart from the irreversible Bodhisattvas, any other Bodhisattvas whom the Buddhas honour in such a manner?

The Lord: Yes, there are. They are persons belonging to the vehicle of the Bodhisattvas, who are strong in resisting the enemy. They are [451] just now engaged in learning the course of a Bodhisattva under the Tathagata Akshobhya, and the Bodhisattva Ratnaketu, course there on the pilgrimage of a Bodhisattva, and dwell engaged in learning it. In addition, those Bodhisattvas who course in perfect wisdom, and who resolutely believe that "all dharmas fail to be produced" without, however, having so far acquired definitely the patient acceptance of dharmas which fail to be produced; as well as those who resolutely believe that "all dharmas are calmly quiet," without, however, having entered into the attainment of the irreversible domain over all dharmas; those Bodhisattvas who dwell in this dwelling are honoured by the Buddhas in the above manner. [452] But Bodhisattvas of whom the Buddhas proclaim the name, etc., and over whom they exult, must have forsaken the level of the Disciples and Pratyekabuddhas, and one must expect them to be on the level of the Buddha. And they shall be predicted to full enlightenment. For Bodhisattvas of whom the Buddhas proclaim the name, etc., and over whom they exult, they also shall stand in irreversibility.

4. ENLIGHTENMENT AND SUCHNESS

Moreover, Subhuti, Bodhisattvas will stand in irreversibility if, when they hear this deep perfection of wisdom being taught, they resolutely believe in it, are not stupefied, do not hesitate or doubt; if in the resolute belief that "so it is, as the Tathagata has taught" they go on listening to it in greater detail; and if they make up their minds that they will want to listen in still greater detail to this perfection of wisdom in the presence of the Tathagata Akshobhya; and if they will resolutely believe when they listen to just this perfection of wisdom in the presence of persons belonging to the vehicle of the Bodhisattvas who in his Buddha-field lead the holy life. [453] Thus I teach that merely to hear the perfection of wisdom achieves much. How much more will be achieved by those who resolutely believe in it, who, after that, take up a position in relation to Thusness and progress to Thusness, and who, after that, stand firmly in Suchness and who, standing firmly in Suchness and in all-knowledge, will demonstrate dharma.

Subhuti: If, O Lord, one cannot get at any different dharma, distinct from Suchness, then what is that dharma that will stand firmly in Suchness, or that will know full enlightenment, or that will demonstrate this dharma?

The Lord: One cannot get at any different dharma, distinct from Suchness, that will stand firmly in Suchness. The very Suchness, to begin with, is not apprehended, how much less he who will stand firmly in Suchness. Suchness does not know full enlightenment, and no dharma is got at that has known full enlightenment, that will do so, or that does so. Suchness does not demonstrate dharma, and that dharma cannot be got at which would be demonstrated. [454]

5. EMPTINESS AND DWELLING IN PERFECT WISDOM

Sakra: Deep, O Lord, is the perfection of wisdom. Doers of what is hard are the Bodhisattvas who want to know full enlightenment. For, indeed, no dharma stands in Suchness, no dharma knows full enlightenment, no one demonstrates dharma. And yet that does not cow them, nor do they hesitate, nor are they stupefied.

Subhuti: You say, Kausika, that "doers of what is hard are the Bodhisattvas who, when dharmas as deep as these are being taught, feel neither hesitation nor stupefaction." But, where all dharmas are empty who can therein feel hesitation or stupefaction?

Sakra: Whatever the holy Subhuti may expound, that he expounds with reference to emptiness, and he does not get stuck anywhere. The holy Subhuti's demonstration of dharma does not get stuck anywhere, no more than an arrow shot into the air. Then perhaps, O Lord, I, if I take into consideration Subhuti the Elder, as he thus teaches and expounds, may become one who correctly preaches the Tathagata-truth, a preacher of Dharma, and one who declares also the logical sequence of dharma.

The Lord: So it is, Kausika. When you teach and expound as he does, then you become one who correctly preaches the Tathagata-truth, a preacher of dharma, and one who declares also the dharma's logical sequence. For whatever [455] the Elder Subhuti makes clear, that he makes clear with reference to emptiness. Because the Elder Subhuti does not, to begin with, even review or apprehend the perfection of wisdom, how much less him who courses in the perfection of wisdom. Even enlightenment, to begin with, he does not get at, how much less at him who will know full enlightenment. Even all-knowledge he does not get at, how much less at him who will reach all-knowledge. Even Suchness he does not get at, how much less at him who will become a Tathagata. Even non-production he does not get at, how much less at him who will fully awake to enlightenment. Even the powers he does not get at, how much less at him who will possess the powers. Even the grounds of self-confidence he does not review, how much less him who will be self-confident. Even the dharma he does not get at, how much less at him who will demonstrate dharma. For Subhuti the Elder dwells in the dwelling of the isolatedness of all dharmas, in the dwelling of the baselessness of all dharmas. And it is quite certain that this dwelling in the isolatedness and baselessness of all dharmas, on the part of Subhuti the Elder, is of infinitesimal value compared with the dwelling of a Bodhisattva who courses in perfect wisdom, and who dwells in it. Because, except for the dwelling of a Tathagata this dwelling of a Bodhisattva who courses in perfect wisdom, who dwells in it, surpasses all other dwellings. [456] This dwelling has been described as the foremost of all dwellings, as the best, the choicest, the most excellent, the most sublime, the highest, the supreme, the unequalled, the incomparable. It surpasses the dwellings of all Disciples and Pratyekabuddhas. Therefore then, Kausika, a son or daughter of good family who wants to arrive at what is the highest possible degree of perfection for all beings, to arrive at the best state, the choicest state, the most excellent state, the most sublime state, the incomparable state, —they should dwell in this dwelling of the Bodhisattvas who course in perfect wisdom, who dwell in it.

Chapter XXVIII

AVAKIRNAKUSUMA

1. PREDICTION OF AVAKIRNAKUSUMA

Thereupon, at that time, one of the Gods of the Thirty-three seized Mandarava flowers, magnificent Mandarava flowers, and came to where the Lord was. And just at that time, six thousand monks were assembled and seated in that assembly. They rose from their seats, put their upper robes over one shoulder, placed their right knees on the earth, and saluted the Lord with their folded hands. Through the Buddha's might their hands were then filled with Mandarava flowers, with magnificent Mandarava flowers. They scattered those flowers over the Lord, and said: "We, O Lord, shall course in this perfection of wisdom! We, O Lord, shall dwell in the supreme dwelling of perfect wisdom!" Thereupon, on that occasion, the Lord smiled. But such is the nature of the Buddhas and Lords that, when they manifest a smile [in an assembly of Bodhisattvas], then various-coloured rays issue from the Lord's mouth,—rays blue, yellow, red, white, crimson, crystal, silverish and golden. These rays illuminate endless and boundless world systems with their lustre, they rise right up to the world of Brahma, again return from there to the Lord, circulate thrice round the Lord, and then vanish again in the head of the Lord. [458] Thereupon the venerable *Ananda* rose from his seat, put his upper robe over one shoulder, placed his right knee on the earth, bent his folded hands towards the Lord, and said: It is not without reason that the Tathagatas manifest a smile. What is the reason for your smile, O Lord?

The Lord: Those six thousand monks, Ananda, shall in a future period, in the Starlike aeon, know full enlightenment, and after that demonstrate dharma to beings. They all shall bear the same name. With Avakirna-kusuma for their name these Tathagatas shall be teachers in the world. They shall all have an equal congregation of disciples. They shall all live the same length of time, i.e. twenty thousand aeons. Each one of them shall have an extensive holy writ, that shall spread widely among Gods and men. In each case their good law shall abide for the same length of time, for twenty thousand aeons. And showers of flowers, of all the five colours, shall descend on all of them—wherever they may leave the home which they had in village, town or marketplace, wherever they may turn the wheel of dharma, wherever they may dwell, wherever they may appear [among people]. [459]

2. PRAISE OF PERFECT WISDOM

Therefore then, Ananda, Bodhisattvas who want to dwell in the highest dwelling, who want to dwell in the dwelling of the Tathagata, should dwell in the dwelling of perfect wisdom. And with any Bodhisattva who courses in perfect wisdom one can be quite certain that he had, before he was reborn here among men, deceased among men or among the heavenly hosts of the Tushitas. For it is among men and the Tushita Gods that this perfection of wisdom circulates in its full extent. One can be certain that the Tathagatas behold those Bodhisattvas who course in this perfection of wisdom, who learn it, bear it in mind, study, preach, repeat, or merely write it, and who also instruct the other Bodhisattvas, admonish, instigate and encourage them. One should know that they have planted wholesome roots with the Tathagatas. They have not only in the presence of Disciples and Pratyekabuddhas planted wholesome roots so as to train in perfect wisdom, but, without any doubt, those Bodhisattvas who train in this perfection of wisdom and remain unafraid, they have planted wholesome roots with the Tathagatas. [460] Those who take up this perfection of wisdom, bear it in mind, study, preach, repeat and write it, who pursue it,—its meaning, contents and method—one should be quite certain that they have been face to face with Tathagatas. If Bodhisattvas do not revile this perfection of wisdom, do not oppose, deny or reject it, then one should know that they have fulfilled their duties under the Jinas of the past. But if a Bodhisattva does not go back on his vow to win full enlightenment, then he does not give the wholesome root, which he has planted in the presence of the Tathagatas, over to Discipleship or Pratyekabuddhahood as his reward. And as a rule such Bodhisattvas are grateful and practise the perfection of wisdom.

3. TRANSMISSION OF THE SUTRA TO ANANDA

Therefore then, Ananda, again and again I entrust and transmit to you this perfection of wisdom, laid out in letters, so that it may be available for learning, for bearing in mind, preaching, studying and spreading wide, so that it may last long, so that it may not disappear. If, Ananda, you should again forget all the demonstrations of dharma which you have learned directly from Me—the perfection of wisdom alone being excepted—should cast them away, and allow them to be forgotten, that would be but a slight offence against Me. But if you should forget, cast away and allow to be forgotten only one verse of the perfection of wisdom, or merely a part of a verse, that would be a very serious [461] offence against Me, and it would displease Me greatly. And if, after you have learned the perfection of wisdom, you again forget it, cast it away, allow it to be forgotten, then you fail in the respect, reverence and worship which you owe to Me, and to the other Buddhas and Lords, past, future and present. Therefore, Ananda, remember that it would be a seriour offence against Me if, after you had learned the perfection of wisdom, you should again forget it, cast it away, and allow it to be forgotten, and that would greatly displease Me. For the Tathagata has said that "the perfection of wisdom is the mother, the creator, the genetrix of the past, future and present Tathagatas, their nurse in all-knowledge." Therefore then, Ananda, do I entrust and transmit to you this perfection of wisdom, so that it might not disappear. This perfection of wisdom should be learned, should be borne in mind, studied, repeated, written and developed. You should attend well to this perfection of wisdom, bear it well in mind, study it well, and spread it well. And when one learns it, one should carefully analyze it grammatically, letter by letter, syllable by syllable, word by word. [462] For as the dharma-body of the past, future and present Tathagatas is this dharma-text authoritative. In the same way in which you, Ananda, behave towards Me who at present reside as a Tathagata—with solicitude, affection, respect and helpfulness—just so, with the same solicitude, affection and respect, and in the same virtuous spirit, should you learn this perfection of wisdom, bear it in mind, study, repeat, write and develop it, respect, revere and worship it. That is the way for you to worship Me, that is the way to show affection, serene faith and respect for the past, future and present Buddhas and Lords. If Ananda, I, the Tathagata, am dear and pleasant to you, and you do not abandon Me, may thereby this perfection of wisdom become dear and pleasant to you, and may you not abandon it, so that you may not forget even one single word of it, so that it may not disappear. For long could I speak to you about this bestowal of the perfection of wisdom, for one kalpa, or for the remainder of a kalpa, for one hundred kalpas, for up to hundreds of thousands of kotis of kalpas, and more. But, to cut it short, in the same way in which I am your teacher, so is the perfection of wisdom. In the same way in which the past, future and present Buddhas and Lords are the teachers of the world with its Gods, men and Asuras, just so is the perfection of wisdom. Therefore then, Ananda, [463] with a measureless bestowal I entrust and transmit to you the perfection of wisdom, which itself is measureless, for the benefit and happiness of the world with its Gods, men and Asuras. If one does not want to abandon the Tathagata, or the Dharma, or the Samgha, if one does not want to abandon the enlightenment of the past, future and present Buddhas and Lords,—may one not abandon the perfection of wisdom! And there is this further admonition that those who learn this perfection of wisdom, bear it in mind, study, repeat, write and develop it, they assist in the enlightenment of the past, future and present Buddhas and Lords. For, whoever assists this perfection of wisdom when it is crumbling away, he assists the enlightenment of the past, future and present Buddhas and Lords. Because from the perfection of wisdom has the enlightenment of the Buddhas and Lords come forth. And that holds good of all the Tathagatas, whether past, future or present. Therefore, a Bodhisattva who wants to know full enlightenment and to train in the six perfections should listen to this perfection of wisdom, study, repeat and write it, [464] and he should train in this very perfection of wisdom, and make endeavours about it. For this perfection of wisdom is the mother, creator and genetrix of the Bodhisattvas. It is thanks to the perfection of wisdom that any Bodhisattvas ever train in the six perfections, and at any time go forth to full enlightenment. It is thanks to just this perfection of wisdom that they all go forth in the six perfections. Because all the perfections come to nourish the supreme enlightenment after they have come forth from the perfection of wisdom. Therefore then, Ananda, again and again, for a second time, for a third time, do I entrust and transmit this perfection of wisdom to you, so that it might not disappear. For this perfection of wisdom is the inexhaustible storehouse of dharma for the Tathagatas. The dharma which the Buddhas and Lords have demonstrated to beings in the past period, in the world of birth-and-death which has no beginning or end, all that came from just this storehouse of dharma, from the perfection of wisdom. And also the dharma which the Buddhas and Lords will, after their full enlightenment, demonstrate to beings in the future period, in the measureless world of birth-and-death, also that will come from just this storehouse of dharma, from the perfection of wisdom. And also the Buddhas and Lords who just now reside in countless world systems, and demonstrate dharma, they also have derived their revelation from just this storehouse of dharma, from the perfection of wisdom. Inexhaustible therefore is this storehouse of dharma, the perfection of wisdom. [464a] If, Ananda, you should demonstrate dharma on the Disciple-level to persons belonging to the vehicle of the Disciples, and if as a result of your demonstration of dharma all the beings in the great trichiliocosm would realize Arhatship, you would not have done your duty as My disciple if in that way you would keep moving after Me the wheel of dharma, and demonstrate dharma. But if, on the other hand, you would demonstrate and reveal but one single verse of the dharma associated with the perfection of wisdom to a Bodhisattva, then I should be pleased with you, who as My disciple turns after Me the wheel of dharma, and demonstrates dharma. If you consider that demonstration of dharma of yours through which the beings in the great trichiliocosm have all been induced to attain Arhatship, and of those Arhats the meritorious work founded on giving, on morality, and on meditational development, would all that constitute a great heap of merit?

Ananda: It would, O Lord.

The Lord: A person belonging to the vehicle of the Disciples begets a greater merit than that if he demonstrates to Bodhisattvas the dharma associated with the perfection of wisdom. The merit is still greater if it is a Bodhisattva who demonstrates to another Bodhisattva [a verse of] dharma associated with the perfection of wisdom,—for even one single day only, for a morning, for an hour, for half an hour, for a minute, nay for a second, for a moment, for the incidence of a single moment. For the gift of dharma on the part of a Bodhisattva surpasses all the wholesome roots of all those who belong to the vehicle of the Disciples or Pratyekabuddhas. It is quite impossible that a Bodhisattva who is thus endowed with wholesome roots, who thus brings to mind that wholesome root, could possibly turn away from full enlightenment. That cannot be.

4. AKSHOBHYA'S BUDDHA-FIELD

Thereupon the Lord on that occasion exercised His wonderworking power. The entire assembly—monks, nuns, laymen and laywomen, Gods, Nagas, Yakshas, Gandharvas, Asuras, Garudas, Kinnaras, Mahoragas, men and ghosts—they all, through the Buddha's might, [465] saw the Tathagata Akshobhya surrounded by the congregation of monks, accompanied by a retinue of Bodhisattvas demonstrating dharma, in an assembly which was vast like the ocean, deep and imperturbable, surrounded and accompanied by Bodhisattvas who were endowed with unthinkable qualities, all of them Arhats,—their outflows exhausted, undefiled, fully controlled, quite freed in their hearts, well freed and wise, thoroughbreds, great Serpents, their work done, their task accomplished, their burden laid down, their own weal accomplished, with the fetters that bound them to becoming extinguished, their hearts well freed by right understanding, in perfect control of their entire hearts. Thereupon the Lord again withdrew His wonderworking power. The Lord Akshobhya, the Tathagata, then no longer appeared, and all those Bodhisattvas and great Disciples, and that Buddha-field no longer came within the range of vision of the members of the Lord's assembly. For the Tathagata had drawn in His wonderworking power. And *The Lord* said to Ananda: In the same way, Ananda, all dharmas do not come within the range of vision. Dharmas do not come within the range of vision of dharmas, dharmas do not see dharmas, dharmas to not know dharmas. For all dharmas are of such a nature that they can be neither known nor seen, and they are incapable of doing anything. For all dharmas are inactive, they cannot be grasped, because they are as inactive as space. All dharmas are unthinkable, similar to illusory men. All dharmas are unfindable, because they are in a state of non-existence. When he courses thus a Bodhisattva courses in perfect wisdom and he does not settle down in any dharma. [466] When he trains thus, a Bodhisattva trains in perfect wisdom. If a Bodhisattva wants to attain the great enlightenment, which is the highest perfection of all training, then he should train in perfect wisdom. For the training in perfect wisdom has been described as the foremost of all trainings, as the best, the choicest, the most excellent, the most sublime, the highest, the utmost, the unequalled, the incomparable, it has been said to bring benefit and happiness to all the world, it has been described as a protector of the helpless, it has been ordained and extolled by the Buddha. The Tathagatas could, as a result of training in this perfection of wisdom, of having stood in this training, lift up this great trichiliocosm with one big toe, and then just let it drop again. But it would not occur to those Buddhas and Lords that "this great trichiliocosm has been lifted up, has been dropped again." For perfect wisdom is endowed with immeasurable and incalculable qualities. As a result of training in this training of perfect wisdom, the Buddhas and Lords have reached a state of non-attachment to past, future and present dharmas. Of all the possible trainings in the past, future and present period, this training in perfect wisdom is the foremost, the best, the choicest, the most excellent, the most sublime, the highest, the utmost, the unequalled, the incomparable.

5. EXTINCTION, NON-EXTINCTION AND PERFECT WISDOM

For perfect wisdom has no limits, it is inexhaustible and boundless. [467] Because limits, exhaustion and bounds are absent in perfect wisdom. To attribute limits, exhaustion and bounds to perfect wisdom would be like attributing them to space. For the perfection of wisdom is unlimited, inexhaustible and boundless. I have not taught that the perfection of wisdom has any limits, that it can be exhausted, that it has any bounds. The sum total of the words contained in this Sutra on perfect wisdom certainly has its limits, but not so the perfection of wisdom itself. For the sum total of the words in this Sutra is not identical with the perfection of wisdom itself. Perfect wisdom itself is not subject to any limitations, it is without any limits whatever.

Ananda: For what reason again has the Lord not taught any limits to perfect wisdom?

The Lord: Because it is inexhaustible and isolated. One cannot even apprehend the isolatedness of an isolated dharma, how much less can there be a definite circumference to it? Thus, as beyond all measurements the perfection of wisdom is unlimited, without any limits whatever. The Tathagatas of the past have drawn their strength from just this perfection of wisdom, [468] and yet it has not been exhausted, nor become extinct. The Tathagatas of the future also shall draw their strength from just this perfection of wisdom, and yet it shall not be exhausted, shall not become extinct. Those Tathagatas also who just now reside in countless world systems, they also draw their strength from just this perfection of wisdom, and yet it does not become exhausted or extinct. I also, who am a Tathagata just now, I also draw My strength from just this perfection of wisdom, and yet it does not become exhausted, or extinct. One can exhaust the perfection of wisdom no more than one can exhaust space. This perfection of wisdom is therefore quite inexhaustible.

Thereupon it occurred to the venerable *Subhuti*: Deep is this station which the Tathagata has taught. Let me then now question the Tathagata about this station. And Subhuti said to the Lord: Inexhaustible, O Lord, is perfect wisdom!

The Lord: Because it cannot become extinct, since, like space, it cannot be extinguished, and since all dharmas have not been produced.

Subhuti: How should a Bodhisattva consummate the perfection of wisdom?

The Lord: Through the non-extinction of form, etc. [469] Through the non-extinction of ignorance, of the karma-formations, of consciousness, of name and form, of the six sense-fields, of contact, of feeling, of craving, of grasping, of becoming, of birth, of decay and death, of grief, lamentation, pain, sadness and despair. In this manner the Bodhisattva surveys conditioned coproduction in such a way that he avoids the duality of the extremes. He surveys it without seeing any beginning, end or middle. To survey conditioned coproduction in such a manner, that is the special dharma of the Bodhisattva who is seated on the terrace of enlightenment. When he thus surveys conditioned coproduction, he acquires the cognition of the all-knowing. For a Bodhisattva who, while he courses in perfect wisdom through this consummation of non-extinction, surveys conditioned coproduction, cannot stand on the level of Disciple or Pratyekabuddha, but he must stand in all-knowledge. Some Bodhisattvas may turn away from supreme enlightenment, if, because they have failed to resort to these mental activities [which aspire to the consummation of non-extinction] and to this skill in means, they do not know how a Bodhisattva who courses in perfect wisdom should consummate perfect wisdom through the consummation of non-extinction, [470] and how conditioned coproduction should be surveyed in the perfection of wisdom through the consummation of non-extinction. All Bodhisattvas who at any time turn away from full enlightenment do so because they did not resort to this skill in means. All those Bodhisattvas who at any time do not turn away from full enlightenment, do so thanks to this perfection of wisdom. In this way should a Bodhisattva who courses in perfect wisdom consummate perfect wisdom through the consummation of non-extinction. And in this way should conditioned coproduction be surveyed in the perfection of wisdom through the consummation of non-extinction. A Bodhisattva who thus surveys conditioned coproduction, does certainly not review any dharma that is being produced without a cause nor does he review any dharmas as permanent, stable, eternal, not liable to reversal, nor does he review any dharmas as a doer or a feeler. This is the surveying of conditioned coproduction on the part of a Bodhisattva who consummates this perfection of wisdom through the consummation of non-extinction, and who courses in this perfection of wisdom. At the time when a Bodhisattva, consummating the perfection of wisdom through the consummation of non-extinction, surveys conditioned coproduction, at that time he does not review form as if it were a real separate entity, nor feelings, perceptions, impulses or consciousness; nor ignorance, karma-formations, etc., to decay and death, [471] sorrow, lamentation, pain, sadness and despair; nor does he review the fact that "this is my Buddha-field" as if it were real, nor the fact that "that is another Buddha-field," nor does he review as real any dharma by which he could distinguish between this and other Buddha-fields. This, Subhuti, is the perfection of wisdom of the Bodhisattvas, the great beings.

6. ADVANTAGES DERIVED FROM PERFECT WISDOM

When a Bodhisattva courses in perfect wisdom, Mara the Evil One feels struck with the dark of great sorrow, just as a man does when his mother or father have died.

Subhuti: Is this affliction confined to one Mara, or does it affect many Maras, or does it extend to all the Maras in the great trichiliocosm?

The Lord: At the time when Bodhisattvas dwell in the dwelling of perfect wisdom at that time all the Maras in the great trichiliocosm feel struck with the dart of great sorrow, and they cannot sit still on their respective thrones. [472] For the entire world, with its Gods, men and Asuras, cannot gain entry to a Bodhisattva who dwells within the dwelling of perfect wisdom, it cannot gain a foothold which would allow it to take possession of him, to hurt him, to turn him away from full enlightenment. Therefore then, Subhuti, a Bodhisattva who wants to know full enlightenment should course in perfect wisdom. For in a Bodhisattva who courses in perfect wisdom the perfection of giving arrives at its most perfect development, and so do the perfections of morality, patience, vigour, and concentration. In him all the six perfections arrive at their most perfect development, and also all the varieties of skill in means. Whatever deeds of Mara may arise in a Bodhisattva who courses in perfect wisdom, he shall wisely know them when they are taking place, and he shall get rid of them again. A Bodhisattva who wants to acquire all the varieties of skill in means should course in perfect wisdom, and develop it. At the time when a Bodhisattva courses in perfect wisdom, and aspires for it, he should bring to mind not only the Buddhas and Lords who reside in countless world systems, but also their all-knowledge which has come forth from this perfection of wisdom. He should then produce the thought that "also I shall reach those dharmas which those Buddhas and Lords have reached!" [473] For a day, or even down to the time taken up by a finger snap, should a Bodhisattva who courses in perfect wisdom raise such thoughts and aspire to them. But a Bodhisattva who would even for one day, or even for the duration of a fingersnap, aspire for this perfection of wisdom would beget more merit than a Bodhisattva who leans on a basis, and who for countless aeons gives gifts. Such a Bodhisattva will stand in irreversibility. A Bodhisattva who courses in perfect wisdom and who, even for a day, or even for the duration of a finger snap, raises such thoughts, has, we know, been brought to mind by the Tathagatas. How much more so one who daily pursues such thoughts. What future destiny should one expect a Bodhisattva to have whom the Tathagatas have brought to mind? No other destiny except full enlightenment can be expected of him. He cannot possibly be reborn in the states of woe. One must expect that he will be reborn in heaven, and that even there he will not be without the Tathagatas, and that he will mature beings. These are the qualities and advantages of a Bodhisattva who courses in perfect wisdom, who aspires for perfect wisdom, and who raises such thoughts, [474] if even for the length of a finger snap. How much greater will be the advantage of one who pursues such thoughts daily, as for instance the Bodhisattva Gandhahastin who just now leads the holy life in the presence of the Tathagata Akshobhya.

Chapter XXIX

APPROACHES

Furthermore, Subhuti, a Bodhisattva should approach the perfection of wisdom as follows: Through non-attachment to all dharmas. From the non-differentiatedness of all dharmas. From the fact that all dharmas cannot possibly come about. In the conviction that "all dharmas are equal in remaining unaffected by change." Because he has recognized by wisdom that all dharmas, as without self, give us no hint [about their true nature or intentions]. In the conviction that "all talk about dharmas [is extraneous to them], consists in mere words, mere conventional expression,"—but the conventional expression does not refer to anything real, it is not derived from anything real, nor is itself anything real. In the conviction that "all dharmas lie outside conventional expression and discourse, that it is not they that have been conventionally expressed or uttered." From the unlimitedness of all dharmas. From the unlimitedness of form, etc., from the signlessness of all dharmas. [476] By penetration into all dharmas. From the fact that all dharmas are perfectly pure in their original nature. From the fact that all dharmas are beyond words. Because all the different kinds of forsaking are really equal [in value and kind], since all dharmas have never been stopped. Because Suchness is everywhere the same, since all dharmas have already attained Nirvana. In the conviction that "all dharmas do not come, nor do they go; they cannot be generated, they are unborn, their non-birth being absolute." Because he observes neither himself nor others. In the conviction that "all dharmas are holy Arhats, perfectly pure in their original nature." In the conviction that "all dharmas have put down their burden, because no burden had ever been put on them." From the fact that all dharmas have neither place nor locality. For form, etc., is without place and locality, in accordance with the own-being of its original nature. Because he is exhilarated by the cessation of all dharmas. Because he feels neither content nor discontent. Because he becomes neither impassioned nor dispassionate. For form, etc., in their true reality, in their own-being, do not become either impassioned or dispassioned. In the convinction that "the original nature [of all dharmas], is perfectly pure." In the conviction that, "all dharmas are non-attached, free from both attachment and non-attachment." [477] In the conviction that "all dharmas are essentially enlightenment, because they are all equally understood by the Buddha-cognition." From the emptiness, Signlessness and Wishlessness of all dharmas. In the conviction that "all dharmas are essentially a healing medicine, because they are controlled by friendliness." In the conviction that "all dharmas are dwellers in friendliness, dwellers in compassion, dwellers in sympathetic joy, dwellers in impartiality." In the conviction that "all dharmas are identified with the supreme universal spirit, because in their being no faults can arise, because in their essential being all faults remain unproduced." In the conviction that "all dharmas are equally neither hopeful nor hostile."

One should approach the boundlessness of the perfection of wisdom through [the analogy of] the boundlessness of the ocean; through [the analogy of] the multicoloured brilliance of Meru. One should approach the boundlessness of the perfection of wisdom: from the boundlessness of form, etc.; through the [analogy of] boundless illumination shed by the circle of the sun's rays; from the boundlessness of all sounds; from the boundlessness of the final achievement of all the dharmas of a Buddha; from the boundlessness [of the excellence] of the equipment of the whole world of beings with merit and cognition; from the boundlessness of the element of earth; and so from the boundlessness of the elements of water, fire, air, space and consciousness. [478]

One should approach the unlimitedness of the perfection of wisdom from the unlimitedness of the collection of wholesome and unwholesome dharmas; from the unlimitedness of the collection of all dharmas.

One should approach the boundlessness of the perfection of wisdom: through the acquisition of the boundlessness of the concentration on all dharmas; from the boundlessness of all Buddha-dharmas; from the boundlessness of all dharmas; from the boundlessness of emptiness; from the boundlessness of thought and its constituents; from the boundlessness of thoughts and actions.

One should approach the measurelessness of the perfection of wisdom from the measurelessness of wholesome and unwholesome dharmas. One should approach the resounding declarations of the perfection of wisdom through the [analogy of the] roaring of the lion's roar.

One should approach the fact that the perfection of wisdom cannot be shaken by outside factors from the fact that all dharmas cannot be shaken by outside factors. For form, etc., is like the ocean. Form, and each skandha, is like the firmament; like the brilliant and multicoloured Meru; like the production of the rays of the disk of the sun; boundless like all sounds; boundless like the whole world of beings; boundless like the final achievement of the dharmas of a Buddha; boundless like the equipment with merit and cognition of all beings in the world; [479] it is like the earth, like water, fire, air, space and consciousness; it has no definite boundary like the collection of all wholesome and unwholesome dharmas;

it has no definite boundary like the collection of all dharmas. Form is the departure [into Buddhahood], the own-being of form is the Buddha-dharmas which are essentially the Suchness of form; etc., to: consciousness is departure [into Buddhahood], the own-being of consciousness is the Buddha-dharmas which are essentially the Suchness of consciousness. Form, and each skandha, is the boundless true nature of all dharmas; the empty, boundless true nature [of things]; the boundlessness of thought and its constituents; it gives rise to thoughts and actions; it is wholesome or unwholesome until there is non-apprehension; it is like the lion's roar; it cannot be shaken by outside factors.

In such ways should a Bodhisattva approach perfect wisdom. [480] If the Bodhisattva approaches perfect wisdom in this way, apperceives it, enters into it, understands it, reflects on it, examines, investigates, and develops it,—with acts of mind that have abandoned all deception and deceit, all conceit, the exaltation of self, all laziness, the deprecation of others, the notion of self, the notion of a being, gain, honour and fame, the five hindrances, envy and meanness, and all vacillation,—then it will not be hard for him to gain the full perfection of all virtues, of the Buddha-field and of the supreme dharmas of a Buddha.

Chapter XXX

SADAPRARUDITA

1. SADAPRARUDITA SETS OUT TO FIND PERFECT WISDOM

Furthermore, Subhuti, one should search for perfect wisdom as the Bodhisattva Sadaprarudita has done, who at present leads the holy life in the presence of the Tathagata Bhishmagarjitanirghoshasvara.

Subhuti: How then did the Bodhisattva Sadaprarudita search for the perfection of wisdom?

The Lord: First of all Sadaprarudita, the Bodhisattva, searched for perfect wisdom in such a way that he did not care for his body, had no regard for his life, and gain, honour and fame did not interest him. He found himself in the seclusion of a remote forest, and *a voice* up in the air said to him:

Go East, son of good family! There you shall hear the perfection of wisdom! And on your way you must not pay any attention to the weariness of your body, you must not give in to any fatigue, you must pay no attention to food or drink, to day or night, to cold or heat. You must not make any definite plans, either about inward, or about outward things. You must not look to the left or right, to the South, East, West or North, upwards or downwards, or in any of the intermediate directions. And you must not allow yourself to be shaken by self or individuality, or by form or the other skandhas. [482] For one who is shaken by those, he is turned away from the Buddha-dharmas. When he is turned away from the Buddha-dharmas, then he wanders in birth-and-death. And when he wanders in birth-and-death, then he does not course in perfect wisdom, then he cannot reach the perfection of wisdom.

Sadaprarudita said to the voice: That is how I shall act. Because I want to bring light to all beings, because I want to procure the dharmas of a Buddha.

The Voice answered: Well spoken, son of good family!

Thereupon the Bodhisattva Sadaprarudita again listened to *the voice*, and what he heard was this:

Son of good family, you should search for perfect wisdom after you have produced the firm conviction that all dharmas are void, signless and wishless. You must shun signs, existence, and the false view that there are beings. You must shun bad friends. Good friends, however, you should tend, love and honour. They are those who demonstrate dharma, and who teach that "all dharmas are void, signless and wishless, not produced, not stopped and non-existent." When you progress like this, you shall before long be able to study the perfection of wisdom either from a book, or from the mouth of a monk who preaches dharma. And you should treat as the Teacher that person from whom you may come to hear the perfection of wisdom, you should be grateful and thankful, and you should think [483]: "This is my good friend. When I have heard the perfection of wisdom from him, I shall soon become irreversible from full enlightenment, shall be quite near the Tathagatas, shall be reborn in Buddha-fields in which Tathagatas are not lacking, and, avoiding the unfortunate rebirths, I shall accomplish an auspicious rebirth!" When you weigh up these advantages, you are bound to treat that monk who preaches dharma as the Teacher. You should not follow him with motives of worldly gain, but from desire for dharma, out of respect for dharma. You must also see through Mara's deeds. For there is always Mara, the Evil One, who may suggest that your teacher tends, enjoys and honours things that can be seen, heard, smelled, tasted or touched, when in actual fact he does so from skill in means, and has really risen above them. You should therefore not lose confidence in him, but say to yourself: "I do not know that skill in means as he wisely knows it. He tends, enjoys and honours those dharmas, in order to discipline beings, in order to win wholesome roots for them. For no attachment to objective supports exists in Bodhisattvas." After that you should contemplate the true reality of dharmas, i.e. that all dharmas are without both defilement and purification. For all dharmas are empty in their own-being [484], they have none of the properties of a living being, they have no life, no individuality, no personality, they are like an illusion, a dream, an echo, a reflected image. When you thus contemplate the true reality of all dharmas, and follow the preacher of dharma, you shall before long go forth into the perfection of wisdom. But you must watch out for yet another deed of Mara. If the preacher of dharma should dishearten you by what he says, that should not make you averse to the perfection of wisdom; but with a mind that desires only dharma, that respects only dharma, you should, unwearied, follow the monk who preaches dharma.

After receiving this admonition from the voice, the Bodhisattva Sadaprarudita journeyed East. Before long it occurred to him that he had not asked the voice how far he ought to go. He stood still just where he was, cried, sorrowed and lamented. For seven days he stayed in that very spot waiting to be told where he could hear the perfection of wisdom, and all that time he paid no attention to anything else, and took no food, but simply paid homage to perfect wisdom.

A man, Subhuti, who had lost his only child, would be very sad and unhappy, [485] and he could think of one thing only, his son and the sorrow he feels from him. Even so the Bodhisattva Sadaprarudita could at that time think of nothing else, except "when then shall I hear this perfection of wisdom?"

2. DESCRIPTION OF GANDHAVATI, AND OF DHARMODGATA'S LIFE

When Sadaprarudita thus sorrowed and pined away, a *Tathagata-frame* [suddenly] stood before him, gave his approval and said: Well spoken, son of good family! For the Tathagatas of the past, when they were Bodhisattvas, have also searched for perfect wisdom in the same spirit in which you just now search for it. In this same spirit of vigour and determination, of zeal and zest,—do you go East! There, five hundred leagues away from here, is a town called Gandhavati. It is built of the seven precious things. It is twelve leagues long and twelve leagues broad, and enclosed by seven walls, seven moats and seven rows of palm trees. It is prosperous and flourishing, secure from attack, contains abundant provisions and is full of beasts and men. Five hundred rows of shops run through the town from one end to the other, beautiful to behold like a well-coloured painting, arranged one by one in regular succession, and in between them well-constructed sites and passages are erected, respectively for vehicles drawn by animals, for palanquins, and for pedestrians, so that there is plenty of room for all. The walls all round that town are made of the seven precious substances. [486] Their well-founded copings slope into the golden river Jambu. And on each coping grows a tree, made of the seven precious things, laden with various fruits, also made of precious things. All around, between each tree and the next, hangs a string, also made of precious substances. A network of small bells is fastened on the strings, and thus surrounds the entire city. When stirred by the wind, the small bells give out a sweet, charming and delightful sound, just like the sound from the five musical instruments when they are played in harmony by the Gandharvas, skilled in songs. And that sound causes those beings to divert, enjoy and amuse themselves. The moats all around the city are full of water which flows gently along, neither too cold nor too hot. The boats on that river are brilliant with the seven precious things, beautiful to behold, and their existence is a reward of the past deeds of the inhabitants who, aboard them, divert, enjoy and amuse themselves. The water is everywhere covered with blossoms of the blue lotus, of the pink lotus, of the white lotus, and with other most beautiful and fragrant flowers. There is no species of flowers in the great trichiliocosm that is not found there. All around that city there are five hundred parks, beautiful to behold, brilliant with the seven precious things. [487] Each park has five times five hundred large lotus ponds, covered with beautiful blossoms, each of the size of a cart-wheel, fragrant,—blue, yellow, red and white. The sounds of geese, cranes, ducks, curlews and other birds fill the air over the ponds. And the exis-tence of those parks which they do not regard as their own private prop-erty is a reward for the past deeds of those beings, for they had coursed for a long time in the perfection of wisdom, their minds faithfully devoted to the Guide of the Buddhas and bent on listening to her and understand-ing her, and for a long time they had been intent on deep dharmas. And there, in that city of Gandhavati, at a place where four roads meet, is the house of the Bodhisattva Dharmodgata,—one league all round, bright with the seven precious things, beautiful to behold, enclosed by seven walls and seven rows of palm trees. There are four parks near the house, for the enjoyment of those who live in it. They are called Nityapramudita, Asoka, Sokavigata, and Pushpacitra. Each park has eight lotus ponds, called Bha-dra, Bhadrottama, Nandi, Nandottama, Kshama, Kshamottama, Niyata and Avivaha. One side of each pond is of gold, the second of silver, [488] the third of vaidurya, the fourth of crystal. The ground at the bottom consists of quartz, with golden sand over it. Each pond has eight stairs to it, decorated with steps, made of variegated jewels. In the gaps between the steps, inside the golden river Jambu, grows a plantain tree. The ponds are covered with various kinds of water flowers, and the air above them is filled with the sounds of various birds. Round these ponds grow various flowering trees, and when they are stirred by the wind, their flowers drop into the ponds. The water in the ponds has the scent, colour, taste and feel of sandalwood. In this mansion lives the Bodhisattva Dharmodgata, with his retinue, among them sixty-eight thousand women. He diverts, enjoys and amuses himself, he feels and tastes the five kinds of sense-pleasure. All the inhabitants of that city, both women and men, divert, enjoy and amuse themselves, they have constant joy in the parks and on the ponds and they feel and taste the five kinds of sense-pleasure. The Bodhisattva Dharmodgata, however, with his retinue, diverts, enjoys and amuses him-self only for a certain time, and thereafter he always demonstrates the perfection of wisdom. And the citizens of that town built a pulpit for the Bodhisattva Dharmodgata in the central square of the town. It has a gold-en base, then a cotton mattress is spread on that, then a woollen cover, a cushion and a silken cloth are put on top of that. High up in the air, half a Kos high, there is an awning, shining with pearls, even and firm. All [489] round that pulpit flowers of the five colours are strewed and scattered, and the pulpit itself is scented with various perfumes. So pure is the heart of Dharmodgata, so great the respect of his hearers for dharma. Seated on that pulpit the Bodhisattva Dharmodgata demonstrates the perfection of wisdom. The citizens of that town listen to his teaching with great respect for dharma, with trust in dharma, with faith in what is worthy of faith, with minds that are lifted up in faith. In addition many hundreds, many thousands, many hundreds of thousands of living beings, Gods and men, assemble there to listen. Some of them explain the perfection of wisdom, some repeat it, some copy it, some follow it with wise attention. All those beings are no longer doomed to fall into the states of woe, and they are irreversible from full enlightenment. Son of good family, go to that Bodhisattva Dharmodgata! From him you shall hear the perfection of wisdom. For he has been for a long time your good friend, he has summoned, instigated and encouraged you to win full enlightenment. He also has, in the past, searched for the perfection of wisdom in the same way in which just now you search for it. Go forth, son of good family, go on day and night, giving your undivided attention to the task! Before long you shall hear the perfection of wisdom!

When the Bodhisattva Sadaprarudita had heard this, he became contented, elated, joyful, overjoyed and jubilant. [490] A man, hit with a poisoned arrow, could not think of anything else except: "Where shall I find a surgeon, a skilled physician, who can pull out this arrow, and free me from this suffering." Just so the Bodhisattva Sadaprarudita at that time pays no attention to any dharma except: "When then shall I see that son of good family from whom I shall hear the perfection of wisdom? When I have heard that dharma, I shall forsake all attentions to a basis." Without leaving the place where he was Sadaprarudita then heard the Bodhisattva Dharmodgata demonstrating the perfection of wisdom.

3. LIST AND SIGNIFICANCE OF CONCENTRATIONS

As a result he produced a perception which did not lean on any dharma. And he came face to face with many doors to concentration. The names of the concentrations were as follows: "It surveys the own-being of all dharmas," "The non-apprehension of the own-being of all dharmas," "Entrance to the cognition of the own-being of all dharmas," "Non-difference of all dharmas," "Spectator of the unchangeability of all dharmas," "Illuminator of all dharmas," "From all dharmas darkness has vanished," "It shatters the cognition of all dharmas," "It tosses all dharmas about," "The non-apprehension of all dharmas," "Bedecked with flowers," "Within its body it consummates all dharmas," "Having abandoned illusion," "Calling forth images reflected in a mirror," "Calling forth the sounds of all beings," "Without any dirt," "Gladdening all beings," "A follower of the vocal sounds of all beings, from skill in means," [491] "Consummation of the whole variety of letters, words and vocal sounds," "The state which comes from feeling no rigidity," "Inexpressible in its essential nature," "Attainment of unobstructed emancipation," "Visit from the king," "Grammatical analysis of speech into words and letters," "It has insight into all dharmas," "It has left the sphere of all dharmas behind," "The unobstructed limit of all dharmas," "Fashioned like the firmament," "Like a thunderbolt," "The king is near," "The unrivalled king," "Victorious," "One cannot avert the eye," "Fixed on the element of dharma," "Come out of the element of dharma," "Granter of consolation," "It has roared like a lion," "No world for beings to be reborn in," "Free from dirt," "Undefiled," "Lotus-array," "Annihilation of hesitation," "Follower of all substantial excellence," "Elevated above all dharmas," "Attainment of the super-knowledges, the powers and the grounds of self-confidence," "Piercer of all dharmas," "Seal of the desisting from becoming on the part of all dharmas," "The ocean in which all dharmas lose their becoming," "Spectator of all dharmas without distinction," "It has left behind the jungle of all views and actions," "Without darkness," "Without a sign of all dharmas," [492] "Freed from all attachment," "Without a trace of laziness," "It sheds light on deep dharmas," "Fashioned like Meru," "Irresistible," "It shatters the circle of Mara's army," "No inclination for anything in the triple world," "Emission of rays," "Sight of the Tathagata," "Spectator of all Tathagatas."

Established in these concentrations, he saw the Buddhas and Lords in the countless worlds in the ten directions, as they revealed this very perfection of wisdom to Bodhisattvas. And those Tathagatas applauded and comforted him, and they said to him:

We also have in the past, when we were Bodhisattvas, searched for the perfection of wisdom in just the same way. We also, while we were searching, acquired just those concentrations which you have acquired just now. After we had acquired them we have gone on our route, established in the perfection of wisdom and the irreversible dharmas of a Buddha. But when we survey the original essential nature and the own-being of these concentrations, then we do not see any real dharma that enters into them, or that emerges from them, that would course towards enlightenment, or that would know full enlightenment. This absence of imaginings about any dharma whatsoever, that is this perfection of wisdom. Because we have stood firm in the absence of all self-conceited imaginings we have acquired our bodies of golden colour, the thirty-two marks of the superman, the eighty accessory marks, and the splendid haloes around us, and we have reached the unthinkable and supreme cognition of Buddhas, the wisdom of Buddhas, the supreme concentration of Buddhas, and the perfection of all the dharmas and qualities of Buddhas. [493] Even the Tathagatas cannot grasp the measure, nor define the boundary, of that perfection of qualities,—how much less the Disciples and Pratyekabuddhas. You should therefore fill your mind with respect for these dharmas of the Buddhas, so that you should increasingly desire them, so that you should become more and more zealous for them. Because the supreme enlightenment is not hard to get for one who desires it, who is zealous for it. For the good friend also should you arouse intense respect and affection, and serene should be your confidence in him. For it is when they have been taken hold of by the good friend that Bodhisattvas shall quickly know full enlightenment.

Sadaprarudita asked the Tathagatas: Who is our good friend?

The Tathagatas replied: The Bodhisattva Dharmodgata has for a long time matured you for the supreme enlightenment, he has upheld you, he has been your preceptor in perfect wisdom, in skill in means, and in the dharmas of a Buddha. It was he who has upheld you, and for that friendly deed you must honour him in gratitude and thankfulness, and you must bear in mind what he has done for you. If, son of good family, you should for one aeon, or for two aeons, or for up to one hundred thousand aeons, or more, carry about the Bodhisattva Dharmodgata like a turban on your head, would furnish him with everything that makes beings happy, and would present him with as many forms, sounds, smells, tastes and touch-ables as there are in the great trichiliocosm, [494] —even then you would not have repaid that son of good family for what he has done for you. For it has happened through his might that you have acquired these concentra-tions, that you have heard of the perfection of wisdom and of skill in means, and that you have gained the perfection of wisdom.

4. SADAPRARUDITA AND THE MERCHANT'S DAUGHTER

After the Tathagatas had comforted the Bodhisattva Sadaprarudita, they again disappeared. But *Sadaprarudita* emerged from his concentra-tions, and asked himself "whence have those Tathagatas come, and whither have they gone?" Since he could no longer see thoseTathagatas, he was worried and pined away for them. He thought to himself: "The holy Bodhisattva Dharmodgata has acquired the dharanis, he possesses the five superknowledges, he has performed his duties under the Jinas of the past, he is my patron and good friend, who for a long time has done good to me. When I have come to him I must ask him about this matter, ask him to explain whence those Tathagatas have come, and whither they have gone." Sadaprarudita thereupon nursed affection and confidence, esteem and respect for the Bodhisattva Dharmodgata. He then reflected: "With what kind of honoring gift could I now approach the Bodhisattva Dharmodgata? But I am poor, and have nothing of any value [495] with which I could express my respect and reverence for him. It would not be seemly for me to come without anything at all. But I am poor, and that now makes me sad and regretful."

Such were the feelings, such was the attitude of reverence, with which the Bodhisattva Sadaprarudita proceeded on his journey. In due course he reached a town, went to the midst of the marketplace, and decided that he would sell his own body, and with the price thereof do honour to the Bodhisattva Dharmodgata. "For through the long night of the past, in the measureless cycle of birth-and-death, thousands of bodies of mine have been shattered, wasted, destroyed and sold, again and again. I have experienced measureless pains in the hells for the sake of sense pleasures, as a result of sense pleasures, but never yet on behalf of dharmas of this kind, never yet for the purpose of doing honour to beings of such a kind." Sadaprarudita then went to the middle of the marketplace, lifted up his voice, and cried: "Who wants a man? Who wants a man? Who wants to buy a man?"

Thereupon *Mara* the Evil One thought to himself: "Let obstruct this Bodhisattva Sadaprarudita. For if he succeeds in selling himself out of concern for dharma, if he then goes on to honour the Bodhisattva Dharmodgata, and to ask him, with regard to the perfection of wisdom and to skill in means, how a Bodhisattva coursing in perfect wisdom may quickly achieve full enlightenment, then he is bound to reach the ocean of sacred knowledge, shall become inaccessible to Mara and his host, [496] and will reach the perfection of all qualities, after which he will work the weal of all beings, and take them away from my sphere, and others again he will take away after he has known full enlightenment." Mara, the Evil One, thereupon so disposed the Brahmins and householders in that town that they could not hear the voice of Sadaprarudita. When *Sadaprarudita* could not find a buyer for himself, he went on one side, wailed, shed tears, and said: "Alas, it is hard on us that we do not find a buyer even for our body, so that we could, after selling our body, honour the Bodhisattva Dharmodgata."

Thereupon *Sakra*, Chief of Gods, thought to himself: "Let me weigh up the Bodhisattva Sadaprarudita. Will he now, filled with earnest intention, renounce his body out of concern for dharma, or will he not?" *Sakra* then conjured up the guise of a young man, went to the Bodhisattva Sadaprarudita, and said to him: "Why do you, son of good family, stand there dejected, pining away and shedding tears?" [497] *Sadaprarudita* replied: "I want to sell myself, but I cannot find anyone to buy my body." *Sakra*, in the form of the young man, said: "On behalf of what do you want to sell yourself?" *Sadaprarudita* replied: "From love for dharma I want to sell myself, so as to do worship to dharma, and to honour the holy Bodhisattva Dharmodgata. But I do not find a buyer for this body of mine. I have therefore thought to myself that, alas, I must be a person of exceedingly small merit indeed." The *young man* said: "I myself have no need of a man. But my father is due to offer sacrifice. For that I require a man's heart, his blood and the marrow of his bones. Those you may give me, and I shall pay for them." *Sadaprarudita* then thought to himself: "I have exceedingly easily got what I desired. Now I know that my body is sufficiently perfect for me to win perfect wisdom, skill in means and the dharmas of a Buddha, since in this young man I have now found a buyer for my heart, blood and marrow." With his mind bristling with joy, and all ready, he said: "I will give you my body, since you have need of it!" The *young man* asked: "What price do I give you?" *Sadaprarudita* answered: "Give me whatever you will!" [498] Sadaprarudita then took a sharp sword, pierced his right arm, and made the blood flow. He pierced his right thigh, cut the flesh from it, and strode up to the foot of a wall in order to break the bone.

A *merchant's daughter*, from her upper window, saw this, and she thought to herself: "Why should this son of good family do that to himself? Let me go to him, and ask him." She went up to Sadaprarudita, and said: "Why do you inflict such fatal treatment on yourself? What shall you do with this blood, and with the marrow of your bones?" *Sadaprarudita* said: "When I have sold them to this young man, I shall go to worship the perfection of wisdom, and to do honour to the holy Bodhisattva Dharmodgata." The *merchant's daughter* said: "What is the kind of quality, what is the excellence of the qualities, which you will create in yourself by your wish to honour the Bodhisattva Dharmodgata after you have sold your own heart, blood and marrow?" *Sadaprarudita* replied: "Dharmodgata will explain to me the perfection of wisdom and the skill in means. [499] In them I shall train myself, and, as a result, I shall become a refuge to all beings; and, after I have known full enlightenment, I shall acquire a body of golden colour, the thirty-two marks of the superman, the eighty accessory marks, the splendour of a halo the rays of which extend to infinitude, the great friendliness, the great compassion, the great sympathetic joy, the great impartiality, the four grounds of self-confidence, the four analytical knowledges, the eighteen special dharmas of a Buddha, and I shall acquire the five superknowledges, an unthinkable purity of conduct, an unthinkable purity of concentration, an unthinkable purity of wisdom, and the ten powers of a Tathagata. I shall fully awake to the supreme cognition of a Buddha, and acquire the supremely precious jewel of the dharma, which I shall share with all beings."

The *merchant's daughter* replied: "It is wonderful, son of good family, how exalted and sublime are the dharmas which you have proclaimed. For the sake of even one of these dharmas should one be willing to renounce one's bodies even for countless aeons, how much more so for the sake of many of them. These dharmas which you have proclaimed please me also, and seem good to me. But see, son of good family, I shall give you whatever you may require, and with that you may [500] then honour that Bodhisattva Dharmodgata! But do not inflict such treatment on yourself! I also will come with you to the Bodhisattva Dharmodgata! I also will, together with you, plant wholesome roots, which will help to win such dharmas!"

Sakra, Chief of Gods, thereupon threw off his disguise as a young man, and in his own proper body he stood before the Bodhisattva Sadaprarudita, and said to him: "I applaud your firm sense of obligation. In the past also the Tathagatas have had so great a desire for dharma, and it was that which helped them to know full enlightenment and to gain the precious jewel of the Dharma, after they had first coursed in the course of a Bodhisattva, and asked questions about the perfection of wisdom and skill in means. I have no need of your heart, blood or marrow. I only came here to test you. Now choose a boon. I shall give you any boon whatever!"

Sadaprarudita answered: "Give me the supreme dharmas of a Buddha!" *Sakra,* Chief of Gods, replied: "That lies not within my province. That lies within the province of the Buddhas, the Lords. Choose another boon!" *Sadaprarudita* replied: "Do not trouble your mind about the mutilated condition of my body! I shall myself now make it whole again by the magical power of my enunciation of the Truth. As I am in truth irreversible, have been predicted to full enlightenment, and am known to the Tathagatas by my unconquerable resolution,—may through this Truth, through this utterance of the Truth this my body be again as it was before!" [501] That very moment, instant and second, through the Buddha's might and through the perfect purity of the Bodhisattva's resolution, the body of the Bodhisattva Sadaprarudita became again as it had been before, healthy and whole. And Sakra, Chief of Gods, and Mara, the Evil One, reduced to silence, just vanished from that place.

The *merchant's daughter* then said to Sadaprarudita: "Come on, son of good family, let us go up to my house. I shall ask my parents to give you the riches with which you can express your desire to worship that perfection of wisdom, and to honour that Bodhisattva Dharmodgata, a desire which is due to your love for dharma." The Bodhisattva Sadaprarudita and the merchant's daughter went together to her house. When they got to it, Sadaprarudita remained standing on the threshold, while the merchant's daughter went into the house, and said to her parents: "Mummy and daddy, you must give me a part of your wealth! I want to go away with the five hundred maidens you gave me for servants! Together with the Bodhisattva Sadaprarudita I want to go to the Bodhisattva Dharmodgata, in order to worship him. And he shall demonstrate dharma to us, and that way we shall acquire the dharmas of a Buddha." [502] Her *parents* replied: "Who then is this Bodhisattva Sadaprarudita, and where is he just now?"

The *merchant's daughter* said: "This son of good family stands at the threshold of the door to our house. And he has set out determined to know full enlightenment, in other words, he wants to set all beings free from the immeasurable sufferings of birth-and-death." And she told them all that she had seen and heard, [503] how Sadaprarudita had sold his body, and mutilated it, and how she asked him for his reason, and how he praised and revealed to her the unthinkable qualities of a Buddha and the immeasurable dharmas of a Buddha, which he had in mind as his goal. She went on to say that "When I had heard of those unthinkable qualities of a Buddha, I felt an exceeding joy and elation. And I thought to myself: 'It is wonderful to what an extent this son of good family is a doer of what is hard, and how much he must love the dharma to endure oppression and pain in his body. For it is from love for dharma that he renounced himself. How can we fail to worship dharma, and to make a vow to reach such stations, we who have vast and abundant possessions?' [504] So I said to that son of good family: 'Do not inflict such fatal treatment on yourself! I shall give you abounding riches, which you may use to worship and honour that holy Bodhisattva Dharmodgata, I also shall go together with you to that Bodhisattva, and I shall worship him, too. I also shall accomplish those supreme dharmas of a Buddha which you have proclaimed!' Mummy and daddy, allow me to go, and give me the riches I have asked for!"

Her *parents* replied: "It is wonderful how well you have related the hardships of that son of good family. Unthinkable, for sure must be the dharmas for the sake of which he endures these hardships, they must be the most distinguished in the whole world, a source of happiness to all beings! We will give you our permission to go. We also should like to come

with you, to see, to salute, to honour, to worship that Bodhisattva Dhar-
modgata." The *daughter* replied: "Do as you say. I would not oppose
those who are on the side of what is right."

5. THE MEETING WITH DHARMODGATA

It was thus that the merchant's daughter set out to worship and
honour the Bodhisattva Dharmodgata. [505] She took five hundred car-
riages and ordered her five hundred servant girls to get ready. She took
abundant riches, and ample provisions, mounted one carriage together
with the Bodhisattva Sadaprarudita, and proceeded East, surrounded by
the five hundred maidens on their five hundred carts, accompanied by a
huge retinue, and preceded by her parents. After some time the Bodhisat-
tva Sadaprarudita saw the city of Gandhavati from afar. In the middle of
the marketplace he saw the Bodhisattva Dharmodgata on his pulpit,
demonstrating dharma, surrounded and revered by an assembly of many
hundreds, of many thousands, of many hundreds of thousands. The
moment he saw him he was filled with that kind of happiness [506] which
a monk feels when with one-pointed attention he has obtained the first
trance. He looked upon him and thought to himself: "It would not be
seemly for me to approach the Bodhisattva Dharmodgata seated on a
carriage. Let me therefore alight from it!" Thereupon he alighted from his
carriage, and the merchant's daughter with her five hundred maidens fol-
lowed suit. Sadaprarudita, with the merchant's daughter and her five hun-
dred maidens then went up to where the Bodhisattva Dharmodgata sat
amidst a magnificent display of religious aspirations. For the Bodhisattva
Dharmodgata had at that time created, for the perfection of wisdom, a
pointed tower, made of the seven precious substances, adorned with red
sandalwood, and encircled by an ornament of pearls. Gems were placed
into the four corners of the pointed tower, and performed the functions of
lamps. Four incense jars made of silver were suspended on its four sides,
and pure black aloe wood was burning in them, as a token of worship for
the perfection of wisdom. And in the middle of that pointed tower a
couch made of the seven precious things was put up, and on it a box made
of four large gems. Into that the perfection of wisdom was placed, written
with melted vaidurya on golden tablets. And that pointed tower was
adorned with brightly coloured garlands which hung down in strips.

The Bodhisattva Sadaprarudita and the merchant's daughter with her
five hundred maidens looked upon that pointed tower, so magnificently
decorated as a display of religious aspirations. They saw thousands of
Gods, with Sakra, Chief of Gods, scattering over that pointed tower heav-

enly Mandarava flowers, heavenly sandalwood powder, heavenly gold dust, and heavenly silver dust, [507] and they heard the music of heavenly instruments. *Sadaprarudita* then asked Sakra, Chief of Gods: "For what purpose do you, together with many thousands of Gods, scatter over that pointed tower, which consists of precious substances, heavenly Mandarava flowers, etc., and why do the Devas up in space play heavenly music on their instruments?"

Sakra answered: "Do you not know the reason, son of good family? This is the perfection of wisdom, the mother and guide of the Bodhisattvas. When Bodhisattvas train in it, they soon reach the perfection of all qualities, and, consequent on that, all the dharmas of a Buddha and the knowledge of all modes."

Sadaprarudita replied: "Where is this perfection of wisdom, the mother and guide of the Bodhisattva?"

Sakra answered: "The holy Bodhisattva Dharmodgata has placed it in the middle of this pointed tower, after he had written it on golden tablets with melted Vaidurya, and sealed it with seven seals. We cannot easily show it to you."

Thereupon the Bodhisattva Sadaprarudita and the merchant's daughter, with her five hundred maidens, all paid worship to the perfection of wisdom—with the flowers which they had brought along, and with garlands, wreaths, raiment, jewels, incense, flags and golden and silvery flowers [508] and, one after another, they deposited their portion in front of it, for the greater honour of the Bodhisattva Dharmodgata. They then worshipped the Bodhisattva Dharmodgata by scattering flowers, etc., over him, and played heavenly music on their instruments—motivated by a desire to worship dharma.

The flowers then rose high above the head of the Bodhisattva Dharmodgata and formed a pointed tower of flowers. And those flowers of various colours, golden and silvery, stood high in the air, like a canopy. And also the robes, raiment and jewels stood high up in the air, like a pavilion in the clouds. When the Bodhisattva Sadaprarudita and the merchant's daughter with her five hundred maidens beheld this wonder, they thought to themselves: "It is wonderful to see how much wonderworking power this Bodhisattva Dharmodgata possesses, how great a might, how great an influence. So far he courses but in the course of a Bodhisattva, and now already he possesses so much power to work wonders. How much more will he have after he has known full enlightenment!" [509] The merchant's daughter and the five hundred maidens thereupon felt a longing for the Bodhisattva Dharmodgata. All of one mind, they resolutely raised their hearts to the supreme enlightenment, and said: "May we, through this wholesome root, become Tathagatas in a future period! May we come to course in the course of Bodhisattvas, and may we receive those very dharmas which this Bodhisattva Dharmodgata has received! And may we just so honour and respect the perfection of wisdom as this Bodhisattva Dharmodgata honours and respects it, and may we reveal it to the many just as he has done! And may we become as endowed with perfect wisdom and skill in means, and as accomplished in them as this Bodhisattva Dharmodgata is!"

The Bodhisattva Sadaprarudita, and the merchant's daughter with her five hundred maidens, after they had worshipped the perfection of wisdom and honored the Bodhisattva Dharmodgata with their heads, respectfully saluted him with their folded hands, and stood on one side. The Bodhisattva Sadaprarudita then told the whole story of his quest for the perfection of wisdom, beginning with the voice he had heard in the forest, that bid him go East. [510] He told Dharmodgata how he had stood in many concentrations, and how the Buddhas and Lords of the ten directions had comforted and applauded him, and had said: "Well done, son of good family! These concentrations have issued from the perfection of wisdom. By firmly standing in the perfection of wisdom have we achieved all the dharmas of a Buddha." He went on to relate that: "The Tathagatas then vanished again, and I emerged from that state of concentration. I then asked myself 'wherefrom now did these Tathagatas come, and whither have they gone?' I thought to myself that 'the holy Bodhisattva Dharmodgata has received the dharanis, [511] he possesses the five superknowledges, he has done his duties under the Jinas of the past, he has planted wholesome roots, and is well trained in perfect wisdom and skill in means. He will explain to me this matter as it really is, and tell me where those Tathagatas have come from and whither they have gone to.' Now I have come to you, and I ask you, son of good family: 'Where have those Tathagatas come from, and whither have they gone to?' Demonstrate to me, son of good family, the coming and going of those Tathagatas, so that we may cognize it, and so that we may become not lacking in the vision of the Tathagatas."

Chapter XXXI

DHARMODGATA

1. THE COMING AND GOING OF THE TATHAGATAS

Dharmodgata: Tathagatas certainly do not come from anywhere, nor do they go anywhere. Because Suchness does not move, and the Tathagata is Suchness. Non-production does not come nor go, and the Tathagata is non-production. One cannot conceive of the coming or going of the reality-limit, and the Tathagata is the reality-limit. The same can be said of emptiness, of what exists in accordance with fact, of dispassion, of stopping, of the element of space. For the Tathagata is not outside these dharmas. The Suchness of these dharmas and the Suchness of all dharmas, and the Suchness of the Tathagata are simply this one single Suchness. There is no division within Suchness. Just simply one single is this Suchness, not two, nor three. Suchness has passed beyond counting, because it is not. A man, scorched by the heat of the summer, during the last month of summer [513], at noon might see a mirage floating along, and might run towards it, and think 'there I shall find some water, there I shall find something to drink.' What do you think, son of good family, has that water come from anywhere, or does that water go anywhere, to the Eastern great ocean, or the Southern, Northern or Western?

Sadaprarudita: No water exists in the mirage. How could its coming or going be conceived? That man again is foolish and stupid if, on seeing the mirage, he forms the idea of water where there is no water. Water in its own being certainly does not exist in that mirage.

Dharmodgata: Equally foolish are all those who adhere to the Tathagata through form and sound, and who in consequence imagine the coming or going of a Tathagata. For a Tathagata cannot be seen from his form-body. The Dharma-bodies are the Tathagatas and the real nature of dharmas does not come or go. There is no coming or going of the body of an elephant, horse, chariot or foot-soldier, which has been conjured up by a magician. Just so there is neither coming nor going of the Tathagatas. A sleeping man might in his dreams see one Tathagata, or two, or three, or up to one thousand, or still more [514]. On waking up he would, however, no longer see even one single Tathagata. What do you think, son of good family, have these Tathagatas come from anywhere, or gone to anywhere?

Sadaprarudita: One cannot conceive that in that dream any dharma at all had the status of a full and perfect reality, for the dream was deceptive.

Dharmodgata: Just so the Tathagata has taught that all dharmas are like a dream. All those who do not wisely know all dharmas as they really are, i.e. as like a dream, as the Tathagata has pointed out, they adhere to the Tathagatas through their name-body and their form-body, and in consequence they imagine that the Tathagatas come and go. Those who in their ignorance of the true nature of dharmas imagine a coming or going of the Tathagatas, they are just foolish common people, at all times they belong to birth-and-death with its six places of rebirth, and they are far from the perfection of wisdom, far away from the dharmas of a Buddha. On the contrary, however, those who know as they really are all dharmas as like a dream, in agreement with the teaching of the Tathagata, they do not imagine the coming or going of any dharma, nor its production or stopping. They wisely know the Tathagata in his true nature, and they do not imagine a coming or going of the Tathagatas. And those who wisely know this true nature of a Tathagata, they course near to full enlightenment and they course in the perfection of wisdom. These disciples of the Lord do not consume their alms fruitlessly, [515] and they are worthy of the world's gifts. The gems which are in the great ocean do not come from any place in the East, or West, or in any other of the ten directions, but they owe their existence to the wholesome roots of beings. They are not produced without cause. And when, dependent on cause, condition and reason, these gems have been coproduced and stopped by conditions, they do not pass on to any place anywhere in the world in any of the ten directions. And nevertheless, when those conditions exist, the gems are augmented; when those conditions are absent, no augmentation takes place. Just so the perfect body of the Tathagatas has not come from any place anywhere in the ten directions, and it does not go to any place anywhere in the world with its ten directions. But the body of the Buddhas and Lords is not without cause. It has been brought to perfection by their conduct in the past, and it has been produced dependent on causes and conditions, coproduced by subsidiary conditions, produced as a result of karma done in the past. It is, however, not in any place anywhere in the world with its ten directions. But when those conditions exist, the accomplishment of the body takes place; when those conditions are absent, the accomplishment of the body becomes inconceivable. When the sound of a boogharp is being produced, it does not come from anywhere. When it is stopped, it does not go anywhere, nor does it pass on to anywhere. But it has been produced conditioned by the totality of its causes and conditions,—namely the boat-shaped hollow body of the harp, the parchment sounding board, the strings, the hollow arm of the boogharp, the bindings, the plectrum, the person who plays it, and his exertions. [516] In that way this sound comes forth from the boogharp, dependent on causes, dependent on conditions. And yet that sound does not come forth from that hollow body of the harp, nor from the parchment sounding board, nor from the strings, nor from the hollow arm, nor from the bindings, nor from the plectrum, nor from the person who plays it, nor from his exertions. It is just the combination of all of them that makes the sound conceivable. And when it is stopped, the sound also does not go anywhere. Just so the perfect body of the Buddhas and Lords is dependent on causes, dependent on conditions, and it has been brought to perfection through exertions which have led to many wholesome roots. But the augmenting of the Buddha-body does not result from one single cause, nor from one single condition, nor from one single wholesome root. And it is also not without cause. It has been coproduced by a totality of many causes and conditions, but it does not come from anywhere. And when the totality of causes and conditions has ceased to be, then it does not go to anywhere. It is thus that you should view the coming and going of those Tathagatas, and that you should conform to the true nature of all dharmas. And it is just because you will wisely know that the Tathagatas, and also all dharmas, are neither produced nor stopped, that you shall become fixed on full enlightenment, and that you shall definitely course in the perfection of wisdom and in skill in means.

When this disquisition on the fact that the Tathagatas neither come nor go had been taught, the earth and the entire great trichiliocosm shook in six ways, it stirred, quaked, was agitated, resounded and rumbled. And all the realms of Mara were stirred up and discomfited. All the grasses, shrubs, herbs and trees in the great trichiliocosm bent in the direction of the Bodhisattva Dharmodgata. [517] Flowers came up out of season. From high up in the air a great rain of flowers came down. And *Shakra,* Chief of Gods, and the *Four Great Kings* scattered and poured heavenly sandalwood powder and heavenly flowers over the Bodhisattva Dharmodgata, and said: "Well spoken, son of good family. Through your might we have heard a sermon which has issued from ultimate reality, which is contrary to the whole world, and which gives no ground to any of those beings who are established in any of the views which involve the assumption of an individuality, or who have settled down in any of the views which assume the existence of something that is not."

Sadaprarudita then asked Dharmodgata: "What is the cause, what is the reason why this great earthquake is manifested in the world?"

Dharmodgata: In consequence of your asking for this disquisition on the not-coming and not-going of the Tathagatas, and through my exposi-

tion of it, eight thousand living beings have acquired the patient accept-
ance of dharmas which fail to be produced, eighty niyutas of living beings
have raised their hearts to full enlightenment, and of sixty-four thousand
living beings has the dispassionate, unstained dharma-eye been purified for
the vision of dharmas.

2. SADAPRARUDITA'S SELF-SACRIFICE

The Bodhisattva *Sadaprarudita* then had a supreme, a most sublime
feeling of zest and joy: "It is a gain to me, a very great gain that, by asking
for the perfection of wisdom and for this disquisition, I have wrought the
weal of so many beings. [518] That alone should bring me merit sufficient
for the accomplishment of full enlightenment. Unquestionably I shall be-
come a Tathagata." In his zest and joy he rose seven palm trees high into
the air, and, standing at the height of seven palm trees, he reflected: "How
can I, standing here in the air, do honour to the Bodhisattva Dharmod-
gata?" *Sakra*, Chief of Gods, saw him, read his thoughts, presented him
with heavenly Mandarava flowers, and said to him: "Honour the Bodhisat-
tva Dharmodgata with these heavenly flowers! For we feel that we should
honour the man who helped you. Today your might has wrought the weal
of many thousands of living beings. Rare are the beings who, like you,
have the strength, for the sake of all beings through countless aeons to
bear the great burden."

The Bodhisattva *Sadaprarudita* then took the Mandarava flowers from
Sakra, Chief of Gods, and scattered them over the Bodhisattva Dharmod-
gata. He presented the Bodhisattva Dharmodgata with his own body, and
said to him: "I give you myself as a present, and I shall be your attendant
and servant from today onwards." And with folded hands he stood before
Dharmodgata. [519] The merchant's daughter and her five hundred maid-
ens then said to the Bodhisattva Sadaprarudita: "We in our turn make a
present of ourselves to you, son of good family. Through this wholesome
root we also shall become recipients of just those dharmas, and together
with you we shall again and again honour and revere the Buddhas and
Lords, and the Bodhisattvas, and we shall remain near to you." Sadapra-
rudita replied: "If you, maidens, in imitation of my own earnest intention,
give yourselves with earnest intentions to me, then I will accept you." The
maidens replied: "We imitate you, and with earnest resolution we give
ourselves as presents to you, to do with us as you will." Thereupon the
Bodhisattva Sadaprarudita presented the merchant's daughter and her five
hundred maidens, embellished and adorned, together with their five hun-
dred well-decorated carriages, to the Bodhisattva Dharmodgata, and said:

"All these I present to you as attendants and servants, and also the carriages for your own use." Sakra, Chief of Gods, applauded him and said: "Well done, son of good family! A Bodhisattva must renounce all his property. Through that thought of renunciation he soon wins full enlightenment, and the worship he pays thus to the preachers of dharma enables him to hear about the perfection of wisdom and skill in means. [520] Also in the past the Tathagatas, when they still were Bodhisattvas, have, by the fact that they renounced everything, procured a claim to full enlightenment; and they also have asked questions about perfect wisdom and about skill in means." The Bodhisattva Dharmodgata accepted Sadaprarudita's gift, so that his wholesome root might reach fulfilment. Immediately afterwards he returned it to Sadaprarudita. After that, the Bodhisattva Dharmodgata went into his house. The sun was about to set.

The Bodhisattva *Sadaprarudita* then thought to himself: "It would not indeed be seemly for me, who have come here out of love for dharma, to sit or to lie down. I will remain either standing or walking, until the time when the Bodhisattva Dharmodgata shall again come out of his house, in order to reveal dharma to us."

The Bodhisattva Dharmodgata then remained for seven years immersed in one uninterrupted state of trance, and he dwelt in countless thousands of concentrations, peculiar to Bodhisattvas, issued from perfection of wisdom and skill in means. For seven years *Sadaprarudita* never adopted any other posture than the two just mentioned, and he did not fall into sloth and torpor. For seven years he never felt any preoccupation with sense desires, or with ill will, or with harming others, he never felt any eagerness for tastes, nor any self-satisfaction. But he thought: "When then will the Bodhisattva Dharmodgata emerge from his trance, [521] so that we may spread out a seat for him, whereon he may demonstrate dharma, and so that we may sprinkle well the place where he will reveal the perfection of wisdom and skill in means, anoint it well and bedeck it with manifold flowers?" And the merchant's daughter with her five hundred maidens followed his example, passed their time in two postures only, and imitated all his works.

One day the Bodhisattva Sadaprarudita heard a *heavenly voice* which said: "On the seventh day from today the Bodhisattva Dharmodgata will emerge from his trance, and he will then, seated in the center of the town, demonstrate dharma." When Sadaprarudita heard the heavenly voice, he was contented, elated, joyous, overjoyed and jubilant. Together with the merchant's daughter and her five hundred maidens he cleansed the ground, spread out the seat made of the seven precious things, took off his upper garment, and spread it on top of the seat. The maidens also took off their upper garments, spread their five hundred upper garments on that seat, and thought: "Seated on that seat will the Bodhisattva Dharmodgata demonstrate dharma." [522] And they also were contented, elated, joyous, overjoyed and jubilant.

When the Bodhisattva Sadaprarudita wanted to sprinkle the ground he could not find any water, though he searched all round. For Mara, the Evil One, had hidden all the water. And he did this so that Sadaprarudita, if he could not find any water, should become depressed and sad, or change his mind, with the result that his wholesome root would vanish, or the fervour of this worship be dimmed. The Bodhisattva *Sadaprarudita* then thought to himself: "Let me pierce my own body, and sprinkle the ground with my blood. The ground is full of rising dust, and I fear that some of it may fall on the body of the Bodhisattva Dharmodgata. What else can I do with this body which is of necessity doomed to break up? Better surely that this my body should be destroyed by such an action rather than by an ineffectual one. For the sake of sense pleasures, as a result of sense pleasures many thousands of frames of mine have again and again, while I wandered in birth-and-death, been broken up, but never in conditions as favourable as these, never for the sake of gaining the good law. If they must once more be broken up, let them in any case be broken up in a holy cause." He [523] then took a sharp sword, pierced his body on every side, and everywhere sprinkled that piece of ground with his own blood. The merchant's daughter with her five hundred maidens followed his example, and did as he did. But there was no alteration of thought in either the Bodhisattva Sadaprarudita, or in all those maidens, which would have given Mara, the Evil One, a chance of entering in order to obstruct their wholesome roots.

Sakra, chief of Gods, then thought to himself: "It is wonderful how much this Bodhisattva Sadaprarudita loves dharma, how firm is his sense of obligation, how great the armour he has put on, and how he disregards his body, his life, and his pleasures, and how resolutely he has set out with the goal of knowing full enlightenment, in his desire to 'set free all beings from the measureless sufferings of birth-and-death, after he has known full enlightenment." Sakra then changed by magic all that blood into heavenly sandalwood water. And all round that piece of ground, for one hundred leagues, an inconceivably sublime scent, the scent of that heavenly sandalwood water, filled the air. And *Sakra* said to Sadaprarudita: "Well done, son of good family! I applaud your inconceivable vigour, your supreme love and search for dharma. The Tathagatas in the past [524] also have procured the right to full enlightenment through this kind of earnest intention, vigour, and love for dharma."

The Bodhisattva *Sadaprarudita* then thought to himself: "I have spread out the seat for the Bodhisattva Dharmodgata, and I have well swept and sprinkled this piece of ground. Now I must still get flowers with which to cover this piece of ground, and to scatter over the Bodhisattva Dharmodgata when he demonstrates dharma." *Sakra* then said to Sadaprarudita: "Accept these heavenly Mandarava flowers for that twofold purpose!" And he presented him with a thousand heavenly Khara measures of heavenly flowers. And the Bodhisattva Sadaprarudita accepted those flowers, and used some of them to cover the piece of ground, and, later on, he strewed others over the Bodhisattva Dharmodgata.

3. DHARMODGATA'S DEMONSTRATION OF DHARMA

After the lapse of seven years the Bodhisattva Dharmodgata emerged from his trance, went up to the seat spread out for him, sat down on it, and, surrounded and attended by an assembly of many hundreds of thousands, he demonstrated dharma. The moment the Bodhisattva Sadaprarudita [525] saw the Bodhisattva Dharmodgata, he was filled with that kind of happiness which a monk feels when, with one-pointed attention, he has obtained the first trance. And this is the demonstration of the perfection of wisdom by the Bodhisattva *Dharmodgata*:

"The perfection of wisdom is self-identical, because all dharmas are the same. Perfect wisdom is isolated because all dharmas are isolated. Perfect wisdom is immobile because all dharmas are immobile. Perfect wisdom is devoid of mental acts because all dharmas are devoid of mental acts. Perfect wisdom is unbenumbed, because all dharmas are unbenumbed. Perfect wisdom has but one single taste because all dharmas have one and the same taste. Perfect wisdom is boundless because all dharmas are boundless. Perfect wisdom is non-production because all dharmas are non-production. Perfect wisdom is non-stopping because all dharmas are not stopped. As the firmament is boundless, so is perfect wisdom. As the ocean is boundless, so is perfect wisdom. As Meru shines in multicoloured brilliance, so does the perfection of wisdom. As the firmament is not fashioned, so is perfect wisdom not fashioned. Perfect wisdom is boundless, because form, and the other skandhas are boundless. Perfect wisdom is boundless because the element of earth, and the other elements, are boundless. Perfect wisdom is self-identical, because the adamantine dharma is self-identical. Perfect wisdom is undifferentiated because all dharmas are undifferentiated. The non-apprehension of perfect wisdom follows from the non-apprehension of all dharmas. Perfect wisdom remains the same whatever it may surpass because all dharmas remain the same whatever they may surpass. [526] Perfect wisdom is powerless to act because all dharmas are powerless to act. Perfect wisdom is unthinkable because all dharmas are unthinkable."

Thereupon on that occasion there was born in the Bodhisattva Sadaprarudita the king of concentrations called "the sameness of all dharmas," and, consequent on that, the concentrations called "isolation of all dharmas," "immobility of all dharmas," "absence of all mental acts in all dharmas," "lack of numbness in all dharmas," "the one taste of all dharmas," "the boundlessness of all dharmas," "the non-production of all dharmas," "the non-stopping of all dharmas," "boundless like the firmament," "boundless like the ocean," "brilliant and multicoloured like Meru," "not fashioned, like the firmament," "boundless like form, etc.," "boundless like the element of earth, etc.," "adamantine," "non-differentiatedness of all dharmas," "non-apprehension of all dharmas," "sameness of all dharmas whatever they may surpass," "all dharmas are powerless to act," "all dharmas are unthinkable." Beginning with these, the Bodhisattva Sadaprarudita acquired six million concentration doors.

Chapter XXXII

ENTRUSTING

1. END OF THE STORY OF SADAPRARUDITA

In conjunction with the acquisition of the six million concentration doors, the Bodhisattva Sadaprarudita saw the Buddhas and Lords,—in all the ten directions in countless trichiliocosms—surrounded by their congregations of monks, accompanied by multitudes of Bodhisattvas, teaching just this perfection of wisdom, through just these methods, in just these words, in just these letters, even as I just now in this great trichiliocosm demonstrate dharma,—surrounded by the congregation of monks, accompanied by multitudes of Bodhisattvas, and teaching just this perfection of wisdom, through just these methods, in just these words, in just these letters. He became endowed with inconceivable learning and a sacred knowledge vast like the ocean. In all his births he never again was deprived of the Buddha. He was reborn only where he could be face to face with the Buddhas, the Lords. Even in his dreams he was not lacking in the Buddhas, the Lords. All unfortunate rebirths he had abandoned, and he had secured the circumstances which allowed him to accomplish one auspicious rebirth after another.

2. THE PERFECTION OF WISDOM ENTRUSTED TO ANANDA

The Lord thereupon said to the Venerable Ananda: In this manner also should you know this perfection of wisdom as the one who nurses the cognition of the all-knowing in the Bodhisattvas. Therefore then, Ananda, a Bodhisattva who wants to acquire the cognition of the all-knowing should course in this perfection of wisdom, [528] hear it, take it up, study, spread, repeat and write it. When, through the Tathagata's sustaining power it has been well written, in very distinct letters, in a great book, one should honour, revere, adore and worship it, with flowers, incense, scents, wreaths, unguents, aromatic powders, strips of cloth, parasols, banners, bells, flags and with rows of lamps all round, and with manifold kinds of worship. This is our admonition to you, Ananda. For in this perfection of wisdom the cognition of the all-knowing will be brought to perfection. What do you think, Ananda, is the Tathagata your teacher?
Ananda: He is, O Lord.
The Lord: The Tathagata is your teacher, Ananda. You have minis-

tered to me, Ananda, with friendly acts of body, acts of speech, acts of mind. Therefore then, Ananda, just as you have given affection, faith and respect to me as I am at present in this incarnation, just so, Ananda, should you act after my decease towards this perfection of wisdom. For the second time, for the third time, I entrust and transmit to you this perfection of wisdom, so that it may not disappear. No other man would be as suitable as you are. [529] As long as this perfection of wisdom shall be observed in the world, one can be sure that "for so long does the Tathagata abide in it," that "for so long does the Tathagata demonstrate dharma," and that the beings in it are not lacking in the vision of the Buddha, the hearing of the dharma, the attendance of the Samgha. One should know that those beings are living in the presence of the Tathagata who will hear this perfection of wisdom, take it up, study, spread, repeat and write it, and who will honour, revere, adore and worship it.

Thus spoke the Lord. Enraptured, the Bodhisattvas, headed by Maitreya, and the Venerable Subhuti, and the Venerable Ananda, and Sakra, Chief of Gods, and the entire world with its Gods, men, Asuras, Garudas and Gandharvas delighted in the Lord's teaching.

APPENDIX

LIST OF TOPICS

I. The Absolute

All-knowledge (*sarva-jñātā*), i 11, 15-16, 19, 23-25; ii 42-43, 48; iii 57-58; iv 95; vii 170, 175; viii 188; x 210-11, 227; xi 237, 239, 240, 249; xii 254, 255; xiv 289, 290; xv 292, 302-3; xxii 408

Enlightenment (*bodhi*), and dharmas, xvi 313; xix 360-361; xxii 409

Nirvana, i 9, 20-21; ii 36-37, 40; iii 53; vi 151; ix 204; xi 234; xii 273; xiii 283; xv 293, 296; xviii 342

Reality-limit (*bhūta-koṭi*), i 15; v 105; x 215; xi 250; xxiv 416; xxvii 444

Tathagata, i 9; iii 58; iv 100; xii 272, 274; xxii 402; xxvi 442; xxxi 512. Relics of, iii 57 ff.; iv 94 ff.

Beyond (*pāram*), viii 189, 196; xiv 286; xv 295

Thought (*citta*), i 5-6

Thusness (*tathā-tva*), iii 79; x 208, 222; xxiii 412; xxiv 419; xxvii 453

Suchness (*tatha-tā*), v 133; xi 235; xii 271-73; xvi 306 ff.; xvii 323; xviii 342; xix 345-46; xxiv 419; xxv 424-25; xxvii 453; xxxi 512

Dharma, described, xvi 306

Dharmabody (*dharma-kāya*), iii 58; iv 94, 99; xvii 339; xxviii 462; xxxi 513

Dharma-element (*dharma-dhātu*), viii 197; xii 273; xvii 327

Dharmahood (*dharma-tā*), i 4, 9, 21; ii 48; vi 153; viii 196; xii 274; xiii 278; xvii 323; synonyms, xvii 329, 339; xxxi 514

II. The Perfection of Wisdom *(pra-jñā-pāram-itā)*

A. *In itself, in ultimate sense*
   described: ix 205-7; xxii 399
   32 characteristics: vii 170-71

Emptiness (*śūnyatā*)
   synonyms, xviii 341, 347; xxx 482
   ii 35; vii 177; ix 204; xi 243; xii 256; xv 298; xvi 313-14; xxiii 410; xxvii 454-55
   familiarity with (*paricaya* [*parijaya*]), xix 365; xx 370 ff.
   own being (*sva-bhāva*), i 10-11; vii 175-76; viii 185-86; xii 256-57; xix 360; xxx 483
   empty (*śūnya*), xii 273, 275, 276; xxii 399, 405; xxiv 419; xxvii 448

Signless (*a-nimitta*), xii 273; xix 356; xx 371

Wishless (*a-pra-ṇi-hita*), xii 273

Extinction,. and inextinguishable (*kshaya; a-kshaya*), xii 272; xxv 424; xxviii 467-68

Purity (*vi-śuddh̆-i*), viii 186-89, 192; ix 200 ff.; x 220; xii 276; xxv 428

Described by way of negation

    i 7, 21; vii 173 ff.; xii 271; xv 294-95, 301, 303

No-discrimination, non-duality, i 27; viii 192; xv 295; xvii 323; xix 357-58; xxvi 441 ff.

No-production and no-stopping, i 25 ff.; ii 43; vii 174; viii 197; xii 273; xv 297; xix 353-54; xxii 408

No defilement and purification, xii 273; xxii 399 ff.; xxx 483

Neither bound nor freed, i 21-22; viii 185-86, 195; ix 200

Not brought together (*an-abhi-saṃskāra*), xii 273

No growth or diminution, ii 42; xviii 348-51; xix 357; xx 376; xxii 405

Not coming and not going (*anāgamana, agamana*), xv 303, 304

No basis, vi 151 ff.; vii 172 ff.; xx 376

Not relying on (*a-ni-ŚRi-ta*), i 31; xii 273-75; xxx 490

Calmly quiet (*śānta*), xii 276

No is or is not, i 5-6, 14-15

Non-existence (*abhāva*), xii 273

No connection (*na sam-baddha*), xv 300

No attachment (*a-saṅga*), xii 274

Without end (*an-anta-tā*), ii 46

Inexpressible, xviii 347-48; xix 360

Unthinkable (*a-cint-ya*), iii 81; viii 193; x 219, 220; xii 276; xiii 277 ff.

Unknowable, etc., xii 275

Isolated (*vi-vik-ta*), vi 149-50; vii 177; viii 192; ix 204; xii 276; xxii 399, 405; xxvii 445-46

No coverings (*an-ā-var-aṇa*), xvi 322

Like space (*ā-KĀŚ-a-upama*), i 24; viii 193, 196, 197; ix 201, 205; x 220; xii 273; xiii 279-80; xv 297, 299, 301, 303, 304; xvi 306, 314; xxiii 410, xxv 424; xxvi 441; xxvii 445; xxviii 465, 467, 468

Described by way of attitude

No reviewing or getting at, i, 5, 7, 10, 13-14, 23-25; ix 203

Coursing in, viii 193-94; xxii 406-7

Standing in, i; ii 35 ff.; x 211-12

Following it, xxix

Go forth to, i 3

Fearlessness, i 5, 7, 17, 26; iiii 56; iv 98-99; vi 139; x 213, 226; xv 302; xvii 323, 326; xx 381

B. *In relation to deeds of struggling individuals*

The Bodhisattva's stages:
Beginner, i 17; vi 139; xiii 282, xv 292
Irreversible, i 6, 8; ii 40; iii 61; v 128, 130; vi 139; x 212-13; xv 302;
xvii; xviii 341; xx 379 ff.; xxi 387; xxiv 419; xxvii 450 ff.
Prediction, i 13
Worthy of gifts, ix 204; xxii 402-3; xxv 433; xxxi 515
Threefold complete purity, i 11; xvii 326-27
Thought of enlightenment, i 5
In relation to Disciples, etc.
a) Excludes them, i 8; xi 234 ff.; xv 293; xvii 327, 329
b) Identical with it, i 6-7; xiii 281; xv 300 ff.; xvi 319, 320; xvii 323,
339; xxv 432-33
Arhat, i 3; xiii 282
Hell, vii 180 ff.; xx 382
Rebirths, vii 176 ff.; xi 233; xiv 284 ff.; xxv 426-27; xxvi 437-38; xxvii
459; xxviii 473-74
Conditions which lead to perfection of wisdom, iii 79; vii 177-78; x 208
ff., 227; xiv 285; xv 299; xxx; xxxi
Conditions which keep away from perfection of wisdom, vii 178 ff.; viii
185; xiii 282; xvi 313
Help for a Bodhisattva, xxvii 447
Worldly advantages from perfection of wisdom, iii; ix 201; xxiii 414; xxv
427
Perfect Wisdom as mother of Buddhas, xii 253 ff.
Perfect Wisdom as a spell, iii 54 ff., 72 ff.
Counterfeit Perfect Wisdom, v 112-13

C. *Relation to other perfections*

5 perfections, vi 163 ff.; xv 292-93; xvi 310, 322; xxiii 412-13
Patience, ii 38-39
Relation, iii 51, 80 ff.; iv 100-101; vii 172-73; xxii 396-97; xxv 430-31;
xxviii 464
Merit, iii 57 ff.; v 103 ff.; vi 154 ff.; xiii 283; xviii 344-46; xxii 401-3; xxiii
410 ff.; xxv 431-32; xxvi 435-36; xxviii 464a
Relation to cult of Buddha, iii 58 ff.

III. **Skill in means**

iii 58, 75; xi 243; xiv 287; xvi 310 ff.; xix 356; xx 375; xxv 427

IX.   Definitions

X.   Various

GLOSSARY

Compiled by William Powell

ABHIRATI. 'Delightful.' The Buddha land located in the East which Akshobhya Buddha rules.

ACT OF TRUTH (*Satyādhiṣṭhāna*). The magical belief that the enunciation of a true statement can modify events and work wonders.

ACTS OF MIND (*manasikāra*). Focusing of attention, concentration of the mind.

AEON. *See* KALPA.

AJITA. 'Invincible.' Epithet of Maitreya.

AKANISTHA GODS (*Akaniṣṭhā devā*). The highest of the five classes of Gods of the Pure Abode, which is the highest level in the realm of form (*rūpa-dhātu*).

AKṢOBHYA. Literally: 'imperturbable.' A Buddha who rules the Buddha land of Abhirati, which is in the East.

ALL-KNOWLEDGE (*sarva-jñatā*). The omniscience of a Buddha.

ANALYTICAL KNOWLEDGE (*pratisaṃvid*). Four: analysis of meanings, of dharmas, of languages, of ready speech.

ĀNANDA. Renowned for his faith and devotion. He is said to have recited from memory the words of the Buddha at the Council of 500 Arhats. It is he who is understood to have introduced each Sutra with the words, "Thus have I heard at one time."

ANIMAL (*tiryagyoni*). The third lowest of the six destinies, the class includes Nagas and other mythical beasts and birds.

ARHAT (*arhan*). Literally: 'worthy of respect.' The perfect Hinayana saint. He knows what is useful for his own salvation and is content to win enlightenment for himself alone.

ASSEMBLY. *See* COMMUNITY.

ASURAS. Titanic beings, forever at war with the Gods.

ATTAINMENTS (*samāpatti*). Generally of 'the nine successive stations,' i.e. four trances, four formless attainments, and the trance of cessation of perception and feeling.

AVAKĪRṆAKUSUMA. 'Covered with flowers,' said of a group of future Buddhas.

AVĪCI HELL. A hot hell in which suffering is "uninterrupted."

BECOMING (*bhava*). Continuous coming into existence. The tenth in the twelve links of conditioned coproduction.

BEING (*sattva*). A living, sentient creature.

BHADRAKALPA. Auspicious aeon in which one thousand Buddhas are to appear. The Hinayana admits only five.

BHIKṢU. A monk, one who has left home and taken the vows of a monastic.

BHĪṢMA-GARJITA-NIRGHOṢA-SVARA. A Tathagata. The one with an awe-inspiring voice. Alternatively: The one whose soundless voice emits a frightful roar.

BIMBISĀRA RĀJA. A king of Magadha during the time of the Buddha.

BIRTH-AND-DEATH (saṃsāra). Undergoing transmigration. Not different from Nirvana in the Mahayana teaching.

BLESSED REST (nirvṛti). Nirvana of the Hinayana, the ultimate attainment of the Arhat.

BODHISATTVA (bodhi-sattva). Literally: 'Enlightenment-being.' The Mahayana ideal, who through infinite compassion seeks the enlightenment of all beings rather than of himself alone.

BODHISATTVA-VEHICLE. Another name for Mahayana, the great vehicle.

BRAHMĀ. A very high deity. Reputed creator of the world in the Brahmanic tradition.

BRAHMA DWELLINGS (brahma-vihārā). The four Unlimited.

BRAHMIN, YOUNG (mānava). Member of the caste traditionally regarded as the repositors and communicators of sacred knowledge. In a former life the Buddha was a member of this caste.

BUDDHA, AUTHORITY OF THE (buddhādhiṣṭhāna). The inspiration or charisma of the Buddha by which he infuses thoughts into the minds of men and sustains the advocates of the dharma.

BUDDHA-DHARMAS. Qualities or attributes of a Buddha. Also the teaching (dharma) of the Buddha.

BUDDHA EYE (buddha-cakṣus). Direct intuition of all dharmas without exception.

BUDDHA-FIELD (buddha-kṣetra), A world system in which a Buddha teaches the dharma and brings beings to spiritual maturity. Such fields are numerous. Also, Buddha land.

CANDALA OF A BODHISATTVA (bodhisattva-caṇḍāla). A Bodhisattva who behaves like an outcaste.

CARAVAN LEADER (sārthavāha). Epithet of the Buddha.

CHILIOCOSM, SMALL (sāhasra-cūḍika-lokadhātu). A universe consisting of 1,000 suns, moons, heavens, hells, etc.

COMMON PEOPLE (pṛthag-jana). Ordinary people who have not yet reached the Path, and who are dominated by greed, hate and delusion.

COMMUNITY (*saṃgha*). Four assemblies: monks, nuns, laymen and lay·women. One of the three jewels.

COMPASSION (*karuṇā*). Second of the four Unlimited. A mere social virtue in the tradition of the Elders, it is the desire to help beings because of an inability to endure their suffering. In the Mahayana it is ranked with wisdom, being self-generated and not aroused from without.

CONCEIT (*māna*). Ninth of the ten fetters (*saṃyojana*).

CONCENTRATION (*samādhi*). A narrowing of the attention that results in quiet calm. The eighth step in the eightfold path. Traditionally consists of three kinds of practices: 1) the eight trances (*dhyāna*), 2) the four Unlimited, 3) occult powers.

CONCENTRATION DOORS (*samādhi-mukha*). Concentration on various truths which open the door to peaceful calm.

CONDITIONED COPRODUCTION (*pratītya-samutpāda*). Twelve conditions, beginning with ignorance and ending with death and decay, which cause everything that happens in this world.

CONSCIOUSNESS (*vijñāna*). Depending on the context it means: 1) the fifth of the five skandhas. (The other four skandhas depend on it in that it conditions and determines them, and it is that which is aware of the functions of the other four), 2) pure awareness, 3) a thought, 4) a mind, or 5) the sixth material element.

COURSE, TO (*carati*). Verb from the Sanskrit root *car*, meaning to move and, by extension, to live, practice, undertake, or observe.

DEDICATION (*pariṇāmanā*). The transfer of one's own merit to the welfare and utmost enlightenment of all beings.

DEFILEMENT (*kleśa*). Impurity or depravity; 'passion' or 'vice.'

DELUSION (*moha*). The third of the three roots of evil. Confusion, folly, bewilderment, stupidity.

DESTINIES (*gati*). Six classes of animate beings; they are: 1) gods, 2) men, 3) asuras, 4) animals, 5) ghosts, 6) beings in the hells.

DEVAS. See GOD.

DHARANIS. Short formulas which enable us to remember the salient points of the doctrine.

DHARMA. 1) The one ultimate reality; 2) an ultimately real event; 3) as reflected in life: righteousness, virtue; 4) as interpreted in the Buddha's teaching: Doctrine, Scripture, Truth; 5) object of the sixth sense organ, i.e. of mind; 6) a property, e.g. mental states, thing, quality.

DHARMA-BODY (*dharma-kāya*). 1) The absolute body of Buddhahood, free of all definite qualities, or 2) the collection of the Buddha's teachings.

DHARMA-ELEMENT (*dharma-dhātu*). 1) The Absolute Dharma or simply the Absolute, 2) the sphere of religion, 3) the sphere of mind-objects.

DHARMA EYE (*dharma-cakṣus*). Capable of knowing, with regard to individual people, by which expedient and teaching they can be made to find the path to salvation.

DHARMAS, NON-APPROPRIATION OF ALL (*sarva-dharmāparigṛhīta*). Not clinging to any of the mental states.

DHARMAS PECULIAR TO A BUDDHA. See BUDDHA-DHARMAS.

DICHILIOCOSM, MEDIUM (*dvisāhasra-madhyama lokadhātu*). A universe which contains one million suns, moons, heavens, hells, etc.

DIFFICULT PILGRIMAGE (*duṣkara-cārika*). A technical term for the career of a Bodhisattva with its many hardships and acts of self-sacrifice.

DĪPAṂKARA. 'Light-bringer.' A Buddha, the 24th predecessor of the Buddha Gautama, who predicted to him that one day he would win Buddhahood.

DĪPAVATĪ. The capital city of Dīpaṃkara.

DIRECTIONS (*diś*). Ten: the four cardinal, the four intermediate directions, and above and below.

DISCIPLE (*śrāvaka*). One who listens; technically only those who have heard the law directly from the Buddha, but also applied to followers of the Hinayana in Mahayana texts.

DISCRIMINATION (*vikalpa*). Considered to be false and vain imagining.

DOORS OF DELIVERANCE (*vimokṣa-dvāra*). Three: 1) emptiness, 2) signlessness, 3) wishlessness. The Path having been reached, these doors are the approach to Nirvana.

ELDER (*sthavira*), 1) Title implying orthodoxy, 2) member of the early sect adhering to 'the doctrine of the Elders.'

ELEMENT (*dhātu*). 1) The four material elements: earth, water, fire, and air. Space-ether and consciousness are sometimes added to make six. 2) The eighteen elements, i.e. the six sense-objects, six sense organs, six kinds of sense consciousness. 3) The Element of Dharma. 4) The Element of the Tathagata.

EMPTY (*śūnya*). 1) Futile and vain when applied to the things of this world, 2) non-existence of a self (see SELF), 3) an unconditioned dharma.

ENLIGHTENMENT, FULL (*anuttara-samyak-sambodhi*). Literally, utmost right and perfect enlightenment. Peculiar to Buddhas. The Mahayana goal superseding the private Nirvana goal of the Arhats.

ENMITY (*upanāha*). One of the ten subsidiary defilements.

EVENMINDEDNESS (*upekṣā*). 'To overlook.' The fourth Unlimited. An attitude of indifference or equanimity towards all conditioned things, which reflects itself as an attitude of impartiality with regard to all living beings. See IMPARTIALITY.

EYES (*cakṣus*). Five dimensions of vision, partly physical, partly spiritual: 1) fleshly eye, 2) heavenly eye, 3) wisdom eye, 4) Dharma eye, 5) Buddha eye.

FACULTIES (*indriya*). Five: 1) faith, 2) vigour, 3) mindfulness, 4) concentration, 5) wisdom. The cardinal virtues of early Buddhism.

FAIRY (*yakṣa*). A semi-divine, generally benevolent being. A 'gnome.' Primarily tree spirits, present in the sap and living water, causing fertility and growth.

FAITH (*śraddhā*). First of the five faculties. A provisional state that becomes less important as spiritual awareness increases. It has four objects: 1) belief in karma and rebirth, 2) acceptance of the basic teachings about the nature of reality, such as conditioned coproduction, 3) confidence in the three refuges: the Buddha, the Dharma and the Samgha, 4) belief in the efficacy of the prescribed practices, and in Nirvana as the final way out of all difficulties.

FEELINGS (*vedanā*). They may be analysed as pleasant, unpleasant, and neutral. The second of the five skandhas.

FETTERS (*saṃyojana*). Ten: view of individuality, contagion of mere rule and ritual, doubts, greed for sensuous passions, greed for the form world, greed for the formless world, ill-will, excitedness, conceit, ignorance.

FINAL NIRVANA. See PARINIRVANA.

FLESHLY EYE (*māṃsa-cakṣus*). The ordinary eye with which visible objects are seen; its range is very limited.

FORM (*rūpa*). The first of the five skandhas: matter.

FORM-BODY (*rūpa-kāya*). The material body, the body that can be seen by the fleshly eye. Contrasts with the Dharma-body.

FORMATIVE INFLUENCE (*abhisaṃskāra*). 'The karmic formations' which are the second link in the chain of conditioned coproduction.

FORMLESS ATTAINMENTS (*ārūpya-samāpatti*). Four: 1) endless space, 2) infinite consciousness, 3) nothing whatever, 4) neither perception nor non-perception.

FOUR-CONTINENT WORLD-SYSTEM (*cāturdvīpaka lokadhātu*). The earth seen as containing four mythical continents of which Jambudvipa is the most important.

FRIEND, BAD (*pāpa-mitra*). One who distracts from the dharma. A bad teacher.

FRIEND, GOOD (*kalyāṇa-mitra*). One who helps in conversion to or progress in the dharma. A spiritual teacher.

FRIENDLINESS (*maitrī*). First of the four Unlimited. Consists in bestowing benefits on others, is based on the ability to see their pleasant side, and results in the stilling of ill will and malice.

FRUIT (*phala*). Effect resulting from good and bad action.

FULLY CONTROLLED (*vaśibhūta*). A quality especially attributed to the Arhat.

GANDHARVA. 1) A being about to enter a womb, 2) a heavenly musician.

GARUDA. A mythical bird of prey, enemy of the serpent race.

GHOST (*amanuṣya*). 'Not man,' superhuman being, demon.

GIVING (*dāna*). The first of the six perfections. Consists in giving material things, dharma instruction, one's body and one's own life and the merit accrued thereby for the benefit of other beings.

GNOSIS (*jñāna*). Religious knowledge that leads to salvation.

GOD (*deva*). Literally: 'Shining One.' In no sense a creator, neither omniscient, nor omnipotent; simply a denizen of heaven.

GODDESS OF THE GANGES (*gāṅgadevī-bhaginī*). A well-known figure of Indian mythology.

GODS IN THE INTERMEDIATE REALM (*antarīkṣa-deva*). Gods who appear in the sky.

GODS OF THE PURE ABODE (*śuddhāvāsa*). Five classes of Gods dwelling in the five Heavens of Pure Abode. These are the highest classes of the 18 classes of gods dwelling in the realm of form (*rūpa-dhātu*). and are said to be in the fourth and highest level of that realm.

GODS OF THE THIRTY-THREE (*trayastriṃśakāyikā deva-putrā*). Associated with Indra and dwelling on thirty-three peaks of Mt. Sumeru in the second of the six realms of desire (*kāmadhātu*).

GOLDEN FLOWER (*suvarṇa-puṣpa*). Name of a predicted future Buddha.

GOOD LAW (*saddharma*). Buddhist doctrine.

GRASPING AGGREGATES (*upādāna-skandha*). The five skandhas.

GREAT BEING (*mahā-sattva*). Standard epithet of a Bodhisattva. Also 'great spiritual hero' because his aspirations are on a heroic scale.

GREAT COMPASSION (*mahā-karuṇā*). More comprehensive than ordinary compassion in that it 1) is aroused not only by obvious, but by concealed suffering, 2) extends beyond the world of sense desire to the world of form and the formless world, 3) is felt equally for all beings, 4) abandons, in addition to hate, delusion, 5) does not merely commiserate, but protects as well.

GREAT DISCIPLES (*mahā-śrāvaka*). The eighty more important disciples of the Buddha.

GREAT HELLS (*mahā-niraya*). Places of punishment, marked by excessive heat or cold, or by manifold tortures.

GREAT KINGS, FOUR. *See* WORLD-GUARDIANS.

GREAT SERPENTS (*mahā-nāga*) Epithet of the Buddha's Disciples, which indicates their great wisdom. *See* DISCIPLE.

GREAT VEHICLE. *See* VEHICLES

GREED (*rāga*). First of the three roots of evil. The antidote is faith.

GROUNDS OF SELF-CONFIDENCE (*vaiśāradya*). Four: the self-confidence of the Tathagata which comes from 1) having fully known all dharmas, 2) having dried up all outflows, 3) having correctly described the impediments to emancipation, 4) having shown how one must enter on the path which leads to deliverance.

GUIDE OF THE BUDDHAS (*buddha-netrī*) The Prajñāpāramitā.

HATE (*dveṣa*). The second of the three roots of evil. The antidote is wisdom.

HEAVENLY EYE (*divya-cakṣus*). Considers the decease and rebirth of beings in the universe in all the six destinies, without meeting with any obstacles and remaining unimpeded by mountains, walls and forests.

HELL (*niraya*). 'Purgatory,' a place of punishment and purification.

HINDRANCES (*nīvaraṇa*). Five: 1) sense desire, 2) ill will, 3) sloth and torpor, 4) excitedness and sense of guilt, 5) doubt.

HOLY LIFE (*brahma-caryā*). Being a monk or nun. A chaste life.

HOUSEHOLDER (*gṛhapati*). A Buddhist layman who is not a *ksatriya* or a brahmin.

I-MAKING (*ahaṃ-kāra*). The conception of one's individuality, thinking of self.

IGNORANCE (*avidyā*). The ultimate cause of transmigration, it is the negative corollary of gnosis; the first of the twelve links of conditioned coproduction. Also 'nescience.'

ILL (*duḥkha*). The second of the three marks.

ILL WILL (*vyāpāda*). Malice. One of the four bonds.

ILLUSION (*māyā*). Deception, fraud, the nature of phenomena.

IMPARTIALITY (*upekṣā*). From: upa-ĪKṢ, 'to overlook,' i.e. differences. The fourth Unlimited. The perfect man's attitude to living beings.

IMPULSES (*samskārā*). The fourth of the five skandhas. There are fifty-five, springing from six roots, i.e. greed, hate, delusion, and their opposites.

INDRA. A great Aryan god, usually known as Śakra or Kauśika.

INFERIOR VEHICLE. *See* VEHICLES

IRREVERSIBLE STAGE OF A BODHISATTVA (*avinivartanīya bodhi-sattva-bhūmi*). The stage at which a Bodhisattva can no longer fall back, or turn back, on his march to the full enlightenment of a Buddha.

ĪṢĀṆA. One of the older names for Śiva-Rudra, both creator and destroyer.

JAMBU RIVER (*jambu-nadī*). A fabulous river flowing from Mt. Meru, formed by the juice of the Jambu (rose-apple) tree on that mountain.

JAMBUDVĪPA. Buddhist name for India.

JEWELS (*ratna*). Three: Buddha, Dharma, Samgha.

JINA. 'Conqueror,' epithet of the Buddha.

JUBILATION (*anumodanā*). Expression of thanks, gratification, or approval for the spiritual achievements of others.

KALPA. Aeon, world period.

KARMA. A volitional action, which is either wholesome or unwholesome, it is that which passes in unbroken continuity from one momentary congeries of the skandhas to another, either during the life of a person or after his death, until the result (*vipāka*) of every volitional activity of body, speech or thought, that has been done, is arrived at.

KARMA-FORMATIONS (*saṃskāra*). Complexes, conditioned things, impulses. 1) The fourth skandha, 2) the second link of conditioned coproduction, 3) the opposite of the unconditioned.

KAUŚIKA. Name for Indra.

KINNARA. Fabulous beings, represented with the upper half of a human body, and the lower half that of a bird.

KOS (*krośa*). A distance of about 2½ miles.

KOṬI. A very high number.

KṢATRIYA. A member of the warrior class.

LAYMAN (*upāsaka*). One who professes faith in the Buddha's wisdom and formally takes refuge in the Buddha, the Dharma, and the Samgha. May be a householder and need not give credal assent to such tenets as the four truths.

LAYWOMAN (*upāsikā*). See LAYMAN.

LESSER VEHICLE. See VEHICLES.

LIMBS OF ENLIGHTENMENT (*bodhy-aṅga*). Seven: 1) mindfulness, 2) investigation of dharmas, 3) vigour, 4) tranquility, 5) rapture, 6) concentration, 7) evenmindedness.

LIMBS OF THE PATH (*mārgāṅga*). The steps of the Eightfold Noble Path.

LORD (*bhagavan*). An epithet of the Buddha. Also: 'Blessed One.'

MAHĀKĀŚYAPA. A disciple of the Buddha, foremost of those who keep the ascetic rules.

MAHĀKĀTYĀYANA. A disciple of the Buddha.

MAHĀKOSṬHILA. A disciple of the Buddha.

MAHĀYĀNA. *See* VEHICLES.

MAHORAGAS. 'Great serpents,' a group of demons.

MAITREYA. He is the next Buddha.

MANTRAM. Spell, incantation.

MĀRA. Death. The slayer and foe of what is skilled and wholesome. The Buddhist 'Tempter,' the personification of all evils and passions, whose baits and snares are the sensory pleasures. Sometimes identified with the five skandhas, and with what is impermanent, suffering and not self.

MĀRA, ARMY OF (*māra-sena*). An army of hideous and grotesque demons and monsters that attack Bodhisattvas. They represent the human passions.

MARK (*lakṣaṇa*). 1) A characteristic of entities. In this sense one distinguishes special and general marks. Special marks are the features characteristic of different things, 'general' marks those found in all conditioned things, i.e. impermanence, suffering and the absence of self. 2) The 32 marks of a superman. Physical particularities found in a Buddha's body, as well as in that of a Universal Monarch.

MEANS OF CONVERSION (*saṃgraha-vastu*). Four: 1) giving, 2) kind words, 3) helpfulness, 4) consistency between words and deeds.

MERIT (*puṇya*). The fruit of good deeds and the condition for greater happiness or for spiritual progress.

MINDFULNESS (*smṛti*). Third of the five faculties, seventh of the steps of the holy Eightfold Path, first of the seven limbs of enlightenment. The act of remembering which prevents ideas from 'floating away,' and which fights forgetfulness, carelessness and distraction.

MORALITY (*śīla*). The second of the six perfections, it consists in following the ten wholesome ways of acting, or the five precepts.

MOTHER OF THE BODHISATTVAS (*bodhisattva-mātā*). The perfection of wisdom.

NĀGAS. Water spirits, serpents or dragons, either protective or destructive.

NEVER-RETURNER (*anāgāmin*). A saint who, after death will not return again to this world, but wins Nirvana elsewhere. The third of the Four Paths.

NIRVANA. 'Blowing out, expiration.' Quiet calm, sublime, really existing, unperverted.

NIYUTA. A large number.

NOT-SELF (anātman). The third of the three marks. Expressed in the formula, 'Whatever there is, all this is not mine, I am not this, this is not my self.'

ONCE-RETURNER (sakṛdāgāmin). Destined to have one more incarnation. Second of the Four Paths.

ONE WHO DWELLS IN PEACE (araṇā-vihārin). A person who brings to pass freedom from defilements and who is thereby free from passion and non-passion. Subhuti is considered to have attained this state.

OUTFLOWS (āsrava). Four: 1) sense-desire, 2) becoming, 3) ignorance, 4) false views. Their extinction constituted arhatship.

OWN-BEING (sva-bhāva). Natural or inherent condition of something existing through its own power alone, having an invariable and inalienable mark, and having an immutable essence. In its 'own-being' a thing is just itself, and not merely as it is relative to ourselves, or to other things.

PARINIRVĀṆA. Complete nirvana, final nirvana.

PATHS, FOUR. Streamwinner, Once-Returner, Never-Returner, Arhat.

PATIENCE (kṣānti). The third of the six perfections. Non-anger and non-agitation with regard to pain, hardship, abuse, and difficult and uncongenial doctrines.

PERCEPTION (saṃjñā). Concept, notion, idea. There are six, corresponding to the six sense organs. The third skandha.

PERFECT(ION OF) WISDOM (prajñā-pāramitā). The sixth perfection. The most important of the perfections in Mahayana doctrine, it is often personified as a goddess. Its function is purely spiritual and leads to the insight that all dharmas are 'empty.'

PERFECTION(S) (pāramitā). Six: 1) giving, 2) morality, 3) patience, 4) vigour, 5) concentration, 6) wisdom.

PERIODS OF TIME, THREE (tryadhva). Past, future and present.

PERSON (pudgala). A permanent entity which migrates from rebirth to rebirth.

PERVERTED VIEWS (viparyāsa). Four: ignorance analysed as attempting to seek or find: 1) permanence in what is essentially impermanent, 2) ease in what is inseparable from suffering, 3) selfhood in what is not linked to any self, and 4) delight in what is essentially repulsive and disgusting.

PILLARS OF MINDFULNESS (smṛtyupasthāna). Four: the application of mindfulness to: 1) the body, 2) feelings, 3) thought, 4) dharmas (conditions of existence).

PIŚĀCA. An impish devil.

PLACES OF REBIRTH (gati). See DESTINIES.

POWER OF THE BUDDHA (*buddhānubhāva*). His charisma or authority.

POWERS (OF A TATHĀGATA) (*bala*). Ten, such as: 1) knowing wisely, as it really is, what can be as what can be, and what cannot be as what cannot be.

PRAJĀPATI. 'Lord of Creatures,' name for prominent Hindu deities.

PRASENAJIT RĀJA. A king of Kośala.

PRATYEKABUDDHA. Single Buddha. Self-enlightened, but unwilling or unable to teach others.

PRETA. Hungry spirit haunting the earth. One of the six destinies.

PURE ABODE (*śúddhāvāsa*). Five heavens. See GODS OF THE PURE ABODE.

PŪRŅA. Son of Maitrāyanī; a disciple of the Buddha.

RĀJAGŖIHA. The chief city in Magadha.

RĀKṢASA. An evil or malignant demon.

REALITY-LIMIT (*bhūta-koṭi*). The point where reality as we know it comes to an end; synonym for the Hinayanistic Nirvana.

REALM OF BRAHMA (*brahma-kāyika*). Also of 'Brahma's group,' the lowest devas of the realm of form.

REALM OF FORM (*rūpa-dhātu*). The second realm of the triple world.

REALM OF SENSE DESIRE (*kāma-dhātu*). The lowest realm of the triple world.

REPULSIVE (*aśubha*). A feature of all aspects of sensuous experience. It is often added to the three marks.

RIGHTS EFFORTS (*samyak-prahāṇa*). Four: to rouse one's will, make an effort, put forth vigour, make one's thought tense, correctly exert oneself: 1) so as to bring about the (future) non-production of evil and unwholesome dharmas which have not yet been produced, 2) the forsaking of the evil and unwholesome dharmas which have been produced, 3) the production of wholesome dharmas which have not yet been produced, 4) the maintenance, non-disappearance, further development and perfect fulfilment of those wholesome dharmas which have been produced.

RISHIS. 'Seers,' legendary wise men, composers of the Vedic hymns, raised to heaven and a status comparable to that of the gods.

ROADS TO PSYCHIC POWER (*ŗddhi-pāda*). Four: 1) desire-to-do, 2) vigour, 3) thought, 4) exploration. Also 'Bases of Psychic Power.'

ROOTS, WHOLESOME (*kuśala-mūla*). A term for past merit which will bring its rewards.

ROSE-APPLE ISLAND (*jambudvīpa*). Buddhist name for India.

SAHĀPATI. 'Lord of the World of Men.' Buddhist name for Brahmā.

ŚAKRA. Name for Indra, the 'Chief of the Gods.'

ŚĀKYAS. A tribe of landowners and *kṣatriyas* in Kapila-vastu from whom Gautama was descended.

SAṂGHA. One of the three jewels. *See* COMMUNITY.

ŚĀRIPUTRA. One of the Buddha's principal disciples. Renowned among the Elders for wisdom and skill in Abhidharma (analytical contemplation of events). The Mahayana however considered his an inferior wisdom.

SELF (*ātman*). A substantial entity that remains one, unchanged and free.

SENSE-FIELDS (*āyatana*). Twelve, corresponding to the six sense organs and their objects.

SENSUOUS PLEASURES (*kāma-guṇa*). Five: derived from sight, sound, smell, taste, touch.

SERPENTS. *See* GREAT SERPENTS.

SIGN (*nimitta*). 1) Object of attention, 2) basis of recognition, and 3) an occasion for entrancement.

SIGNLESS (*a-nimitta*). Second of the three doors to deliverance. The state of the cessation of all sense-perceptions which is the entry to Nirvana. Said to be an attainment of the Arhat.

SINGLE BUDDHA. *See* PRATYEKABUDDHA.

SINS, DEADLY (*ānantaryāṇi*). Five actions bringing immediate retribution: 1) killing one's mother, 2) killing one's father, 3) killing an Arhat, 4) causing dissension in the order of monks, 5) causing a Tathagata's blood to flow.

SKANDHAS. Literally, 'aggregates.' Five: 1) form, 2) feeling, 3) perceptions, 4) impulses, 5) consciousness. These are the constituents of what is mistaken for a self or person.

SKILL IN MEANS (*upāya-kauśalya*). The Bodhisattva's skill in doing whatever is necessary for the salvation of sentient beings.

SON OF A GOOD FAMILY (*kulaputra*). A polite form of address for Buddhist believers implying a good spiritual endowment, or a good social position, or both.

SOUL (*jīva*). Unifying and vivifying force within an organism.

ŚRAMAṆA. Celibate, ascetic, striver. A religious mendicant.

ŚREṆIKA. Name of a wandering mendicant. *See* WANDERER.

STARLIKE AEON (*tārakôpama-kalpa*). Name of a future aeon.

STREAMWINNER (*srotâpatti*). One who has entered the Path. Literally: 'entrance into the stream.' It is the first of the four stages of Hinayana religious development.

STŪPA. A reliquary, cairn, tope, often bell-shaped and built in the open to contain relics of the Buddha or his disciples, or to commemorate the scene of their acts.

SUBHŪTI. One of the chief disciples of the Buddha, he is noted for friendliness and compassion according to the tradition of the Elders. In the Mahayana he is regarded as the foremost disciple. He is the principal interlocutor of the Prajnaparamita Sutras, speaking without error through the power and authority of the Buddha.

SUCHNESS (*tathatā*). Also: thusness, true reality, nothing added or subtracted.

SUDHARMĀ. 'Maintaining Justice.' The assembly hall of the Gods.

SUMERU. A mountain located in the middle of the world and surrounded by seven concentric rings and mountain ranges. Also, Meru.

SUPERKNOWLEDGES (*abhijñā*). Six: 1) psychic power, 2) heavenly ear, 3) cognition of others' thoughts, 4) recollection of past lives, 5) heavenly eye, 6) cognition of the extinction of outflows. Sometimes five omitting (6). Arhats have attained all six.

SUPREME OBJECT (*paramārtha*). Ultimately true, the Absolute.

SŪTRA. A text which claims to have been spoken by the Buddha himself.

SŪTRĀNTA. A Buddhist text, or the doctrines contained in it.

SYMPATHETIC JOY (*muditā*). To rejoice in the material and spiritual successes of others. The third Unlimited. Enriched by the dedication of merit doctrine of the Mahayana.

TATHĀGATA (*tathā-gata* or *tathā-āgata*). A title of the Buddha meaning either "Thus-gone" or "Thus-come."

TATHĀGATA-FRAME (*tathāgata-vigraha*). The figure or shape of a Tathagata.

TEACHER (*śāstar*). A Buddha.

TERRACE OF ENLIGHTENMENT (*bodhi-maṇḍa*). Name given to the spot under the bodhi tree on which the Buddha sat when he became enlightened. Also: place of enlightenment.

THOROUGHBREDS (*ājāneya*). Of noble race, generally said of animals, but extended to men, especially Buddhas and Bodhisattvas.

THOUGHT (*citta*). 1) Mental activity, or 2) 'Thought,' Spirit.

THOUGHT OF ENLIGHTENMENT (*bodhi-citta*). The thought in which the Bodhisattva first decides to win the full enlightenment of a Buddha, *anuttarasamyaksambodhi*.

TRANCE (*dhyāna*). Four progressive states: first, second, third and fourth.

TREE OF ENLIGHTENMENT (*bodhi-vṛkṣa*). The sacred fig tree under which the Buddha attained enlightenment.

TRICHILIOCOSM, GREAT (*trisāhasra-mahāsāhasra-lokadhātu*). A universe which comprises 1,000 million suns, 1,000 million moons,

1,000 million heavens and hells, etc.

TRIPLE JEWEL (*tri-ratna*). 1) The Buddha, 2) the Dharma, 3) the Saṃgha. These are also the 'refuges' of the layman.

TRIPLE WORLD (*traidhātuka*). 1) The world of sense desire, 2) the world of form, 3) the formless world.

TUSHITA GODS (*tuṣita deva*). 'Satisfied gods' dwelling in the fourth level of the realms of desire. A Bodhisattva spends his last life here before he becomes a Buddha.

UNCONDITIONED (*asaṃskṛta*). Not dependent on causes or conditions for existence. Often an epithet for Nirvana.

UNEFFECTED (*anabhisaṃskāra*). That which is not brought about by reaction to a stimulus.

UNEQUALLED THOUGHT (*asama-citta*). The thought that comprehends the sameness of all things and principles. Attained in the seventh stage of the Bodhisattva.

UNFORGIVABLE OFFENCES (*mūlāpatti*). Four: fornication, theft, killing a human being, and falsely claiming spiritual attainments. Part of early monastic discipline (*prātimokṣa*).

UNLIMITED (*apramāṇa*). Four: 1) friendliness, 2) compassion, 3) sympathetic joy, and 4) impartiality. These are regarded as social virtues and are of secondary importance in Hinayana doctrine, but given greater emphasis in the Mahayana.

VAIDŪRYA. Lapis lazuli.

VAIJAYANTA PALACE (*prasāda*). Indra's palace.

VAJRAPĀṆI. 'With a thunderbolt in his hand,' an imposing guardian yakṣa residing at Rājagṛha. May be conjured up by a Bodhisattva to frighten evildoers. Often seen in frescoes accompanying the Buddha.

VEHICLE(S) (*yāna*) Methods of salvation as analysed by the Mahayana. Three: 1) Disciples, 2) Pratyekabuddhas. These two constitute Hinayana, inferior or lesser vehicle: pejorative for those Buddhists who did not accept the new Mahayana teaching. 3) Mahayana, great vehicle: The movement within Buddhism that arose about the beginning of the Christian era espousing the Bodhisattva doctrine, the aim of which is Buddhahood or supreme, perfect enlightenment, and combining it with a metaphysical doctrine of universal emptiness.

VENERABLE (*āyuṣmat*). Respectful appellation of a monk.

VIEW (*dṛṣṭi*). Opinion, almost always wrong.

VIGOUR (*vīrya*). Second of the five faculties. Derived from the word for hero (*vīra*) and implying heroic endeavor to benefit other living beings as well as unremitting effort in overcoming one's own faults and cultivating virtue.

VINAYA. One of the three divisions of the scriptures. It deals with monastic discipline.

VULTURE PEAK (*Gṛdhra-kūṭa-parvata*). A mountain near Rājagṛiha.

WANDERER (*parivrājaka*). A non-Buddhist wandering mendicant, possessing limited wisdom.

WELL-GONE (*Sugata*). Epithet of the Buddha who has gone on the right path and to the right place.

WHEEL OF THE DHARMA (*dharma-cakra*). Set in motion by the Buddha when he first preached his doctrine.

WHOLESOME WAYS OF ACTING (*kuśalakarmapatha*). Ten: Abstention from taking life, taking what is not given, sexual misconduct, false speech, slander, harsh speech, frivolous talk, covetousness, ill will, and wrong views.

WINGS OF ENLIGHTENMENT (*bodhipakṣa*). Thirty-seven: four applications of mindfulness, four right efforts, four bases of psychic power, five dominants, five powers, seven limbs of enlightenment, eight limbs of the path.

WISDOM (*prajñā*). The fifth of the five faculties. In early Buddhism this consisted of the methodical contemplation of the dharmas, and insight into their 'own-being.' *See* PERFECT WISDOM.

WISDOM EYE (*prajñā-cakṣus*). Cognizes the true characteristics of the various dharmas.

WISHLESS. (*apraṇihita*). 'Placing nothing in front,' a state in which one makes no plans for the future. The term could also have been rendered as 'aimless.' It is the third of the three doors to deliverance.

WORLD-GUARDIANS, FOUR (*cātur loka-pāla*). Indra's four god-kings who dwell on the four sides of Mt. Meru in the first of the six realms of desire (*kāmadhātu*). They ward off attacks on the world by malicious spirits. East *Dhṛtarāṣṭra*, south *Virūḍhaka*, west *Virūpākṣa*, north *Vaiśravaṇa*. Also called the Four Great Kings (*mahā-rāja*).

WORLD-KNOWER (*loka-vid*). Epithet of the Buddha.

WORLD-SYSTEM (*loka-dhātu*). A world with all the heavens or hells it may contain.

WRATH (*krodha*). One of the ten subsidiary defilements.

YAKSHA. *See* FAIRY.

CORRECTIONS

Work done on the text of this Sutra, since this translation was published in 1973, has brought to light a few mistakes. First of all, Professor J. W. de Jong, of Canberra, has taken the trouble to check much of this translation against the sources, —not only the Sanskrit and Tibetan, but at times also the Chinese. His detailed study will be published in *Indologica Taurinensia.* He very kindly let me have his typescript, and most of the alterations proposed in the following list result from his observations. Secondly, freed from academic responsibilities I have now completed my study of the variant readings of the Sanskrit text, and this has led to some more corrections. The entire study, indicating all my departures from the printed editions, will be published in due course in some Festschrift or other.

First I indicate the page of this book, followed by the line. Those who are too impatient to count can assume that five lines are two centimetres. Then the words which should be changed are given in italics.

107, 14	he should *readily* and continually
, 17-18	In any case, *whether* the Tathagata *remains* [*in this world*] or has disappeared into final Nirvana,
118, 11-14	of dharma. *As a servant of the king fears nothing on account of the king's might* [99] *and is worshipped by a great body of people,* so also the preacher of dharma, because, through the might of the Dharma-body *he is fearless and worshipped* by a great body of people.
121, 8-7 fr.b.	not understand [*what the true perfection of wisdom is*] should beware of *being ruined* [*by listening to it*],
130, 8 fr.b.	down in *the turning* over, and
140, 21-23	are persons *whom I do not even agree to you seeing, —how much less should you become intimate with them, or* [*give them*] wealth,
, 8-7 fr.b.	wither away, lest *he who is guilty of these offences hear of that frightful length of time during which his body* [*has to stay in the hells*]. —So the Lord

151, 12	all dharmas *are the same in that* [*as unproduced*] *they cannot be* apprehended.
152, 7	because all dharmas are *undifferentiated.*
156, 6-5 fr.b.	wholesome roots, *acquired in the past,* that this deep perfection of wisdom has *been bestowed upon him.*
175, 18-19	look the same, *since* in their own-being
182, 22	*Beings* who resolutely
186, 9	the water. *His goods will be at one place and his ship will perish somewhere else. In this way* that stupid merchant
194, 3 fr.b.	in six ways, *and exhibited the eighteen great signs,* it stirred
201, 3-1 fr.b.	dharma. *He does not see any dharma which he does not yoke to the nature of dharmas and he sees everything as being associated with it.*
204, 3	Who can *cognize,* who fully know it?
, 7	space, *in vain do you exert yourself,* revealed
, 10	this *attempt to dissuade him* is just
205, last line	They praise *the absence of*
209, 14	because you *desire to be instructed.*
215, 19-20	wisdom, then *because of his repeated practice of the perfection of wisdom he will also in his dreams develop it in abundance.*
229, 8 fr.b.	felt, *realized* and fully known.
246, 11 fr.b.	which are *undesirable,* disagreeable
247, 6-5 fr.b.	listening to. *I should not allow myself to be deflected from my earnest intention* [*to win full enlightenment*]. When I
259, 11 fr.b.	One would decide to *fight* space
275, 2-1 fr.b.	consciousness; it *is free from the accumulation* of all wholesome
279, 15-14 fr.b.	Their *copings made of gold from the Jambu river rose loftily.*
280, 23-24	jewels. *And inside every hole of the slabs of the*

staircase, which is made of gold from the Jambu river, there* grows a plantain tree.

280, 5-4 fr.b.

town built for the Bodhisattva Dharmodgata in the central square of the town *an elevated seat [to serve as his pulpit]*. It

280, last line
to 281, 2

shining with pearls. *To keep the seat firmly established, [the citizens], all equally united and full of delight,* [489] *sustained it through the well-established karma-result which had matured from their various deeds, they strewed and scattered all round that place flowers of the five colours, and scented it with various perfumes.* So pure

E.C., December 1974